AF060982

Destroying the Other's Collective Memory

Studies in the
Postmodern Theory of Education

Joe L. Kincheloe and Shirley R. Steinberg
General Editors

Vol. 141

PETER LANG
New York • Washington, D.C./Baltimore • Bern
Frankfurt am Main • Berlin • Brussels • Vienna • Oxford

Ilan Gur-Ze'ev

Destroying the Other's Collective Memory

PETER LANG
New York • Washington, D.C./Baltimore • Bern
Frankfurt am Main • Berlin • Brussels • Vienna • Oxford

Library of Congress Cataloging-in-Publication Data
Gur-Ze'ev, Ilan.
Destroying the other's collective memory / Ilan Gur-Ze'ev.
p. cm. — (Counterpoints; vol. 141)
Includes bibliographical references (p.) and index.
1. Education—Social aspects—Israel. 2. Zionism—Study and
teaching—Israel. 3. Critical pedagogy—Israel.
I. Title. II. Counterpoints (New York, N.Y.); vol. 141.
LA1441 .G87   370.11'5—dc21   00-038949
ISBN 0-8204-4942-3
ISSN 1058-1634

Die Deutsche Bibliothek-CIP-Einheitsaufnahme
Gur-Ze'ev, Ilan:
Destroying the other's collective memory / Ilan Gur-Ze'ev.
−New York; Washington, D.C./Baltimore; Bern;
Frankfurt am Main; Berlin; Brussels; Vienna; Oxford: Lang.
(Counterpoints; Vol. 141)
ISBN 0-8204-4942-3

Cover design by Dutton and Sherman Design

© 2003 Peter Lang Publishing, Inc., New York
275 Seventh Avenue, 28th Floor, New York, NY 10001
www.peterlangusa.com

All rights reserved.
Reprint or reproduction, even partially, in all forms such as microfilm,
xerography, microfiche, microcard, and offset strictly prohibited.

Contents

Acknowledgments		vii
Introduction	Counter-Education and the Exile of Spirit	1
Chapter 1	Holocaust/Nakbah as an Israeli/Palestinian Homeland	25
Chapter 2	Beyond the Destruction of the Other's Collective Memory	51
Chapter 3	Hitler and Philosophy in the Israeli Curriculum	68
Chapter 4	The Tower of Babel and Western Phalogocentrism in Israel	108
Chapter 5	The Vocation of Female Teachers in a Changing Society	119
Chapter 6	The Vocation of Higher Education	157
Chapter 7	Multiculturalism and Education in Israel	176
Chapter 8	Literacy, Education, and Violence: The Israeli Example	204
Chapter 9	The Philosophical Revolution in the Israeli Army	243
Chapter 10	Humanistic-Oriented Education in Context	276
Chapter 11	The Metaphysics of Traffic Accidents and Education Toward an Alternative Public Sphere	318
Index		347

Acknowledgments

I am most grateful to Dr. Ilan Pappe, co-author of the chapter "Beyond Destroying the Other's Collective Memory", for permitting me to include it in this book. I am grateful to the poet Almatukal Teah for permitting me to publish an extract from his collection. I thank Professors Ron Rubin and Bo Strath for permitting me to publish a reworked version of "Holocaust-Nakbah Memories as Israeli-Palestinian Homeland", due to appear in their forthcoming book "Homeland". Some chapters of this book are based on "Philosophy, Politics, and Education in Israel", published in Hebrew (1999) by the University of Haifa Press and Zemora-Bitan. I acknowledge with thanks permission to rework these chapters for this book.

Ilan Gur-Ze'ev

Introduction
Counter-Education and the Exile of Spirit

The relations between philosophy, politics, and education are those of war and creativity.[1] Violence as enforced productivization of the self, as control and as camouflaging of internalized representations of conflicting violences is central to education as a concept and as politics. The ultimate product of systematic violence is order, peace, satisfaction, and normalized subjects.[2] This does not stand in opposition to Levinas's understanding, according to which

> Being's interestedness takes dramatic form in egoisms struggling with one another, each against all, in the multiplicity of allergic egoisms which are at war with one another and are thus together. War is the chronicle or the drama of the essence's interestedness. No entity can await its hour. . . . Essence thus is the extreme synchronism of war.[3]

As normalized subjects humans are devoted to the reproduction of the violences which created them as subjects, on the one hand, and to the destruction of rival violences, on the other. The more efficient is normalizing education the more humans tend to arrest themselves with ever more devotion to their de-humanization. They apprehend themselves to the chains which prevent them from being other than they are, shackles, which prohibit them from detecting, questioning, and challenging the violences of the apparatuses which construct them and determine their horizons. These apparatuses and developments are responsible even for orchestrating the possibilities of their resistance or revolt against the present order and surely their adjustment to "their" arena and its governing *violences*.

A precondition for the very existence of these apparatuses and relations is the successful hiding of a dreadful secret, the secret of the creativity of power (relations). Normalizing education is committed for its concealment and for the constitution or protection of conditions for the abandonment of its deciphering, reconstruction, and destruction. Normalizing education is committed to lead humans to abandon the quest for *the totally other*[4] for surrendering themselves to the governing facts of the day. It manipulates humans to disregard their becoming products of a system and to forget, despise, or ridicule their unrealized potentials, which are the essential characteristics of them as subjects, as "not-objects." It constitutes and protects humans' devotion to the self-evidence within whose framework they are imprisoned. Normalizing education fabricates the subject as *some-thing* and prevents her from becoming *some-one*, even as a rebel. Normalized humans are always thrown between "them," the Others, the "we" or the "I." Their possibility, their imperative, to struggle over the possibility of realizing their unfulfilled possibilities, and their readiness for the *not yet*, is abandoned. These possibilities relate to a kind of intersubjectivity where the *otherness*[5] of the Other is being acknowledged. It acknowledged that only from outside, by the Other in her otherness, can the constitutive apparatuses of the soul, consciousness, skills, and social performance be recovered. These relations enable reflection and empower the subject as an active player in the constitution of her self. The normally unfulfilled human potentials contain the possibilities of taking a greater part in the representation of her interests, yardsticks, knowledge, and identity. These potentials contain changing her self and creating essentially new possibilities for intersubjectivity, where individual—even if never totally "free"—evaluations and autonomous moral decisions and the possibilities of spiritual stance, and not mere efficient resolutions, are central to life.[6] Such possibilities contain openness for moral-political judgment and a kind of practice, which actively changes reality into a more human arena. The very possibility of distortion, the very possibility of manipulating humans, however, presupposes a human subject, which is not a mere construct of normalizing education. The existence of normalizing education not only opens the way for counter-education—it also refers to the subject as not-an-object, and as such, as some-one,[7] whose otherness will ultimately be never totally destroyed. The normalized subject is the "proof" that education can never have the last word. Life is undefeatable even by itself.

Normally, to the degree that education is successful, men and women commit themselves to a struggle over their existence as a systematic degradation, denial, and distortion of their humanity as the manifestation of their "efficiency" or "success" or even "humanity." They abandon themselves in a struggle over survival and success within the horizons of the hegemonic realm of self-evidence (body, psyche, culture, society) in which they are imprisoned as victims and agents of "their" system.[8] In a certain sense in both aspects they contribute, time and again, to the de-humanization processes within the hegemonic order of things. In another sense the way they actualize themselves as normalized humans actualizes the order of things. The order of the system has no meaning if detached from the human intersubjectivity, its productivity, and potential resistance.[9] The same holds also in regard to the quest for "humane life," emancipated from the realm of scarcity and from the very presence of need. In this respect humans are never "enslaved" nor can they be "emancipated." The only open gate is the gate of transcendence from the *Illusion* of emancipation.

Within the framework of normalizing education they are unable to "emancipate" themselves from what they are *not-yet*. Nor can they liberate themselves from that "self" who they already became—as part of the system and a construct of its power relations. This is since it is always that self as "I" which will realize itself by destroying the otherness of the Other and who will realize "itself" as a productive element of the system even when rebelling against that "I" or against the hegemonic order and its discourses.

> Discourse is not life: its time is not your time; in it, you will not be reconciled to death; you may have killed God beneath the weight of all that you have said; but don't imagine that, with all that you are saying, you will make a man that will live longer than that.[10]

All that the "I" can do is to *dance* on the borders between and among rival fields, forces, and conflicting dynamics which create for it changes, ruptures, and new possibilities within the horizons of the systems within which humans realize their constructed, contingent, identities, strives, and Utopias.[11] Within normality they actually experience the death of the subject or the triumph of the system, which is committed to prevent the birth of the human or the realization of the potential of the struggle over the elevation of human life into a worthier conflict.

The dialectics between the forces which form the various fields and networks within which the human intersubjectivity and "self-realization" are actualized simultaneously also enables the constitution of the human subjects as the agents of the subjugating system. They are servants and creations of apparatuses of control, representation, and creation of new conceptual possibilities within the hegemonic order of things. By the same token they are also prisoners and victims of this order of which they are the sole executioners. All this concerns solely the existing order. It relates to current education, which is responsible for reproducing the power relations, hierarchies, and dynamics in which there is room for a positive Utopia which relates to the flourishing of women and men as authentic, original, natural, or future ideal "I." Within positive Utopia this "I" is one with himself or herself to the degree that he or she denies the external or internal Other and is committed to destroy the "external" and "internal" otherness. The otherness in the Other and in one's self becomes an archenemy to be destroyed, redeemed, exiled, or educated.[12] The "I" becomes one with the forgetfulness of the limitless openness of being and of *the totally other* as an absolutely Other human being.[13]

Normalizing education is committed to the advancement and camouflaging of this aim. As such it is a process of systematic de-humanization of humans. It serves the system by containing even the structural folly of challenging the hegemonic realm of self-evidence and the futility of resistance within positive utopianism. In other words the aim of normalizing education is safeguarding the constant transformation of the human subject into an object. As such she becomes a thing among other things. The subject becomes a product of a subjectification process.[14] It becomes meaningless to separate between it and the fields and dynamics within which it has a role, which determines its function and "meaning." As such the subject becomes a construct of mythologizing dynamics and forces which constitute the *Same*[15] of the hegemonic order in which there is no room for the otherness of the Other nor for reflection, dialogue, and transcendence.

Even in an era which deciphered naiveté toward ideology critique and positive revolutionary critique, this book refuses the conclusion according to which there is no more in humans than that which was internalized in them by mere natural or cultural systems. Life is much richer. *Life* is not to be conceived without the realization of potentiality, of the unexpected outburst of *the totally other*, without the messianic moment.

This suggests a concept of the human which refuses to give the last word to factuality.[16] According to the concept of the human in critical philosophy, human beings have the potential of being more than mere constructs or relations of the systems within which they are nothing but a function. Even the given factuality is not to be reduced to mere constitutive and representative apparatuses. Being by its essence includes and promises *Infinity*.

> The ethical relationship is not grafted on to an antecedent relationship of cognition; it is a foundation and not a superstructure. To distinguish it from cognition is not to reduce it to a subjective sentiment. The idea of infinity, in which being overflows the idea, in which the other overflows the same, breaks with the inward play of the soul and alone deserves the name experience, a relation with the exterior. It is then more cognitive than cognition itself, and all objectivity must participate in it.[17]

Within infinity the possibility of essential change—and not only relative change—is always present, even if only in a negative manner by the presence of its absence. This is why human reality is never totally determined and ultimately is never closed. The attempts of the violences of politics is never totally victorious over the violence of the poet

> who speaks in the name of a creative power, capable of overcoming all orders and representations in order to affirm Difference in the state of permanent revolution which characterizes eternal return.[18]

It contains an eternal invitation for *transcendence* from the present order and for otherness than the *Same*, which the educational violence gives birth to.

It is wrong to conceive human reality as disconnected from the utopian moment, from the possibility of the outburst of *the totally other* into the continuum of violence.[19] Critical philosophy functions on the edges of, between, and across border zones. Borders, which divide between the utopian possibilities and the given facts as represented by the hegemonic representation apparatuses, and its limitations and possibilities. At the same time it is crisscrossed by local, unexpected, possibilities for resistance, critique, and change which are constituted by the same developments.[20] These possibilities and the *difference* they manifest are always part and parcel of the system, of the *Same*, and by themselves do not offer an essential change or transcendence but an eternal repetition. Lyotaed defines this situation as *differend*. It is a case in which "a plaintiff is deprived of means of arguing, and so becomes a victim." It is a situation in which the rules of conflict, which apply to a case, are articulated in the idiom of the hegemon, in such a way that the other party cannot explain how he was manipulated and victimized.[21] Essential change must overcome this victimization, not only unveil the productivity of violence. In this sense essential change or transcendence is an abyss.

However, it is exactly from here, from the gulf of oblivion of human destiny, from the edge where the walls of the self-evident are erected, from the trust in self-abandonment and human enslavement, that counter-education becomes an open possibility. Counter-education abandons the invulnerability which is promised by normalizing education and its self-evidence, with no alternative self-evidence. It cannot offer any kind of pleasures, success, or confidence. It cannot even offer the relevance offered by normalizing education in the era of advanced capitalism and the electronic production/representation of reality, its consumption, and its venues for abandoning the utopian call.

Normalizing education is accountable for the representation of the current order as self-evidence, while veiling its violences and the problematic abyss of their contingent productivity. It is committed to "internal" and "external" *colonization* of humans, which the system produces and controls—as well as "their" Others, which are identified and represented as strangers within the system and beyond its borders. The aims of the colonization processes of normalizing education are to castrate, destroy, detain, swallow, or make the "I" to forget the otherness of the Others. This process is actualized in a parallel fashion as part of the production of the normalized subject.

As a unique kind of violence education cannot fulfill its potential and produce the *Invisibility* of the control on the representation apparatuses without pinpointing the unordinary, the deviation, the exotic, the Other. It cannot avoid the commitment to distract otherness. The peak of the success of this violence is in its veiling itself as violence and in presenting its yardsticks, conceptions, borders, and enemies as self-evident, avoiding legitimization crisis. Here the ethical I,[22] which is committed to challenge this order, to unveil its violences, its production of the legitimacy criteria of knowledge, its evils and its ultimate goals or mere performance, is presented as a specially dangerous manifestation of the Other.

The more efficient the educational violences are, the less visible, speakable, and resistible they are. The consensual and legitimate transparency of the educational politics works, sometimes, as a fortress of the self-evidence, preventing addressing the violence of education and the essense of violence itself.[23] As education as violence is being unveiled and its relation to the politics of education is being articulated it manifests a dangerous weakness of the order it serves and a serious threat for the fortunes of its reproduction. Educational violence triumphs daily by its enabling the enslavement of humans to the veiling apparatuses, to the reproduction of the networks within which humans reproduce their lives and its surrounding networks while changing themselves and their reality, their normality, stability, well-being, knowledge, and pleasures.[24] These social-material-historical processes are paralleled and fertilized by individual-psychological-symbolic realities. It is wrong to disconnect reality from the violences competing on its production, representation, distribution, consumption, and change. This holds also to the subject:

> Subjectivity in this sense is abstract. And within human societies at least, it is always inscribed or distributed within cultural codes of differences that organize subjects by defining social identities. Such codes differentially value particular positions within the field of subjectivity. In other words, although everyone exists within the strata of subjectivity, they are also located at particular positions, each of which enables and constrains the possibilities of experience, representing those experiences and of legitimizing those representations.[25]

All of these are meaningful only within a context, which is always a battlefield of conflicting powers and diversities. This is the arena within which the normalized subject can question the subjectification of others and the production of her self by powers, which ensure their invisibility as well as the concepts, the passions, and the limits of their potential unveiling.

In this sense, it is not only that the normalized subject is never "authentic"—she is never with her self since her self is always a construct of the system which produces it for reproducing the system. The urge for the origins or for a positive Utopia as well as the disenchantment from them are fundamentally a manifestation of the contingent power relations, representation apparatuses, and reproductions processes which constitute knowledge, identities, and consciousness as well as morality and aesthetics.[26] Within this arena do the revolt and the quest for demythologization of reality dwell, accompanied by other myths, illusions, and material life possibilities.

Normal disenchantment and revolt against normalizing education by itself cannot guarantee *the totally other*, only "revolution" or "emancipation," even when it "succeeds." Such disillusion will not even give birth to a great philosophy or an essentially different politics from the ones which were overcome. This is so even when the oppressed dream on authenticity or when they struggle against the hegemonic factuality in light of a positive Utopia. The pronouncement about the end of Utopia, or the overcoming of the naiveté of the ideal of authenticity can offer comfort to those praising "the death of the subject," "everything goes," "the futility of the ideal of reflection." But it cannot constitute counter-education, new conceptual possibilities, meaning, love, happiness, or hope. The most it can bring is pleasure, cynicism, pragmatism, and more effective normalization within post-modern conditions. In this book it will be exposed and reconstructed in the Israeli context within a historical framework.

In this book I will try to show that education, all education, is essentially *violence* which represents and serves the politics of the existing order. As such it is positioned in opposition to the negative Utopia of critical philosophy. Critical philosophy is not neutral or objective. It has a commitment to refuse injustice and the hegemonic apparatuses of producing truths, norms, needs, identities, and enemies. It inevitably collides with the ruling powers[27] and its normalizing education. It manifests a refusal to accept the present facts as the last and ultimate yardstick to evaluate reality, and it is committed to the effort of its own questioning and its own transcendence. It questions the self-evident and traces for the absent, for the forgotten, for the unrecoverable silenced voices and for the unfulfilled potentials. In this project philosophy is not afraid of the Nietzschean *grand refusal* in a post-revolutionary, post-critical, and in many respects post-nihilistic, era. It negates the forces, powers, facts, and demands of reality. Its utopian negativism is conceptualized within a counter-educational framework.

Counter-education differs essentially from the various versions of normalizing education. Within it there is no strict separation between philosophy, politics and the various positive alternatives for normalizing education. Here education is not to be reduced to mere socialization or acculturation, and counter-education is not a mere negation of normalizing education.

This orientation is realized in this book in a concrete context—the Israeli arena. Each of the enclosed chapters represents the realization of critical theory within a specific context while addressing the possibilities of counter-education in the Israeli arena. Some of the most hidden secrets of the normalizing education in the Israeli arena are here unveiled and historically addressed. In this sense it is also a re-reading of the history of Israeli education in the broadest meaning of the term.

It is an attempt to show in a concrete and detailed manner how the violence of normalizing education constitutes the images of knowledge, the conceptual apparatus, the consciousness as well as emotional, moral, and aesthetic dimensions which determine the horizons of humans in each specific historical stage. All these enable the successful function of the human subject as a brave soldier, efficient consumer/producer, or a reformator. The Israeli and the Palestinian contexts manifest to what degree the *symbolic violence* is impossible without its material and historical contexts. This book will try to reconstruct in a detailed manner how direct, unmediated, physical use of force is determined by symbolic, invisible, unspeakable violence. Only when the forces which determine education are unveiled, acknowledged, and become speakable, namely when it becomes "real" and conceived as threatening the self-evidence and its material, conceptual, and psychological defenses is it represented as improper, illegitimate, and as such it is exposed and denounced as violence. Worthy educators, curriculums, and (formal or informal) pedagogies are preconditions for the construction of (always) enforced collectives that send brave armies to battlefields such as de-humanizing factories, cinema halls, commercial centers, and to the various links in the cyberspace.

The present book tries to offer a historical concretization to normalizing education. By referring to eleven different Israeli/Palestinian contexts it tries to show how within different networks such as transportation, army, and academy the efficiency of good educators or cultural politics can preserve and advance the traditional work of prophets, priests, censors, and executioners. Education and teaching as obliteration, as reproduction, and as the destruction of collective memories, identities, and knowledge and education as the cultivation of skills, knowledge, and values of the chosen ones has not changed their fundamental principles. However, they do change dramatically in their appearances in the various historical stages and diverse cultural settings. There are important changes in the techniques of control of the representation of reality and its production, reproduction, and change. As will be shown, the obliteration of the Other and the reproduction of the relevant or legitimate passions and knowledge do change dramatically over time.

While comparing various historical stages of the West and by comparing cultural developments in Israel, Palestine, and the West, this book presents the claim that the present displays an important improvement in the efficiency of the production as well as in the productivisation and subjectification of humans. The reduction in the possibilities of protecting and developing one's autonomy as an intellectual and as a citizen parallels the degradation of central and direct censorship, the lessening of explicit and direct assaults on "dangerous" knowledge, marginal identities, memories, and narratives. In the post-modern condition the symbolic violence sophisticated the modernist educational apparatuses and empowered normalizing education and its subjectification apparatuses. This, while being conceived by its disciples and protagonists alike as an alternative to the modernist hierarchies, as a threat to dogmatism, to central control, and to illusions concerning universally valid "true" or "objective" knowledge and values.

The Israeli context in this book manifests wider developments and more general valid questions, principles, and practices. The essence of the post-modern educational violence in its philosophical and political contexts is questioned here contextually without rejecting altogether its sensibilities, topics, and critique. In this light the present work is an attempt to show how agents and practices of production and control of teachers are used in post-modern settings in new ways that give birth to new cultural, social, and political realities, new limitations, and new possibilities. Addressing specific test cases will show how today both in the centers of the affluent society and in its modern and pre-modern margins education as creative violence is not being replaced by more democratic and open strategies. It only changes practices, rhetorics, and affects, not its fundamental commitment and ultimate dehumanizing results.

In contrast to the politics of modern educators and the armies they daily create and empower, and in opposition to its post-modern alternatives, critical philosophy as well as critical theory of culture and society cannot offer counter-violence. At best the critical philosophy that is here presented can show that every human is more than what the system has invested in her. As a human subject she has the potential of resisting the normalization processes, becoming different than expected, and even transcending the hegemonic order. As a project such a resistance can be realized even in microscopic spaces or for a blink of a moment. It can become a struggle for self-reconstruction and it can become part of a post-colonial political/cultural alternative.

Every human is "something" that might elevate herself and distance herself from the thingness by developing "something" peculiar, unexpected, and uncontrolled into a small crack in the system. Individually and socially it will manifest that the human can become different than she was constructed to be by the hegemonic educational violences. This otherness has an ethical and ontological existence as well as a historical, pedagogical, and political nonrelativistic dimensions. The "Principle of Hope," Utopia, the Principle of Indeterminability, or even a mutation in natural evolution all manifest this possibility. According to Derrida

> chaos and instability, which is fundamental, founding and irreducible, is at once naturally the worst against which we struggle with laws, rules, conventions, politics and provisional hegemony, but at the same time it is a chance, a chance to change, to destabilize. If there were continual stability, there would be no need for politics, and it is to the extent that stability is not natural, essential or substantial, that politics exists and ethics is possible. Chaos is at once a risk and chance, and it is here that the possible and impossible cross each other.[28]

Critical philosophy gazes at *the totally other* rather than the given, it represents the potential readiness of the human to be called on, to take part in regeneration. This readiness contains no guarantee, or a certain promise—only the possibility of a promise. Yet it enables the quest to overcome the *Same* in all its forms, such as the present hegemonic apparatuses, which produce the generally accepted truths, hopes, values, and kaleidoscopic mixtures of these as long as they function in accordance with the logic of the capitalistic system. It represents a quest for overcoming, not solely deconstruction or recycling, critique, and negation, not endless, meaningless fashioned replacement and recycling within "differences," which are mere reflections of the hegemonic system, aestheticization of its morals and drives.

This is why critical philosophy must become a theory of critique of society and culture. The theory underlying this work is well aware of its historicity and its commitment to self-critique and change, in light of the fact that as an involvement in actual life it has always existed in limited, specific, dynamic contexts. Today, in the era of the Internet, it is so important to emphasize that, like its rivals, current critical theory too is working within a historical context which is determined by ontological as well as technological, sociocultural, and conceptual limitations and possibilities which are reconstructed, criticized, and transformed. This is the reason for its addressing concrete and sometimes microscopic settings as part of a comprehensive critique of the social, as part of the development and change of society and culture—as well as being part of its own transformation. Such changes and possible transformations are paralleled, initiated, and manifested by concrete social struggles.

As a dweller in the political arena, critical philosophy is committed to a critical theory that will introduce a counter-education which will challenge the success of the violence of normalizing education. Critical theory gave birth to various educational strategies, which traditionally were developed within the framework of critical pedagogy. In the last four decades critical pedagogy, in its diverse forms, had an important impact on Western educational thought and to a lesser degree in the realization of alternative pedagogies. It had its voice heard also in the third world, sometime indirectly via feminist, multiculturalist, and post-colonialist discourses and pedagogical practices. In Israel, however, it was hardly felt. Until now even in the Israeli academia there was very little presence to these counter-educational theoretical perspectives. One should note that historically critical pedagogy did not succeed to elevate itself to more than an advanced, progressive, educational alternative. This might be partly explained by that as a pedagogical practice and theory it lost its intimate relations with philosophy in general and especially with critical philosophy.

One of the aims of this work is to offer an intermediate component between critical philosophy and counter-education as an alternative to both the hegemonic education and to current standard versions of critical education. This book tries to propose the need, the possibilities, and the limitations of such counter-education in context. It represents two spaces within which this alternative might be struggled for. One is that of the ethical "I." In light of Horkheimer and Levinas's works here, the ethical "I" represent a stance, which precedes rationality, moral, and politics. The other manner in which counter-education might be concretized is a moral-political one. Within this framework it refers heavily to theoretical sources as diverse as ideology critique, cultural studies, post-colonial discourse, and certain feminist trends which culminate into a social struggle over the possibility of autonomy, reflection, and transcendence as a dialogical, communal, and anti-violent existence.

While this book finds much relevance in some aspects of the recent radical thought, it refuses to be overwhelmed by the politics of identity or the relativism which use assertions such as "there is nothing exterior to the text" or "anything goes." It refuses to abandon erotic *responsibility* toward the actuality, toward *the totally other* of the given actuality. It does it in a multicultural context without abandoning the quest for love but while resisting the various conflicting ethnocentric solidarities.[29] As such this book should not be considered as a mere revisionist or post-Zionist research in the history of the Israeli education, culture, and society. It tries to propose a philosophical framework for actual counter-education in Israel in action, not only an additional contribution to the important work of "the new historians"[30] who realize in Israeli academia the new possibilities of the post-Zionist era.

Even when contextualized, counter-education as here presented cannot be reduced to positive educational frameworks in accordance with any fixed ideal. However, while refusing any institutionalization, counter-education is not an abstract Utopia either. It is present as a de-mystification of reality, which is not to be transformed into a positive alternative nor to a mere, empty "critique." In its appearance as a stance of the ethical "I" it appears as a total commitment to *the totally other* as the otherness of the Other. This commitment must negate the present order, which dehumanizes the Other and negates her or his otherness. This negation, however, affirms the system's supreme existence. By so doing it does not establish the total defeat of Utopia, it only emphasized the ways within which positive utopianism is part of the system. It is exactly the supremacy of factuality and its refusal to give room for negative utopianism which establishes the undecidability of *the totally other*, of the Messianic moment in being. Counter-education is unimaginable in the absence of a messianism without a Messiah. As such in the era of the Internet, in face of the capitalist globalization,[31] it challenges the function of the apparatuses of the production of commodities, producers, and consumers which reduce knowledge, love, and even mystery fetishized signs of "freedom" and fabricated pleasures such as driving fast or luxurious cars. In Western societies today, the alternative suggested by counter-education cannot be realized in revolutions such as those realized or dreamed of in modernity. And it certainly does not sell an attractive reform or a new educational fashion in pleasurable/tempting conditions. It has no positive Utopia that is to be enforced by normalizing education. The words of Roland Barth are still relevant on this matter:

> In a sense, the mythologist is excluded from this history in the name of which he professes to act. The havoc which he wreaks in the language of the community is absolute for him, it fills his assignment to the brim: he must live this assignment without any hope going back or any assumption of payment. It is forbidden for him to imagine what the world will concretely be like, when the immediate object of his criticism has disappeared. Utopia is an impossible luxury for him: he greatly doubts that tomorrow's truths will be the exact reverse of today's lies. History never ensures the triumph pure and simple of something over its opposite: it unveils, while making itself, unimaginable solutions, unforeseeable syntheses. The mythologist is not even in a Moses-like situation: he cannot see the Promised Land. For him, tomorrow's positivity is entirely hidden by today's negativity.[32]

Counter-education cannot offer more than critical practices, emotional possibilities, and disenchantment of the kind produced by the current subjectification process—even while initiating and exposing its ruptures, distortions, deconstructions, and resistances. These, however, are of much value, sometime even in "practical," constructive aspects, opening new symbolic and material possibilities for a more humane coexistence. It is a kind of human existence, which faces its anti-human horizons, as well as the futility of grand expectations for a current "revolution" or for "emancipation" brought about by the imperatives of reason and its self-justified interpreters and prophets. The struggle, which manifests negative Utopia, relates to the possibilities of reflection, of transcendence from the self-evidence of the hegemonic order. It addresses the possibilities of humans' self-constitution, articulation, and representation as part of reality, of which they are agents of change, antagonism, resistance, and transformation but also of solidarity and responsibility. The constitution of dialogical arenas and networks of solidarity within the present system manifest that the negation of the present system and the resistance to its hegemonic logic have also positive, constructive dimensions. These, however, cannot be institutionalized, frozen, and guaranteed; they are determined to remain temporal, partial, fragile, and risky.

With all its "positive" dimensions, however, counter-education has no illusions: it is a *battle* that cannot offer "success" in the sub-lunae world, nor detection of the "authentic" I. Central to counter-education is the acknowledgment that the attempts to negate the present order or to develop a critical distance even when fulfilled to some degree are not to be totally separated from the production, control, representation, and consumption of the system against which it turns. Yet it is not a mere manifestation of the system, its logic, and its practices. It is also something else, something *more* than the relations, contexts, and constructs of power relations within contingent systems and networks. That "something" is a manifestation of the human subject as not-an-object, as transcendence from the continuum of the *Same*.

At the same time, as always local, temporary, and immanently fragile, any achievement of counter-education cannot become "true," "fundamental," guaranteed, universalized, or frozen in time. It does, however, offer humans, as individuals—never as collectives—moments of transcendence and emancipation from the burden of the hegemonic ideals, strives, fashions, and forces which determine the pleasures, reflectivity, and horizons of the normalized subject. It takes part in the messianic tradition and seriously relates to "emancipation" from meaninglessness. Yet it cannot offer an alternative, positive, solid "genuine normality" or indisputable "meaning." It is a kind of "emancipation" in which there is no rest, no Garden-of-Eden on earth, and it is to be struggled for again and again, with no guarantee, no consolation, and no reward.

In other words, counter-education cannot offer anything more than a struggle, and in the present conditions this too only as a Utopia, even if a concrete Utopia. The realization of this concrete Utopia can be advanced here and now by every expression of displeasure, hatred, and discontent which gives birth to "border identities" and sites of "occult instability."[33] Its greatest obstacles are the disappearance of the consciousness to alienation, the demolition of the critical distance, and the lack of relevance of the problematization of the *Same* by challenging the apparatuses and conditions which produce its becoming self-evident and invisible. In other words, its greatest obstacle is the current general identification with the present order and its given or promised pleasures and conventions.

Wearing down these cracks in the system might become a gate for dialogical alternatives and for counter-educational possibilities. This is so even if under normal conditions they serve as knowledge images and conceptual apparatuses, and inner drives which represent only an additional, alternative, violent version of normalizing education. Peter McLaren is not completely wrong when he asserts that

> Such a project does not work from an "ideal unity which represents and mediates multiple interests." It works instead from univocal multiplicity of desires whose process secretes its own system of tracking and regulation. There is no unique objective, no totalizing unity.[34]

It is wrong, however, to abandon the relation to infinity and totality in the name of contingency, anti-foundationalism, and contextualism. At the same time, however, in light of Adorno's thought, today's critique should see itself dialectically, and be aware that the concepts are not only "refusing" to be identical with the objects—they are not even identical with themselves. This concept of dialectics is foreign to McLaren, Giroux, and most other prominent thinkers of today's critical pedagogy. Adorno's negative dialectics,[35] however, should be reformulated, in light of the segmentation and disappearance of the concept[36] and the psychological and intellectual world in which the challenge of the concepts and allegories was vivid, meaningful, dangerous, and could offer transcendence and *redemption*. This is in face of the total reification within today's culture industry. And yet counter-education insists that even in today's electropolis the ethical experience can offer transcendence, responsibility, and meaning, even if only dialectically, temporarily, and with no total and eternal salvation. As Jan Maschelein shows, it is a rich source of meaningful educational alternatives.[37]

As will be shown in this book, normally the alternatives to the present order are not less committed than the hegemonic normalizing education to hinder the possibilities of non-ethnocentristic, non-violent versions of solidarity and support the refusal to love and to dialogical reflection and transcendence. As will be shown by the Israeli context, the inequalities, systematic oppression, and the violent control within hegemonic capitalistic, ethnocentristic, and technologically advanced networks may even infuse and fertilize religious-nationalistic-oriented, anti-modern, and declared anti-humanist alternatives. These are explicitly committed to the formation of a theocracy, which will enforce by all means harmony, truth, and discipline on a diverse, fragmented, disoriented, and antagonistic society. At the same token, it would destroy post-modern discourses which concern the politics of representation, the conflicting violences which constitute identities and the competition between narratives, memories, and passions within and between competing

Introduction

and complementing networks. And so, counter-education is not only facing the hegemonic normalizing education—it is also confronted by its most successful and vivid rival alternatives, which are not less violent than the hegemonic normalizing education they struggle against. This, even when the slogans of resistance and emancipation are held by the marginalized, oppressed, and victimized.

Practically, counter-education can and has to address the concrete, specific, contextual logic of the hegemonic order within "its" system. This should be always historically contextualized while reconstructing and challenging material, general, and social developments.[38]

Counter-education de-mystifies reality by unveiling the connections between control of social resources and politics of representation. To the degree that it is being realized it does so in concrete and specific manners. Its aim can be struggled for in arenas such as cyberspace, economic, and culture industry, gender, and the ethnic within which while being crisscrossed by different networks of power relations the human is being produced, controlled, emancipated, destroyed, and falsely cherished.

The starting point of such a utopian project is always actuality, as part of the reproduction of cultural tradition and the hegemonic power relations. This actuality includes the various oppositions to the present order. Counter-education is worthy of its name when and if, when addressing the various levels and networks, their synchronization and their crisscrossing, it acknowledges that they also contain important *new* possibilities for reflection, transcendence, resistance, and change—and it works for their elevation and fulfillment. By itself counter-education, as critical theory, cannot offer a new, "true" positive vision as an alternative to the present order of things[39]. And it is part of this world especially when it gazes toward the *not-yet*, toward the messianic moment,[40] when it furthers the tradition of negative theology.[41]

And so, current counter-education should refer critically yet relate very seriously to the alternatives offered by critical pedagogy. Much relevance it can find in current post-colonial, cultural studies, postmodern feminism, and in multicultural discourses.

The struggle against the self-evident of the capitalist system and its cultural logic is under different settings in the affluent West and in the third world, but there are also important differences if we compare The Netherlands and Israel or Palestine.

In this book the Israeli context is used as an arena for the realization of critical philosophy, which is being formulated in a critical theory of Israeli society and culture. The theoretical attempt of the Frankfurt School thinkers is being here reformulated in a multicultural context, which is partially already a post-modern setting. The present work offers a re-reading of the Israeli history while developing a dialogue with Jewish traditions. As it addresses the triumph of Zionism and its violences, it reconstructs central developments in Western society and its culture industry.

The Israeli arena which incubates rich, violent, creative, contradictory, multicultural collisions, however, is not a mere test case for a Western-oriented critical pedagogy. It is part of a struggle over the formation/deconstruction of an Israeli identity and narrative, which is at the same time part and parcel of the destruction/constitution of a Palestinian identity, memory, and homeland. It is wrong to refer to "Israel" without addressing the transformation of "Palestine" into "Israel" as an unusual case in the history of Western education. It is an unusual successful case of realizing symbolic violence.[42] This success is manifested also in counter-reactions to the Zionist project, as one can see in the current Palestinian creation and representation of its identity and collective memory as natural, self-sufficient, original, and potentially harmonious. As if Jews and Arabs struggle only for land and honor, not over the symbolic might to conquer each other's collective memory, identity, will, and productive violence.

In the Israeli side this uncompleted, *not-yet* traceless transformation was a two-tier process. It included negating the fundamentals of Judaism and of social Jewish life in the Diaspora, while defeating the Palestinian identity of the land and its representations. Acquiring, digesting, and putting into oblivion the Palestinian symbolic, economical, political, and military presence in Palestine[43] was preconditioned by the triumph over the traditional Jewish *Galutiut* (Diaspora identity) within the psyche of "the new Jew" from the *Halutz* (the new Hebrew farmer-warrior) in the beginning of the twenties to the Israeli high-tech expert of the nineties. This twofolded victory is accompanied by leave-taking from the Jewish religious tradition and partially departing from the traditional Jewish way of life. It was accompanied by the constitution of a fragile Israeli identity which was never actualized by more than a tiny minority, even if by a leading elite, in Israel.[44] The Israeli normalizing education was committed to universalizing this identity under the titles such as "the new Jew," "the *Sabra*" (Jewish Israeli born), or "the Israeli soldier," and it was committed to a "melting pot" politics against the diversity and the richness of traditional Jewish memories, narratives, identities, and interests, which were acknowledged as representations of the Other which is to be destroyed at all costs.

The wrecking of the melting pot politics[45] and the fragmentation of the Israeli identity into new, unforeseen, conflicting identities[46] was possible because of the success of the Zionist project. It took place during more than a generation in conditions of an economically, technologically, and militarily

Introduction

strengthening affluent society in which imparity ever grows, and structural violence and systematic injustice to various groups become ever more sophisticated and less bearable. The culture industry which reflected and served these developments did not and even now refuses to spare much room for the collective memory of the Other. It does not allow relevancy and legitimacy to alternative narratives—unless they are presented in the form of recycling fashions and meaningless symbolic dynamics, as mere information or fetishized folklore, as in the cyberpunk. In any case there is no room in such a culture for Spirit. The absence of Spirit and the presence of contingency as described by Adorno and Horkheimer[47] to Derrida and Laclau[48] will be here contextualized and challenged.

Both of these conflicting twofold aspects of normalizing education—the idealistic and the anti-idealistic dehumanization—manifest the power of *life*. It realizes itself even by its current post-modern rebelling against, and making into playtools the attempts to subvert, limit, explain, fetishize, and mystify reality by technologically oriented rationality.

The myths which are produced and recycled in the current Israeli culture industry become "a second nature," represent the capitalistic logic as a manifestation of a globalization process. They represent today's exile of Spirit and the intensification of rational de-humanization processes. This is possible since life can manifest itself not only by Eros, but also through Thanatos. It is also because Eros itself has endless ways to realize itself, some of which are accomplished by the de-humanization of the human subject and/or his Other.

This book reconstructs the rise and fall of Zionism as a modern Jewish Spirit who gave birth to an effective educational violence, which enabled its victories. It reconstructs the wrecking of a project which for three turbulent generations committed itself to offer a secular substitute for the eternal Jewish readiness to fulfill its aim and its readiness to be called on, as manifested in Jewish messianism for thousands of years. In this context the infiltration of instrumental rationality and the demolition of idealism and collective solidarity within the secular Israeli society will be reconstructed in face of the transformation of Jewish messianism on the one hand, and the deconstruction of the solidarity and its collective ethnocentric goals, on the other.

The various chapters such as those which refer to the control over the representation of the Holocaust and the obliteration of the Nakbah, the rationalization of traffic "accident," or the stance of language and the status of teachers, articulate in a historical context the establishment of the hegemony of instrumental rationality. This reconstruction pays special attention to the context of transformation from modernity to post-modernity within Israel—a context which is partially still pre-modern. The book presents as a central theme a neglected topic in current post-modern discourses: the political and educational possibilities and limitations of coexistence of pre-modern, modern, and post-modern spaces, which crisscross each other. As a partially Western and partially colonial and partially post-colonial Middle-Eastern arena, the Israeli scene contains some unique developments which are of outmost importance for the general elaboration of current counter-educational possibilities.

In the present book the various chapters reconstruct the ways by which strategic orientations, and functionalist and instrumental-oriented perspectives became supreme criteria in the Israeli military, economical, political, and cultural centers. At the same time a special effort is made to reconstruct (especially when dealing with multiculturalism in Israel) the ways by which pre-modern and anti-modern alternatives currently become rapidly stronger both politically and "spiritually."

Fertilized by frustration and oppression of Palestinian and *Mizrahi* Jews in the margins of the Israeli society, the anti-modern and anti-democratic, anti-liberal margins are threatening the Israeli center.[49] It is a social, political, and cultural alternative which offers a vivid, attractive educational alternative, which is gathering momentum both in the Jewish and Palestinian collectives in Israel and in the self-governed Palestinian territories. Already now these developments threaten the self-confidence of the relatively affluent middle class, which are still widely (and partially wrongly) called "secular."

The current work tries to relate to the practices by which the transformation of Palestine to Israel and the appropriation of Palestinian identity by the Israeliness in many respects did succeed[50] and why the "internal" colonization, that which was supposed to defeat the separate, particular, and diverse Jewish identities ultimately turned out to be far less successful. In both of these respects this work tries to reconstruct the strategies of the attempt to constitute a harmonious new Jewish collective on the wreckage of another, non-Jewish, not-yet fully self-aware collective. This version of normalizing education was from its very beginning anti-humanistic, while being committed to the ideals of the Enlightenment, to socialism, or to liberalism.

The critical reconstruction of one hundred years of Zionist normalizing education will elaborate the general trends of modern education and its violences by historically reconstructing in detail the ways by which normalizing education actually works. A special place will be here reserved for the denotation of the construction, control, distribution, and consumption of the collective Israeli memory, identity, and consciousness within modernistic-oriented images of knowledge and political practices. This work will try to

Introduction

show how their success enabled new knowledge images and new strives, new bodies-of-knowledge, new identities and new manifestations of self-evidence —some post-modern and some pre-modern, which have today a fantastic renaissance within the Jewish and the Palestinian collectives.

The current educational successes of the post-modern and the pre-modern alternatives threaten the achievements of a hundred years of Zionism, which even its military contributions is being today put into question. Here, too, the military efficiency is to be explained by the efficient educational violence, which is a philosophical issue even in a post-modern era. Critical philosophy is relevant to this project as a research program and as a political stance; yet first of all it is meant to become a first step toward a counter-education. As such it relates to every human, in every place on this earth where de-humanization processes determine the context and the means by which humans try to constitute themselves, relate to their responsibilities, or strive to enter into or escape from meaningful intersubjectivity.

In this respect the present work is a call for emancipation which cannot even hope that "emancipation," "successful revolution," or universal "truth" will be realized by counter-education. It acknowledges its limitations, not only its responsibilities. It cannot hope for establishing an alternative, positive, enduring reality which will be strong enough to defend itself from colonizatory practices of "exterior" normalizing education and from "internal" alternatives. Within counter-education there is no room for collectivism, only for the Utopia of a dialogical community.

Two ways are open for the negative Utopia of counter-education to come into being. One open way for it is to be realized as an existential totality, a state of existence that is not to be institutionalized. It is an ethical sphere and it is not even to be reduced to an existential experience. It is a self-creating human moment in which the ethical "I" becomes a reality. In such a moment a bridge is erected, a relation is established to *the totally other* as an Other who is a totality to be faced,[51] to be conquered. It is wrong to conceive this relation as a strategic decision of the subject, which establishes relations with the Other. It is more being called on by her responsibility[52] toward the otherness of her fellow human and toward the not-yet-realized potentials within the given reality that the subject becomes an ethical "I."

The normalized subject *cannot* decide to become something essentially different than she is directed and constituted to be. Yet sometime the power of the system, its structure, and its hegemonic symbolic and material dynamics are challenged by something much superior to its might. From time to time an unknown, uncontrolled otherness *bursts* into the system, as if it comes from beyond its historical horizons and as if it can bring about changes and even a transformation of the entire realm of self-evidence. As part of this change or as its only manifestation, the normalized subject can be transformed by being faced with new possibilities. In this respect the ethical "I" is a possibility which is being enforced and not chosen. And so the emancipation becomes fundamentally something which is not solely self-created or initiated by the subject. If it were a manifestation of free will it would have shown the factuality as free, and as such, there would be in it no room for real choice, exactly as in a totally closed and determined system.

Under these circumstances the unexpected might present itself in any unconsummated moment, like the appearance of the messiah in the Jewish tradition. And so the "I" as some-thing might become some-one, uncontrolled by the conflicting violences of normalizing education. As Levinas tells us, this alternative is pre-rational[53] and has no language, political platform, or moral agenda. It is always a possibility which challenges the hegemonic order and the invisibility of the violences of normalizing education. Yet as a negative Utopia, even as a concrete life possibility, it is determined to impotency in political terms, since it cannot offer counter-violence and institutional successes.

There is, however, another way by which counter-education can be realized. It can be struggled for within a dialogical arena by men and women as moral-political subjects who realize their responsibility as socially active agents. In a dialogical-moral-political arena there is room for rational dissuasions, compromises, and critical spirit. Here the resistance to the hegemonic order can formulate itself into dialogical reflections, oppositional politics, and alternative agendas. However, it is important to see that even as such, in a temporary, limited arena, counter-education cannot promise a universal durable alternative while insisting on refusing counter-violence, manipulative education, and abandonment of dialogical co-existence. Its Utopia must be a negative Utopia even in its most "positive" and concrete manifestations. Not less important is the problematic bridging of the gap between the private and the public, the philosophical and the political, the ethical "I" and the moral "I." This book would like to contribute to the erection of such bridges.

This book is not a solely academic work. It sees itself also as an element in a moral and political dialogue and struggle for more equality, for more possibilities, for silenced "voices," for recollections of distracted memories, identities, and rights of women, ethnical, national, and sexual, and cultural minorities, and others. But it is at the same time also part of a demystification of their traditional ways for emancipation, not only part of a reconstruction and of their victimization and resistance to their oppressors.

This work cannot offer a one-dimensional separation between the victim and the victimizer, the system, its agents, and its products. Michel Foucault is right: power is everywhere.[54] Yet, this does not mean that there is nothing but power. This book, which reconstructs the educational powers, their victories, victims, and transformations, attempts to show that power is *not* all that there is; de-humanization processes relate to the infinity, to the openness, to the possibilities for uncontrolled and for totally other, human prospects for men, women, and children.

"Moments" of such an alternative are present even in the history of the construction of Israel and Palestine. In some respects humans can work for changing reality and for transforming themselves, open new spaces for dialogical possibilities, for actualizing counter-education. But it is only a limited, always suspicious, dangerous project.

As such this book is more of an invitation to counter-education than counter-education in action. An invitation for refusal to abandon religiousness which manifests the infinitude of the openness of being and of human being to become different than they are directed to be by "their" normalizing system. The forgetfulness of this human potential is being here challenged without a promise for the pleasures of truth or of victories of the oppressed. Normally, if not totally destroyed, the oppressed will change their position and become oppressors of others, maybe of their former victimizers, and normalizing education will change its tactics and achievements. Counter-education must acknowledge it not only when referring to the rival collectives as the Hoottus and the Tuttzi in Rwanda, the Serbians and the Kosovonians in Kosovo, or opposing factions of the American society in Seattle, or Palestine/Israel. It is exactly the ever-assured presence of *the totally other* and its possible presence in the form of a new Hitler, Jesus, earthquake, or volcano which manifests the possibility of hope and meaningful life. In such a world love is an open possibility and transcendence from meaninglessness enables dialogical coexistence. In such a world counter-education becomes a concrete Utopia, a way of life which contains new possibilities and worthy struggles.

NOTES

1. Ilan Gur-Ze'ev. *Philosophy, Politics and Education in Israel.* Tel-Aviv: Zemora-Bitan and The University of Haifa Press, 1999.
2. Ilan Gur-Ze'ev. "Towards a non-repressive critical pedagogy." *Educational Theory* 48: 4 (Fall 1998), 463-486.
3. Emmanuel Levinas. "Essence and disinterestedness," in Adriaan T. Peperzak, Simon Critchley, and Robert Bernasconi (eds.), *Emmanuel Levinas; Basic Philosophical Writings.* Bloomington and Indianapolis: Indiana University Press 1996, 111.
4. Max Horkheimer. "Die Sehnsucht nach dem ganz Anderen," *Gesammelte Schriften* 7, Frankfurt a.Main: Fisher, 385-404.
5. Immanuel Levinas. "Is ontology fundamental?", in Adriaan T. Peperzak, Simon Critchley, and Robert Bernasconi (eds.), *Emmanuel Levinas; Basic Philosophical Writings.* Bloomington and Indianapolis: Indiana University Press 1996, 9.
6. Jan Masschelein. "Schoepfung und absoluter Anfang," 7.
7. Jan Masschelein. "Wandel der Oeffentlichkeit und das Problem der Identitaet," *Zeitschrift fuer Paedagogik* 28 (1992), 62.
8. Jonathan Friedman. "Narcissism, roots and postmodernity," in Scott Lash and Jonathan Friedman, *Modernity & Postmodernity.* Oxford: Blackwell 1992, 333.
9. Michel Foucault. *Power/Knowledge: Selected Interviews and Other Writings 1972-1977.* Translated by Colin Gordon, Leo Marshall, John Mepham, and Kate Soper. New York: Harvester Wheatsheaf 1980.
10. Michel Foucault. *The Archeology of Knowledge.* Translated by A. M. Sheridan Smith, Bristol: Routledge 1995, 211.
11. Lawrence Grossberg. "Identity and cultural studies: is that all there is?", in Stuart Hall and Paul du Gay (eds.), *Questions of Cultural Identity.* London: Sage Publications 1997, 102.
12. Ilan Gur-Ze'ev. "Toward a non-repressive critical pedagogy," *Educational Theory* 48: 4 (Fall 1998), 463-486.
13. Emmanuel Levinas. "Meaning and sense," in *Emmanuel Levinas; Basic Philosophical Writings*, 62-63.
14. Stuart Hall. "Introduction," in Stuart Hall and Paul du Gay (eds.). *Questions of Cultural Identities.* London: Sage Publications 1997, 2.
15. Emmanuel Levinas. "Transcendence and height," in *Emmanuel Levinas; Basic Philosophical Writings*, 12.
16. Max Horkheimer. *Eclipse of Reason.* New York: Oxford University Press 1974, 91.
17. Immanuel Levinas. "Philosophy and the idea of infinity," *Collective Philosophical Papers*, 56.
18. Gilles Deleuze. *Difference & Repetition.* Translated by Paul Patton, New York: Columbia University Press 1994, 53.
19. Herbert Marcuse. "Nachwort," in Walter Bebjamin, *Zur Kritik der Gewalt und Andere Aufsaetze.* Frankfurt a.Main 1971, 100.
20. Michel Foucault, *Power/Knowledge.*
21. Jean-Francois Lyotard. *The Differend; Phrases in Dispute.* Translated by G. van den Abeele, Manchester: Manchester University Press, 1988.
22. Ilan Gur-Ze'ev, Jan Masschelein, and Nigel Blake. "Reflectivity, reflection and counter-education," *Studies in Philosophy and Education* 20 (2001) 93-106.

23 Walter Benjamin. *Zur Kritik der Gewalt und Andere Aufsaetze*, 60.
24 Ilan Gur-Ze'ev. "Cyberfeminism and education," *Educational Theory* 49: 4 (Fall 1999), 447.
25 Lawrence Grossberg. "Identity and cultural studies: is that all there is?", 99.
26 Ernesto Laclau. "Introduction," in Ernesto Laclau (ed.), *The Making of Political Identities*. New York: Verso 1994, 1-10.
27 Max Horkheimer and Theodor Adorno. *Dialectic of Enlightenment*. Translated by John Cumming, New York: 1973, 219.
28 Jacques Derrida. "Remarks on deconstruction and pragmatism," in Chantal Mouffe (ed.), *Deconstruction and Pragmatism; Simon Critchley, Jacques Derrida, Ernesto Laclau & Richard Rorty*. London and New York: Routledge 1996, 84.
29 Peter McLaren, *Revolutionary Multiculturalism*, 298.
30 Uri Ram. "The 'new historiography' or the privatization of memory," in Yehiam Weiz (ed.), *Between Vision and Revision; Hundred Years of Zionist Historiography*. Jerusalem: Merkaz Zalman Shazar 1997, 311-343 (in Hebrew).
31 Jonathan Friedman. *Cultural Identity and Global Process*. London: Sage 1996, 239.
32 Roland Barthes. *Mythologies*. Translated by Annette Lavers, London: The Trinity Press 1972, 157.
33 Peter McLaren. *Critical Pedagogy and Predatory Culture; Oppositional Politics in a Postmodern Era*. London and New York: 1995, 139.
34 Peter McLaren. *Revolutionary Multiculturalism*, 147.
35 Theodor Adorno. *Negative Dialectics*. Translated by E. B. Ashton, New York: Continuum, 1999.
36 Adam Tenenbaum. "Anti-human responsibilities for a post-modern educator," in Ilan Gur-Ze'ev (ed.), *Conflicting Philosophies of Education in Israel/Palestine*—a special issue of *Studies in Philosophy and Education*. Doedrecht: Kluwer 2000, 7-24.
37 Jan Masschelein. "Critical education as problematization. Some remarks on the 'other' value of knowledge, science and technology," *Educational Theory* 48: 4 (Fall 1998), 521-530.
38 Lawrence Grossberg. "Identity and cultural studies: is that all there is?", in Stuart Hall and Paul du Gay (eds.), *Questions of Cultural Identity*, London: Sage 1997, 92.
39 Max Horkheimer. *Traditionelle und Kritische Theorie*. Frankfurt a.Main: Fischer 1974, 35.
40 Walter Benjamin. *Gesammelte Schriften*, II.1, Frankfurt a.Main: 1974, 203.
41 Max Horkheimer. *Gesammelte Schriften* 7, 294.
42 Edward Said. *After the Last Sky*. London and Boston: Faber and Faber 1986, 106.
43 Edward Said. *The Question of Palestine*. London: Routledge & Kegan Paul, 1980.
44 Oz Almog. *The Sabra; A Profile*. Tel-Aviv: Am Oved 1997, 162 (in Hebrew).
45 Moshe Lissak. *The Mass Immigration in the Fifties; The Failure of the Melting Pot Policy*. Jerusalem: Bialik Institute 1999, 74 (in Hebrew).
46 Gadi Yatziv. *The Sectorial Society*. Jerusalem: Bialik Institute, 1999, 151-156 (in Hebrew).
47 Max Horkheimer. "Was wir 'Sin' nennen, wird verschwinden," in Max Horkheimer, *Gesammelte Schriften* 7. Frankfurt a.Main: Fischer, 1985, 345-357.
48 Ernesto Laclau. "Universalism, particularism, and the question of identity," *October* 61 (Summer 1992), 83-90. See also: Ernesto Laclau. "Deconstruction, pragmatism, hegemony," in Chantal Mouffe (ed.), *Deconstruction and Pragmatism; Simon Critchley, Jacques Derrida, Ernesto Laclau & Richard Rorty*. London and New York: Routledge, 1996, 61.

49 Henriette Dahan-Kalev. "Mizrahi Jews in Israel: a postmodern point of view," in Ilan Gur-Ze'ev (ed.), *Modernity, Postmodernity and Education*. Tel-Aviv: School of Education and Ramot, Tel Aviv University, 1999, 226.
50 Edward Said, *After The Last Sky*, 135.
51 Emmanuel Levinas. "Philosophy and the idea of infinity," *Collected Philosophical Papers*. Translated by Alphonso Lingis, Dordrecht: Martinus Nijhoff Publishers 1987, 55.
52 Jan Masschelein. "Wandel der Oefentlicheit und das Problem der Identitaet," *Zeitschrift fuer Paedagogik* 28 (1992), 59-75.
53 Immanuel Levinas. "Freedom and command," *Collected Philosophical Papers*, 21.
54 Michel Foucault, *ibid.*

CHAPTER 1
Holocaust/Nakbah as an Israeli/Palestinian Homeland

The quest for homeland, even the reflection on homeland, is never at home. The moment "homeland" enters the linguistic space and receives its "voice" it comes to the brink of loss, of distance or of exile from what homeland refers to. Entering the language of homeland, quest for homeland, or overcoming being exiled from homeland as it is, or as it should become, entails entering the Platonic cave within which a collective or a realm of self-evidence and *Same* is created. It is constituted by powers, that are effective enough to secure the invisibility of their manipulations for the collective, which it creates, activates, represents, and victimizes. It is exactly the depths of the evidence of selfhood, orientation, yardsticks, and aims of the individual that feel at home in their "homeland" which represents their effective victimization and loss of themselves. In this sense the language of homeland or Heimat as its history reveals, might also open new possibilities of overcoming the hegemonic system.

Homeland as well as the quest for homeland or Heimat, as part of individual and collective identity formation, representation, and reconstruction are one of the products of normalizing education. It reflects the efficiency of the hegemonic educational violence. At the same time, however, the longing for Heimat or for returning to "home-land" also manifests an immanently alternative quest, antagonistic, totally other than the continuum of the *Same* of which national homeland is but one, historically short-lived, example. This other, non-collectivist, never formed and given quest, enables the never-determined presence of *the totally other*,[1] as *transcendental* element. It calls for a struggle, which is also a breakthrough, to overcome the temptations of the Platonic cave of homeland. Such a call is a challenge and a threat to the triumph of normalizing education and its actualized or promised Heimat. It endangers not only the attitude to one's homeland in terms of identification with one's-self, patriotism, willingness for sacrifice, or hate/fear of the Other; much more than that, this possible transcendental *call* endangers being at home in all other manifestations of the *Same*, the continuum, and the self-evidence, namely of the manifestations of Thanatos. Still, this call it is a great danger. It includes suffering albeit a worthy suffering and transcendence which have no determined "aim," "goal," "truth," or nirvana. This messianic moment is a religious element, which offers not an alternative concept of homeland or sweet Garden of Eden on earth—but an alternative presence of exile or homelessness. In this respect it is inseparable from the presence of the quest for, or love of, homeland or the miseries of its loss.

The academic treatment of the issue of homeland is not irrelevant to our topic. "Heimat is where one is born, where one receives an education, comes to consciousness of selfhood, adjusts oneself to family and society, or constructs a 'social entity.'"[2] Sociologists and social psychologists have explained Heimat as a basic human need, comparable to eating or sleeping.[3] According to Celia Applegate, political scientists have also spoken of Heimat in terms of natural human tendencies, in particular tendencies to form political allegiances, whether on either the local or the national level.[4] This scholar maintains that Heimat is not only a source of security in the patria, fatherland, and motherland. It is much more than that: it is, as Karl Phillip Moritz and the romantic tradition understood, an image of "home, tranquility and happiness."[5] Rolf Petri, too, emphasizes Heimat as a social stabilizing element.[6] He denotes the importance of Heimat as a relation and as a sense of place of origin, as familiar land, as the opposite of facing a strange place. Petri is right in emphasizing that the concept of Heimat as being one with oneself (Bei-Sich-Sein) also had a metaphysic element which allowed and fertilized the feeling and the expressions relating to a semantic field that stretches from conceptions such as "father Rhein" to conceptions such as "the German blood"[7] as unifying and elevating elements. Petri advances the academic discussion on this issue by showing the instrumentalization of the Heimat feelings, conceptions, and cultural activities within the framework of changing economic and national struggles.[8] At the same time, Petri argues, Heimat also functions as a subjective space where a person who is not one with himself or herself can introspect and experience himself or herself, meeting and reassuring his or her identity.[9]

We will try to make clear the conceptions of homeland and the role of the quest for homeland as well as the human situation within two different conceptions of homeland or Heimat by first reconstructing the role of normalizing education in establishing, representing, and reproducing notions of homeland. After showing it in relation to homeland as a safe haven, we will try to elaborate on it in another version, from the point of view of the Exiled. This second version will be at the center of this elaboration, the focus being on the case of the Israelis and the Palestinians.

The Israeli/Palestinian concepts of homeland and exile will be reflected with special attention to the function of the instrumentalization of the memories of the Holocaust and Nakbah as a manifestation of normalizing education. This will be done from a counter-educational perspective which does not offer an alternative concept of homeland but positions itself in an alternative exile as a locus for a struggle for overcoming both Israeli and Palestinian, indeed all normalizing collectivist-oriented concepts of homeland (and loss of homeland/striving to reestablish the lost homeland). This alternative to the concept of loss and victimhood will challenge the concepts of victimhood; suffering and exile of these two rival collectives and the essential *Same*, which they represent. A different concept of homelessness represents a readiness for, and sensitivity to, counter-education, and not the victory of its alternative symbolic bombardment. This is the most we can do, and even in this we already represent normalizing education and the other manifestations of the *Same* as our homeland. The acceptance of this contradiction is a gateway to much greater dangers and possibilities of self-articulation and love of the otherness of the Other's exile.

Normalizing education manifests itself in many ways, arenas, and compositions. One of its central manifestations is in constructing collectives and individuals. "*Home*," here, is essential. The ability of normalizing education to reproduce itself while using its victims as its agents is determined by effectiveness in establishing a totality in which there is no alarming or awakening gap between the normalized individual and the normalizing system. The system produces realms of self-evidence in which the yardsticks to evaluate identifications and characterizations are self-assurance, of which the individual becomes a part, an agent, and a symbol. If the identification of the individual with the system ensures a safe closure and a comfortable totality, the individual, who has became some-thing will not feel alienation toward his or her normalizing space of manipulation and he or she will regard it as his or her "home." Concrete and specific contextual, historical, material, and symbolic conditions always determine the construction of such agents of the hegemonic realm of self-evidence.[10] It is always vulnerable, always on the edge of being colonized by another system and alternative ideologies, collectives, power relations, consciousness, interests, and social formations and interests.

The collective, as a close grouping of normalized individuals and as a manifestation of the efficient reproduction process of hegemonic normalizing education, is committed to internal and external colonization processes. Its effective violence is a precondition for its reproduction and enhancement. The ultimate victory of normalizing education over its alternatives is in its ability to *veil* efficiently its creative violence. Its effective violence is tested by its competence in ensuring an unproblematic identification of its victims with its violence, turning it into a present or a promised "home". The space of this violent process of normalizing education becomes "home" when the violence is efficient enough. It gives birth and cultivates the safeguards of the horizons of its prisoners. One of the most efficient policing powers is the prisoners' love of this "home" or "home-land," their commitment to disregard, destroy, or redeem their own and their Others' internal or external love of homeland. It is of vital importance in constituting peace, tranquility, and love of the kind that will make possible the prosperity of the "we." Fundamentally this means the safe reproduction of the hegemonic system and the impotence of its victims to unveil the violences which create their identity, their quests, their fears, their enemies, and their love of their selves, their "we," "their" "homeland," and the "they," the "enemies."

Nationalism is but one of many possible manifestations of the production of collectives by the violence of normalizing education. The concept of homeland or Heimat and the love and devotion to one's homeland are a manifestation of a successful de-humanization of humans, by constructing not only their identity, love, fears, and hatreds but also their identification with this process and committing themselves to it as its guardians and agents. Normally such systems and ideologies collide with their Others in a creative meeting in which each side manifests its love of homeland by destroying the Other and *colonizing* its rivals as heroes, patriots, good citizens, or devoted fellows. These clashes need not always erupt into an explicit violence, war, or conquest of physical spaces.

In different historical situations and social and cultural contexts it has different manifestations and is never fixed, stable, and secure. The production of collectives and their closure has many different versions. Some of these use the rhetoric of openness, pluralism, anti-dogmatism, kaleidoscopic, hybrid, contingent educational processes, and so forth. This is manifested, for example, in cyberspace, in actualizing consumerism, or activating the McDonald'sization of intersubjectivity, all of which are manifestations of normalizing education which create collectives, their sense of homeland, its horizons, and its Others.

The Israeli-Palestinian context manifests a clash between two normalizing educational systems, which produced and reproduce two collectives committed to negating the otherness of the Other as a vital part of each one's self-constitution. This self-constitution of the collective is actually the act of the negation of self-constitution of the individual human. It is the act of robbing by the system of human potentials for overcoming collectivism and false love and relation to Spirit, creativity, and responses to a *call* of something higher than life as the aim of life. It demolishes the potentials for dialogical self-constitution. It is actually the self-realization of the system. It uses the consciousness of self, identity, collective memory, and quests for a freed homeland in each collective for self-reproduction. It is committed to denying the concept of the homeland of the Other and to "liberating" the geographical space as well as the symbolic arena as part of its normalizing education, which also has its explicit and occasionally military violences. It is not the absence of a common discourse or bridge between the narratives of Israeli and Palestinians that is responsible for the successful veiling of the symbolic violence which is responsible for the visible violence between the two collectives. Quite the contrary: it is their concept of homeland and their concept of the collective and its Other that binds them in a common narrative, fertilized daily by the conflicting normalizing education.

Israelis and Palestinians represent a unique concept of homeland. This model is unique in its composition of the concept of homeland in opposition to the normal concepts of homeland, fatherland, motherland, or Heimat as a safe, familiar, tranquil place, which constitutes the identity of the individual and the collective. In the Israeli-Palestinian case it is the Diaspora which is the constitutive element. For both the Israelis and the Palestinians being exiled as a collective experience and consciousness is the central dimension of normalizing education. Its effects are essential for constituting the collective identity, the memories, the quest for home-land, and the commitment to defend its borders, interests, and imperatives against the Other.

The Israelis and Palestinians are also united by another essential element: each of the rival collectives conceives the same space as its home-land and itself as the sole legitimate reflection of its identity and metaphysical meaning, goals, and imperatives. For all the differences, and they are of vital importance, both share a commitment to destroy the Other; and rival normalizing education, its narrative, and its commitment to struggle against what it conceives as criminally violent practices against the legitimate and original inhabitants of the country. The instrumentalization of the memories of the Holocaust and the Nakbah are essential for this discourse between the two normalization processes and narratives to such a degree that the two should be conceived also as one. It is a single process, manifesting and realizing the essence of normalizing education and the mechanism of constructing homeland or Heimat as "home." It has not only its "land" but also its Others, who are committed to colonize it and make the land into their "home," as part of destroying the identity and all that is dear and of value in the other "we."

In Israel the memory of the Holocaust is not left to contingency. It is officially instrumentalized and institutionalizes by a special law. A governmental agency (*Mosad Yad Vashem*) was established to preserve and represent its memory and implications. The history of the changing representations of the Holocaust memory and the official educational "lessons" of the Holocaust are beyond the scope of this paper. The focus here is on the centrality of the memories of the Holocaust to the goals of the Israeli normalizing education in general and especially in its relations to the concept of homeland.

Since its beginning, the Israeli instrumentalization of the Holocaust memory has treated the memory of the Holocaust as part of the polemics with the Jewish non-Zionists and the rest of the world. The goal has been to establish "the lessons of the Shoa" as an ultimate justification of the Zionist claim for establishing Palestine/Israel as a "national home" or as the realization of "home coming" to Zion, to Israel. This is both the only way to secure the safety of the Jews and as the realization of the inner imperative of the Jewish history.

The mainstream Zionist attitude to Israel/Palestine is to be understood as a secular political theology. It conceived an unbreakable tie between the true identity and telos of the Land of Israel and the Sons of Israel. It saw Israel/Palestine as the "historic homeland" of the Jews; the passage of time had not lessened their legitimate right to live and gather themselves in it while building it, or "redeeming" it. All the more "since it is almost a desert, and almost unpopulated by others, and we, for our part never abandoned our hope to return to this land, as manifested by the 12th of the pillars of our faith, all our prayers and all our history."[11] A. D. Gordon, one of the greatest and most influential figures of the Zionist labor movement, was very clear on the connection of the secular Zionist claim to Israel/Palestine as a Jewish homeland with the Jewish essentialism of the Zionist project, even in its most radical secular forms. "Judaism," he asserted, "is one of the foundations of the 'I' of each one of us."[12] Accordingly he saw the Bible as the source of the Jews' right to the land, as its eternal legitimization. To this he added the argument of work and creativity as manifestations/creating power of the identity of the land, constituting it into a "home":

> We have an historical right on the land, and this right remains ours as long as another, alternative, power of life and creativity has not acquired it entirely. Our land, which beforehand was 'the land of milk and honey' or, at any rate, produced a high culture, became wasteland, poor, distressed of all cultural countries, and almost empty. As if it is a sign that the country is waiting for us, reassurance of our right on the land.[13]

The position from which the "purification" or reclaiming the homeland is viewed as justified is *exile*, and the locus from where it is articulated is the Diaspora, even when the viewer is in Israel/Palestine. This is contrary to what we can find in discussions of other Heimat or homeland. In the Israeli case this is where the call for fearless "creativity" and struggle comes from, as manifested in the mystization of Josef Trumpeldor and the *halutz* (pioneer) as creative, innocent, ethnocentrist, fearless, farmer-warrior. The national-religious and the secular nationalist trends in Zionism were united in their essentialism, conceiving the essence of Palestine to be Israel, or, Zion, where Zionism, if successful, will realize a renaissance of the nation and its religion/spiritual-cultural creation.[14] One trend emphasized the spiritual-religious aspect, and saw Israel/Palestine as the revival of *Yaveneh* and the rabbinic-halachic tradition. Its secular version was represented by Ahad Ha'am, who introduced a concept that distinguished the spiritual homeland from the physical homeland. His project too was vitalistic and ethnocentristic, demanding of the recapture of the Jews' connection to the *essence* of Palestine/Israel. Yet this was not in order to guarantee political domination: within this concept of homeland the imperative was to reestablish Israel/Palestine as a Jewish spiritual center, while most of the Jews could continue their physical lives in the Diaspora as their relevant political, economic, and social context. This second trend saw in Israel/Palestine the revival of *Beitar* and the vitalistic-nationalistic tradition. A third trend adopted a rationalist Eurocentrist orientation, seeing Israel/Palestine as an ancient home from a rationalist Eurocentristic orientation, according to the ideals and the self-image of the contemporary Western bourgeois. While conceiving Israel/Palestine as the historical homeland of the Jews, Theodor Herzl was prepared to accept any refuge place to solve the immediate threats on the existence and security of Jewish life, and develop it into an independent Jewish state free of emotional, religious, mythological, and other irrational bonds of a collective to its homeland. When the Zionist congress rejected his "Uganda project" he vowed in the traditional words "if I forget you Jerusalem. . . . may my tongue cling to the roof of my mouth." While committing himself to the struggle for making Zion once more the homeland of the Jewish people as the ultimate goal of zionism, his commitment was more of an internal political maneuver (to avoid the disintegration of the Zionist movement) than a reflection of his deep feelings for Israel/Palestine.[15]

Historically, the fourth trend emerged victorious in the Zionist history, while being influenced by, and containing elements of, the other trends, of which the one represented by Ahad Ha'am was by far the least influential.

Both the right and left wings of the hegemonic Zionist movement were committed to an uncompromising negation of the Diaspora. This was founded on the perception of the Diaspora as a perverted, unnatural way of Jewish life, not just dangerous; and certainly not primarily on the Jews' harsh circumstances in it or on the actual and potential dangers that the Diaspora incubated. In Zionist secularized political theology, Jewish life had a universal and a national telos. The fulfillment of the historical-cosmic mission of the Jewish nation originated in the revelations and experiences of the founding fathers and their birth through and with the religious significance of the sites and symbols of the space. Within the Jewish tradition and the Zionist narrative this telos of Israel did not end with the gift to the world of the book of books, with begetting Christianity and Islam, and not by Jewish fertilizing modern Western culture with some of its most important figures and ideas. The imperative of the telos of the Jews is to negate the Diaspora and recreate national political and cultural life in its homeland. The realization of its telos within its universal and national Utopia is formulated in modern Western revolutionary leftist or rightist articulations yet essentially it draws from and continues the ancient Jewish religious conception of the special role that the Children of Israel have in this world, with its metaphysical foundations on the one hand, and on its Messianic attitude toward the future and its presence, on the other. Moshe Hess, Berdiczewski, Abaa Ahimeir, Borochov, Uri-Zvi Grinberg, Jabotinsky, Arlozorov, Ben-Gurion, and Menahem Begin are all united in this secularized vitalistic political theology.

The conception of homeland here has three dimensions. One is of seeing Palestine, in its essence, as Israel, namely, seeing the land's Palestinian identity as a historical stage, which manifests its decline and downfall, paralleling the downfall of the Jewish people in the Diaspora. It is conceived as an "almost unpopulated land" or as desolated land ("*Midbar shemama*"), which calls for its flourishing, purifying, and elevation by its returning owners, who are by no means immigrants, and certainly not colonizers. This project of the renewed connection between "a land without a people and a people without a land" ("*eretz lelo am leam lelo eretz*") is also a political project of literally conquering the land, establishing a Jewish majority, and enforcing a Zionist hegemony. This project was conditioned by the success of Zionist education, which was committed to give birth to "the new Jew" as a pioneer (*Halutz*), as an Israeli-born (*Sabra*), or as a soldier. Zionist education had the mission of colonizing the *soul* of the individual and creating a new collective harmonious totality as a precondition for the success of the political and military struggle over colonizing physically, politically, militarily, and culturally the space and establishing a Jewish hegemony that would reflect its essential identity and its Messianic mission. Here the concept of homeland as a future political struggle over creating a nation and its homeland is inseparable from the metaphysical foundation of a concept of revolution or struggle as homeland, on the one hand, and from the Utopian axis or a positive Utopian concept of homeland, on the other. This is so because the political-activist-present-oriented trend in the Zionist movement is revealed as a movement which is inconceivable outside its orientation toward the past and future and is also to be understood only in its metaphysical foundations and spiritual mission. The violence of normalizing education and its manipulations are revealed here as a precondition for the struggle of the realization of this project of creating a new collective and a new country on the foundation of the Diaspora identity of the Jewish people and by overcoming the Palestinian identity of the land. The purification of the Diaspora mentality and the purification of Palestine and its transformation into Israel became part and parcel of the project of re-entering history and returning to the track of fulfilling the supra-political mission of the Zionist politics. During the last 120 years the Zionist hegemonic normalizing education which created the Israelis and Israel could not create this collective and "its" space without the otherness of the Diaspora mentality and the Diaspora economic, social, and cultural conditions, on one hand and without the otherness of the Palestinian people and the Palestinian identity of Palestine, on the other. This clash was a vital element for its self-constitution—as it was for the Palestinian normalizing education and its nation-building project.

For the Israeli normalizing education it was of vital importance to establish a unified, coherent narrative of a collective memory. Its starting point was biblical Zion and its utopian axis was purified Israel. This narrative, which created the Zionist subject, was constructed by a sense of telos, which was founded on the logic of *migalut legeula* ("from exile to redemption"). After the Holocaust this narrative made that catastrophe and its lessons central, and *migalut legeula* concept was concretized and realized by the concept of *mishoa litekuma* ("from Holocaust to resurrection"). In its various articulations this narrative was founded on a concept of the all-embracing presence of the absence of homeland, on the one hand, and on the presence of violent injustice against the Jews, on the other. Being the ultimate victim of human history while being the subject of history was essential for this secularized political theology. In both of its poles—the Jews as historical victims of unredeemed world and as the claimants for universal and national justice—the concept of home was essential. The dispersion of the Jews and their life as permanent victims of human history did not reflect solely the exile of the Jews from their country and their loss of sovereignty alone. They also reflect a general human condition of living in an unjust, unredeemed world. In this sense Zionism was only one manifestation of a more general and much richer Jewish utopian commitment, realized within various and conflicting revolutionary projects, ranging from anarchism and Marxism to scientific revolutions in modern Western culture and society. In the Zionist narrative the history of homelessness—as the history of overcoming the *exile* of human reality as a real home for all people—is inseparable from the issue of the presence of historical violence. Historical violence or the whole-presence of the conditions, that Marx called "pre-history," is conceived as manifested with special clarity and immeasurable toll in the evil, which was committed throughout history against the Jews. After the Holocaust this secularized political theology became a central challenge for Zionist normalizing education. It became instrumentalized in support of the Jewish claim for Israel as a sovereign Jewish state as well as against the Palestinian narrative and its concrete challenges for the realization of the Zionist narrative.

The concept of victimhood and the self-conception of the Jews as the paradigmatic victims of secular history were essential for the fabrication of the narrative of *migalut legeula* and *mishoa litekuma*. Within the hegemonic Zionist narrative the concept of victimhood was historically paralleled to the period of Jewish life in the Diaspora. The normalizing Zionist education presented an equation between the termination of Jewish victimhood and the self-emancipation from the Diaspora mentality (*galutiut*) and from the Jewish "unnatural" life in the Diaspora by returning to the Jews' "homeland." Within this perspective the land of Israel itself was presented as captive, perverted, humiliated, and deserted, or inhabited by strangers and primitive people at times conceived as "Arabs" and at times as "Bedouins," but never as Palestinians. A special educational and political effort was recruited for *geulat akarka*, for "the redemption of the land." The return to the homeland itself was conceived as an emancipatory and expurgatory element, and it was the grand mission of "the new Jew" to redeem the land and emancipate her/himself: to (re)build and be built (*livnot uleibanot ba*). There was no way to separate the two, according to the Zionist normalizing education. The memory of the Holocaust was instrumentalized to this conclusion and the central claim of Zionism was presented as tragically and undisputedly manifested by history and *Amalek*, its agent.

The Zionist educators presented *Amalek* as a historical agent, who was responsible for Jewish victimhood. "Amalek," wrote Ben-Zion Dinner, the central figure in the history of Israeli education, "is constant (element) eternally present within the gentiles" (*Mida amealehet bein aumot*). The Holocaust was presented as one of the picks of a continuum of the history of Jewish victimhood while Jews lived in the Diaspora. Hitler or Hitlerism was paralleled with the eternal essence, which the historical *Amalek* represented. In this sense, while Hitler was presented as synonymous with *Amalek*, the defeat of Nazism was presented as not synonymous with the defeat of *Amalek*. This figure, while presented as the agent responsible for the victimization of the Jews in the Diaspora, was still more set forth as presence at home too, in Israel. The

Palestinians became present-day *Amalek* and the distorted reality of Israel as Palestine. Likewise the victims of the effort to reclaim, recapture, and "redeem" it were presented as martyrs (*Kedoshim*), equaling the Palestinian martyrs/their victims/victimizers (*Shaid*).

Victims of the refusal to the Zionist road to homeland and the victims of the struggle for "the liberation of Israel" as the homeland of world Jewry were united by the Zionist hegemonic education. Under slogans such as *Migalut legeula*, the school curriculum reflected and fabricated a Zionist subject who did not question the foundations, the practices, and the aims of this narrative, its rivals, and its enemies. History textbooks, school rituals, memorial days, memorial books, and special ceremonies, even art, the media, and the museums, were committed to the reproduction of the hegemonic narrative and helped to mobilize in a constructive manner daily symbolic and nonsymbolic violence. Thus, in the realization of the lessons and ideals of this narrative against "the *Amalek* of our generation," the Palestinians, who are said to be one of its manifestations, Remembrance Day for the Holocaust (*Yom Ashoa*) is very close in time to Remembrance Day for Israeli solders who fell in Israeli's wars for independence (*Yom Azikaron Lehalelei Ma'arahot Israel*); and this day is followed at once, with no separation by the eve of Independence Day (*Yom A'atzemaut*), celebrating the Jewish state of Israel.

While rejecting the Jewish concept of Diaspora as an ontological sign and as a precondition for the fulfillment of Jewish mission in the world and as a manifestation of its being the chosen people, Zionism rejected exile, being out of the secular/violent history or homelessness, as the homeland of Jews. The negation of the *Gola* (Diaspora) as a mentality and as social-cultural historical context for Jewish life was a precondition for the hegemonic Zionist movements who struggled for a political, historical negation of the Diaspora and for the constitution and development of Israel as the homeland and sovereign state of the Jews. This project could not be struggled for without a parallel negation, that of the legitimacy of the Palestinian claim to Palestine as the homeland of the Palestinians and the negation of their negation of the Zionist project. It is impossible to separate the Israeli-Palestinian explicit and visible struggle from the symbolic and direct violences. The struggle over place-names, for example, Jerusalem/al Kuds or Ein Hod/Ein Hud, or Heifa or Haifa, and the struggle over their Israeli or Palestinian identity (and the kind of their "Palestinian" or "Israeli" identity) are inseparable.

The refusal to acknowledge the legitimacy of the existence of the Other and/or the legitimacy of its claim to Israel/Palestine as its homeland *unites* the two collectives in a dialectics which simultaneously makes possible/enhances the visible and the invisible violence among the two rival groups while constituting their very existence as a collective. Each of the struggling collectives sees itself as the sole legitimate owner of the place and accepts the Other as a threat or perversion of the authentic or ideal identity of its homeland. Each of the rival normalizing educational systems gives special place to the relations between the victim and the victimizer. For the Israelis as Jews, the remembrance of their history as a chain of victimizations which manifest the evil in this world and the special goal and the uniqueness of the Jewish people in history, is not only a religious imperative. It is also a constitutive element of their traditional education and the formation of their traditional identity as Jews, and it became a formative element in the hegemonic Zionist education right up to the changes wrought by the last generation. Here, within the history of victimhood the remembrance of the Holocaust became of vital importance for the Zionists. Within this project the memory of the Holocaust was, and is, still instrumentalized and reproduced in relation to four interconnected and sometimes conflicting challenges. *1.* Following the traditional strife with the Jewish non-Zionists and anti-Zionists, as the ultimate "proof" of the fundamental claim of Zionism, its negation of the Diaspora and its claim for a Jewish returning to its homeland as the only guarantee of Jewry's security as a collective and as a guarantee of its return into normal national life. *2.* The tension between the imperative of "back to national normality" and the self-conception of a unique nation with an unmatched history and human telos among the nations even within the secularized return home. Not only the fathers of Zionism, such as Hess, Borochov, Jabotinsy, Gordon, and Arlosorov, but even post-independence leaders of the Zionist left and right such as Ben Gurion and Begin, reproduced and further developed this secularized political theology. The issue of Jews as the ultimate victims in world's history and reestablishing a Jewish homeland and a *Sabra* mentality as opposed to the Diaspora mentality (*Galutiut*) demanded and justified the instrumentalization of the Holocaust memory. *3.* The instrumentalization of the Holocaust memory and its ever greater role in the hegemonic Zionist narrative was enhanced in face of the Palestinian *Nakbah*, the constitution of a rival Palestinian narrative which challenged the Zionist narrative. And it was enhanced in face of the Palestinian (counter) violence and its negation of the Zionist instrumentalization of the Holocaust, its lessons and its commitment to the establishment and strengthening of Israel as a Jewish homeland as the ultimate answer to the Holocaust. The Palestinian transitional denial or minimization of the Holocaust, their denial of the right of Jews to return to Israel as their homeland, and for that matter their denial of the legitimacy of any Jewish existence in Israel, along with their violent resistance to the realization of the Zionist project became unified. These denials and violence became unified into a Zionist-conceived reality of a new Holocaust not in the Diaspora but in Israel itself. The response to this existential and ideological threat was combined with the refusal to acknowledge the suffering inflicted on the Palestinians and the injustice done to them by the realization of the Zionist project. The fear of a new Holocaust and the fear of acknowledging responsibility for the *Nakbah* became inseparable. So did the denial of the otherness of the Other by National Socialism, the denial of the otherness of the Other, his/her suffering and aspirations by the Palestinians toward the Jews as such and as Israelis, and the denial of the otherness of the Other by the Israelis toward the Palestinians, their suffering, and aspirations. Palestinians and Israelis were united by their refusal to acknowledge not only historical tragedies and suffering, but also present suffering and aspiration for homeland as a peaceful, secure Heimat. Each side's refusal to recognize the Other's right to homeland became a *constitutive* element for collective identity formation and articulated an exiled point of reference for the conception of each collective's homeland. More and more Israelis have become aware of this, within a process of the formation of a post-modern reality in which the constitutive myths of Zionism and its creative violences are rapidly being disintegrated. Within this process more and more Israelis recognize Israel as Palestine, for the Palestinians, namely, acknowledge Palestine as the legitimate homeland of the Palestinians as well as the historical injustice done to them during the *Nakbah*, before that tragedy, and after it to the present day. Parallel to this process, fewer Israelis see Israel as the legitimate homeland of the Jews alone and a growing minority no longer see it anymore as the legitimate homeland (historically or presently) of the Jews. In the face of this development and as part of it the mythization of the Holocaust memory has become more efficient then ever. The instrumentalization of the Holocaust memory within this process, however, was not realized so effectively by the hegemonic Zionist normalizing education, which has almost disintegrated completely and lost its manipulative potentials for most segments of the Israeli middle class. 4. Within the post-modern conditions in the Israeli arena and its culture industry the Holocaust memory was not lost. It has become integrated into the system and is being produced, distributed, and consumed as any other reified commodity in the representation market. The McDonald'sization of this arena makes "Holocaust experiences" and "Auschwitz trips" into commodities, which incubates a special value. Here not a modern conception of a given or promised homeland is being produced but is its postmodern alternative. This process does not carry with it much potential for Israelis' recognition of the Palestinian Others' suffering and responsibility toward their distress, and even when it does it de-politicizes this recognition. More than that, it deconstructs the quest for homeland as well as sensibility to homelessness. It not only dismantles the commitment toward the national solidarity and willingness to self-sacrifice for the realization of collective ideals and imperatives. At the same time it dissolves the ability to assume responsibility for the Other's being exiled, uprooted from the homeland, and the potentials for resisting injustice and struggling for a dialogue. Meaninglessness as a pleasure machine becomes home.

Palestinian normalizing education parallels and corresponds with the Zionist one. Without being a mere reaction to the Zionist project it cannot be conceived without or outside the life-and-death struggle between the two. For the Palestinians too, the formative collective experience is that of being exiled, of being a suffering, homeless people, even when not uprooted from their land.[16]

Edward Said is very clear on this point: "There is no doubt that we do in fact form a community, if at heart a community built on suffering and exile."[17] The point is not that the Palestinians do not give up their identity in face of their tragedy and ongoing daily suffering. Much more than that it is the suffering, the loss of the homeland, which formulates their identity. Mahmoud Darwish writes on this issue in his poem "The Palestinian wound":

> We are discharged of remembering, the Carmel hills are within us, and on our eyelashes the grass of the Galilee. Do not say: I wish we would run toward her like a river, do not say! We are in the flesh of our homeland and she is within us![18]

The longing for the "actual" Palestine, for the land as essentially, and therefore actually is, becomes a formative element of the identity as represented by the normalizing apparatuses and its agents. The representation apparatus, the symbol, and its agents as authentic "Palestinians" are united. Darwish himself is partially aware of that in one of his interviews where he writes:

> This is an attempt at fixing the land in the language and in the body. In the Palestinian case there is something specific and special, namely that when the Palestinians went away and were exiled they took their keys with them. They were careful to keep the keys in safe places. No matter that it was in exile or in a country to which they emigrated. In this sense the key itself took the house along. In this sense the house is attached to the one who left. Not the man alone left, the land itself went away with the Palestinian wherever the Palestinian went. Consciously and unconsciously he had the need to feel that he carries the place with him, and the lost homeless one was both the man and land. This is why I have many expressions of homeland as a suitcase. My homeland is simultaneously not a suitcase and a suitcase.[19]

This present experience of homeland is in tragic contradiction to a traditional unformulated homeland, as part of self-evidence and inner-self; it was destroyed in the *Nakbah*. Its destruction is articulated in the word *Nakbah*, or, it is to be seen in light of the absence of an equivalent word in Arabic to Heimat or homeland. In literate Arabic the closest word is *mauten*. Another close term is *muskat al ras* (where put my head to rest) or the house of the grandfathers.[20] This conception of homeland as *mauten* becomes much closer to the word Heimat, yet is very different in face of a direct experience of the Palestinians

> like the one experienced by the Jafaites and all the others who immigrated from the Palestinian towns and villages—then, the longing and the quest become *mauten* or *muskat al ras*. The experience of the town or the neighborhood and the house in which one grew up, in which one tasted the first bits of happiness in one's life, part of one's inner life that is impossible to strip one from, becomes something much higher then a tangible thing. It becomes a symbol.[21]

Here the Jewish concept of homeland in exile and the Palestinian concept of homeland, as well as their concepts of loss and victimhood become very close on the one hand (without losing their differences) and part of a dialectical unity, on the other.

The Jewish presence is conceived here as a contamination of the pure land of Palestine, and in many cases as a daily rape of the land and its innocence.[22] Homeland as the place of the most contaminated, distorted, and perverted and raped by its unlawful violent conquerors is shared by the Jews/Israelis and the Palestinians. Some Palestinian thinkers who acknowledge the similarity position the two conceptions share in the framework of rival narratives struggling over hegemony in a symbolic clash, which is also a political and existential tragic struggle.[23] In the Palestinian view, however, there is no symmetry between the two claims for homeland and the two conceptions of the contamination or blasphemy, *rape* of the land, as there is no symmetry between the two concepts of Diaspora and returning home.

The Palestinian narrative is not yet formed and there is much contention over the construction and the legitimate presentation of the Palestinian identity. Still, all Palestinian political activists, most Palestinian intellectuals, and most of the Palestinian population are united in their conception of the illegitimacy of any Jewish presence in Palestine, the Israeli conception of Israel as a Jewish homeland, and on the attitude of Jews to the Palestinians and their responsibility for the *Nakbah*.

The ethnocentric attitude of the Zionist hegemonic narrative is reflected in the Israeli Declaration of Independence and is matched by the ethnocentrism of the Palestinian narrative and in its realization in its constitutive texts such as the National Charter (1964 and 1968) and the Declaration of Independence (November 1988). According to article 1 of the 1968 version of the National

Charter, "Palestine is the homeland of the Arab Nation and is an integral part of the great Arab homeland. The Palestinian stock is part of the Arab nation." Article 3 says that "The Arab Palestinian nation has a lawful right on his homeland" and in article 4 the Palestinian identity is articulated in relation to the land: "The Palestinian identity is an essential rooted character, which does not disappear. The sons from their fathers inherit it. The Zionist occupation and the disintegration of the Arab Palestinian nation, as a result of the Holocausts that it suffered, do not harm the personality of the Arab Palestinian people and its Palestinian membership of the nation and do not negate them." In the Palestinian Declaration of Independence this position of a relationship between the land and the Palestinian identity is quite explicit. It says there: "On the land of God's delivery to humanity, on the land of Palestine was born the Palestinian people, there it grew, developed and created its human and national existence which is an organic, inseparable relation between the nation, the land and history." It is important to note, however, that both official texts were written by Palestinian exiles in the Diaspora. The view of exile is very present here in special centrality when it speaks of the Palestinian identity as a reflection of the identity of the land and as an essential dimension, not a historical, contingent construct. In the unofficial texts, in stories, poems, stage plays, and essays the experience of the *Nakbah,* the exile, and the daily experience of loss of the homeland and enrichment of remembrance are explicitly presented as the constitutive element in the formation of the Palestinian collective identity. Edward Said, who defines this constitutive element,[24] emphasizes also the constitutive function of the collective suffering and violence inflicted on the Palestinians.[25] This aspect, too, parallels the Zionist narrative of the Jews as the paradigmatic victim in human history also in this respect. The formative power of the loss of homeland is explicitly paralleled with the Jewish one but within an ideological framework, which presents the Zionists as mere colonizers.[26] Many scholars, writers, and poets emphasize this theme.[27] The loss of the homeland did not make it unreal or remote for the Palestinians, as for the Jews who prayed for it daily and committed themselves to "next year in Jerusalem" wherever they were and in all central events of Jewish life. For the Palestinians this is an attitude toward homeland that might be represented by Mahmoud Darwish when he writes, "We have a country of words. Speak speak so I can put my road on the stone of a stone. We have a country of words. Speak speak so we may know the end of this travel."[28] The Palestinian existence as an experience of people uprooted from the land that is daily raped by its victimizer.[29] The Palestinian experience of exile, according to Said manifests the "unhealable rift forced between a human being and a native place, between the self and its true home."³⁰ Exile, victimhood (or the presence of the *Nakbah*), and suffering or Palestinian identity and Israeli victimization, become inseparable. A central role in this Palestinian narrative is played by the resistance to the Israeli instrumentalization of the Holocaust memory as part of their effort to present the Palestinian tragedy as a terrible price they had to pay for the realization of the Jewish colonialist project.

The Palestinians did not only reject any Jewish claim for being the legitimate owners of Israel. They rejected and to this day maintain a general rejection of any true relation between the Jews and Israel as their homeland, not solely those Zionist and Jewish non-Zionist claims to be the sole legitimate owners as the Children of Israel. The suffering of Jews in the Diaspora in itself was never a central Zionist argument for the justification of the right to the country as a Jewish homeland, yet suffering and victimhood were undeniably central to the Jewish political theology. As a mirror image of the Zionist narrative the Palestinian national movement traditionally bound its refusal to acknowledge and offer empathy to the historical victimization of the Jews to its refusal to acknowledge the special relation of the Jews to Israel. This attitude is manifested even today in the negotiations of the Israelis and the Palestinians. Israel's offer to relinquish its sovereignty over the site of the Jewish temple (*har habait*), which is also a Moslem mosque and an important religious site (*al aksa*), in exchange for official Palestinian recognition of the Jewish relation to the site is unconditionally rejected. The struggle over the power to represent the space as "Israel" or "Palestine," the clash over political control over collective sovereignty between the two parties, and the disagreement as to who is the victim and who is the victimizer and the power to construct and represent the identity of the Israel/Palestine have become inseparable. The philosophical and the political relations between the Holocaust and the *Nakbah* and who owns Israel/Palestine and whose homeland it is have become a unified element for Israeli and Palestinian internal and external violence, which at the same time is also a fruitful *constitutive* element of reproducing each of the warring side's ethnocentric collectivism. Within the framework of each collective the Other is a threat for the very existence of the collective and is perverting the homeland by its very existence, so that the land itself is victimized, not only its authentic owners. The Zionists changed the Palestinian names of the sites—many of which still conserve their Hebrew building blocks, foundations and linguistic roots— renaming them according to their "authentic" *Hebrew* names or inventing new names. This act—from a Palestinian perspective—is inseparable from uprooting the *Palestinian* dwellers or from changing the topography, the architecture, or the demographic and political *arche* of spaces and sites in Palestine. This is why when Palestinians counter this violence and traditionally they do not direct their counter-violence to the Israeli army or police but to the civilian population, they target factories, traffic lights, or post offices and even forests. Directing their violence to the fruits of the love/rape of Palestine by/to the Israelis aims at killing the Spirit of their Israelihood; overcoming the forbidden love affair/reunion of the land of Palestine/Israel and the colonialists/Jews, which became raped Palestine/flourishing Israel.

Setting the forests on fire is a repeated occurrence in Israeli-Palestinian coexistence which normally does not receive much attention when the Israeli/Palestinian violence is analyzed in light of the cost of these exchanges in terms of human life, property, and additional political barriers to dialogue. Yet it is a factor that merits far more attention then it usually receives.

The returning to Israel and the constitution of the New Jew was for the hegemonic Zionist narrative connected with the ideal of reentering into an intimate relation with the land, farming it as a way of life and hard labor as an ideal for the reconstitution of the individual and the nation. Already at the beginning of the twentieth century A. D. Gordon acknowledged the presence of Arabs—not of Palestinians; in 1909 he writes:

> The country is ours as long as the Jewish people is alive and did not forget its homeland. On the other hand, it is wrong to decide that the Arabs have no share in it. . . . One thing is for certain. The country will belong to that side which will be willing and able to suffer more and work harder for the land. . . . that is the imperative of reason, this is also the conclusion of justice—and this goes along also with the nature of things.[31]

The "redemption" of the country was conceived and actualized by buying the land and farming it. Those who position Zionism as a colonialist movement fail to recognize the uniqueness of this colonization process. It involved buying the land at any price from its owners, thereby increasing the value of the Palestinian property and also causing Palestinian farmers to leave their homes and the land they had worked, in some cases for centuries. But simultaneously it created a huge Arab immigration movement from the neighboring countries, which came to constitute most of today's Palestinian population, and consequently their competition with the Jewish immigrants on the labor market with the Palestinians. They fail to see the idealistic dimension of this process, which was a vital element in the construction of a new, "Israeli," collective. They fail also to see the meaning of the conception of entering a desolated and neglected country, foresting its bare mountains, drying its swamps, and farming its valleys. The drying of the Hadera swamps, as an example by the Jewish immigrants at the beginning of the last century, became an important myth within the Zionist normalizing education at schools, in literature, on the stage, and in other apparatuses, the trees are central figures here. In the play *"The gathering of the boxes,"* by Andre Finkerfeld-Amir, the desolation of the country is symbolized by the mosquitoes (who carried the diseases around the areas of the swamps). The drying of the swamps, the farming of the fertile land, which recovered at a high cost in human life, the eucalyptus trees take part as central heroes. They are called "the heroes of Hadera" and together with trees from other redeemed lands they drive out the desolation.[32] The planting of the land became celebrated by a national holiday and was adopted as a compulsory element of schooling; but in addition it became internalized in the collective psyche, joined to the traditional Jewish attitude to the holiness of the country and the religious-mystic essence of trees and of planting trees.

The planting of trees in the bared and neglected country, as the Jewish *Halutz* saw/found/imagined it, became a symbol of the redemption of the country from its desolation, a focal point of the exile who returns home and of the homeland that returns to him. In school rituals the reunion was often celebrated in the form of marriage. At the same time it had a political dimension of controlling the space, manifesting the presence and the power of the Zionist project, preventing Palestinian settlement and empowering the violent colonization of the Jewish Diaspora mentality and replacing it with Israeli mentality — if not in reality at least as an ideal.

The Palestinian resistance to the Zionist project had and has many forms, one of which is to set the forests ablaze. There is hardly any natural woodland in Israel/Palestine, and most of the forests were planted as part of the Israeli settlement. This activity is conceived by the Palestinian intellectuals and politicians as a successful colonialist aggression and the blooming or afforested land is taken as the daily *rape* of the homeland; therefore, setting the forests on fire has a special meaning. The total negation of the Zionist project, rejection of its hegemonic narrative, denial of its instrumentalization of Jewish victimization and suffering in the Diaspora and its claim for Israel/Palestine as its homeland—all are united in this burning. Its point of reference can be addressed in other, more articulated positions and actions, such as the refusal to acknowledge the Holocaust or the minimization of its extent and moral implications, or the current official rejection of any Jewish connection with Jerusalem and the Temple Mount. And yet, in such sporadic, individual, but still consistent acts of setting alight the "forests of the Jewish National Fund," which pervert so successfully and pleasurably the view of the Palestinian homeland, there is special manifestation of the Israeli-Palestinian struggle. The forests are set on fire, like the beloved daughter who, according to the Palestinian tradition, has to be put to death by the males of the family if she "offended the family honor." In Arabic the land and the family honor are both called *ard*, although they are spelled differently. Poets, writers, educators, and politicians play on the two homophones: the land gave itself, abandoned itself in total surrender even to a love affair with Israelihood and with the actualization of the ideal of forcing/rediscovering the Jewish identity of the land of Israel. Exile from the homeland, then, is also the lot of those who held on and did not leave (*zumud*), against all the odds and difficulties inflicted by the Israeli presence. Hisham Sharabi's words are paradigmatic on this issue: "Man," he says, "does not really embrace his homeland unless he loses it. Immigration is essentially different. Facing the rape of my land and losing my homeland, my grandfather's house and the vies of my childhood is a kind of assassination."[33] This has occurred alongside the uprooting of its Palestinian identity. For Palestinian intellectuals accepting this process means acquiescence in, and even siding with the rape of Palestine as homeland, the betrayal of a holy marriage; this deed has to be cleansed and purified, and what is more purifying than blood and fire?

The Palestinian commitment to liberate Palestine is unconditional and uncompromising, as manifested by its intellectuals; even when politically there is a desire for a pragmatic settlement. However, even the politicians such as Yaser Arafat, when they delve deep into the foundations of the conflict and come upon the principles of rival concepts of homeland, refuse to accept the Jewish right, even as a partial or a moderate right or even attitude, to Israel/Palestine. Traditionally this was the hegemonic attitude of the Zionist movement. Yet from its very beginning it was accompanied by an active opposition which argued for the rights of the Palestinians, resisted the injustice inflicted on them and protested against it within the Zionist movement and as opposition to it. Both sides have changed their positions, to various degrees. The empowerment of the Palestinian national movement in the shadow of the victory of the Zionist project by establishing a strong state in economic, technological, military, and cultural respect, as well as the presence of ever stronger influence on the Israeli society of Instrumental Rationality, global capitalism, and multi-cultural realities—all have exerted their influence. In the Israeli society one important influence was the demolition of the Zionist ideology and its idealistic-collectivist concept of homeland, of which the exile was the locus of relating to and struggling for, at least for the secular part of the Israeli society. These processes have deep and diverse effects such as the rise of strong individualism and the McDonald'sization of this advanced techno-scientific consumption-oriented society. In face of these developments the traditional Zionist-propagated concept of homeland has lost its vitality and much of its relevance. As part of this development, growing sections of Israeli society acknowledge not only the presence of the Palestinians as a nation but also their narrative and their legitimate rights, their aspirations as well as their *Nakbah*. This process is paralleled by an ever stronger Palestinian negation of the justification of any Jewish claim. Not only an equally just claim to a legitimate narrative in which Israel is a homeland of the Jews, but even of partial or less just claim to its homeland. Today, no Palestinian intellectual will question Zionism as a mere violent Western colonizing movement, which uprooted and destroyed the Palestinian homeland and its peaceful normal life.

This asymmetry is especially notable when post-modern Palestinian intellectuals treat the issue of the Israeli-Palestinian conflict, its roots and future. While conceiving the Palestinian identity as historically developed and contingent (and, therefore, not a "right" or a "wrong," "authentic" or "inauthentic"), intellectuals such as Edward Said will reject the Israeli narrative as "false," "violent," "manipulative," or "colonialist," and refuse to acknowledge *any* claim to a legitimate Jewish conception of Israel as the homeland of the Jewish people. The most advanced move in this respect is the attempt to appropriate the Jewish narrative and introduce the Palestinians as the true Jews of today.

Edward Said joins Azmy Bishara and some other Arab intellectuals who today call for a halt to the traditional Arab denials of the Holocaust and even to Arab attempts to minimize its scale and moral implications. Yet while favoring a Jewish-Palestinian dialogue and not an Israeli-Palestinian dialogue, Said sets a condition: one side—the Jewish—will accept that it is the victimizer and the other side is its victim. "There is no symmetry in this conflict. I must say it and I deeply believe in it. Here there is one side who is guilty and another side, which is the victim. The Palestinians are victims."[34] Said so insists on acknowledging the Holocaust and Jewish suffering not solely out of his empathy with Jewish suffering and life in exile from the homeland. He does so within a dialectical argumentation within which the ultimate victims of Hitlerism in the Holocaust are not the Jews in the Holocaust but the Palestinians in the *Nakbah*. This is since the victims of the victims are the ultra victims. The struggle about who's homeland is Israel/Palestine or does, in its essence, the space worthy the name Israel, Palestine, both or neither becomes inseparable from the question not of who suffered more but who is the ultimate victim in human history. It is a life-and-death struggle over whose narrative is the right one and who is its perpetrator. Stated otherwise, it concerns what apparatus controlling the representation of the narrative is stronger in destroying the rival narrative and hiding the violences which make possible a simplistic justification of the "authentic" the "right" or the "justified" claim, interests, suffering, and "counter-violence" against its Other.

But Edward Said, like some other Palestinian intellectuals, wants more than that. He is not satisfied with negating the Jewish claim to Israel as homeland and with convicting them as victimizers. By the same token he, like other Palestinian intellectuals, also wants to inherit their Jewishness and he proclaims himself as the authentic Jew of today: Jewishness as an existence in a permanent exile, Jewishness as homelessness.

> Theodor Adorno said that in the twentieth century the idea of home is pushed away. I guess that part of my critique of Zionism is based on its overestimation of a home. It claims that we need a home, that we will do anything to appropriate an home, even if it means making others homeless.... I never understood the claim that this place is mine and you get out. I dislike also the drive to one's roots, to the pure origin. I believe that the great intellectual and political disasters of the twentieth century were actualized by condensing movements that attempted to simplify and purify. They said that we have to build here the tenants or the *Kibbutzim* of our army and start all over again. I would not like it even for myself, I do not believe in it. Even if I had been a Jew I would struggle against it. And it will not last for long. ... believe me. ... I am the last Jewish intellectual. You do not know anyone else like that. All the other Jewish intellectuals are masters from the suburbs. From Amos Oz to those who live here in America, so that I am the last one, the authentic follower of Adorno. I will articulate it like this: I am a Jewish Palestinian.[35]

This trend is part of a wider trend, which represents the Zionist and very often any Zionist as a present-day Nazi. It is a widespread phenomenon in the Arab world of which Saria, Bishara, and Said explicitly distance themselves. However, is it fair to ask if Said is really presenting an alternative to this trend? Or does he actually offer a more sophisticated project? In its first stage the Israelis are presented as today's Nazis and in the second stage the Palestinians inherit not only the Jews' victimhood but also the historic moral mission of Judaism, along with the establishment of the hegemony of the Palestinian narrative and sovereign homeland. The reply should be that while Said insists on a difference between the evil of the National Socialist regime and the Israeli injustice inflicted on the Palestinians he is more violent toward the essence of Judaism, its moral historic mission, its Messianism, and its claim for Israel as a Jewish sacred place and homeland. This attempt of his merges with a wider Palestinian trend to equalize the *Nakbah* and the daily life conditions under Israeli role with *Auschwitz* and with the moral implications of the Holocaust. This is so even with the explicit rejection of this part of the Palestinian normalizing education. While agreeing the Holocaust had a tragic influence on present-day moral behavior of the Israelis[36] we disagree with the conclusions of Said, his goal, and his followers' post-colonialist and nationalistic-oriented projects.

In his special way Said contributes to the equation of the Holocaust and the *Nakbah* or at least to the representation of the *Nakbah* as an outcome of the communization to the Jewish victimization—at the price of victimizing the Palestinians. This trend does not challenge the general Palestinian trend of presenting the Israelis as the present-day Nazis, as is reflected in a relative modest way in the poem of Taha al Matukhal: "Many years ago you collapsed under the deeds of the butchers in Dachau/ Your father was slaughtered in the Warshao Ghetto/ You cried in the face of your sisters rape in the hell of Auschwitz/ Have you forgotten? How did you dare to reestablish Auschwitz in the midst of the desert?/ How did you dare to uproot a nation from its homeland? How did you dare to burn the children/ Have you forgotten?"[37] The Palestinian shift to the next stage, that of declaring themselves as "the real Jews," is exemplified by the Palestinian poet Kamil Bulata, who declared "I feel that I am a Jew." But Mahmoud Darwish reacts to this with an admonition: "[it is a must] to warn the too-easy writers among the Arabs of the danger of these tempting metaphorical images, when all of the sudden the oppressed Arab Man sees himself as 'the new Jew" in a moment of a difficult loneliness."[38] For Darwish it is but a manifestation of the violence of the Israeli oppression, which transforms the victimizer into the victim and the Arab into "the new Jew." According to Darwish the Israeli cannot be satisfied with empowering his memory with the inclusion of the armed narrative and donning the garb of the victim: he has also to destroy the Palestinian memory and deprive the Palestinian from his relation to the place, the history, and the Arab space. It will not take long, says Darwish, before the Israeli claims to be the real Palestinian.[39]

This position of Said is a rich, deep, and challenging position. A central element of it, however, is that it is committed to justify one violence against its opposing violence on the ground that one narrative and one claim for a homeland is more valid than the other. More specifically, in the Israeli-Palestinian struggle over the representation of rights, victimhood, and authenticity, Said sides with the Palestinian side, while denouncing the Jewish symbolic and nonsymbolic violence—neglecting the essential lesson of Adorno, which he claims to follow, that any collectivism, any use of violence, any normalizing apparatus is a challenge to overcome. Palestine, which swallows Israel and Palestinian identity, which swallow Judaism, are Said's colonialist project. Deconstruction is here recruited for Palestinian ethnocentricity, which becomes a universal transcendental project. By conquering the Jewish claim for justice, swallowing its narrative and its sites of origin, legends, and pretensions, the Palestinian people becomes not "simply" a collective less than a hundred years old, only recently formed. It becomes far more, a historical power and an ancient, rich, universally valid moral voice and an unmatched cultural project.[40] Within it Said, as a Jew, can find nowhere his home, but everywhere his homelessness. Here the loss of the homeland is inseparable from the actual violent struggle for its recapture. On this matter Said is uncompromising, as one can see in his rejection of the present "peace process" and the attempt at appeasement between the Israelis and the Palestinians. Said's favoring actual continuation of the war until the final defeat of the Israelis, their surrendering of the land/hegemony, and their acceptance of their historic role as victimizers represents a devotion to ethnocentrism. At the same time it also shows he too refuses to face the implications and challenges of normalizing education—and avoids the struggle of overcoming its violences for which his project is one of the most advanced apparatuses. The struggle over who is the ultimate victim of history, who's homeland is Israel/Palestine, and who is the real Jew is a unique manifestation of the ongoing-general function of normalizing education. It must produce collectives, their quest for territorial homeland, and their realms of self-evidence, which simultaneously produces also their Other as a danger/threat/colonizer.

While both the Israeli and the Palestinian sides are committed to control the space, they are also committed to control its "true" representation or effectively to destroy the rival narrative within a framework in which homeland is a metaphysical entity. Here the Palestinian patriots and the Israelis join forces. Here it is seen in special clarity how normalizing education creates both rivals as essential agents for its own self-reproduction. Refusing to dwell in the narrative of each of the sides, or overcoming not only both narratives—but also the play within which they are actualized, destroyed, and replaced by other, more effective and violent, is the aim of counter-education. As such it has no "homeland" and *homelessness* is its home. Jewish negative theology, Heidegger's concept of unconcealing the *Ge-stell* and Benjamin and Adorno's concept of Messianism without a messiah, or negative utopianism, are some of the places a counter-education committed person will visit in order to empower the struggle against normalizing education. The Holocaust and the *Nakbah*, as well as the struggle over the uncontested status of being the ultimate victim and the owner of the authentic claim for homeland, are inseparable. They represent the tragic essence of every education. Education is inseparable from reality in the sense of being, which necessarily produces war over existence, over representation and over space. Within this process and as part of its manifestation it produces struggles for national liberation and ideology critiques, which are, aimed at defeating and conquering the other's representation apparatuses, claims for homeland, and even its homelessness.

NOTES

1. Max Horkheimer. "Ueber den Zweifel," *Gesammelte Schriften*, 7, Frankfurt a.Main: Suhrkamp 1985, 218.
2. Wilhelm Brepohl. "Heimat und Heimatgesinnung als soziologische Begriffe und Wirkichkeiten," in Kurt Rabl (ed.), *Das Recht auf die Heimat. Vortraege, Thesen, Kritik.* Muenchen 1965, 43.
3. Celia Applegate. *A Nation of Provincials—The German Idea of Heimat*. Berkeley, Los Angeles, Oxford: University of California Press, 1990, 5.
4. *Ibid.*
5. *Ibid.*, 7.
6. Rolf Petri, "Deutsche Heimat 1850-1950," 3.
7. *Ibid.*, 5.
8. *Ibid.*, 35.
9. *Ibid.*
10. Ilan Gur-Ze'ev. "Introduction" in Ilan Gur-Ze'ev (ed.), *Conflicting Philosophies of Education in Israel/Palestine*. Dordrecht: Kluwer, 2000, 1-6.
11. Moshe Lilenblum. "On the revival of Israel on the land of our ancestors," in *M. L. Lilenblum; A selection of His Essays*. Jerusalem: The Zionist Agency 1952, 76.
12. Aaron David Gordon. *The Nation and The Work*. Jerusalem: The Zionist Library 1916, 366.
13. *Ibid.*, 244.
14. Ze'ev Ya'avetz. "The unity," in Y. Obsey, Hilel Bavly, M. Fiershtein and others, (eds.), *Becoming a Nation* I. New York: Keren Israel, 122 (in Hebrew).
15. Anita Shapira. *Land and Power*. Tel Aviv: Am Oved 1993, 26-27 (in Hebrew).
16. Glen Bowman. "'Acountry of words': Conceiving the Palestinian nation from the position of exile," in Ernesto Laclau (ed.), *The Making of Political Identities*. London and New York: Verso 1994, 139.
17. Edward Said. *After the Last Sky*. London: Farber and Farber 1986, 5.
18. Mahmoud Darwish. *Dewan Mahmoud Darwish*, Beirut 1989, 342.
19. Mahmoud Darwish. "There is no holiness to the executioner," *El Carmel* 52 (Summer 1997), 221.
20. Hisham Sharabi. *Jafa, an Aroma of a City*. Beirut: Dar el Fatah 1991, 15.
21. *Ibid.*
22. *Ibid.*, 15-16.
23. Edward Said. "Keynote essay," in Ghada Karmi (ed.), *Jerusalem Today; What Future for the Peace Process?* Ithaca 1996, 16.
24. Edward Said, *After the Last Sky*, 5.
25. *Ibid.*
26. *Ibid.*, 120.
27. Glen Bowman, "'A country of words,'" 145.
28. Mahmoud Darwish. "We travel like other people," *Victims of a Map*. Translated by Abdullah al-Udhri, London: Al Saqui Books 1984, 31.
29. Hisham Sharabi, *ibid.*, 15-16.
30. in Janet L. Abu Lughod. "Palestinians: exiles at home and abroad," *Current Sociology*, 36: 2 (Summer 1988), 61.
31. Gordon, *ibid.*, 96.

32 Yoram Bar-Gal. *An Agent of Zionist Propaganda; The Jewish National Fund 1924-1947*. Haifa: Haifa University Press 1999, 240.
33 Hisham Sharabi, *ibid.*
34 Edward Said. "My right of return"—an interview, *Ha'aretz* 18,8.2000, 22.
35 Edward Said. "My right of return," *ibid.*
36 Ilan Gur-Ze'ev. "Was Hitler really defeated?" in *Philosophy, Politics and Education in Israel*, Haifa: Haifa University Press and Zemora-Bitan 1999, 57-98 (in Hebrew).
37 Taha Almatukal. *A Song from Ansar 3*. Ramallah 1989, 63 (in Arabic).
38 Mahmoud Darwish. "The identity of absence," *Mifgashim* 7-8 (Autumn 1987), 27.
39 *Ibid.*
40 Ibrahim Abu-Lughod. "The Search for Identity," in *Palestine and Education: the "Teaching Palestine" Project*. Almawird: Teacher Development Center Almawird 1997.

CHAPTER 2
Beyond the Destruction of the Other's Collective Memory[1]

The destruction of the collective memory of the Other, through the construction of one's own, is a central element in the formation of national identities. *Violence*, direct as well as symbolic, plays thereby a crucial part as collective memories are produced, reproduced, disseminated, and consumed within concrete historical power relations, interests, and conceptual possibilities and limitations. In the case of Palestine/Israel, control of the collective memory is part of the internal and external violence, each of the rival collectives applies to secure its reconstruction. That is, the way the two sides to the conflict construct their collective identity is a dialectical process whose impelling force is the total negation of the Other. Within this dialectic, each side sees itself as a sole victim while totally negating the victimization of the Other. The violence used in order to conquer the centers of power relations and dynamics aims at positioning more "effectively" one's own narrative, interests, values, symbols, goals, and criteria while at the same time securing those of the Other are marginalized, excluded, or destroyed. The incommensurability has the upper hand and dialogue has no chance of finding a starting point. Collective self-constitution, negation of the legitimacy of the Other's otherness, victimizing the Other and refusing to acknowledge the Other's suffering become inseparably bound up with each other. The self-proclaimed victimhood, the refusal to acknowledge the evil inflicted on the Other and the insistence on being sole victim, are fused into the kind of practice which reflects the position of the Other. In the case of the Israeli/Palestinian coexistence, the struggle over the control of the memory of victimization is a matter of life and death, and suffering and death, as actuality and as memory, are philosophical, political, and existential issues.

Palestinian Mainstream Responses to the Holocaust Memory

A synchronic and diachronic reconstruction of Palestinian intellectual responses to the Holocaust enables us to identify four major attitudes. These, naturally, vary and coexist while remaining fluid. There is also a historical change in the self-positioning of each of these responses in the Palestinian intellectual self-reflection and in its cultural politics.

The few scholars who have looked into the question of the Holocaust/ Nakbah representation among the Palestinians agree that responses to the Holocaust move from total denial of the event, through indifference toward it, to acknowledge that it happened while minimizing its dimensions and its moral significance, to full acknowledgment not just of the event but also of its universal moral implications as a unique stage in the history of human evil (Bishara, 1995, 56-74, Nevo, 1989, 2241-2250). Until recently the main development had been the move away from a total denial toward acknowledgment with minimization of its moral significance, as is manifest in the works of journalists, historians, and political writers ever since the Nakbah of 1948.

Zionism has worked systematically on mystifying the Holocaust and structuring modes of control over the representation of its memory; it has become a salient feature of the Zionist educational system. At the same time, Zionism insists on denying the Nakbah and refuses to admit Israel's role in the Palestinian suffering as victimizer. The 1953 Knesset made control of the Holocaust memory a matter of law, and a special governmental agency was created, *Mosad Yad Vashem*, to protect, represent, and police the official *memory* of the dead as part of the Zionist narrative to which *galut* (life in Diaspora) inexorably leads to *geula* (redemption), and *shoah* (Holocaust) to *tekuma* (resurrection) (Gur-Ze'ev, 1998, 161-177).

On the Palestinian side equation between the Nazi regime and crimes it committed on the one hand, and the state of Israel and the way it has treated the Palestinians, on the other, re-occurs in many studies. Israel is often seen as a "Nazi-Zionist entity" and its practices characterized as "Nazi Zionist crimes" (Rabin and Horowitz, 1993).

Adding to Palestinian unease in dealing with the Holocaust memory is the counter-equation Israelis have made of Palestinian nationalism with Nazism, embodied in the persona of the Mufti, Hajj Amin al-Husayni, and his notorious handshake with Hitler. The Mufti spent part of the war years in Nazi Germany and served for a while as a main propagandist voice for the Arab world.

The way Palestinians refer to this chapter in their history reflects the general attitude toward the Other among Israeli and Palestinian intellectuals: a total negation of the otherness of the Other as well as the realization how an instrumentalist attitude toward historical knowledge does service in the present constitution of collective identity. When some Palestinian historians admit that it has been a mistake for the Mufti to work so closely with the Nazis, they add that Hajj Amin should not be judged so severely as the Holocaust occurred in a period of Palestinian history in which they themselves suffered growing defeat and despair (Alush, 1967, 151). Moreover, the Mufti was a product of his time. As Naji Alush states, the sympathy of the masses throughout the Arab world was with the enemies of French and British colonialism. Recently a more critical approach of the Mufti's actions has emerged.

Some Palestinian historians concede that the Fascist ideology itself attracted some young radicals in the Arab world as well (Alush, 1967, 151-153), but in the case of large segments of the Arab world in general and in that of the Mufti in particular, most see the pro-Nazi attitude as "pragmatism": hatred of Britain rather than love for the Nazi regime (Mattar, 1988, 99-107).

In the 1980s, as it became quite unacceptable both among Western and Eastern intellectuals, Arab historians turned their back on this kind of apologetics. When writing on the episode, they have begun using a discourse similar to the one Israeli historians employ when discussing the relations between Jewish leaders of the Stern Gang and the Nazis, or when writing about those Zionist emissaries who negotiated with the Germans on behalf of the Jewish Agency. "The Mufti," writes Ali Muhafaza, "was willing to cooperate with the devil" (Muhafaza, 1981, 259).

Admittedly there is another trend according to which since the Mufti had no involvement in the extermination of the Jews there is no room here for postulating a moral dilemma or adjudicating wrong-doing. In the assessment of most of the Palestinian historians, the Nazi Germans simply exploited Hajj Amin for their own purposes (Muhafaza, 1981, 268-270).

The whole problem of the Mufti's cooperation with the Nazis was pushed to the side not least because Israeli biographies of the Mufti began appearing at around the same time, which accepted the Palestinian perspective on the Mufti's stay in Germany and apportioned the same pragmatic nature to his activities and partly due to growing criticism of the Mufti altogether in the Palestinian histgraphical milieu (Al-Ghuri, 1973, II, 181-189).

Denial was replaced by a strategic acknowledgment of the Holocaust and the Jewish suffering which questioned the uniqueness of the Jewish tragedy and made its best to normalize it. As the power to tell the story and to eliminate the counter-narrative is an integral part of the actual military and political struggle over non-symbolic resources such as land and political power, the war over the land, the struggle over the legitimization of sovereign national existence, and the fight over who is the victim and who is the victimizer became inseparable parts of the overall symbolic and the military confrontation between the two collectives. By the same token, as it was regarded a vital element in the ability of each side in eliminating the Other, or the Other's legitimacy, the control of the collective memory and the destruction of the Other's memory have become central elements in each of the rival education systems.

Normalizing the Holocaust entailed a continued refusal to acknowledge the scale and moral significance of the Holocaust (Nevo, 1989). Some Palestinians, among them Azmi Bishara, have criticized this attitude as an educational and political mistake (Bishara, 1995). Indeed, it seems that until recently there has been no analysis of the systematic extermination by Nazi Germany of the Jews or a reflection on the horrendous magnitude of the killings; in short, there is still today in many Palestinian intellectual circles a consistent effort at marginalizing, if not normalizing, the event and presenting it as a Zionist exaggeration (Hadawi and John, 1960, I, 349-351).

We hardly find any articles on the subject during the 1970s and 1980s in the central Palestinian academic stages (Nevo, 1989). At the same time, there was a dominant trend which presented the Palestinians as the real Jews and as the ultimate victims. This was in effect a way of appropriating the moral capital that the Jews had gained through their suffering. Taha Almatukal, the general secretary of the Palestinian writers, and himself a well-known Palestinian poet, conveyed this idea as follows:

> Many years ago you were collapsing under the murderers of Dachau/ Your father was slaughtered in the Warsaw Ghetto / You suffered the agony of your sister's rape at Auschwitz/ Have you forgotten? How could you constitute a new Auschwitz in the center of the desert/ How did you dare to transfer a people from its land? How did you dare to burn the children/ Have you forgotten? (Almatukal, 1989, 63).

In a similar way Mahmoud Darwish addresses the very same connection between the use the Jews in Israel have made of the Holocaust memory and the uncompromising struggle the Palestinians are waging over the land and its identity. Darwish warns against coming out with such declarations as "I am a Jew," as Kamil Bulata had done. In his eyes, this way of self-identification is but another aspect of the Israeli occupation of the Palestinian identity. The danger, as far as Darwish is concerned, is that this dialectic could make the Israeli aggressor appear as having the upper hand in the battle over who is the ultimate victim:

> As he needs to load his memory with the armed legend and the uniform of the victim, the Israeli has to empty the Palestinian memory from its ties to the Arab place, history and space, and equip him with the newly developed Jewish consciousness of the time. It won't take long and the Israeli will also claim to be the authentic Palestinian (Darwish, 1987, 46-47).

But how "empty" is the Israeli memory that it needs to be loaded? Does it now have its own content of suffering and victimhood? While safeguarding the Palestinian collective memory from the destructive means of the Other side, Darwish seems to ignore the otherness of the Israeli and the dialectics of its/his collective memory, which necessarily collides with the legitimacy and needs of the Palestinian otherness.

Recently there has been a call to abandon the way of refusal and to overcome the inability to acknowledge the Holocaust and its universal implications. It was first heard among Palestinians in Israel who were members of the Israeli Communist Party, such as the writer Emil Habibi.

When he spoke out in favor of a Palestinian acknowledgment of the Holocaust and its universal moral implication, Habibi did so from a humanistic perspective. Habibi's dialectical presentation of the Jewish Holocaust memory becomes important when we want to clarify the special link that connects Palestinians and Israelis and challenge the ethnocentrism on both sides which enables the victimization of the Other while maintaining the self-conception of victim. Habibi's was a general Palestinian conception in which the Holocaust is acknowledged as a Jewish tragedy, for which the Jews are being compensated at the expense of the Palestinians. Habibi explicitly states that one cannot equate between the Nazi extermination of the Jews and the Israeli expulsion of the Palestinians. He then brings up another, new notion, according to which Palestinians too are the victims of the Nazi regime since they were victimized by a second generation of Nazi victims who not only did not learn the lesson of the Holocaust, but defiled the Holocaust memory by perpetrating similar crimes against the Palestinians (Habibi, 1986, 27).

While Habibi appears to be one of the first Palestinians to confront the question of the Palestinian attitude toward the Holocaust memory head-on, two Palestinian intellectuals, Edward Said and Azmi Bishara, and several authors in the wider Arab world as well, have since gone even further in criticizing past attitudes and are now developing a new approach that has led not only to the universalization of the Holocaust memory, but also to some conclusions that bear heavily on the examination of the Holocaust/Nakbah dialectics. We will focus on the works of Said and Bishara for the simple reason that until now they are the only Palestinian intellectuals who challenge the traditional Palestinian reaction to the Holocaust.

As he already has done in his earlier works, Said has written recently that the full cost of the Jewish Holocaust is to be seen in a kind of moral handicap for the Jews which came to be with their dispossession of the Palestinian people (Said, 1997). Said's depiction of the Zionist instrumentalization of the Holocaust could not be more apt. The Zionist, and later Israeli, educational network instrumentalized the Holocaust memory in the service of practical needs and in order to justify or veil a systematic immoral treatment of the Palestinians and other Others. Elsewhere we have called this kind of revivification of the dead Israel's "evil industry" (Gur-Ze'ev, 1999).

For Edward Said and Azmi Bishara, their familiarity with neo-Marxist and postmodern discourse, and, in the case of Said, the pivotal role he has played in shaping the post-colonialist approach, is behind their deconstructive attitude to the Palestinian collective memory, which enabled them to further the deconstruction begun by Habibi of the Palestinian attitude to the Holocaust memory. Similarly, post-Zionist scholarship, not least under the influence of Said himself, has developed a critical deconstructive approach toward the Israeli collective memory (Gur-Ze'ev, 1999; Pappe, 1995, 66-90).

Openly criticizing the Palestinian tendency to marginalize the Holocaust, both Said and Bishara in recent publications argue that for the Palestinians themselves, confronting the subject of the Holocaust memory within the Palestinian context is of vital importance. In this they are supported by the Lebanese writer, Hazim Sarayah, and the Sudanese Salih Bashir, who in the columns of *Al-Hayat* and *al-Ahram* have taken a similar stance (Sarayah and Bashir, 1997).

The new approach they represent to the Holocaust memory contains four new possible avenues for future Palestinian treatment of the issue at hand. All four directions can be found as well in the works of these few Israelis who recently also have begun to deconstruct their side's instrumentalization of the Holocaust memory.

The first direction is one that adopts a critical, albeit empathic, stance toward the past Palestinian and the Arab denial and minimization of the Holocaust (Bishara, 1996, 102-107). In the case of Bishara, the empathy follows directly from the Arab nationalism he claims himself beholden to. Thus, it is important to him to convince his audience that a different approach is not necessarily tantamount to an a- or anti-nationalist approach. His commitment to the nationalist discourse appears also when he writes about the question of Jewish nationhood. Bishara declares that there is no such thing as a Jewish nation—as also stated in the Palestinian charter, Judaism is a religion, not a nation.

Bishara's particular angle, as a supporter of Arab-nationalism, not only Palestinian nationalism, leads him to examine not just Palestinian attitudes, but also, and mainly, other Arab positions. From our point of view, Bishara's parameters distance him from head-on confronting the dialectics of the Holocaust/Nakbah memories, a distancing which leaves him within an ethnocentric framework of discussion.

Thus, from within the national perspective, Bishara directs a systematic and forceful deconstruction at a range of Palestinian and Arab responses: from total disregard to support of the Nazi solution to the Jewish question (Bishara, 1995, 60-64). According to him, the Arab response to the Holocaust was not framed by anti-Semitic tendencies, but rather by its reaction to the Zionist project. That is, for Bishara, the past denial of the Holocaust by the Arabs formed a natural response to the instrumentalization of the Holocaust memory by the Zionist movement and, later, Israel.

As to the particular Palestinian attitude, Bishara attributes the roots of the Palestinian denial to the necessity for them to come to grips with the European crime, before it becomes possible to discuss their own tragedy. The Holocaust memory is that other memory, more awesome, more horrific, through which the Palestinians are expected to deal with their own memory. No wonder that one of the more effective ways of dealing with the predicament this created, claims Bishara, was to deny the authenticity of that other memory.

Bishara's main point is that in the 1950s the Palestinians developed an anticolonialist counterprism to help them deal with the Holocaust memory: the Holocaust was denied as a Zionist invention, as part of a general Palestinian perception of Israel as omnipotent and a crypto power. Israel was conceived as so powerful it could engineer a myth of such horrendous content for its own purposes.

Anti-Holocaust attitudes, prevalent among radical circles in the Arab world at the same period, were somewhat different. Here, the treatment of the Holocaust was an integral part of the production of anti-Jewish literature, consisting of a history of Jewish evil, that found its culmination in the crimes committed against the Palestinian people. The Holocaust was not so much denied as it was explained as something the Jews had brought upon themselves. This was hardly a coherent stance: at times the event had never occurred, at times it was minimized, and at times it was even justified (Nevo, 1989).

Bishara shows how the Arab denial and minimizing of the importance of the Holocaust favor, rather than harm Israel in its struggle while it cultivates the image of the victim (Bishara, 1995, 56). The explicit argument of Bishara is that acknowledging the Holocaust is instrumentally justified for the Palestinian cause.

Thus, Said, too, strongly criticizes the traditional Palestinian response to the Holocaust. He views it in the context of lost opportunities to develop a different approach: "Perhaps the Eichmann trial was useful to the Arab side during the psychological battles of the 1960s as a way of exposing Israeli callousness to the Arabs, and not especially as an attempt to acquaint Arab readers with details of the Jewish experience (Said, 1997)." Said warns particularly against any cynical instrumentalization of the Holocaust memory, of the kind exercised by the Zionist movement and the state of Israel. In claiming this, Said is joined by a small number of critical Israeli writers (Diner, 1986, 20-23; 1996, 50-53; Ben-Naftali, 1993, 57-78; Ben-Amos, 1988; Gur-Ze'ev, 1998a).

Implicit in Said's thesis is the argument that the Palestinian instrumentalization of the Holocaust memory in the past as in the present makes them as guilty as Ben-Gurion and Netanyahu, who have justified Israeli crimes against Palestinians on the basis of the Holocaust memory. As a recent example of the cynical exploitation he deplores, Said refers the recruitment of Roger Garudy to the Palestinian cause in Europe, which in Said's eyes is entirely counter-productive. Like Bishara, Said claims that such acts not only work to diminish the universal lesson to be learned from the Holocaust memory control, but also obstruct rather than serve the Palestinian cause and the possibility of a peaceful coexistence between Israelis and Palestinians (Said, 1998).

As to Said's demand to the Palestinians to acknowledge and learn from the universal lessons of the Holocausts, we may see it as generated either by his modernist commitment to humanism or by his postmodernist commitment to overcome collective identities and ideological frameworks.

Said, however, also reveals a pragmatic concern for counter-productive Palestinian conduct. As does Azmi Bishara, for example, when he inveighs against allowing a stage in *al-Hayat* for David Irving as counter-productive exploitation, and joins earlier calls to the paper to refrain in the future from publishing the work of someone who is a Holocaust denier, a psychopath, and an anti-Semite (al-Hayat, 1992).[2]

Said and Bishara both voice their dissatisfaction with the more recent writings on the Holocaust among other Arab and Palestinian writers. Denial and minimization have been replaced by a repressive tendency to "exile" the Jewish Holocaust from the general discussion of the horrors of Nazism. Thus, they find in Palestinian and Arab writings total condemnations of Nazism, or for that matter, condemnation of race ideologies, but without any mention of the historical context in which these politics had been practiced against the Jews. Bishara points out that even Charles Issawi, an established expert on race theories, nowhere in his studies mentions a link between general race ideologies and past practices against the Jews of Europe (Bishara, 1995, 67).

What preoccupies Bishara is that while in the 1990s there has been a tendency in the Arab world to accept the moral and universal lessons of the Second World War, these were not applied to the Jewish Holocaust. Even humanists in the Arab world, remarks Bishara, are still afraid of mentioning the Holocaust, since they feel it may harm the general Arab interest.

The second direction singled out by Said and Bishara is a continuous recognition and criticism of the way Israel and Zionism have instrumentalized the Holocaust. But, unlike in the past, this is not done in a way so as to minimize the Holocaust memory. In his *The Politics of Dispossession*, Said has already explained how functional the Holocaust memory is for the young state of Israel by showing how the meaning of the "redemption" changed in Zionism after the Holocaust. Palestine became the refuge, an affirmative action for those dispossessed Jews not massacred by the Nazis (Said, 1994, 34).

Nevertheless, Said does not object to the refutal of the Zionist instrumentalization of the Holocaust, but urges the Palestinians to concentrate on defending present-day Palestinian politics from the defamation cast upon them by Israel and its supporters in the West in the name of the Holocaust memory. He recalls that when Barbara Walters in 1979 interviewed Arafat, she acted as a prosecutor bent on exposing Arafat's latent Nazism, by referring again and again to the PLO charter's vow to destroy Israel. "She was, in fact, raising the specter of the Holocaust before her audience's eyes" (Said, 1994, 66).

But even these and other examples of American Jewish instrumentalization of the Holocaust memory for contemporary political purposes—such as the elevation of the Jewish community's *suffering* above that of the African-Americans and Indians whose history of suffering has not been given a museum such as the Jews got in Washington—should not diminish the universality of the Holocaust memory. In fact, Said goes even further, and adds that despite the occurrence in the past, before and after the Holocaust, of mass massacres and ethnic cleansing, "the uniqueness of what had been done to the Jews, in terms of our horror and collective human guilt, should not be minimized" (Said, 1997, 2).

Sarayah and Bashir, mentioned above, show in their own work how the world at large has succeeded in facing its conduct during the Holocaust, more courageously, i.e., without succumbing to Israeli manipulation of the Holocaust memory. Thus, France brought Maurice Papon to trial and the Republic's president admitted that France bears responsibility for sending Jews to their death; the Swiss are now willing to examine the behavior of their banking system during the war, the Catholic church has issued an apology for its role in the Holocaust, and Germans have begun looking in the mirror when they decided to pick up a copy of Daniel Goldhagen's book. But in all these places, there is nonetheless strong criticism of Netanyahu's Israel as a stubborn, racist, and occupying state (Sarayah and Bashir, 1992).

A third new avenue of examination offered in these works is the reassessment of the Mufti's connection with the Nazis. Bishara criticizes the

Israeli historiographical attempt to create an alliance between the Mufti and the Nazis in the collective Western and Israeli memories and sets out to put the episode within a different context. That is, Zionism and not Nazism was the main issue for the Palestinians; this was true in the past and is true today. Nazism and Fascism were marginal and quite often misunderstood phenomena for the Palestinians, including for the Mufti during his honeymoon with Hitler. Unlike Haj Amin al-Husayni, there were members of the Palestinian political and social elites who still hoped during the war years that Britain would adopt a more pro-Palestinian policy.

The final avenue that has opened in the new approach we are outlining here is the beginning of a search into the possible connection between Holocaust memory and Nakbah memory as part of a more general effort to find a basis for a viable Israeli-Palestinian coexistence. Admittedly any sensitivity to this connection, not to mention its critical analysis, is almost totally absent in the Israeli and Palestinian intellectual discourse and cultural politics.

Bishara and Said, each from his own particular location, are aware of the difficulties inherent in such a dialogue. Bishara circumvents the need to face the dialectics of the Holocaust/Nakbah memory constitution, by focusing on a pragmatic, national, approach to the question. Hence, he sees a new Palestinian attitude to the Holocaust memory as leading to a Palestinian recognition of the state of Israel, notwithstanding the unjust events on which the state was founded; it cannot and should not be discredited, and it has its needs and rights.

Bishara's, in a way optimistic, conclusion is that the principal step to be taken in order to enter a substantial dialogue is a Palestinian recognition of the legitimacy of Israel, and, of course, a complementary Israeli recognition. Moreover, his partner in such a dialogue is the essential Israeli, be he a soldier or a politician. Said, on the other hand, not only is more cautious but also seeks a dialogue with Jewish, not only Israeli, intellectuals. Said warns against a headlong dive into a dialogue that can only be of the utmost sensitive nature and suggests beginning it among Arabs and Jews outside Palestine, who "are capable of fully appreciating and, in a sense, transcending" the tragedies of each other[3] (Said, 1997, 3).

For us, one of the most impressive and constructive conclusions emerging from Bishara and Said's journey into the past, is their clear assertion that Holocaust and Nakbah cannot be equated. In the words of Said, it is foolish to equate mass extermination with mass expulsion because they are not the same; neither can the one justify the other. Neither event should be minimized. In fact, argues Said, the equation, so common in Arab and Palestinian literature, is one of the main reasons why the Palestinians have not been able to cope effectively with the Israeli instrumentalization of the Holocaust.

Bishara too argues strongly against any comparison. The instrumental justification Bishara adduces for this is that comparison relatives and contextualizes the Israeli occupation of Palestine in a way that could entail relativization and contextualization of the Holocaust, on the one hand, and the Palestinians' dispossession, on the other. The Palestinians ought to be able to grasp the Holocaust as leading to the creation of Israel, without in any way diminishing the severity of what Israel did to them in 1948. Said recognizes that the task is a most difficult one. For one thing the total absence of the Palestinians from Jewish thought and philosophy does not bode well for a promising start on the part of the Israelis. The equality that is demanded is one that makes room for attention, consideration, integrity, respect vis-à-vis the validity of the horrors and fears of the other side (Said, 1994, 167).

Responses

Bishara and Said herald a new approach among Palestinians toward the mechanisms of constitution and control of the Palestinian/Israeli collective memories, particularly in the way they challenge the place of the Other and its memory within it. We would like to take this point further and suggest possible explorations of the Holocaust/Nakbah connection as proposed by Bishara and Said.

We discern three possible avenues from here. One is to navigate cautiously, as Bishara and, to a lesser extent, Said do, between continued commitment to the nation, accepting its discourse and collective memory, and a refusal to succumb to attitudes that minimize the universal—or even if one allows for it, the subjective—significance of the Other's catastrophe.

For both Bishara and Said, Holocaust and Nakbah are connected as two horrendous, albeit unequal, crimes: the one is presented as a prelude to the second. The Palestinian cause is strengthened not by denying the Holocaust, or disregarding or minimizing it but, rather, by showing the full magnitude of its evil and horror while asserting that its ultimate victim is the Palestinian through his systematic victimization by the victims of the Holocaust.

A second option is the one suggested by Ilan Gur-Ze'ev (but rejected by Ilan Pappe). Gur-Ze'ev sees it as most important that, when calling for a dialogue, this dialogue will be between parties who are not committed to asymmetrical claims for suffering, hierarchical conceptions of victimhood, and ethnocentric conceptions of justice. "There is suffering and injustice enough for everyone," says Said, and one could not agree more. According to Gur-Ze'ev, the dialogue that we are invites us to become equal partners facing each other's suffering, united in responsibility to the Other, responding to its suffering. Said and Bishara, however, insist on the supremacy of the Palestinian narrative and on the supremacy of the Palestinian suffering. There is a clear hierarchy and a sharp asymmetry within this invitation for a dialogue: Jews suffered from the injustice perpetrated against them by the Nazis, not from any injustice by the Palestinians. The Palestinians, on the other hand, suffered not from the Nazis, but from the Israelis. "Unless the connection is attempted which shows the Jewish tragedy as having led directly to the Palestinian catastrophe by let us call it necessity rather than pure will, we cannot coexist as two communities of detached and uncommunicatingly separate suffering" (Said, 1997, 3).[4] Said rightly sees the dialogue as a "moral imperative," which demands from the Palestinians to acknowledge the Jewish suffering inflicted on them by the Nazis and from the Jews to acknowledge the tragedy they inflicted on the Palestinians. This means that, as Palestinians, we demand considerations and reparations from them" (Said, 1997, 4).

For Gur-Ze'ev what is "missing" is the Palestinian recognition of the injustice inflicted on the Jews throughout their history in the Diaspora and the Palestinian part in their present tragedy. He maintains that the Holocaust is the story of death, while the Nakbah is the legacy of suffering. The first is a manifestation of total evil and has no justificational moderation or dialectical dimension. The second is manifestation of injustice and thus totally different. They meet on the ontological level, and it is this which enables the dialectics of Holocaust and Nakbah memories. Gur-Ze'ev does not accept the representation of the Palestinians as mere victims nor does he subscribe to the view of the Zionists as colonizers and the Zionist project as but a local version of Western colonialism. Gur-Ze'ev demands equality in judgment and argues that the asymmetrical perception of reality and its reflection in the "dialogue" does promise a life-and-death struggle which dehumanizes both parties. Within the ethnocentristic rhetoric, argues Gur-Ze'ev, there is no reason not to accept the Zionist ideology and its justification of the Jewish claim on Israel. The same manipulation can successfully be achieved for the Palestinians within the framework of nationalist to justify their claim to be the ultimate victims of Nazism and of Western colonialism. The aim of counter-education is to overcome this dialectic which victimizes both collectives as part of their self-construction and as a moral imperative to destroy the Other—as his victim.

A third option is the one suggested by Pappe which refers not only to the distinction between evil and injustice insisted on by Gur-Ze'ev, but also to the chain of victimization. Both authors agree that the direct relationship between the Palestinians as victims of the Israelis and the Israelis as past and present victims of the Palestinians plays an important role in determining the conditions of the dialogue. For Pappe this conclusion means that the imbalance of power and blame is rooted in a "relative" evil: the colonial and post-colonial history of the place. The historiographical assessment leads him to accept different levels of deconstruction vis-à-vis the contemporary victimizers, the Israelis, and the present victims, the Palestinians.

While agreeing with Gur-Ze'ev that Zionism is not a case of pure colonialism, Pappe nevertheless supports the principal definition of Zionism as a colonialist movement and thus accepts that the Palestinian violence and counter-violence cannot be judged in the same way as Zionist violence and counterviolence. Both Pappe and Gur-Ze'ev find a more complicated, not to say anti-colonialist, context for the examination of violence. Bishara, to a point, shuns this kind of examination as he presents himself as both a Nasserite and a student of the Enlightenment and the Frankfurt School (Bishara, 1997, 7-25), two affiliations that in their different perceptions of violence in the human experience cannot coexist.

Pappe claims that although there was violence, no injustice was inflicted by the Palestinians on the Israelis, as no injustice was inflicted by the Algerians on the French colonialists, though there certainly was violence. In the reformulation of collective memory currently underway in South Africa, the Africans are not diminishing the catastrophes that propelled white settlers to come to South Africa. While reintroducing the crimes of Apartheid into the collective memory, the dialogue here creates space for the traumas that led whites to leave Europe in search of another "homeland." Similarly, one cannot equate injustice and Palestinian resistance to Jewish expulsion and ethnic cleansing.

Both writers of this article agree that whichever avenue for dialogue is suggested as forming an adequate response to this Palestinian challenge, nothing justifies the hegemonic Israeli representation of the Holocaust memory or the Israeli denial of major responsibility for the suffering of the Palestinians and their Nakbah.

Accepting that ideology, critique, and non-ethnocentric oriented multicultural reconstruction will lead to more reflective attitudes and more humanistic orientations toward the suffering of both sides, the next important step to be taken is probably to formulate what conclusions we can draw from this recognition of the connection between the Holocaust and the Nakbah memories for a continued Israeli/Palestinian dialogue. The starting point, we think, is overcoming nationalism and ethnocentrism. Critical theory and postmodern elaboration of the historical constitution of the subject, knowledge, identity, and memory, together with empirical studies, should impel this deconstruction and reformulation of the hegemonic Palestinian and Israeli narratives.

But those who go down this road will encounter many obstacles. Adopting a critical "humanist" or "universal" approach which does not simply dismiss humanism, they will find themselves set apart from the accepted intellectual, cultural, and emotional levels within the history of "their" societies. They are in eternal exile. Can they still be considered as "Palestinians" or "Israelis"? This is but one question to be answered within this future dialogue. Moreover, theirs is a realistic as well as constructive position. Or would it be better if one still could navigate, as Bishara suggests, between the national collective will and memory and a humanist and universal approach? Or should we first wait, as Said suggests, for the fruits of a dialogue between Diaspora groups less captivated by the national collective memory and its control? Or should we do this as part of a continued decolonization process, as suggested by Pappe? Or should we do it as part of a counter-education which will challenge all forms of collectivism and strive for dialogical communities which are anti-ethno-centristic-oriented as advocated by Gur-Ze'ev?

Our main query in this chapter is how far can both sides emancipate themselves from the narrative of their own collective, distance themselves from the realm of self-evidence, needs, criteria and perspectives, and move toward a deconstructive posture and how important it is for coexistence. Our intention is to deconstruct the scheme which produces not only this "both sides," but also the symbolic and direct violence they perpetrate.

Should a deconstructive approach be directed equally to all narratives, collectives, and the power relations which historically constitute them? This question, as far as the Palestinian case is concerned, has not as yet been fully answered by even the most open and critical among Palestinian intellectuals.

Conclusion

After years of denial and minimization of the event's memory and its universal implications, a new Palestinian attitude has recently been formulated toward the Holocaust memory.

In their bold challenge of mainstream and past Palestinian perceptions and utilization of the Holocaust memory, Edward Said and Azmi Bishara have exposed the tension between the collective national memory on the one hand, and critical a-national positions on the other. Neither is ignoring the one for the sake of the other. Thus even in this new approach the national narrative or interpretation always hovers in the background, even if minimized and censured. It may be argued that, if this is so, a certain level of violence, mainly symbolic, will remain. Symbolic violence enables non-symbolic violence to operate according to both its positive-creative and negative-destructive potentials. The bottom line is that where there are remnants of any unwholesome destructive approach, the way is left open for turning human subjects into objects, mere symbols of the system (Baudrillard, 1983, 5). At the end of the day they may still be agencies of the self-reproduction of the system and its internal and external colonization practices, which will culminate in the destruction, digestion, marginalization, or disregard of the Other and its otherness. To put it more bluntly, will Israelis and Palestinians then still be educated as potentially either victims or perpetrators?

On the theoretical level the new Palestinian approach outlined above calls for a continued dialogue which will address the gaps and the tensions between critique and commitment to emancipation, between the understanding of power relations and the production of collective identities, as narratives, between the contingent apparatuses of self-affirmation and the victimization of the Other. A thorough look into the moral imperative of such an analysis is warranted.

The hope of the authors of this chapter is that relativism, contingency, and anti-foundationalism, however important they are, will not have the last word, and that even in a post-modern, post-colonialist and multicultural world one can and should address questions of injustice and be a politically active ironist, without the confinement of the iron cage or ethnocentrism or the false naiveté of an easygoing optimism.

NOTES

1 This chapter was written with Ilan Pappe. I would like to thank Ilan for enabling the publication of this chapter in this book.
2 See *al-Hayat*, 1 and 2 August, 1992.
3 Said, "Bases for existence," 3.
4 Said, "Bases for coexistence," 3.

BIBLIOGRAPHY

al-Ghuri, Emil. (1973). *Palestine Through Sixty Years*, Volume 2, Beirut: PLO Publication: 181-189 (Arabic).
Almatukal, Taha. (1989). *Poetry Space: Poetry from Ansar 3*, Ramallah (Arabic).
Alush, Naji. (1967). *Arab Resistance in Palestine, 1917-1948*. Beirut: no publisher (Arabic).
Baudrillard, Jean. (1983). *Symbolic Exchange and Death* (trans. I. H. Grant). London: Sage.
Ben-Amos, Avner. (1988). "Close Proximity," *Ha'aretz*, 3 March (Hebrew).
Ben-Naftali, Meir. (1993). "The Israeli Philosophers and the Holocaust," *Teoria ve-Bikoret* 4 (Autumn): 57-78 (Hebrew).
Bishara, Azmi. (1995). "The Arabs and the Holocaust," *Zemanim* 53 (Summer): 56-74 (Hebrew).
———. ed. (1997). "Introduction" in *The Enlightenment: An Unfinished Project?* Tel-Aviv: Hakibbutz Ha-Meuchad, 7-25 (Hebrew).
———. (1996). "On Chauvinism and Universalism," *Zemanim* 55 (Winter): 102-107 (Hebrew).
Darwish, Mahmoud. (1987). "The Identity of a Space," *Mifgash* 7-8 (Autumn): pp. 46-47 (Hebrew).
Diner, Dan. (1986). "Israel and the Annihilation Trauma," *Politika* 8: 20-23 (Hebrew).
———. (1996). "Accumulative Cognition: On History and Self-Justification in the Israeli Discourse," *Alpaim* 12: 50-53 (Hebrew).
Gur-Ze'ev, Ilan. (1998a). "The Morality of Acknowledging/Not-acknowledging the Other's Holocaust/Genocide, *Journal of Moral Education*, 27\2: 161-177.
———. (1998b). "The Mythification of the Holocaust and the Industry of Evil", *Ha'aretz*, 24 March (Hebrew).
———. (1999). *Philosophy, Politics and Education in Israel*. Haifa: Haifa University Press and Zemora-Bitan (in Hebrew).
Habibi, Emil. (1986). "Your Holocaust is Our Disaster," *Politica* 8: 27-30 (Hebrew).

Hadawi, Sami and John, Robert. (1960). *The Palestinian Diary*, Part 1, Beirut: Institute of Palestine Studies.

Mattar, Philip. (1988). *The Mufti of Jerusalem; Haj Ain al-Husayni and the Palestinian National Movement.* New York: Columbia University Press.

Muhafaza, Ali. (1981). *The German-Palestinian Relations 1841-1945.* Beirut: PLO Publication.

Nevo, Joesph. (1989). "The Attitude of Arab Palestinian Historiography toward the Germans and the Holocaust," in Y. Bauer and others (eds.), *Remembering for the Future: Working Papers and Addenda*, Vol. 2. London: Maxwell: 2241-2250.

Pappe, Ilan. (1995). "Critique and Agenda: The Post-Zionist Scholars in Israel," *History and Memory*, Vol. 7: 66-90.

Rabin, Eitan, and Horovitz, Moshe. (1993). "The Five Expelled were Returned," *Ha'aretz* (February 8) (Hebrew).

Said, Edward. (1997). "Bases for Coexistence," *Al-Ahram Weekly*, 15 November.

———. (1998). "Israel-Palestine: A Third Way," *Le Monde Diplomatique*, 7 September: 6.

———. (1994). *The Politics of Dispossession.* London: Chatto and Windus.

Sarayah, H. and Bashir, S. "Knowing the Holocaust or the Breaking of the Jewish Monopoly Over It?" *Al-Hayat*, 18 December 1997, p. 19.

Shavit, Ari, "Citizen Azmi," interview with Azmi Bishara, the Supplement of *Ha'aretz*, 29 May 1998, p. 23.

CHAPTER 3
Hitler and Philosophy in the Israeli Curriculum

The mission of education is to control the representations of reality, consciousness, conceptual schemes, apparatuses of identifying reality, its cataloging and its interpretation and meanings production, as well as the psychic structure of men and women. In the educational act, knowledge about knowledge and knowledge about the self and the world are transmitted in various teaching practices in the social, economic, technological, linguistic, and psychological fields, according to their locus in the dynamics of these fields and according to the historical stage in which a given project is situated. The curriculum in its narrow sense and in its broader sense, in its formal and its informal sense, the explicit curriculum and the hidden one, are all to be understood within this context. The curriculum is both an instrument of warfare and a means of production, and it has a negative and a positive side. It should never be understood in itself but rather on the background of alternative curricula, as well as the forces and interests that struggle for their hegemony; curricula that are to be eliminated, digested, or marginalized as part of a successful normal education. This is how the normalized subject is produced and the system reproduced, a subject that always has something "different" and Other than that which one was educated to be.

The production and reproduction of the realm of self-evidence[1] is the real agenda for the normalized subject, which is educated to act as an agent of the system; education is supposed to regulate it in an unproblematic manner. The images of knowledge,[2] bodies of knowledge,[3] the conceptual apparatus,[4] and the consciousnesses that are created and regulated by normalization education determine the possibilities and limitations of the subject's function. This function, that transforms the subject into an object, is at the same time a yardstick for the nature and limits of the possibilities of communication and the normal intersubjectivity possible within the limits of the space where the hegemonic educational ideology is present. The subject functions as an object to the degree that he/she functions as an agent of reproduction determined by the nature of its normalization and the limits of possibilities for transcendence from this realm of self-evidence.

Hitler and Philosophy in the Israeli Curriculum

The normalized person functions as the agent of the system that creates his/her possibilities and limitations for change, improvement, and the ability to criticize reality within which he/she is functioning or struggling for change and transcendence.[5] In modern societies human beings are never totally normalized, and there is no sole power that creates and controls identities without being challenged by fearful legitimate alternatives and antagonisms within itself. This dimension of education is rapidly changing in the post-modern condition.

The secular Jewish educational system in Israel[6] is involved today in a rapid transformation[7] that includes a serious identity crisis.[8] It is unavoidable for this development not to be represented in the practice of the established educational system, as well as in the other social and cultural dynamics that represent and reproduce collective and private consciousness and the reflections on them. Historically, the constitutive Zionist myths have been almost totally eroded, and they are being replaced by a new set of myths that can supply the needed impetus for the kind of normalizing education that suits the demands of current technological advances, the present needs of advanced capitalist production, and the local post-industrial social organization.[9] In contrast, the rhetoric of institutionalized public education did little to adjust itself to the post-industrial or post-modern reality, paralleling a political structure (in the narrow meaning of the term) that is still devoted to modern and, in some instances, even pre-modern jargon.[10] Here special attention should be given to the national conflicts that are manifested in armed practice and fights over "space" and control of instruments of representing identities and criteria for legitimacy of knowledge, identities, collective memories, and intersubjectivity. In Israel, this is a struggle in which power is reduced to its traditional material and symbolic manifestations. Their development demands the constitution of such a kind of private and collective identity that not only does not fit the possibilities and needs of a pre-modern world, but the kind that must reject even the local humanistic manifestations of modernity.

The Israeli/Arab dialectic of blood/land and knowledge/power demands an educational practice that will produce *agents* with a sufficient aggressive potential for the reproduction of the national manifestations of the struggle. It demands such an organizational structure that will represent and enable the preservation and development of the aggressive potential of the two collectives, the Israeli and the Palestinian.

In the secular Israeli arena, the influence of the post-industrial trend is gathering momentum in the cultural, social, and technological senses, and the unofficial, anti-collectivist and anti-idealist education is rapidly melting the traditional achievements of Zionist education. These conflicting trends cause the official educational system to face and challenge the new myths that arose within the inner logic of the post-industrial system. It challenges the new trend in order to support and serve the institutionalized Zionist educational targets. However, it cannot be efficient in its struggle unless it accepts at least some of the new myths and uses the new technologies of representation as well as its concepts of knowledge. This brings the system into an organizational anomaly[11] in which one has to look for its ground in its ideological disarray and philosophical confusion. The formal institutionalized system cannot be satisfied with borrowing fashions like "literacy," "media consumption," and with culture heroes like Madonna, Aviv Geffen, and Steff Wertheimer which vitalize its downfall. It must recruit to the struggle alternative *educational violence* that is produced from modern national myths whose potential is even today very high, especially in the new social and cultural context.

The mythicization of Holocaust memory and the representation of other Holocausts or genocides might serve as an example for the traditional system's way of trying to challenge the new myths, the new images of knowledge, the conceptual apparatus, the consciousness, and the new identities that are transmitted by current unofficial production practices, namely, by the relevant education in the Israeli secular arena. These are the horizons of the critique of teaching the Holocaust in today's Israel.

The recognition of the Other's identity[12] or the Other identity's negation is a partial dimension of the struggle over self and collective consciousness' constitution, or part of a struggle over its emancipation from the imposition of another force claiming to represent an authentic self-consciousness. As one can see in Hegel's dialectic between lordship and bondage,[13] the ontological conditions remain as a foundation of the movement toward being recognized by a foreign self-consciousness. Subjective violence is an objective condition for the self-recognition of consciousness and for the re-formation of identity: "Self-consciousness has before it another self-consciousness. . . . it must set itself to sublet the other independent being, in order thereby to become certain of itself as true being."[14]

Knowledge, including moral knowledge, is produced, represented, distributed, and consumed within the horizons of this discursive process about which one has to be aware of the importance of its historical and political concretization. As "education," this moral knowledge is essentially produced and reproduced as part of a two-layer cover—an epistemological one and an ideological one—hiding its roots and its share in the production of the normalized subject, which reflects, serves, and develops the given realm of self-evidence and the production means of hegemonic knowledge and identities.

However, knowledge, with moral educational knowledge included, has *other* sources. These sources have a utopian axis, sources that are being expressed in the dialogical essence of human existence.[15] In contrast to discourse, dialogue has a utopian axis and is committed to struggle over transcendence from the realm of self-evidence.[16] In contrast to the discourse, which realizes itself in reality, the dialogue is always ironic, an open scope for an alternative reality to the prevailing one, which suddenly might explode and enhance skepticism and estrangement. It might call into question the normal function of manipulation and the syntax of the procedural apparatuses that constitute and represent self-evident knowledge, including knowledge about the problematization of this self-evidence. From time to time, the quest for dialogue transforms into partaking in the system's power games and contributes to the efficiency of the control practices of the hegemonic discourses. Normally, the educational discourse presents and reproduces the hegemonic forces and knowledge and portrays the quest to be swept away by them to the degree of total subordination, eternal nirvana or other methods of inhalation. In contrast, education for dialogue, represents the quest for the spirit and the hope for transcendence from the dullness of the profane. It is realized in the demand for recognition, in the self-consciousness as a starting point for a struggle over the possibility of a dialogue in which different subjective and collective identities take part, as well as their knowledge and unique needs that are accepted as legitimate.[17]

The history of Western moral education presents the transformation of the quest for transcendence and the negation of self-evidence into a productive anti-spiritual dimension. It functions within the limits of the power nets of knowledge that produce subjects and constitutes "their" possibilities for reproducing, developing, and conceiving of "their" own "voice," the self-evident knowledge and the cataloging and syllogism apparatuses that are part of this education. It arbitrarily includes as well the justification of the socio-cultural space and the inner logic within which all these are conceivable and necessary.

Criticizing the function of the representation of the Holocaust in the current historical Israeli context might give a specific concretization for the alternative for current "spiritual education." This issue will be dealt with here by evaluating the function of Israeli textbooks in the production of the spiritual world of the secular Zionist subject. I intend to concentrate on a specific textbook, its context, sources, and procedures of consciousness reproduction that it innovates within the framework of its explicit and implicit aims. At the same time, the moral dimensions of its production, the constitution of its legitimacy and relevancy, and its acceptance and elimination by another textbook will be considered. As in Hegel's dialectics of the lord and bondsman, in the case analyzed here, this denial is to be understood as part of a process of constituting the negated self-consciousness. However, while the Hegelian project refers to a teleological-historical process that strives to overcome the contradictions, in the historical stage in which we are framed, and especially in Israel, this violence is not to be understood as part of the historical development of appeasement and overcoming real contradictions. What we are talking about is an *ontological sign* that even in Israel, reality has a universal meaning. Like the struggle over constitution identity, recovering meaning is a struggle over the possibilities of transcending from the reality that is manifested in the dialectic between the two textbooks. The dialectic that binds them is to be understood as a "stretched" text: it is impossible to understand one axis without matching it to its opposite. This effort of understanding is committed to the ability of reconstructing the dialectic that constitutes each of them, an effort which is both a philosophical and a political one, and its telos is the constitution/destruction of self-consciousness and collective/subjective identity. This mission will be elaborated on here as part of an effort to reconstruct the context of the production of the Zionist morality and its subject, a project that historically is ever more desperate for mythicizing and instrumentalizing Holocaust memory. This concept is explicitly contrasted to the standard positivistic trend so popular in teaching the Holocaust in Israel,[18] and it is categorically committed to negating it and exposing its background, motives, and practices, as well as its telos.

The representation of the Holocaust as a constitutive dimension in the production of secular Zionist morality will be treated here while referring to a textbook that explicitly is not meant to deal directly with the Jewish Holocaust, but rather indirectly; herewith, I will treat a textbook whose subject is the teaching of the Genocide that the Armenian people suffered a hundred years ago. In the Zionist arena, this book is unique in its explicit commitment to educate students in sensibility for other people's suffering.[19]

The struggle that occurred for and against this textbook as an alternative to other textbooks approved in secular Jewish schools in Israel might be understood as a manifestation of an alternative moral education to the hegemonic one. It might be interpreted as an essential alternative that negates and challenges the private and collective identity, as formed by Zionist hegemonic tradition, the context and educational manipulation apparatuses of the Zionist system. To my mind, the reconstruction of the power struggles around this educational issue might help us to discover the hidden forces and the coded apparatuses of normalizing education. In a sense, this reconstruction itself is but a dimension of resisting hegemonic Israeli ideology and is a part of an alternative morality, which is, in turn, a *religious* act. This educational praxis is no more than a hint of the desired alternative and is not a positive utopia. It is a positive educational process, even if the alternative it strives for is impossible to realize within the horizons of the current historical possibilities.

The Israeli public education was historically a localized version of the modern educational project, as a central element in the struggle for nation building and liberation. The paradox of building and liberating a nation is the framework within whose borders Zionist education constituted a new philosophical conception of education that was committed to the successful production of "the new Jew," with its collective goals in the Jewish people and in general human culture.[20] The educational Zionist project might be seen as a perfect manifestation of the educational violence that was targeted against Jewish tradition, against inner groups, their collective memory and interests, as well as against external enemies, like the Palestinians. Historically, within the framework of formal Zionist education, the negation of the Diaspora and the colonization/settlement of Israel/Palestine were inseparable. The destruction of the Diaspora as an ethos and as the central political dimension in Jewish private and collective consciousness was a precondition for the constitution of the *halutz* (the pioneer) as the ideal Jew, "the new Jew,"[21] the opposite of *Eved Adonay* (God's servant) as the ideal Jew. Berl Katzenelson, one of the founding fathers of the labor Zionist movement, expresses it in a religious language: "our faith—that this spectacle the *halutz* (the pioneer) is history's faithful messenger, the messenger of the national supreme being (*Hasgacha Eliona*)."[22]

The *halutz* myth was nourished by the evolving Israeli culture, in general, and by its textbooks, in particular, against a Jewish non-Zionist alternative, especially in light of the Holocaust that destroyed the social organization and the traditional culture of the centers of the Jewish people in Europe.[23] Furthermore, the myth of the Israeli soldier, which replaced the pioneer myth, was constituted as an alternative to the traditional Jewish identity, its way of life, values, and morals, or at least that was how it was represented in the Israeli public education in its formative years. Another dramatic change would be seen after 1967 and the Six Day War.[24]

Since the end of the Second World War, Zionist historiography worked hard on the instrumentalization of the knowledge about the Holocaust[25] as part of the project of building a successful Zionist moral education. The hegemonic version of the representation and distribution of Holocaust memory was a central instrument in the constitution of the Israeli collective consciousness. The control of the collective memory and its legitimate criteria of interpretation has become a central element in the project of nation building out of diverse collectives with different contexts, different historical memories, and different interests and goals. The control of the historical memory, its production, interpretation, and distribution have been developed into an instrument for the constitution of "the new Jew." His/her collective identity and ethnocentricity were essential, and their protection was to be ensured by the uniformity of the memory and the engagement of its legitimate interpretations with the nation-building project. Within this framework, *Auschwitz* was developed into an immanent and obligatory expression of the Jewish cultural and social alternatives to Zionism and the refusal to receive the call for joining the struggle for a national independent Jewish state in Israel.[26]

The memory of the Holocaust, the *"Zachor"* ("remembrance"), which was developed as a moral justification for Zionist practices,[27] was based on an instrumentalized interpretation of the biblical *"Zachor"* as explicitly declared by the founding fathers of Israeli public education like Ben Zion Dinur, Israel's most influential minister of education.[28] The word *"Zachor"* appears eight times in the Bible, where it is framed in three different contexts. The first is the one where remembrance is seen as part of prophecy. The second represents the link to the S*abbath* as *the totally other* than the daily power games, an idea that provides for a *utopia* in whose light it is possible to break the self-evidence of the secular reality and erect the demand for transcendence and for the transformation of human beings and their possibilities. The essential principle of the *shabbat* as overcoming secularity, of all daily expression of power as conceived by Judaism as essential, is conceived as mandatory on all levels and dimensions of the Jew, including his/her slaves and animals.

The third context of the *"Zachor"* is the military one. It might be the war against Pharaoh or against Amalek. However, one has to remember that the Bible refers here to God's wars. "Remember what Amalek did unto thee," as written in Deuteronomy 25:17, refers to remembering the godly imperative of devotion to his commandments as mandatory to enter the promised land and fulfill the total demolishing of Amalek: men, women, children, and even their animals—disconnected from any secular explanations of economic, military, or other earthly interests.

"Zachor et asher asa lecha Amalek" ("remember what Amalek has done to you") as God's command, as a warning, and as a constitutive element of collective identity by identifying "Amalek" with any Other, was the grand mission of Israeli public education. It was also internalized in the negation of the Diaspora and became an essential dimension already in the constitution of the myth of the *halutz*, and after that in the production of the *Sabra* and the Israeli soldier myths. The *Zachor* as remembrance of the Holocaust victims was synthesized with the "remember what Amalek has done to you." The remembrance of the German National Socialism was integrated into the

concept of the Jew as an "eternal victim." Within the context of the hegemonic Israeli education, this concept implicitly conceives of any Other or *goy* as a historical realization of "Amalek" as an idea.[29] Under suitable conditions, in times of crisis, or for social groups that are in rapid deterioration or constant crisis, it is easy to concretize personally or collectively: namely, that the justification of the fate of Amalek is suitable for the "fate" of "Amalek of our time" or that of times to come. Rabbi Kahane, as an example, used to freely express these ideas. Yet, even he did not explicitly refer to the physical extermination of "our day's Amalek" (the Palestinians), but rather promoted the expropriation from their civil and political rights and their right to property and conditioned their stay in the country only on the status of *Ger*. These ideas are very popular in Israel, in varying degrees of magnitude. Research on democratic and humanistic stands of Israeli teachers is alarmingly clear on this issue.[30] This is not an accident or some misfortune. It is one of the manifestations of the great success of Zionist education, especially of the (Jewish) orthodox religious education in Israel. Zionist education was very effective in producing the self-evident moral knowledge that the state of Israel is and should be the state of the Jews and not the state of its citizens (Jews and non-Jews alike). In this matter, Ben Zion Dinur, who constituted the hegemonic educational ideology of the secular part of Israeli society, was not an extremist or exotic ideologue. On the contrary, he represented the mainstream trend in Zionism. He explicitly identified "Amalek" as an ideal with the enemies of Israel in their historical context, and after the Holocaust it became self-evident in Israel: "The striving to demolish the Jews did not start with Hitler. . . . it found in Hitler its messenger and performer. Yet by that it was not completed. Amalek is the symbol of Hitler, and his paradigmatic character is in curtailing the ones who are backwards, the tired and the exhausted."[31] Dinur was one of those responsible for the formative educational conceptions and myths in Israel and was very important in his contribution to the effective national endowment of pairs like "Holocaust and bravery" to be commemorated, or "from Diaspora to redemption" to be celebrated. As part of this project, he founded secular Jewish education by propagating the self-evident knowledge that: "We have to remember that Amalek is 'a potential that goes through generations,' and we should not be allowed to forget this terrible potential."[32]

The instrumentalization of the Holocaust was equalized between the Nazi "Amalek" and the Arab "Amalek" by the special use it developed for the traditional Jewish *Zachor*. As I mentioned, it took one element out of three; it did not look for the synthesis between the three in Jewish religion, and even the sole element it denoted was interpreted wrong from the traditional Jewish perspective. This argument is to be defended by referring to the Jewish history of national education by remembrance and holy celebrations: The *Zachor* that referred to the victory over Amalek was not celebrated by the Jews by *halel* (expression of gratefulness to God), and it did not have a special holiday to be celebrated like the victory over the *mityavenim* that wanted the *torah* to be forgotten and dismissed. This is the context of official Zionist equation of Arabs, be it Gamal Abdul Nazer, Sadam Hussein, or Yaser Arafat, to Adolf Hitler. This is how exile and secular redemption are met in secular Israeli public education, Diaspora and independent Israel, Hitler and the Palestinians, memory and power. As educational energy, it conditions the overcoming of external and internal enemies. However, at the same time it is itself conditioned by effective violent education; it is the one to constitute the conceptual apparatus, the psychic structure, and the memory, and through their manipulation, the formation of self-identity and collective identity. These are to make into "natural" the "free decision" of the normalized Zionist person in Israel to sacrifice himself/herself for the collective and the national designation. This is politically articulated in two important Israeli laws that were created at the same time: the law of states education (1953) and the law of remembrance of the Holocaust—*Yad Vashem* (1953).

The Zionist utopia inherited traditional Jewish redemptive thought, in which an important dimension across the Jewish exile was a universalistic and anti-political impulse. Even after the erection of the state of Israel and the distraction of the centers of orthodox Judaism, an important stream stayed faithful in its waiting for the messiah and refusal to enter secular history and politics. In its most extreme version, it is today represented by *neturey karta* ("the guardians of the city"—the most extreme ultra-orthodox Jewish sect).[33] The traditional Jewish religious refusal of secular history represents a refusal of *power* and of the state, and it cannot be adjusted to the Zionist project and its obligatory use of power: "Because the Jewish people is beyond the contradiction that constitutes the vital drive in the life of nations—the contradiction between national characteristics and world history, home and faith, earth and heaven—it knows nothing of war."[34]

Zionist moral philosophy inherited the traditional Jewish moral while introducing an alternative ideal subject and a different world conception that demands the immediate national return to secular history. Zionist education negated the traditional Jewish negation of secular history and the refusal of participation in power games. It was negated both as part of three exile ways of life and as part of exile thinking that should be destroyed. Thinkers such as Martin Buber, Ernst Simon, and Hai Rot, who tried to constitute a Zionist synthesis between humanism and the Jewish tradition, favored the return to synthesis between humanism and the Jewish tradition, favored the return to history. However, they educated for trading history as a sacred space of humanistic intersubjectivity in which the telos of universal emancipation and the advance of reason's realization is taking place.[35] This is the foundation for the synthesis between the concept of redemption in Judaism and the Enlightenment's project of universal emancipation. However, these thinkers were driven to the margins of cultural relevancy in Israel, and the political potential of their educational alternative was minimal. Yet, they managed to disturb the Zionist establishment to a much greater extent than the direct political weight of their educational alternative.

Prior and after the establishment of the state of Israel, the secular Zionist educational institutions saw themselves as being committed to the constitution of "the new Jew" as their conceptual, moral, and political aims. This educational project of Israeli nation building represented and reproduced a unique moral philosophy, in which there was no legitimate place for critical discussion on such issues as the right of a minor intellectual group to reconstruct and propagate a hegemonic version of one, unified, coherent historical memory; the exclusiveness of the violent fabrication of national narrative that represents one group; the meaning of constituting the right to produce a narrative that will attract/build/reconstruct the Israeli collective, produced for violently contradicting another collective which is empowered/produced by a rival narrative with antagonistic demands and claims about the space/ideal called the land of Israel/Palestine. As an alternative to traditional Jewish universalistic morality, Israeli public education concentrated increasingly on an ethnocentric, anti-humanistic, and anti-Jewish concept of history, as claimed by Yesha'ayau Leibowitz. Leibowitz reminds us that in the *Sidur* (the Jewish prayer book), a remembrance prayer is included in memory of 'the Jewish communities (kehilot kodesh) that scarified themselves in God's name, that were lighter than eagles and braver than lions.' These words were directed to Jews who never in their lives held a weapon in their hands, but rather "went as sheep to be slaughtered." Until the Six Day War, the Israeli state's education represented in a very negative way the manner in which millions of Jews "went as sheep to be slaughtered." It was represented as a manifestation of the Diaspora mentality and world view from which Israelites (especially secular *sabras*) had been emancipated. The ideal Israeli was not that of *Eved Adonay* (God's servant), about whom in Isaiah 25 it is said, "As a lamb that is led to be slaughter, And as a sheep that before her sharers is dumb." The barbarization of Judaism by the secular Israeli public education is described by Leibowitz: The violence, the admiration for combat bravery, the rudeness and disrespect for human beings as human creatures—all of these are mutually connected.

barbarization and the infiltration of the spirit of violence to the core of the Jewish consciousness:

> We know the version of the *azkara* that is being said in the funeral of each Jew, *"bema'alot kedoshim uteorim"*. . . . However, people that spoke on behalf of the Jewish faith and that are accepted as representing it dared to add one word to this prayer, when it is recited for our brothers and sons who were killed in the last generation's wars: *"bema'alot kedoshim uteorim vegiborim"*. . . . "Why did they add *"giborim"*? (heroes) because the brothers and sons were brave in battle. But does this bravery represent any form of human virtue? . . . Since when is being a war hero to be praised? I do not mean to say that every war hero is inhuman; some war heroes are *zadikim* (saints) and others evil, some pure and others defiled. Therefore, this addition to the memorial prayer is nothing less than an additional manifestation of the spirit of violence that has penetrated even into today's Judaism.[36]

An essential element in ensuring the efficiency of (secular) Israeli public education was its ability almost completely to avoid an internal critical moral engagement in the constitutive foundations of Zionism. It has been almost impossible to challenge the hegemonic educational manipulations and the representation practices of historical memory and the collective consciousness of the "Israelis."[37] Yet, there were always moral philosophies in the margins of Israeli culture and politics that were educationally challenging. In some cases, like in the case of the Communist Party, *Gedud A'avoda*, or *Hashomer Hazair*, they even had a concrete political formation. However, the Zionist educational ideologies were basically part and parcel of the mainstream Zionist movement and its goals.

Zionist education was always confronted with internal conflicting alternative ideologies and with immanent aporias, which fertilized moral, aesthetic, cultural, and social dialogues and confrontations. To my mind, it is especially important that the critical historians of the hegemonic educational ideologies be aware of this. However, historically, the hegemonic ideology successfully managed to marginalize oppositional political and philosophical alternatives to avoid challenging its educational hegemony. The educational development reconstructed in this study is to be understood in its concrete local context. It includes constant ideological and military conflict with the Arabs, in general, and the Palestinians, in particular. This is a struggle over control, purification, and redemption of the land of Israel from "Amalek," and her coming back to herself, her real self, namely the land of Israel. The identity of the land and the identity of the people are conceived here as inseparable, there can be no compromise here, a matter for a life-and-death struggle. Already, the beginning of the Israeli *Declaration of Independence* reveals the Israeli commitment to denial of the Other as the foundation for educational possibilities, as the struggle of direct military operations, and additional manifestations of institutionalized violence that represent the hegemonic Israeli identity: "The Jewish people was born in the land of Israel, here its spiritual, religious and political identity were formed, here it realized civic independence, here it produced national and universal cultural treasures." In this formative document, there is no place for the recognition of the Other as equal, for the recognition of his name and his place, his right to equal possibilities to express his identity, voice, and rights. The self-evident starting point is ethnocentric. Only within these limits is the Other recognized: as an enemy with whom "we" have to be generous, to "give" him the right and recognition as a citizen in the state of the Jewish people, namely in the state that is not his state even as its citizen. Officially, in the state's educational system, the Palestinian is recognized in one (or more) of three possibilities: as an object of paternalistic generosity, as a collaborator ("good Arab"), and as an enemy who must be defeated. One has to be careful not to acknowledge the big difference between the anti-Semitic recognition of the Jews as "the Jewish problem" and the Israeli popular and official view of the Palestinians as "the demographic problem." Yet, in both cases, it is the "us versus them" ideology that constructs the basis of educational aims. Israeli textbooks have historically manifested this ideology and done their best to ensure its defense and reproduction.[38] This practice is manifested at all levels and disciplines of the hidden curriculum that is also effectively active outside the formal schooling arena, in art, literature,[39] theater,[40] and the mass media. In a study conducted in 1988, 73.8% of the Jewish participants responded that it is justified to prefer Jews over Arabs, and 42.8% supported the prevention of Palestinians from participating in general elections.[41] In a study conducted in 1996, teachers' seminars were surveyed for their response to the statement according to which "Israeli Arabs today are citizens with equal rights in the state of Israel." From the secular seminars, 60% responded that they agree or largely agree, as compared with 25% from the religious seminars.[42] In response to the statement "the state belongs to the Jews and Arabs have no right to participate in state resolutions," 30% of the secular seminar students responded favorably, as compared with 78% of the students from the religious seminars.[43] It shows to what degree Zionist education is effective, especially in the state's funded and pedagogically autonomous national-religious institutions. Practically, it shows the popular support for institutionalized discrimination on a racial or ethnic basis in Israel. In the secular educational institutions, this success is gradually declining, while in the religious institutions, it is becoming stronger and more effective.

Since its beginning, the Zionist self-consciousness was apathetic, negated the Palestinian identity of the land,[44] or paternalistically referred to the

Palestinian identity through an orientalistic perspective,[45] as a deterioration of the old Hebrew identity of the land and its people or as natives who should be recognized and helped as long as they do not develop into "Amalek." They developed the ethnocentric military dimension of the Zachor concept that characterized the entire actual Jewish history and realized it "in peaceful ways" toward the Palestinians. From their perspective, it was the victim's coming home. From the Palestinian perspective, it was economic and political colonization to be resisted by all means. The violent Palestinian reaction to the Zionist "peaceful" colonization that was aimed at changing the identity of the land was interpreted after the Holocaust and interpreted by the Zionists as a reaffirmation of the idea of the Jew as an eternal victim even in his homeland. The uprooted Palestinians became the oppressors, and the attacked Jews, as in the Nazi era, became threatened by a new extermination as a manifestation of being the eternal victim. Yet, ironically, the Holocaust seemed to justify the Zionist claim that there is no other place to protect Jews from extermination but in Palestine/Israel. At the same time, the Zionist project directed a special educational effort toward the majority of the Jewish people which was, until the Holocaust, anti-Zionist or non-Zionist.[46] Until that historical stage, most of the Jews were orthodox or ultra-orthodox and refused to enter into the state's power struggles, but were instead totally devoted to the messianic hope or totally committed to the utopian project of universal emancipation in its Marxist and other versions. Either way, most of them opposed Zionism as a partial, ethnocentric, and reactionary utopia. Many Jews constituted or joined liberal and pragmatic alternatives that enabled them to be indifferent or moderate supporters of the Zionist project, which was far from being relevant for their actual lives.

In my mind, the history of Holocaust memory representation in the state's educational institutions is to be understood in light of the change in the status of knowledge and the change in the moral concepts that took place within the framework of the cultural, social, economic, and technological changes in Israel. Here I will concentrate on the current historical moment. Yet, one has to endorse a development that at first glance might amaze. On the one hand, there is a development according to which the Holocaust issue becomes increasingly central in Zionist education, while on the other hand, the central constitutive myths of Zionism are being ridiculed and demolished, if we refer to ones like the *halutz* (pioneer), the *sabra* (native Jewish anti-Diaspora-mentally-oriented Israeli), or the Israeli soldier. The return to the bravery of the masses that was described by pre-1967 textbooks as "sheeps going to be slaughtered"[47] did not reflect a reinterpretation of the *Eved Adonay* (God's slave) ideal or any reinterpretation of Jewish tradition in general, nor did it manifest a re-binding of the Jews who are within the Zionist framework with the humanistic tradition and the universal emancipatory project. The conscious return to grief and challenging of absolute evil, as manifested in the Jewish Holocaust, are today reflecting the relevance of new needs and new myths. These are related to the symbols' economy, to the post-industrial market, and the post-modern conditions that are not to be grasped except within the framework of the change that took place in the conceptual and material life possibilities.

The second trend is to be understood as a local symptom of a general Western development. Instrumental Rationality replaces the tradition of Objective Reason as source of reproduction and development in current Western societies.[48] Yet, with the dispossession of Objective Reason, the erotic quest for transcendence from the given reality, which is the essence of true religiosity, is eroded, along with the commitment to human solidarity and revolutionary transformation of society.

The Enlightenment's moral philosophy was developed within the framework of the Objective Reason tradition. It represented a critical pretension for the universal validity of its claims for justice, liberty, and equality, in a consistency that very often was realized in a concrete educational practice, at the cost of its transformation to its opposite. However, in the current Western arena, in which Instrumental Rationality has the upper hand, there is no place for such religiosity, nor for its moral concepts, its foundations, and its social aims, as well as its national or religious revolutionary projects. Accordingly, the status of knowledge and production, representation, distribution, and consumption of symbols has changed dramatically.[49] We are facing the constitution of new realities in which new subjects and new limitations, possibilities, and control apparatuses and practices are being implemented. Among the changing conditions, one has to mention the demolishing of the conditions for dialogue and the formation of a system within its framework of Christianity and Judaism, as well as Kantian moral philosophies becoming totally irrelevant. Pragmatic and functionalist concepts of knowledge are becoming hegemonian, and the calculative thinking and the logic of control are become vital for enhancing the productivity of the system.

One of the manifestations of this development is the destruction of the conditions for idealism and solidarity with the collective, as well as the cynicism toward any altruistic behavior. This development is also gathering momentum in the most progressive arenas of Israeli society[50] and has been seriously researched.[51]

One of the local manifestations of this process is the surrender of the "melting pot" cultural ideal, which was a central ideal throughout the history of hegemonic secular Zionist education.[52] In some cultural fields, there is already an explicit recognition of the legitimacy of the multiculturalist discourse, while even in the Israeli group that sees itself as committed to humanistic ideology,[53] there is almost a total negation of its social and philosophical implications. Thus, the recognition of multicultural discourse as legitimate is not paralleled with the acceptance of the claims for transforming the state into a citizens' state, for separating between religion and nationality, or for providing anti-ethnocentric education. The demolishing of the traditional Zionist myths and the progress of Instrumental Rationality's reflections are present in the textbooks being used in the state's educational system. Yet, as Ruth Firer already mentioned in the 1980s, even when the textbooks' authors try or pretend to try to be "objective" and are willing to present the students with values to be judged, the Zionist values remain as the sole center on which the historical description and evaluation are fabricated.[54] Today there is plenty of research on the strengthening of Holocaust memory in restructuring the collective Israeli identity. Its presence in educational programs points to the link between national revival and the Holocaust and the implications of this link for a godless world that is spiritless to the degree that there is less place in it for humanism than for its rivals.[55]

The victory of the Israeli left and the premiereship of Yitzhak Rabin is not to be understood as the victory of humanism, but rather the opposite, as symbolizing the strength of the local instrumental-functionalist trend. It manifests the problematic status of the Zionist left and its immanent anti-humanism. Here were manifested the strength of the trends present in the space between the stock market and the casino, Madonna and Madonna, between the cultural horizon of the "Peace Now" movement and the cultural-social horizon of the league of Israeli industrists who sided explicitly with the "peace camp" and Shimeon Peres in the 1996 elections. All of these do not present a moral-humanistic alternative to traditional Zionist education, but rather its normalization in light of its successes, bureaucratization, and senility. The normalization processes in secular Israeli culture in the centers of the local affluence are representing a pragmatic, anti-idealist, and anti-solidarian trend, which are demolishing the traditional Zionist myths that enabled the constitution, defense, and expansion of Israel.

In light of the 1992 victory in the elections, *Meretz*, the party on the extreme Zionist left, won the administration of the Ministry of Education in the coalition negotiations. It was but natural that a minister of education of that party, committed to humanism and human rights, would call a scholar like Yair Auron to build a new history program for schools,[56] which would challenge the issue of genocide/Holocausts that took place and continue to take place in the twentieth century.

In November 1993, the sketch for the new program was officially confirmed.[57] The program included a textbook, an instruction book for teachers, and a general program for training teachers who would be teaching the new program and would be qualified to deal with the challenges arising from the new program. Auron's history program was based on comprehensive historical research on the issue, which was published under the title *The Banality of Forgetfulness*.[58] From the very beginning, the program was not introduced as it should have been, namely, as symbolized by the metaphor of *tikun hanefesh* (as an exercise in spiritual healing, which is a precondition for *tikun olam*—the improvement of the world), that tried to displace Israeli ethnocentric, anti-Jewish, and anti-humanistic education. Yet, implicitly, it had an immanent humanistic commitment that was immediately identified by its national-religious opponents in the Ministry of Education.[59] It is of some importance to note that its humanistic qualities were the main sources of the left's support for the program. Even the Ministry of Education supported it to the point that they acknowledged its full educational virtues. Then it was immediately abolished. The struggle over the program was not so much about its immediate effects and dangers, since it was intended to be part of the non-obligatory general history program, and high school students who are taking the full history program (about 5,000 in all) could choose many other history programs in preparation for their matriculation examination. The struggle over the program took place because of the symbolic power it represented; it was a fight over Israeli identity, and in this sense, within the state's secular educational system, the program was doomed to fail.

In contrast to the prevailing instrumentalization trend in Israel, the program tried to bridge between education and teaching in an ethnocentric institution. The new history program challenged the "expert" ideology and the neutral-objective pretension of its history teaching programs. It was unjustly received as a direct political challenge to the eroding relevancy of current Israeli moral philosophy and its spirit. However, this recognition evolved gradually, and one can see from the documents that the secular educational administration, perhaps not entirely disconnected from the left's rhetoric, approved central elements of Auron's educational project; namely, the humanistic educational mission of teaching history and its implications for the functionalist scientific ideology. In a letter to be published by the Ministry's spokesman, sent by the Pedagogical Secretariat, it was explicitly and officially stated that according to the committee, the program should deal "with questions of moral values, theology, and philosophical questions that arise out of our acquaintance with others' tragedies. This includes trying to elaborate the special meaning of our being Jews—victims of a genocide (the Holocaust, *shoa*)—to the tragedies of others."[60] Here one can acknowledge the peak of a three-stage historical development of Israeli public education. In the first stage, the curriculum is totally dependent and reflects the nation-building ideology and the accompanying needs as supreme criteria for the selection, interpretation, and representation of knowledge. This represents a continuation of pre-independence trends that were formulated by Ben Zion Dinur. The end of this stage might be marked by the Six Day War. The second stage started with the entrance of big foreign capital and the Israeli economic boom after that war. Parallel to this development, an instrumental-pragmatic concept of knowledge emerged. It was founded on the claim for objectivity, professionalism, and functionalism. The penetration of this trend into such a conservative institution as the state's educational system endured for a generation. Yet, it did not stop from melting its spirit, even if it did not harm its formal structure or make more than minimal changes in the curriculum. Today, we are at the peak of this development, prior to a new stage that might radically change both the curriculum and the bureaucratic structure of Israeli public education. Yet, two counter-reactions to this development are already identifiable. One is the gathering momentum of the national-religious alternative. It is using the possibilities that were opened in the face of the leftist coalition in the 1996 elections, the appointment of Zevulun Hammer, the national-religious party representative to the Ministry of Education, and the appointment of many ultra-religious nationalists to important posts in government ministries. The second development represents the reaction, a deterioration of the secular labor party and the Left's traditional elite. Under the slogan that the diminishing possibilities of defending a humanist secular education in Israel are diminishing, there is a gathering momentum for a separate, independent secular educational system, similar to the one that the ultra-orthodox and the national-religious have achieved since the establishment of the state.[61] It reflects a historical retreat of socio-cultural modernity, that in Israel crosses the left-right political lines of divisions that are concerned mainly in the national conflict issues. We must understand the alternative Holocaust teaching program of Auron in light of these trends. It included much more than what its supporters and enemies saw in it. It offered a trace of *tikun*, of regain, of the soul's purification. After *Auschwitz*, after the establishment of the state of Israel, after the Jews entered secular history and the politics of power, there is a need for *tikun* as part of an educational project that is not disconnected from Jewish religious tradition and its morals. One can explain with historical and sociological tools the constitution of Israeli ethnocentrism and aggressiveness from the heart of Jewish history, by addressing the magnitude of the injustice that was done to the Jews, especially in light of the

Jewish Holocaust, on the one hand, and the injustice done to the Palestinians (that is called by them *Karita*, national relinquishment or *Nakbah*, collective tragedy), on the other. However, human beings are much more than the sociology and psychology attributed to them. This is especially true in the Jewish religion's self-conception and the concomitant obligations rooted in it, as reflected in the *Eved Adonay* (God's servant) ideal, on the one hand, and in its universalistic redemptive vision, on the other hand.

The *tikun*, or purification of the soul as part of world's improvement, should not be a dogmatic one. This purification of the soul is well aware of the absence of God and the irrelevancy of traditional metaphysics and transcendentalism, as well as the disappearance of Spirit and its theoretical foundations. Yet, it should be a (new) Jewish and humanistic *tikun*, in light of the educational spiritual power of Jewish tradition and of the successful violent negation of this educational tradition. An education for recognition and sensitivity to the misery and disaster done to others and for empathy with their tragedy manifests an entrance into universalistic conversation. In the Jewish case, it is the only way to save Judaism from the dogmatism and the violent institutionalism of the barbarization of the religion and its spirit. Such a dialogue reflects a serious attempt to escape and totally avoid, even for a moment, social power relations, the manipulations of the apparatuses producing and representing knowledge, memory, identity, and ethnocentric, egoistic control-oriented practice. The teaching of the miseries of other people—especially those inflicted on them by us—and education for empathy with their grief is not only an alternative to the anti-judaistic moral orientation of the hegemonic Zionist ideology; it also represents a resistance to, and refusal of, the current Israeli instrumentalist-egoistic alternative to dogmatic and ethnocentric interpretations of Judaism and its educational implications. For both reasons, an alternative educational program dealing with the Holocaust is very dangerous, yet not impossible. However, in the current Israeli arena, alternative education as a *tikun hanefesh* is impossible. This is so since the spiritless secular Jewish society in Israel does not have a *nefesh* (soul). Instrumental Rationality, on the one hand, and postmodernism, on the other hand, are not allowed to recognize "soul," "spirit," "goal," and "humanity." Under such conditions, there is no place for education as purification or cultivation of the soul. The attempt to realize the educational ambitions of Auron's Holocaust/genocide teaching could have been a meaningful experience even if it had not accomplished its goals. Yet, even if this experience was finally prevented, the struggle against abolishing this program was valuable nevertheless. The resistance as a moral stand, as a dialogical manifestation of the ethical "I" is what counts, like in the case of prayer. In

Rozenzweig's understanding of Judaism, the essential thing in prayer is not its fulfillment, but the very possibility of a true prayer is what really counts.[62]

However, this history program was never even realized; it was abolished a short time before its official presentation to the teachers and pupils who volunteered to engage it in various schools.[63] It seems to me that the level of consideration on which the program was a threat, which made abolishing it unavoidable, was the hidden politico-educational level and its philosophical prepositions. However, officially the struggle between those who approved of the program and their enemies used professional rhetoric and referred to the "professional" dimensions of the issue.

The professional committee of history teaching in the Ministry of Education, headed by Professor Micelle Avitbul, made its decision—a negative one. The fate of the program is indicative of the fate of the humanistic-oriented educational alternative and the upper hand of its functionalist and ethnocentric ideological rivals. In the issue of representing Holocaust memory, we face a concrete manifestation of the Israeli synthesis between the secular nationalist and national-religious trends, on the one hand, and the pragmatic instrumentalist-functionalist trend, on the other hand. In this case, pragmatic functionalism is being swept into the service of the constitutive Zionist myths and the political project that demands the mythicization of Holocaust memory. Accordingly, there is no place for Auron's educational alternative and for the teaching of other Holocausts/genocides. It is possible to conceive of the development manifested by the rise and fall of the Auron program as representing the way in which the new instrumentalist power is using the traditional ethnocentric rhetoric, its myths and morals, for its own purposes. However, it is also possible to see it as part of the Israeli kaleidoscope, parallel to different and antagonistic powers and orientations. Here I do not refer to the postmodern ontological representation, but rather to a classic critical reconstruction of a historical development in which there is room for more than one trend in a given historical moment. The report of the professional commission of the Ministry of Education reveals that in the Israeli case, the second option is the relevant one, namely, the pragmatic instrumentalist-functionalist orientation using the traditional Zionist myths in its own purpose. It is using them in the service of a Zionist system, even if it is a spiritless system.

The report that abolished the humanistic curriculum did not introduce its critique on ideological-scientific grounds, nor on the grounds of a struggle between two sets of values, but rather on a "professional" one: "genocide studies are a new field of research, in which the people are still undecided and wandering in the darkness…" In addition, Auron's proposals are disconnected "from the general context of the history of the Ottoman Empire toward the end of the Second World War."⁶⁴ In the report, the teaching of others' miseries is blamed as being too "sensitive" to the political issues raised by the media, and it concludes, "in its present form, the program that was introduced to us fits better to 'communal time' in youth movements than to history lessons." The most important quality of the program serves to justify its abolishment: "Though the discussion raises important philosophical and ethical questions, the outlook is not historical, but rather Israeli value-oriented."⁶⁵ In this light, the order of the Ministry was the immediate abandonment of the program.⁶⁶ An alternative program was produced, and for the 1996 school year its basic textbook was published under the title: *Minorities in History—The Armenians in the Ottoman Empire.*⁶⁷

Two main differences arise from comparing the abolished textbook to the one approved by the establishment. First, the winning textbook looks like an ideal tip of positivist scientific ideology. In the history of curriculum, such an ideology appears as totally committed to a neutral representation of relevant "facts" and to the avoidance of value judgments, moral dilemmas, and educational implications.⁶⁸ Secondly, within the framework of this orientation, the new program sees itself as committed to minimizing the issue of historical understanding and reflexivity toward the production manipulations of the Israeli collective identity. It explicitly prefers teaching "relevant facts" of a neglected chapter of the Ottoman Empire. Ironically, the struggle between the two textbooks was not referred to as a "Jewish problem" or "an issue of self-constitution, historical understanding, and the manipulations needed for the production of the Zionist subject in a functionalist-pragmatist era," but rather, as "the Armenian problem."

In the textbook written by Auron, the holocaust of the Gypsies, the Armenians, and others (their suffering is consistently called "genocide" as opposed to the Jewish "Holocaust") is represented as a historical event that has to be addressed. This struggle over understanding is presented as containing moral meanings that are to be deciphered and elaborated, and in this light humanistic education might be realized. However, by that I do not mean that the defeated textbook is less positivistic than its successor. The textbook just did not receive the official approval. The institutionalized power to approve is manifested in its very appearance, which is at the same time a conditioned existence; namely, an existence as a form of *destruction* of the Other, her textbooks, her memory, her identity, and her being acknowledged as a suffering human being with a right to pronounce herself, protest, refuse, and transcend its reality. Within this framework the presentation of the Armenian holocaust is to be understood not as "a fact," but rather as something controversial. It is of special significance for a positivistic history textbook, as well as for the overall issue of critically understanding the possibilities, aims, and procedures of teaching a historical event. It is also of vital importance for challenging the educational and moral implications of doing, writing, teaching, and studying history. This is part of the more general issue of challenging the loss of the possibilities of self-constitution through solidarity with the Other.

The new, approved textbook manifests the principal claim of the positivistic philosophy of science, according to which there is no place for critical humanistic moral education in history lessons. The anonymous writer writes on the issue of the Armenian holocaust as if it were a case of disagreement between objective and neutral experts: "The Armenian, Turkish and the Western researchers who are studying the age and the relations between the Armenians and the Turks disagree about the interpretations of the events between 1915-1916."[69] From studying the documents in light of the general Israeli context within the framework of Critical Theory and its interests, it looks as if the main reason for the abolishing of Auron's program was not its low professional standards, but rather the height of its moral educational potential and the political implications of its humanistic approach. This is where, in the end, "professional level of performance" in its minimalist meaning receives its full impact. It is a specific example of a general phenomenon in the critical study of curriculum, as developed by Critical Pedagogy.[70] Here I will not go into details about this issue, as well as the issue of the level of Turkish involvement in this curriculum debate that became a matter of public interest for quite a long time in Israel. However, it is important to mention not only the depth of the question that was revealed here, but also the "horizontal" line of its development: The struggle between the two textbooks, the context and the powers they represent, received not only wide Israeli public attention, but also some international interest as well. The struggle on the nature of Holocaust pedagogy, even as something referring to "the Armenian problem," received an echo in the German press,[71] in the Palestinian press,[72] and in the Armenian Diaspora.[73] It even had a political dimension in the minimalist meaning of the term. When Deputy Foreign Minister Dr. Yosi Beilin visited Turkey at that time, he was asked at the airport, "did the government of Israel approve the history program?"[74]

Holocaust memory is produced and reproduced as a monopoly by the Zionist establishment within the framework of satisfying very deep quests. The ways of producing and representing the memory fitted the needs of restructuring the institutionalization of Israeli ethnocentrism. These needs included challenging the eroding of the constitutive Zionist myths that represented and served the hegemonic Zionist ideology and its educational practice in the Israeli secular arena.

The 1988 Demjanjuk trial and its representations might be seen as one of the best examples of the conscious effort to instrumentalize Holocaust memory for the sake of the struggle over the preservation and reproduction of the Israeli ideal collective identity, and as a necessary step in the development of the Israeli industry of Holocaust memory. The Demjanjuk trial was explicitly represented as a collective educational catharsis that aimed to reproduce the educational effects that were successfully produced in the Eichmann trial. The retired high court judge, Haim Kohen, called this trial "a spectaculum for the people," and the attorney for Demjanjuk wrote a book entitled *The Demjanjuk Affair: the Rise and Fall of a Show-Trial*.[75] The trial was organized as an educational event in both state and worldwide perspectives, an event that should have been not only a lesson for the mind of the non-believers (in the Zionist ultimate right), but also as a power that would penetrate to the soul and reconstruct it in accordance with "the lessons of the Holocaust" that are constantly delivered by the other organs of the Israeli educational system. An unofficial mass transportation brought many pupils to the scene daily. This was carefully orchestrated for maximum effect. Simultaneously, the architecture of the court was changed in accordance with the demands of Israeli and international media.[76] Even when it was clear that the educational targets would not be fulfilled and the delivery of the official lesson was being destroyed, the Israeli Holocaust industry did not stop. It was obsessed and could not avoid investing huge energies in the symbolic struggle over the justification of collective Zionist identity in the form of the conviction and the killing of Demjanjuk. It looks as if Israeli collective identity could not avoid treating Holocaust memory without a Jewish official hangman on praxis as a symbol of the Zionist victory over traditional Judaism and the Diaspora. Accordingly, the Israeli educational television continued daily for many hours, but in vain. Official Zionism could not do the impossible, not because of the "betrayer" or of the talent of the Israeli advocate of the accused Jon Demjanjuk, who was convicted as "Ivan the Terrible" from the Treblinca death camp, on April 25, 1988, was sentenced to death and released after six years when his appeal was accepted by the Israeli court. The scandalizing demand of his attorney for the court to ask his *seliha umechila* (his forgiveness), words that are ordinarily used in reference to the Nazi victims, was rightly not accepted.

The reason for the educational fiasco of Zionism in the Demjanjuk trial was a historical one. In that the year, 1988, the event took place in the center of Israeli affluent society as a secular, capitalist, technologically advanced yuppie society. Until Demjanjuk's conviction, the issue in question was already framed within the context of local right-left divisions over the vision of Grand Israel, political hegemony, and other issues to be struggled over by the media.

By the end of the eighties and the beginning of the nineties, as part of the success of the Zionist project, the collective secular consciousness in Israel was already characterized by a different orientation than the one that characterized it in the early sixties, when the Eichmann trial took place. One of the manifestations of this change might be seen in Yehuda Elkana's article "in favor of forgetfulness," as an alternative to the *Zachor*, as part of the Zionist instrumentalization of Holocaust memory. Elkana's moral demand was to uproot the control of Holocaust memory over the Israeli collective consciousness so that it would be possible to freely develop the present in the light of a humanistic alternative, in order to free "us" from living in the shadow of a fatalistic memory of the Holocaust.[77] For Elkana this is the essential thing, since the representation of Holocaust memory apparatuses not only served the justification of the existence of the state of Israel, but justified by the same token, occupying the territories liberated/conquered in the Six Day War. From here it is a short distance to justifying the subjugation of two million Palestinians with no civil rights, prevention of their freedom, and negation of their individual and subjective interests and honor while gaining economically and taking advantage of them rationally and systematically. It is important to clarify the relation between moral justification and control of Holocaust memory, and the need for moral justification of controlling by means of "all necessary measures," and "law and order," the conquered/liberated land and its inhabitants during their uprising (*intifada*) at the time of the Demjanjuk trial.

In their refusal to acknowledge their legal defeat and out of their commitment to the challenge of the educational victory, the establishment's representatives refused to acknowledge the changing social and cultural contexts of Israel in 1988. They refused to address and acknowledge the universal implications of the Holocaust, especially in light of the violent ideological, military, and existential struggle between the Israeli and the Palestinian identities, between the social and political manifestations of each identity, and between the power to persist producing the amount of violence needed to ensure the continuation of the struggle. The Palestinians, too, refuse to address the universality of the Holocaust, if they acknowledge it at all. One of the most advanced stands on this issue in the position of Azmy Bishara. He calls on the Arabs, in general, and the Palestinians, in particular, to acknowledge the Jewish Holocaust. This call is strategically grounded on the acknowledgment that "the Palestinians are its indirect victims, since their homeland was taken from them by its direct victims."[78] However, Bishara's position is also far from representing a humanist moral stand, even if he declares himself as "one who tries to constitute out of the Holocaust a universal lesson, a lesson the Arabs too would be able to identify with," in order "to build a road for a more realistic Arab understanding of Jewish collective memory."[79] His position is much more reflective than the Israeli hegemonic one, and structurally he stands where Yair Auron stands in his textbook. Bishara's universalism is committed to a post-colonialist orientation, in which there is a privileged status for the Arab concepts and Palestinian interests. It is reflected even in his criticism of Arab leftist and "enlightened" ultranationalists who refuse to acknowledge the Jewish Holocaust. They are criticized "though the failure of these forces has a reason, the Israeli policy is not damaged at all from the Arab failure to recognize the Holocaust, but rather the opposite, the Israeli monopoly on victimhood grows even stronger as a result. . ."[80] According to Bishara,

> The Holocaust as a historical event is not an issue to be discussed in the Arab context, not to mention the details about the Holocaust or philosophical and historical related questions concerning its hermeneutic understanding or misunderstanding.[81]

Another Palestinian response might be seen in the reception of the hegemonic Israeli representation of Holocaust memory. This reception is to be seen in Muhamad Bakri's response to the Warsaw Ghetto revolt, a response that problematized the Israeliness of his identity as a Palestinian and Israeli citizen: "The Warsaw Ghetto uprising is a source of pride. Every time I was exposed to it I felt as part of it, even though I have never been there."[82] The Palestinian appropriation of the representation of the Warsaw Ghetto identifies the condition of the Palestinians in Israel facing the Israeli oppression with that of the revolting Jews in the Ghetto facing the Nazis. The inspiration of the moral power and the desperateness of the Ghetto's rebels is supposed to support the Palestinian's refusal to accept the violence of the Nazi's victims that were empowered by the Ghetto uprising itself.[83] The instrumentalization of Holocaust memory as seen in Bakri's position is but a reflection of the Zionist instrumentalization of Holocaust memory, and it reaches its peak in Palestinian and Arab refusal to acknowledge the Jewish Holocaust.[84] When they do acknowledge the Jewish Holocaust, they do it within the framework of presenting the evil done by the survivors to the Palestinians as being of equivalent to the evil inflicted on those survivors by the Nazi regime, or even worse. This later version proclaims a special status for evil done by the survivors of a Holocaust dialectically reproduced by their own hands. In both views on the Holocaust, the memory is centered on enabling/causing/preventing future Holocausts such as the one inflicted on the Palestinians. The Palestinian poet Taha Almatukal, the general secretary of the Palestinian writers, presents this theme when he writes:

> Many years ago you were collapsing under the murderers of Dachau / Your father was slaughtered in the Warsaw Ghetto / You suffered the agony of your sister's rape at Auschwitz / Have you forgotten? How could you constitute a new Auschwitz in the center of the desert / How did you dare to transfer a people from his land ? How did you dare to burn the children / Have you forgotten?[85]

Mahmoud Darwish understands the representation of the collective memory and the Holocaust issue as part of the uncompromising struggle over the Palestinian/Israeli land and identity. As for the hegemonic Zionist ideology, for Darwish there is no separation between Holocaust and exile. In the Palestinian consciousness, the Holocaust and the crisis of living in exile drives intellectuals like Kamil Bulata to declare: "I feel I am a Jew." Darwish understands that it is important "to warn the speedy writers among the Arabs from the danger of the seductive power of metaphorical expressions, when suddenly, in a moment of hard loneliness, the oppressed Arab man sees himself as 'the new Jew.'" In his eyes, it is but another aspect of the Israeli conquering the Palestinian identity, a conquest that turns the (Israeli) aggressor into a victim and the Arab into "the new Jew." Implicitly, it is part of the Palestinian Holocaust performed by the Israelis: "Since the Israeli, as he is in need of loading his memory with the armed legend and the uniform of the victim, has to empty the Palestinian memory from its ties to the Arab place, history and space, and equip him with the newly developed Jewish consciousness of the time. It will not take long and the Israeli will also claim to be the authentic Palestinian."[86]

The Palestinian writer and politician Emil Habibi presents quite a different stand. Habibi does not deny the existence of the Jewish Holocaust and does not say that there is no difference between the Jewish Holocaust and the injustice done to the Palestinians. However, even he does not denote the universal meaning of the Jewish Holocaust and does not treat the Holocaust in itself as a manifestation of being. Yet, his dialectical presentation of the Jewish Holocaust memory is important to the clarification of the special link between Palestinians and Israelis and the treatment of ethnocentric morality that justifies Zionist violence:

> In the eyes of the Arabs the Holocaust is conceived as primordial sin, in its power the Zionist movement managed to convince millions of Jews that its way is the right one. If only the Holocaust would not have happened, I can not imagine that the brothers of Heine, Maimonides, Bertold Brecht and Stephan Zweig, Albert Einstein and the Jewish-Arab eternal poet Alsawhal—Shelomo Ben Ovadia—would have allowed that a Jewish administration would deport another Semitic people out of its homeland.[87]

While exposing the Zionist education that instrumentalizes Holocaust memory in order to represent the Palestinians as Nazis that are to be fought to the end,[88] Habibi emphasizes that

> The terrible miseries that the Nazi animal inflicted on the Jews should not be measured only in the six million that were murdered in the concentration and death camps. It should also be measured by the terrible cost the Jewish people paid by [the abandonment] of the Jewish glorious tradition, and in the danger of ruin of what is called 'the Jewish heart.'[89]

Habibi presents an unusual position in the Palestinian acknowledgment/non-acknowledgment of the Holocaust, and he is very close to manifestation of a humanist-universalistic moral stance. Yet, even Habibi's position, which favors the acknowledgment of the Holocaust, is jailed within an ethnocentristic moral framework. In this sense, the fact that Hitler was not really defeated is exemplified even here, not only in the global logic of the post-industrial system and in its Israeli example. The only universalistic-humanistic acknowledgment of the Holocaust in the Palestinian intellectual world is that of Nazem Saria. Saria is not only acknowledging the Holocaust, as Habibi does, and criticizing the Arab refusal to acknowledge its importance for the understanding of the Israeli position in the cultural-national conflict as most of the Arab intellectuals do; in contrast, he introduces a moral humanistic commitment to its acknowledgment. He tackles the Holocaust issue as an event, which has a moral meaning that is universal. From this position he develops his criticism of Arab's refusal to recognize the Holocaust as an essential issue in their own moral development, and as such the universal-valid morality of the Holocaust is of so much relevance to the Palestinians.

The Palestinian's refusal to acknowledge the particular-Jewish and the universal meaning of the Holocaust collides with the Israeli's ethnocentristic acknowledging of "their" Holocaust and refusal to acknowledge other's Holocausts, genocides, and suffering. The victims and their victims alike did not overcome the logic of violence. Hitler was not really defeated.

The instrumentalization of Holocaust memory and its moral implications should not be seen only as a reflection of the erosion of secular Zionist spirit. This trend is to be understood within a dialectical development in which the aging and erosion of the Zionist myths are paralleled by an intensification of the mythicization of Holocaust memory with ever-increasing success. According to some evidence, it saves Israeli identity in the place where other myths failed.

New trends in the Israeli culture industry inherited the relevance and effectiveness of traditional apparatuses of collective identity formation, and are developing at a tremendous pace the mythicization of the memory of the evil that Jews suffered during the Nazi era from the Germans, their allies, and their enemies.

When Auron's textbook was published as the manifestation of a *humanistic* educational alternative, even an implicit and very modest alternative to Israeli ethnocentrism, on the one hand, and to the anti-humanistic instrumentalization of knowledge, including the Holocaust knowledge, on the other hand, it must have faced two main reactions. The first response was that of the traditional idealistic Zionism, and the second was that of Instrumental Rationality and the functionalism that is immanent to it. The abolishing of the humanistic history program produced/reflected a moral space in which we are faced with the Nazi perpetration of the Holocaust, the anti-Semitic refusal to acknowledge the Jewish Holocaust, on the one hand, and the Israeli refusal to acknowledge other people's Holocausts, on the other. The locus of the universalistic meaning of the Holocaust is the dialectic between the "Jewish" and the "other's" Holocausts. The Israeli refusal to acknowledge other people's Holocausts is a negative manifestation of this universality itself that made *Auschwitz* possible. To the degree that Israeli identity has some connection with Judaism, it is evident that Hitler was not completely defeated. Nazism did not defeat Judaism, but inflicted on it a moral downfall in Israel. However, this is not a total ruin, since the Zionist institutionalized religious and secular hegemonic reality in Israel does not represent the essential virtues of Jewish tradition and its attitude toward power, history, and universal morality, but rather its negation.

The universalistic understanding of the implications of Holocaust memory was presented as part of the cultural, social, and political alternative of the Israeli leftist government of 1992-1996, or at least its leftist wing. It was by no means a mistake that its Minister of Education knocked on Auron's door. After all, this universalistic moral attitude was the foundation of the traditional Jewish and leftist protest against oppressive practices used by the IDF and other Israeli organs against the Palestinian population. Yet, this is to be seen as only one part of the politics of the leftist moral attitude in Israel. They were other, ethnocentrist attitudes, which legitimized asymmetrical coexistence and oppressive practices. And yet, the calls for reflection and moral self-critique were always present in the Israeli cultural history, even within the army. This humanistic dimension was traditionally marginal, with a minimal driving force and with no effective educational impact.

The other element in the politics of Israel's leftist moral attitude is to be seen within the framework of the instrumentalization of the knowledge, in the service and as a reflection of the growing needs of the specific realization practices of Instrumental Rationality within rapid technological progress, in the advanced organizational management of production, and in the improved educational practices of the Israeli subject as a sophisticated producer/ consumer. The preferred subject of the Israeli left of today is the yuppie ideal of a successful and productive producer/consumer, who avoids "obstacles" such as transcendental moral imperatives and utopian religious, class, or national quests. There is no room for the ethical "I" within the moral framework of the Leftist cultural politics in Israel. Today, the education most of the Labor Party or *Meretz* can hope for is disconnected from any vision of human beings as characterized by solidarity and unconditioned responsibility for their fellow members of the community, not to mention solidarity with other people as human beings. Last year's critique of human rights abuses and the "Peace Now" movement's call for withdrawal from the "occupied" territories mainly represent Instrumental Rationality and the basic identification with the present order of things, even in the local, ethnocentric context. The Zionist evil industry is neglected, and some of its products are denoted and criticized as obstacles to further progress of the present order. There is no real connection between this "leftist" social critique and humanistic education. Thus, when it became clear that Auron's textbook received attention and implicitly challenged the foundations of Zionist morality and its traditional narrative, the book became untenable even for the mainstream Israeli left. Its ministerial representative, Amnon Rubinstein, then took the responsibility for abandoning it, promising an improved version for the next school year.

However, when criticizing the abandonment of this humanistic history program, one has to take into consideration the geopolitical context of the government's decision to abolish Auron's textbook and his educational program. One can say that in order to counterbalance a peace-oriented Israeli policy toward its Arab population and in facing the challenges of a future Palestinian state, the Israeli government had to come to a defense agreement with a regional power which is not an Arab state. There are two options in the region: secular Iran or secular Turkey. Israel chose the second option and made a defense agreement with Turkey.[90] To the degree that such an agreement is conceived as unavoidable, especially within a policy that strives for a peaceful agreement with the Arab enemies, the moral considerations are to address this geopolitical context. Two conflicting demands are colliding here: One is the obligation for making peace and repairing, even if only partly, the miseries and damage done to the Palestinians within an agreement that has to be counterbalanced by an agreement with Turkey demanding the abolishing of the history program, which holds the Turks responsible for the Armenian holocaust. The other is the moral demand to protest against evil, to acknowledge evil wherever it is done, and to side with the victim. This position is a Kantian moral imperative or a Jewish religious demand that no Jewish or humanistic education should ignore. Yet, the formal argument can follow that doing [even partial] justice to the Palestinians today is morally more justified than teaching the genocide of the Armenians eighty years ago, if the one excludes the other.

Such an argumentation overlooks that there are two different moral concepts involved in this formal argumentation: an obsolete-categorical and a relativistic-procedural one. The Jewish and the humanistic moral commitment demands acknowledging the other as a (potential) partner and as one with rights, needs, knowledge, and identity to be acknowledged and respected. Such a conception demands the recognition of the other as a partner in a dialogue within whose framework the human identity should not only be realized but also be formed and transformed. From this point of view, it is essential to acknowledge the Armenian, Gypsy, or Ruandan's holocausts. This acknowledgment does not imply the forgetfulness of the Jewish Holocaust nor the negation of its uniqueness as an unprecedented event of evil in human history. Yet, such a recognition is the only open gate to the understanding of what the Holocaust is in itself, and what concrete implications it has in the here and now.

The powers and considerations involved in the abolishing of the humanistic history program did not come into being by political pressures from Turkey. It would be wrong to criticize its moral implications by overemphasizing its political dimensions in the narrow meaning of the concept. Other powers were involved that were, to my mind, much more influential. From an institutional point of view, these were manifested in the involvement of *Yad Vashem*, which is the state institution officially responsible for the collective memory of the Holocaust. This institution is the one which operates the Holocaust Museum in Jerusalem and is the best example of secular collective consciousness on the Holocaust and its educational implications.

The antagonistic and complementary secular axis in the secular Israeli consciousness of our day is the ideal of not being a *freier* (a succer). Practically, what this means is avoiding being stupid enough to take moral responsibility for someone else or avoiding a non-egoistic action. This synthesis of Instrumental Rationality and traditional Israeli ethnocentrism is historically contextualized and is united in its negation of care and sensitivity for the *Other's* suffering.

The building of a coherent national narrative is formalized in maxims such as "*megalut legeula*" (from exile to redemption) in order to prevent the possibility of identifying, understanding, and negating the collective realization of evils, and in order to justify them. By that, the very constitution of an "Israeli" identity is justified within its political structure while hiding the secret of its very existence as dependent on the marginalization of the Palestinian identity. The mythicization of the concept of eternal victim is vital to the Israeli that is pretending to include and fulfill the telos of Jewish history, yet barbarically hides in its textbooks traditional Jewish historiosophies and their current moral implications. Within the moral uniqueness and superiority, there was a

Hitler and Philosophy in the Israeli Curriculum 97

complementary universalistic dimension that was developed or negated in different Jewish contexts. Yet in both cases, the education was a religious one, and there was no place for narcissistic moral and violent behavior. The uniqueness of the secular Zionist project was that it released itself from the religious dimension of Jewish history and philosophy and developed the (ideal or actual) uniqueness and superiority of itself on the negation of both traditional Jewish redemptive thought, on the one hand, and Enlightenment's emancipatory project, on the other hand. The moral teaching of not being a *freier* is the supreme diametrical negation of Kant's categorical imperative and the Jewish moral ethos. But this is the last generation's development. Until the Six Day War, Israeli secular society was very collective-oriented and idealistic, at least in its militaristic ethos. Within this moral framework, "we" are not obliged to "their" moral theories as well as their call for mercy, recognition, and decency. Equipped with an education that internalizes a powerful illusion of 3,000 years of united historical consciousness of knowing the *goiim* (all other peoples) as Amalek that is inherently "against us,"[91] the collective Israeli identity formalizes strict moral borders between "we" and "them." This is the essential dimension that unites the morality of Rabi Kahane[92] and the mainstream secular Israeli consciousness. These self-evident moral assumptions were always present in the Israeli left, to varying degrees, especially in the historical Labor Party.[93]

In the current historical stage of the erosion of traditional Zionist ideals and myths that demanded from the individual complete surrender to the collective ends, the mythicization of Holocaust memory is not only holding firmly, but becoming even more central and relevant to both the state's religious and secular educational systems. One of the reasons for this phenomenon is that in contrast to other Zionist myths, the mythicization of Holocaust memory does not demand from the secular Israeli any sacrifice for the collective. Another reason is that it does not collide with the pragmatic-functionalism that flourishes parallel to the technological, economic, social, and cultural manifestations of the local affluent presence of Instrumental Rationality. On the contrary, the mythicization of Holocaust memory becomes a uniting force due to its "spiritual" dimension in a reality where "spirituality" has become a popular commodity, yet with no real challenge to the ethnocentric Israeli orientation. It has strengthened the Israeli collective attitude (that continues as a central dimension in traditional Jewish thought) toward non-Jews as immanently having a moral debt that will never fully be repaid. This is why Israel, as the supposed incarnation of Jewish telos, is ultimately and unconditionally morally superior. The success of this synthesis in the Israeli arena was conditioned by the invention of a common regulative idea. Current Western culture industry and the Nazi death industry share the Thanatos commitment to the presence of *nothingness*. This is the condition for the current success of an institution like *Yad Vashem*. This institution has become the last and the most trusted protector of the Zionist spirit, equipped with an official license to "preserve and develop an atmosphere of concerted memory for the Holocaust's dead"[94] who cannot, but would have liked to, tell us "in order to deliver its lesson"[95] for the sake of the ones who would have liked to but cannot tell us "to deliver its lessons"[96] in the name of those that went to heaven through the smokestacks of the German death industry. The Holocaust lesson and the control of the memory, its production and its representation, received a theoretical formulation, incarnated into a self-evident morality and a bureaucratic-political institution, as in the case of theocracy. That is one source of power for those who speak officially in the name of the dead and in the name of the victims who started to build a normal life in Israel after *Auschwitz*, in the face of the Palestinian *Amalek* who is a constant threat, according to the official narrative and its textbooks. This moral synthesis was explicitly and dramatically exposed in the Gulf War, when the threat of the German gas targeted toward the Jews was real again. Sadam Hussein was represented as holding the power and the will to extinguish the *she'erit hapleita* (the saving remnant of the Holocaust) who had started to build a life in an independent Israel.[97]

The counter-education is immanently a Utopian project, and against all powers and "facts," it is committed not to surrender to the reality. This is the mission of Critical Pedagogy in Israel. Here it has a unique meaning that in the past could have been conceived in religious formulations. However, the starting point of such a counter-education must be rooted in the acknowledging of the absence of God, in the absence of a uniting regulative idea, and in the absence of counter-education itself—while being committed to constituting a concrete position and to acting accordingly in a moral way. This is possible only within the framework of counter-memory that should criticize and transform but not abandon tradition. In this respect, contrary to Elkana, I say, remember and do not forget. Remember Nazism and its Jewish victims, but also its other Others, that were exterminated by the Nazis and by the system in charge of eliminating/creating its memory, the normalizing education, and the false, collective-oriented "we." Remember the violent essence of education that had the upper hand and enabled *Auschwitz*.

The dialectics of acknowledgment and the refusal to acknowledge the other's Holocaust/genocide reflects a central dimension in the collective Jewish soul, its relation to history in general, and especially to the historical Other. At the same time, reflected in it is the ethnocentrism that is invested in the cultural capital of our time. In today's multicultural discourse and in other fields which are under the control of normalizing education, in the name of anti-ethnocentrism, a meaningful momentum is being developed, aimed at negating the humanist-oriented moral philosophy and its claim for universal emancipation. The moral call for cultural pluralism is a javelin edge for the negation of any claim for universal validity or eternal value of truth claims and an immoral criteria for a general theory or commitment to human emancipation. The anti-Nietzscheanistic realm of self-evidence is introduced as the ultimate level for existence and meaning. Its discourses, memories, and collective consciousness are understood as a life-and-death struggle; yet, by the same token, they also call for affirmation and for acknowledging their equal value.

The realization of the Enlightenment's emancipatory educational project turned into the negation of non-Western cultures, of their collective memory and their identity to the degree of their symbolic erosion and its subject's physical extermination. This is also valid concerning ethnic minorities, cultures, and other Others within the hegemonic Western culture. In the second half of the twentieth century, this process became extremely efficient within the framework of intensified rationalization at all levels and dimensions of life and has become a vital part of global instrumentalization of knowledge and the reification of human relations. In the Israeli arena, this trend is manifested in the current reification of Holocaust memory and its transformation into a product within other commodities. This trend is also manifested in new, electronic socialization practices; in mental, philosophical, and political border crossings that enable springing from one field to another field on the same level, for example, from realizing "spontaneity" and "liberation of the senses" in rock and drug festivals, to "memory and purification tours" in *Auschwitz*, and from there to an electronic tour in the moral education site, or rushing to "collective and spontaneous grief" such as the one produced/represented by the media after Yitzchak Rabin's assassination. In such a system, there is no place for tradition nor for spiritual roots or transcendence. There is also no place for historical memory nor for the respect of other's Holocausts. This is so since the recognition of the Other's Holocaust is conditioned by having a "soul" or the presence of spirit, within whose framework it is possible to claim the recognition of the Other as an end in herself, as having values, rights, memory, and identity to be acknowledged and respected as a fellow human being. However, in a post-modern world, there is no place for "spirit," "soul," or for the ethical "I," nor for estrangement and dialectical stress between reality and Utopia,[98] or between reality and its representations.[99] Within the framework of the post-industrial and post-modern arena, there is no place for the conceptual conditions for such a moral ideal of autonomous life that is a precondition on the very subject who is struggling to conceive and realize his/her autonomy in a dialogue as the realization of the utopical dimension, or the godly dimension in the human being.

In Jean Lyotard's *Le Differend*, it is claimed, just as on one side of Hegel's "dialectics of the master and the slave," that between essentially different genres, as in different speech communities, there is no place for dialectics, understanding, or mutual recognition. The *Differend* appears as an unbridgeable gap, which reaches its essence by destroying the other's means for representing his/her case in a manner that will enable him/her to persist in his/her existence and even to win the struggle with the opponent. By losing this power, he/she becomes a *victim*.[100] The *polemos* is "solved" by one of the struggling parties who succeeds from an educational point of view, that is, the one who succeeds in the colonization of the Other by forcing his criteria on the argumentation of the other, who is swept into the promised consensus and justified by the winning side in the struggle. This logic manifests itself even as to the very possibility of acknowledging the Other's identity and the legitimacy of its utopia. It is valid even for the moral ability to recognize the Other's "voice." In this sense, according to Lyotard, the Jews cannot emancipate themselves from the Holocaust and from its reproduction; they are powerless to emancipate the lost memory of those whose voice will never be heard. The Jews are unable to realize this emancipation since as victims, they must incubate something of the power of their former oppressor. Ironically, this Lyotardian determinism is manifested in the official Israeli commemoration of the Holocaust. Lyotard could have developed his argument and claimed that Jews are doomed not to be able to recognize Others' lost memories and Holocausts by the logic of the *Differend*. In this sense, the Holocaust is revealed as representing the essence of being in terms of *galut hashchina* (the exile of God), or in Unesco's words: "The world of the concentration camps.... was not an exceptionally monstrous society. What we saw there was the image, and in a sense the quintessence, of the infernal society into which we are plunged every day."[101]

Essential to this pessimism is a concept of determinate incommensurability, within whose framework there is no place for understanding, meaning, and transcendence. This conclusion is immanent to the thought of Ionesco and Lyotard, as well as to the total instrumentalization of knowledge that is transformed into mere commodity under current capitalistic conditions. From here a moral impotency is derived that is of vital importance for the production and defense of the Zionist ideal and for the Holocaust consciousness it distributes. The new textbook that defeated the humanistic one might be seen as a manifestation of Lyotard's philosophy and should be accepted as relevant, beyond good and evil, beyond a level where a struggle for social and cultural change is possible, but rather as its precondition.

I firmly oppose Lyotard's pessimism, while accepting some vital elements of his thought for two reasons. My reasoning is twofold: first, Lyotard's conception basically suits the ontological reconstruction of discourse, but is totally invalid in regard to the dialogue. Second, the "difference" referred to in Lyotard's thought is the one in which "everything is the same," to the degree of rejecting his postmodern utopia presented in the conclusion of his *The Postmodern Condition*,[102] and certainly refutes any conception of human solidarity and concrete political action of the sort my philosophy of education suggests. The Habermasian concept of the ideal speech situation might help us to define some of the characteristics of the alternative to Lyotard's pessimism.

How ironic is the current situation in which the central trends of today's multicultural discourse that are trying to raise the marginalized "voice" found their alternatives on the philosophies of Jean Lyotard, Michel Foucault, and Jacques Derrida. The current hegemonic multiculturalist discourse is united in its attack on the arrogance and violence of the Enlightenment's project and its "Kantian" moral philosophy that in the end must become violent and ethnocentric. In its consistence version, this attack sums up a new, extreme ethnocentrism, equipped with a self-glorifying rhetoric about the empowerment of marginalized groups, raising the silenced voices, and so on. The demand for a non-abstract equation of all cultures, all values, parameters, and all concepts of discourse between the differences cannot be stopped on the edge of the general theory about anti-general theories and the equal value of all different conceptions of discourse. In such a theoretical framework, the Zionist ethnocentricity becomes legitimate, and its refusal to acknowledge the Other's suffering and the universal implications of the Holocaust inflicted on the Jews receives its philosophical justification and becomes equally moral as its negation. Lyotard's conception of the production and realization of identities and morals is reaffirming power as the ultimate and supreme moral criteria. This is power, not in its negative, anti-moralist sense, but rather in its positive sense, as constituting "the good" and "the evil" as well as the conceptual criteria for their identification, reproduction, and destruction, and the extermination of the human subjects who are their agencies, humans that, according to Lyotard, are to be conceived as mere agencies and products of this system, and that, according to Foucault, are its eternal and determined victims.[103]

These understandings might become a central element for a countereducation to which the concept of the ethical "I" is very relevant. As such it is beyond a reconstructivist-oriented alternative moral critique. This alternative strives to understand the "power's" modes of presence and its specific ways of constituting different moral conceptions, their religious life-and-death collision, and their reactions. Such understandings might be helpful for understanding and resisting the hegemonic conceptions and practices of Zionist moral education. While being anti-metaphysical and anti-foundationalist, this resistance is not anti-religious and it might redeem from its Diaspora the forgotten memory, the "voices" that were silenced, digested, and falsely represented. However, since it has no God, it cannot transcend the concealment plays of being, it cannot transcend *Auschwitz* or introduce a positive alternative. As a new stage in Jewish (negative) theology, the Critical Theory of Walter Benjamin, Theodor Adorno, and Max Horkheimer overcomes some of the failures of today's postmodern discourse. Frankfurt School's Critical Theory introduces a philosophical and political alternative that has a special implication for the Israeli context. While negating some of Judaism's central conceptions, the hegemonic Zionist ideology refuses to acknowledge the other's claim for equal justice and recognition, even as a victim and especially as the victim of Zionism's victory. This is one of the manifestations of the triumph of *Auschwitz*.

This brutal fact must be negated. The starting point of this negation is not to be found in the present reality. It is a utopia, a particle of the Hope Principle. Such a utopia cannot be optimistic toward the possibility of a Jewish humanism like the one held by Hermann Cohen. In Cohen's day, it was still possible to say that

> the time has come to ween again this belief in the moral resurrection of a moral future for humanity. The time has come for the renaissance for the belief, in contrast to people's self-love and classes' materialism. Only in the social morality and only in the humanity of the world's citizens is to be found a vivid Godly Spirit, that the prophets of Israel made into the God of Israel and the entire humanity.[104]

Such a humanistic Judaism offers a universalistic interpretation of the concept of "*vea'avta lerea'cha kamoha*" (thou shalt love thy neighbor as thy self) contrasts with Maimonides's ethnocentric moral stand. Referring to this sentence from Leviticus 19:18, Cohen declares that "the whole Torah, starting with the creation of man, refutes this vexatious opinion."[105] As in today's ultra-orthodox Judaism, this humanist Jewish view firmly negates Zionism and strives to push the Jewish people into secular history with a commitment to look for "success" or "victory" within its frontiers. A Jewish-humanistic stand of the sort held by Leo Beck, Herman Cohen, and Franz Rozenzweig calls for the development of the central ideas of Benjamin, Adorno, and Horkheimer. In a different rhetorical framework and transformed, they continue the Jewish universalistic utopianism. They did it within the horizons of a Critical Theory, referring to the unity of the reason for the plurality of its legitimate voices. It is possible only within the framework of a philosophy where the individual, and not the collective, is the starting point and the end. They developed this concept without being swept into a multicultural rhetoric, on the one hand, and a violent ethnocentrism that is responsible for perpetrating the Holocaust, refusing to acknowledge the Holocaust, or refusing to acknowledge the other's Holocaust, on the other hand. Jewish humanism, if it is a possible stand today, is not the only legitimate form of current humanism. Such a project might contribute to the defense of the claim for the concrete social realization of reason in alternative ways to the ones manifested by Instrumental Rationality. This realization must be concretized into a nonviolent moral philosophy, against all the facts of reality and the possibilities introduced by discourse, where the more aggressive is the one to win. The Armenian dead are lost and it is impossible to save them. The Armenian holocaust is not to be changed. The struggle that is still possible today might be realized only over the memory of the Armenian holocaust and over the legitimacy of its private and universal meaning. At the same time, this struggle is also a form of justification of the resistance to the refusal to acknowledge the other and his/her suffering. Such a resistance is to be concretized in a concrete moral praxis, in a political involvement that is directed toward that which is beyond the deconstruction of the Israeli denial apparatuses and the manipulations for producing the ethnocentric and egoistic Israeli identity.

Utopian Pessimism is a theoretical space from which it is still possible to insist on defending practical reason while saving it from new naturalistic multicultural and instrumentalist-functionalist trends. Since the Hope Principle represents an alternative to the prevailing power that governs reality, in principle, each new moment opens new possibilities for its outburst into the historical time and opens new possibilities. In this sense, and only in this sense, the possibilities are not totally blocked. We are to be committed to counter-education. It is not impossible to struggle for an education that is committed to humanist solidarity, to a universally valid critique. Such a critique should look for deciphering the practices of human moral/immoral existence, while acknowledging the difference of reason's manifestations and facing the open possibility for such a stand to transcend into its negative, as might be seen in the moral education in the current Israeli history textbooks. This is the only form of *hope* that is still possible today.

NOTES

1. Ilan Gur-Ze'ev. *The Frankfurt School and the History of Pessimism.* Jerusalem: Magnes 1996, 26 (in Hebrew).
2. Everett Mendelson and Yehuda Elkana (eds.), "Sciences and cultures," *Sociology of Sciences*, V (1981), 1-77.
3. *Ibid.*
4. Max Horkheimer. *Traditionelle und Kritische Theorie.* Frankfurt a.Main: Fischer 1974, 33.
5. Jean Boudrillard. *Symbolic Exchange and Death.* Translated by Lain Hamilton Grant, London: Sage Publications 1993, 38-39.
6. Ilan Gur-Ze'ev. "Introduction," *Education in the Era of the Postmodern Discourse.* Jerusalem: Magnes 1996, 7 (in Hebrew).
7. Yosi Melman. *The New Israelies.* Tel-Aviv: Brerot 1993, 255 (in Hebrew).
8. Uri Ram. "Society and the social science: Institutionalized and critical sociology in Israel," in *The Israeli Society; Critical Aspects*, Tel-Aviv 1993, 8 (in Hebrew).
9. *Ibid.*
10. Roni Aviram. "Is there a justification for a liberal curriculum in our days," *Studies in Education*, 57-58 (1992), 15-45, (in Hebrew).
11. Roni Aviram. "The schooling system in a post-modern society," in Ilan Gur-Ze'ev (ed.), *Education in the Era of the Postmodern Discourse.* Jerusalem: Magnes 1996, 103-120 (in Hebrew).
12. Charles Taylor. "The politics of recognition," in Amt Gutmann (ed.), *Multiculturalism and the Politics of Recognition*, Princeton: Princeton University Press 1994, 66.
13. Georg W. F. Hegel. *The Phenomenology of Mind.* Translated by George Lichtheim, London: G. Allen and Unwin 1966, 230-240.
14. Hegel, *ibid.* 230.
15. S. H. Bergman. *The Dialogical Philosophy from Kierkegaard to Buber.* Jerusalem: The Hebrew University Press 1974, 140 (in Hebrew).
16. Ilan Gur-Ze'ev. "Total Quality Managment and power/knowledge dialectics in the Israeli army," *Journal of Thought* (Spring 1997), 10-13.
17. Charles Taylor, *ibid.*, p. 25.
18. Ruth Firer. *Agents of Holocaust Lesson.* Tel-Aviv: Oranim 1989, 143 (in Hebrew).
19. Yair Ouron (ed.). *Sensitivity Human Suffering: Genocides in the 20th Century*, Tel-Aviv: Seminar Hakibbutzim 1994 (in Hebrew).
20. Simon Leon. *Hebrew Education in Palestine.* London: The Zionist 1916, 1.
21. Amnon Raz. "Exile within independence; toward a critique of 'Diaspora negation' in the Israeli society," *Theoria Ubikoret* 4 (Autumn 1993), 24 (in Hebrew).
22. Berl Katznelson. "About the Halutz movement," in Moshe Basuck (ed.), *The Halutz's Book.* Jerusalem: The Jewish Agency 1940, 6 (in Hebrew).
23. Yuval Dror. "The Labor Movement's response to the Holocaust in 1943-1948," *Tura* 2 (1992), 255 (in Hebrew).
24. Ruth Firer, *Agents of Holocaust Lesson*, 161.
25. Moshe Zuckermann. *Shoa in the Sealed Room; The "Holocaust" in Israel Press During the Gulf War*, Tel Aviv: Self-publishing 1993, 309 (in Hebrew).
26. Dan Diner. "Israel and the trauma of extermination," *Politica* 8 (June-July 1986), 21 (in Hebrew).

27 Benjamin Beit-Hallahmi. *Original Sins; Reflections on the History of Zionism and Israel.* London: Pluto Press 1992, 181.
28 Ben Zion Dinur. "Zachor," in *Zachor; Words on the Holocaust and on its implication*, Jerusalem 1958, 153-156.
29 Yoel Schvartz. *Zachor; Remembrance of Nazi Germany—Our-Day's Amalek.* Jerusalem 1993, 30 (in Hebrew).
30 Yair Auron and others. *Concepts and Positions of Teacher College Students in Israel Concerning Antisemitism and Racism*, A Research Report, Tel-Aviv 1996 (in Hebrew).
31 Ben Zion Dinur. "Rememberence of the Holocaust and the bravery," in *Zachor; Words on the Holocaust and its Lessons*, Jerusalem 1958, 148 (in Hebrew).
32 *Ibid.*, 153.
33 Aviezer Ravitzky. *Messianism, Zionism, and Jewish Religious Radicalism*, Chicago 1996, 88.
34 *Ibid.*, 356.
35 Martin Buber. *A Believing Humanism.* Translated by Maurice Friedman, New York: Simon and Schuster 1967.
36 Yeshayahu Leibowitz. *War and Bravery in Israel past and Present*, in Shulamit Or (ed.), *Over Violence and Nonviolence.* Jerusalem: Igud Haovdim Hasozialiim 1980, 39-40 (in Hebrew).
37 Uri Ram. "Zionist historiography and the invention of modern Jewish nationhood: the case of Ben Zion Dinur," *History and Memory* 7: 1 (1995), 98.
38 Smuel Zoltek. *The View of the Arab in Textbooks.* Tel-Aviv 1987 (in Hebrew).
39 Drora Berger. "The image of the Arab in the Hebrew literature," *Yiton 77* 168, (1994), 24-25 (in Hebrew).
40 Gideon Efraht. "The image of the Arab in the Israeli Drama," *Emda* 1 (1977), 52-54 and also in Gideon Ofraht, "The image of the Arab in the Hebrew Drama," *Emda* 3, (1978), 39-41 (in Hebrew).
41 Sami Samocha, "Class, group and national divisions in the Israeli democracy," in Uri Ram, *The Israeli Society; Critical Dimensions*, Tel-Aviv 1993, 190 (in Hebrew).
42 Yair Auron and Others, *Concepts and Central Positions of Teacher College Students in Israel Refering to Antisemitism and Racism*, Tel-Aviv 1996, 43 (in Hebrew).
43 *Ibid.* 44.
44 Benjamin Beit-Hallahmi. *Original Sins; Reflections on the History of Zionism and Israel.* London 1992, 69.
45 Edward Said. *Orientalism.* New York: Pantheon Books 1978.
46 Beit-Hallahmi, *ibid.* 173.
47 Arik Karmon (ed.). *The Holocaust* vol. I. Jerusalem: Ministry of Education 1980, 7 (in Hebrew).
48 Ilan Gur-Ze'ev. *The Frankfurt School and the History of Pessimism.* Jerusalem 1996, 200-201 (in Hebrew).
49 Jean-Francois Lyotard. *The Postmodern Condition: A Report on Knowledge.* Translated by Geoff Bennington and Brian Massuri, Manchester: Manchester University Press 1984, 4.
50 Ilan Gur-Ze'ev. "Introduction," in *Education in the Era of the Postmodern Discourse.* Jerusalem 1996, 7-11 (in Hebrew).
51 Jacob Ezrahi and Reuven Gal. "Highschool student's conceptions and ideas over society, security and peace matters," *Research Report*, Zichron Ya'acov 1995 (in Hebrew).

52 Amiram Cohen. "Uniting Jews and values into one nation," *Al-Hamishmar; Hotam*, (25.10.1985), 20-21 (in Hebrew).
53 Ilan Gur-Ze'ev. "Heavy protected secular conservation arena," *Ha'aretz* (26.11.1996), b2 (in Hebrew).
54 Ruth Firer, *ibid.*, xi.
55 Ruth Firer. *Agents of Holocaust Lesson.* Tel-Aviv: Hakibbutz Hameuhad 1989 (in Hebrew).
56 Letter of invitation to Auron, sent by Judith Dumlopm, The Pedagogical Secretariate, to Yzak Tunick, the speaker of the ministry, Ministry of Education, Jerusalem 28 December 1993, 327/10 (in Hebrew).
57 Ministry Of Education—The Pedagogical Secretariat, "Abstract of discussion held by the response-team from the 10.11.1993," 326/10 pp. 1-2 (in Hebrew).
58 Yair Auron, *The Banality of Indifference.* Tel Aviv: Dvir 1995.
59 Maty Dagan, "response-team 10/11/1993," *ibid.*, 1.
60 Letter, 28 December, sent to speaker Tunick.
61 The State-Humanist Educational network, Invitation and manifest of 12.1.1997, Conference at "Zavta," Tel-Aviv.
62 Franz Rozenzweig. *The Star of Redemption.* Translated by William W. Hallo, London: Littman Library of Jewish Civilization 1971, 268.
63 Letter of Michael Yron, Inspector of History teaching to the history teachers from 7.11.1994 (in Hebrew). The new history curriculum was realized for a brief period when Yosi Sarid became Minister of Education under Premier Ehud Barak (2000-2001).
64 Letter of Prof. Mischel Avitbul, Chair of the professional committee for history studies in The Ministry of Education to Michael Yaron from the 6 December 1994 p. 1 (in Hebrew).
65 *Ibid.*, 2.
66 Michael Yaron, chief supervisor for history curriculum, Ministry Of Education—The Pedagogical Secretariat, a letter to the history teachers, 7 December 1994 (in Hebrew).
67 The Curriculum Division, Ministry of Education. *Minorities in History—The Armenians in the Othman Empire*, Jerusalem 1995.
68 Michael Apple. *Cultural and Economic Reproduction in Education.* London 1982.
69 The Curriculum Division, The Ministry of Education, *Minorities in History; The Armenians in the Othman Empire* 1995, 1.
70 Henry Giroux. *Curriculum and Instruction.* Berkeley 1981.
71 Joseph Croitouru. "Schule der Erinnerung; Das Thema Voelkermord im Geschichtsunterricht: Eine Diskussion in Israel," *Frankfurter Algemeine Zeitung* (30.2.1995), 30.
72 Hadas Lahav. "Why was the Armenian Holocaust neglected by the Zionist movement," *El Synara* (6.12.1996), 13 (in Arabic).
73 Yig'al Sarnah. "The last witness of the Armenian Holocaust," *The California Courier* (3.9. 1995) (Translated from the Hebrew daily *Yediot Haharonot*). See also: "Israeli historian approves rejection of Armenian genocide in curriculum," *The California Courier* (3.2.1995).
74 Aluf Benn. "The Turks asked," *Ha'aretz* (2.5.1995).
75 Yoram Sheftel. *The Demjanjuk Affair; The Rise and Fall of a Show Trial.* Tel-Aviv 1993 (in Hebrew).

76 Dan Kaspi. "The Holocaust and the media: the Israeli media in the Denjanjuk trial—the gods that failed," *Otot* 82 (April 1987), 35.
77 Yeuda Elkana. "In favor of forgetfulness," *Ha'aretz* (2.3.1988), 13.
78 Azmy Bishara. "The Arabs and the Holocaust," *Zemanim* 53 (Summer 1995), 55 (in Hebrew).
79 Azmy Bishara. "On ultranationalism and universalism," *Zemanim* 55 (Winter 1996), 102 (in Hebrew).
80 Azmy Bishara. "The Arabs and the Holocaust," 56.
81 *Ibid.*
82 Muhamad Bakri. "The Warshaw Ghetto uprising will not remain the last rebellion," *Hadashott* (21.4. 1993), 35 (in Hebrew).
83 *Ibid.*
84 Azmy Bishara. "The Arabs and the Holocaust," 63.
85 Almatukal Taha. *Poetry Space; Poetry from Ansar 3*. Ramallah 1989, 63.
86 Mahmoud Darwish. "The identity of apsence," *Mifgash* 7-8 (Autom 1987), 46-47.
87 Imil Habibi. "Your Holocaust is our disaster," *Politika* 8 (1986), 27 (in Hebrew).
88 *Ibid.*, 26.
89 *Ibid.*, 27.
90 Ephraim Inbar. "The stretegic alliance between Turkey and Israel," *Discussions in National Security* 10, Tel-Aviv (1996) 29 (in Hebrew).
91 Dan Diner. "Israel and the trauma of extermination," *Politika* 8 (June- July 1986), 22.
92 Raphael Mergui and Philippe Simonnt. *Israel's Ayatollahs; Meir Kahane and the Far Right in Israel*. Londom: Sagui Books 1987.
93 Ze'ev Sterenhel. *Nation-Building or a New Society ? The Zionist Labor Movement (1904-1940) and the Origins of Israel*. Tel-Aviv: Am Oved 1995 (in Hebrew).
94 The Authority for Holocaust and Heroism Memorial—Yad Vashem. *Duties, Organization, Practice*, Jerusalem 1955, 7.
95 *Ibid.*
96 *Ibid.*
97 Moshe Zukerman. *Shoa in the Sealed Room; The "Holocaust" in the Israeli Press during the Gulf War*. Tel-Aviv: Self-publishing 1993 (in Hebrew).
98 Jean Baudrillard. *The Transparency of Evil; Essays on Extreme Phenomena*. Translated by James Benedict, London and New York: Verso 1993, 6.
99 Jean Baudrillard. *Symbolic Exchange and Death*. Translated by Ian Hamilton Grant, London: Sage 1993, 3.
100 *Ibid.*, xi.
101 Eugin Ionesco, in *London Times Literary Supplement* (March 4, 1960).
102 Jean-Francois Lyotard. *The Postmodern Condition; A Report on Knowledge*. Translated by Geoff Benington and Brian Massuri, Manchester: Manchester University Press 1984, 67.
103 Michel Foucault. *Power/Knowledge*. Translated by Colin Gordon and others, New York 1980, 117.
104 Hermann Cohen. *Juedische Schriften* I. Berlin: C. A. Schweschke 1924, 35.
105 Hermann Cohen. *Religion of Reason Out of the Sources of Judaism*. Translated by Simon Kaplan, New York: F. Ungar Pub. Co. 1972, 119.

CHAPTER 4

The Tower of Babel and Western Phalogocentrism in Israel

The Carmel mountain range is supposed to manifest today its Zionist essence. Zionism tore the other cultures into shreds. It effaced their memory, or jailed them, transformed, in its own museums and history books.[1] It exiled the inhabitants, or took over the names and their sites, and transformed the "authentic" Palestinian presence that was left into refuge sites for tourists or for humanist-oriented artists who searched for refuge from the modern metropolitan culture in the innocent nature on Mount Carmel. Zionism accomplished all this on nationalist, capitalist, and humanist foundations—yes, on pacifist strivings too.

"The Tower" or "Eshkol Tower" as it is called officially, rises on one of the peaks of the Mount Carmel in the midst of forests planted by the Jewish National Fund stretching to the West, trying with all its might to detach itself from its factuality. It strives to distance itself from the soil of Asia, to disconnect itself, and it has no choice but to become a Tower suspended in air, undetermined by history, society, culture, and eastern Mediterranean time. The Tower tries to free itself while manufacturing historical, social, and cultural knowledge, which grounds its legitimacy and enhances the suggestive power of the Zionist narrative.

From the sea side, the view of the Tower seems to indicate that its builders deemed it of vital importance that those approaching Palestine from the West would not be able to miss this sign of Zionist-Western triumph. They must willy-nilly behold the glorious erection, symbolizing the Israeliness of Mount Carmel. This victory represents itself by eschewing the construction on the mountain of a monument of military nature. It represents its victory by avoiding that kind of representation, preferring to represent its victory by the university, which is a Tower that almost reaches heaven. This is supposed to manifest the victory of Spirit over brute force—be it nature or other brute forces such as the Palestinian population, dreams, and guns. This control of the representation of the collective "I" also hints at the aims of Zionism while signifying the reasons for its victory. And this is its spirituality, its being driven by and committed to emancipation, progress, and elevation of the soul and Spirit, not only of the body and its political context.

The Tower of Babel and Western Phalogocentrism in Israel

While controlling the representation of the free Spirit on the Carmel it rends the natural structure of the mountain, pokes into the heavens in an unstoppable ugliness. One possible way of disregarding this violence is to be swallowed up into the parochial labyrinth of the Tower and swaddled by its attached honors, intrigues, good intentions, intelligence, and mediocrity, which fill its entire void to its most remote spaces, cracks, and scratches. Another way of avoiding the violence of the temptation of the message of the Tower is to look at it on an ordinary day from the busy industrial city of Haifa, which lies beneath it. On an ordinary day Mount Carmel looks very much like Mount Sinai before God gave the Children of Israel the Torah: covered by dangerous, mysterious smoke, accompanied by undeciphered noises of life and of what transcends it.

According to the hegemonic narrative this poison/sacredness manifests the fulfillment of the Utopian promise: the successful exodus and the Zionist victory of securing the Land of Israel. The artificial clouds that govern Mount Carmel and envelop its Tower unite the Zionist industrial and educational success. At the same time it fulfills the imperatives of Instrumental Rationality: adjusting scientific research to technological-economic needs which refuse to remain at the disposal of nationalistic ideologies and positive Utopias.

The upward thrust of the Tower destroys the calm line of the Carmel crest arrayed with the remnants of Palestinian villages and their not entirely dead gardens. It rises within the remains of a combination of natural forest and monotonous Zionist pine trees, touching-not-touching the edges of the city. It is positioned to manifest its autonomy, as if a Zionist university can really be independent of daily life, political interests, cultural prepositions, and spiritual quests.

The hubris of the traditional Western university receives here an extreme manifestation in a 31-story Tower on the crest, unchallenged by any other building to the West. It manifests the arrogance as well as the naiveté of the only Israeli university which is erected exclusively on humanistic studies and orientation.

The Tower reflects the academic hierarchy. Accordingly, the lower floors contain the offices of the various faculties and departments, and the rooms of the researchers, which in turn are built on the shoulders of lecture halls, the attractive library, and, of course, the students. The higher floors of the Tower are reserved for those who have the upper hand—the administrative ruling class of the university. Here every higher floor represents a higher stage in the hierarchy, right up to the 29th. Here is the meeting room of the university Senate, which is supposed to govern the university as its autonomous, highest decision-making organ. The 30th floor is reserved for a very special lecture hall. Here is the most prestigious site, where the university presents the achievements of its best scholars and invites from afar the most important academics. The lecturers and their listeners face transparent walls, which suggest control over the space, perspective, elevation, and grandeur.

Within the Tower the modernist architecture and power relations already incubate postmodern intercourses. The modern architecture allows the constant flow of "free," uncontrolled, information via electronic communication networks. Yet by the same process the modern power/knowledge architecture and postmodern coexistence unite in preventing dialogical knowledge and intellectual intercourse. Special constraints are inflicted on those who try to escape their architectured isolation, and cross the frontiers and the hierarchies to come into unplanned and uncontrolled contact with other master symbols and architects.

And yet dialogical intersubjectivity is possible even within the Tower of the university. It is made possible by the system itself: by setting off on a tiring climb up a shabby non-air-conditioned staircase, or by using elevators whose uncontrolled technical performance exhibits academic freedom in its height. The crush and the weight of the users reestablish, reproduce, and challenge the order of the Tower. This is in part because of the change from a modern to a postmodern condition. In this process, capitalist globalization forces the university to accept ever more students, and to offer them attractions and services in the offices of the researchers and in the secretariats of the departments, and other "customer services." All these were inconceivable for the modernistic-oriented architectures and engineers who built the Tower and its elevators more than a generation ago. Yet the elevators' being non-air-conditioned, constantly breaking down, and always under repair leaves room for the uncontrolled, for the unexpected academically and existentially stimulating encounters; this is the nice flip side of the Tower of the University of Haifa.

On the one hand, the dynamics within and around the elevators are the breath of the Tower's functioning as a process of productive de-humanizing "academic" life and preventing intellectual dialogical elevation—a project to which the architecture of the power/knowledge is committed. On the other hand, this process of reproducing the logic of the system, its hierarchies and dynamics, the anti-dialogical essence of the Tower and its forced gatherings, its ugliness, and the reactions to its compulsive "productivity" and "efficiency," is also very meaningful for overcoming the logic of the Tower. Out of being locked in an elevator with no light, or of endless, forced, anticipation of its arrival, in the company of departing/exiting partners, and out of other unpleasant events of this nature—the unexpected, the uncontrolled, the inventive dimension or elevation is born. These planned-unexpected meetings incubate potential drives and language of dissent and anger in the private, psychological, sphere. Usually, however, this sphere's political potential soon fades under the manipulations and constraints of the imperatives of efficiency and productivity, as directed by the present culture industry and the market that it serves. Yet sometimes it also enhances reflection, intellectual dissent, and political questioning of the logic of the Tower and the system to which it is subjected. While reconstructing these dynamics we should remember that the Tower of the University of Haifa is far from being a closed system.

The Tower faces out: it views an exterior that suffered rapid Zionization, gave birth to new forces, symbols, and needs—a success that defeated the Zionist myths, values, and dreams such as the realizing a homogeneous, harmonic positive Utopia. New strivings, values, and symbols, and more vital myths accompany new violences that change the space and pre-determine the horizons. These violences are not less arrogant, merciless, and effective than the Zionist violence which they defeated, yet they are better veiled by the postmodern condition.

Today not only global capitalism, the logic of the market, but also Instrumental Rationality are the things that orchestrate the academic symphony. The new symbolic economy and the post-modern context of contingency, hybridity, nomadity, hypertextuality, non-foundationalism, non-essentialism, and speed make their mark alongside the modernist elements, which are still reproduced and have their say too.

With all its traditional humanistic pride today the university does its utmost to participate in the *danse macabre* of the humanist academic tradition and to advance its self-abandonment in face of the emerging post-modern conditions in the Israeli arena. It contributes to the establishment of an arena where there is nothing that can contain and fuel the humanist hope to shine the light of Enlightenment on its surroundings, to re-map the geography, the spirit, and the mind of the entire region. It is explicitly manifested in the politics of the university, which rapidly and efficiently accommodates itself in the practice and the logic of the market and the new, post-modern, demands of the Israeli culture industry. This is so while its past still rules over it, as manifested by the unmarked floor, which every path in the Tower leads to.

This is the 31st story. The elevators do not ascend to it on their regular itinerary, yet it is a floor that no one can ignore, looking at the Tower from outside. But no directory guides you there; no witness testifies to its existence, its nature, and its aims. Is it possible that the Tower with its 30 floors was actually built to sustain the 31st, and its military equipment, secrets, and death? Is this academic-military coexistence, which is unavoidable under the present situation—representing the general relation between Israeli universities and the military-political establishment? Or is it military-academic cooperation, which ultimately serves local capitalism that needs the rhetoric of autonomous academe, patriotism, and military power in the service of a much deeper urge and much broader powers than Israeli higher education and nation-building? The architecture of these questions raises even a more fundamental question, namely the meaning and the stance of the academic idea and the free critical spirit in the university.

The unmarked floor appears to contain huge antennas, communications equipment, radar devices, and other military electronics, whose radiation might affect the health of the workers, not only the real telos of their Tower. Yet no one raises the issue of the present-absent 31st floor and the activity which it hides, radiates, and symbolizes. This silence also accompanies the attitude to the Tower and its telos as a whole.

The Tower fundamentally accommodates the rivalry between the traditional ideal of academia and the politics of the modern university, both of which are today rocked by post-modern violences that threaten the Tower.

The Tower on Mount Carmel confronts another Tower, the ultimate Tower. Here is tension not only between the two Towers and what they represent. No less important is the tension within the very constitution of the Tower of the University of Haifa itself. In the "other," absent, Tower, power and knowledge were of vital importance too, likewise in its elevations, surprises, dramas, tragedies, and hopes. Only from the triumphant voices can we try to recall the silenced story of the builders of that absent Tower, which represented an endeavor whose successful destruction is manifested by the existing Tower on Mount Carmel. According to the story of the destroyers of the Tower of Babel in Genesis 11 the precondition for the first humanist Utopia was that "the whole earth be of one language and of one speech." Only then could the humanists move on to the realization of the Utopia: "They said one to another: Come, let us build a city, and a Tower, with its top in heaven, and let us make us a name; lest we be scattered aboard upon the face of the whole earth." The erotic quest of the builders of Utopia was the fundamental force of human history as the unification of the kingdom of scarsity-plenty and the kingdom of questions-answers.

The utopian eros could not accept human life with no elevation, on the surface of the earth like the snake, after eating from the Tree of Knowledge—good and bad. And humans who at that stage had no answers were in quest of new questions, a stage that precedes formulated answers and questions. They were in search of elevation not toward the neutrality of the good, but toward the Other[2] toward being other than they were. This was possible by the rift already existing between them and heaven, between earth and Eden, and the alienation within themselves. They were all an outcome of a word, a Godly word that violated nothingness, or undeterminateness, and created the world by the power of the word. As such the first humanists still held "one language" and "one speech." There is alienation between the language, which was used but was not necessarily created by them, and the "one speech," which is meaningless without their freedom or innovation.

The alienation is actually alienation from the One, or God, yet at the same time it is also the manifestation of the alienation within God, which is also a precondition for (human) transcendence and (Godly) fear of human transcendence.

Transcendence here manifests the total commitment to overcoming meaninglessness or being externally determined as an unjust situation. Overcoming this injustice was possible for these first humanists by their playing the openness of "one speech" against the closure of "one language" for transcending themselves by themselves, without destroying the ultimate Other, God, but rather deconstructing him (reaching his level or becoming like him). It is dialectics at a pre-philosophical stage, which precedes social and cultural alienation and the very possibility of moral rules and epistemological limits. This intentional phenomenon in which the other apears as Other and lends itself to language is conceived by Derrida as to give oneself to violence, to "transcendental violence."[3] The tension between the language of the builders of the Tower of Babel and our language, does not only reflect transcendental violence, it rather challenges it. This tension enabled the human as Tower builders and their openness toward the question and the injustice without striving to heaven, to the platonic sun, or to the Jewish or Christian God, truth, or *redemption*.

God is threatened by the realization of the human utopia, facing the Tower, which is about to bridge the earth that has been humanized with the godly heavens, and overcome the depths between the godly and the human within the human beings. And he says to them what the destroyers of the story of the builders of Babel dare not utter: "Come, let us go down, and there confound their language." And what was their crime? God's fear of the human "one speech"? Or was it his fear of overcoming the closure and determinateness of the "one language" itself? He says, "Behold, they are one people, and they have all one language; and this is what they begin to do; and now nothing will be withheld from them, which they propose to do."

So God confounded their language and scattered them abroad thence upon the face of the earth. By doing so, God created, out of his fear, the dogmatic, violent, space of the play of "differences,"[4] but also the possibility of philosophy, human diversity, and the new negative utopian struggles over redemption from closure, determinateness, solidarity without total consensus, and love with no absolute truth. He also created the *possibility* of positive utopias that manifest the anti-religiosity of the various dogmas, which block, each in its way, the rearticulation and continuation of the humanistic negative Utopia of the builders of the Tower of Babel. Yet even if the story of the first humanists was silenced it was not erased without trace. The traces, and the eros that is their impetus, are preconditions for the idea of the academia, which cannot be totally defeated even after the victory of God or of the gods over the humans. This victory was always far from complete. This human defeat, like the other defeats that God inflicted on them, ultimately only strengthened the anti-religiosity, dogmatism, and ethnocentrism of human beings. It advanced their power not only to abandon the negative Utopia of the first humanists of the Tower of Babel, but ultimately also to make God and his fears irrelevant, a commodity among other commodities in a post-modern culture industry that does not need Spirit, religiosity, truth, justice, love, or God. This abandonment of God is his greatest victory over human beings. God's victory, however, could not have been complete. Indeed, this was guaranteed since he violently disturbed nothingness and created the world.

Even after the destruction of the Tower and the humanist negative Utopia, God was not completely successful in overcoming the special human qualities. This is to be seen particularly after the destruction of the Tower and the "one language" which fertilized the erotic quest for reflection and the struggle for transcendence. This negative Utopia as love that is not love of the love of God always threatens God and his dogmatic disciples. This is so even when they abandon Utopia altogether and take it as if they liberated themselves of any metaphysical remnants, and they are but efficient producers/consumers watching with cynical eyes every manifestation of thought, responsibility, or love. Even in a postmodern *parody* the struggle between God and human beings has not come to a halt but it continues in various fields and ways. One of the most important of these is the struggle between academia and the university.

The university was ever a daughter of this world, part and parcel of human history, part of an ever-changing system of networks, powers, interests, evils, and naivities, and of worldly love and actual improvements in the human condition. But it was also more. The university also contained the quest for God or the love of dogma and security. Yet at the same time it also contained something foreign, a negative Utopia in the form of the academic ideal. This *quest* is a manifestation of the free human spirit, the quest for overcoming the self-evident and the compulsory, as an ever-renewed building of the Tower of Babel.

This is an arena where the rivalry between God and human beings, or between the quest for "returning home" or for death (or for total devotion to God, last answers, certainty, and so forth), and the eros of the negative Utopia of the builders of Babylonian Tower. This rivalry is present in the tension not only between politics and philosophy, university and society, but also between academia as an idea and the university as institutionalized concrete power/knowledge relations. The Israeli version of this tension has many unique characteristics. It is partly exhibited in the Tower on Mount Carmel and the academic life of its residents, who devote themselves to reproduce the negation of the academic ideal and to the erosion of the eros of the builders of the Tower of Babel and their humanist Utopia.

In a post-modern reality it is not the gods or human rebels who come to demolish the Tower. There is no longer a transcendental absolute that can undertake to confound the language of free critical scientific researchers, distort their ideology, or threaten the social and cultural foundation of their Tower. This scientific Tower reflects, according to some of the post-modernists, the essence of the masculine aggressive-oriented Western logic and science. This is why it strives compulsorily for linear articulations, either-or argumentation, final answers, or at least to achieve efficiency, success, or victory over the Other—in accordance with its essence: the phallus and its urge for triumphant orgasm. This urge, according to this narrative, comes into its full realization in logic, science, and Western technology. In post-modern actuality, the Tower itself can endure, yet the scientific ideology, the image of knowledge, and the fundamental strivings will be replaced with no less efficiency than the drama God orchestrated at the site of the first humanist Tower. However, according to some of the post-modernists, it will not be achieved with the traditional hierarchical order, linear argumentations, historical memories, and the logic of the attainable middle as manifested in the traditional university as a Tower. The modern university as a Tower, according to this narrative as a process of erection toward "the truth" or victory, is about to be replaced by postmodern attitudes to knowledge, textuality, identity, and intersubjectivity. Here, within ever-changing networks, contingent claims, and hybrid constructions, there will be no room for the inner logic of the Tower, its hierarchies, dogmatism, and violence. However, for the foreseeable future all this will be founded on the practice and imperative of the absolutism and universalism of global capitalism. Yet this is something the post-modern critics of the modern Tower neglect or wants us to forget, while they hide the centrality of the new violences that their rhetoric veils.

In Israel it is valid not only in respect of the modern scientific ideology, but also as to its commitment to the nation-building project and the elimination of the Palestinian identity, memory, and productivity. The university on Mount Carmel stands still, yet it is rapidly losing its modernistic rule and possibilities, as a research institute as well as a Zionist reproduction organ.

Many of its dwellers who are awake already acknowledge the fall of the modernistic walls of the Tower. They acknowledge that it has become impossible to maintain academic work and reproduce its ideals as if nothing has happened, as if the university still represents the ideal of the autonomy of the human Spirit, critique that recognizes no authority and limits, and the project of deciphering the reality and spreading of higher education. They acknowledge that the stance and the nature of knowledge have changed, as well as the procedures and the context of the production of the normalized human subject. They know that the university cannot continue to adorn itself in reflection, transcendence, and emancipation as it used to in modernist higher education. Many others are unaware of the changes, yet they feel that something "has gone wrong." And so they search for ways to satisfy the imperatives that enter the Tower from "outside" in order to reproduce the good modern academic life "inside." Still others do their best to sacrifice the Tower and its modernist academic ideals. This is in order to protect their well-being by serving with great devotion (even if without love) the new gods, trying to manifest their efficiency, profitability, instrumentality, according to the standards of the new post-modern fashions and the imperatives of the market. Their tone is heard in the new rhetoric of the administration of the university, in which the student is called "the client" and the researcher is treated as a "service provider" for the market in both its facets: the needs of the clients and the imperatives of technological-economical advance.

Yet what Derrida calls "A community of the question"[5] is still possible. It is possible not within a positive Utopia and as part of a university which was drawn into the present culture industry and the imperatives of globalizing capitalism but as a part of academia as a negative Utopia. "Within that fragile moment when the question is not yet determined enough for the hypocrisy of an answer to have already initiated itself beneath the mask of the question, and not yet determined enough for its voice to have been already and fraudulently articulated within the very syntax of the question. A community of decision, of initiative, of absolute initiality, but also a threatened community, in which the question has not yet found the language it has decided to seek, is not yet sure of its own possibility within the community. A community of the question about the possibility of the question."[6] The erotic impetus of the question promises that even in its remote exile the academic ideal is still alive, even if it is present only negatively, by the presence of its absence, in the Tower on Mount Carmel. The eros of the builders of the Tower of Babel has not been totally defeated by the hubris of the modern university and its Instrumental Rationality, or by the Zionist phallogocentrism. Even the University of Haifa's being swallowed completely into the Israeli post-modern culture industry will not vanquish that which the academic ideal strives for. This is not because of the fruit of the Tree of Knowledge, good and bad. It is because of the openness of beings in relation to "the opening of being"[7] which enabled Eve and Adam to be in the dilemma of eating or not eating. Human subjects are open, undetermined, finite beings within the infinity of being human life, or the struggle of the possibility of a more human life. This signifies the possibility of the continuation of the suffering of God and his followers: this sign incubates a promise that ultimately, "the one," sameness, or the absolute, do not have the upper hand. It is, therefore, impossible to completely destroy the traces, the imperatives, and the potentials of the builders of the Tower of Babel, the negative utopians, and of the academic ideal, which advances, preserves, and transcends this legacy. In this respect the future of academia within the University of Haifa is still anticipated, a reality which is still ahead of it, waiting for the religiosity of its future Dionysian lovers.

NOTES

1. Ilan Gur-Ze'ev. "The morality of acknowleging/not-acknowledging the Other's holocaust/genocide," *Journal of Moral Education* 27: 2 (1998), 161-177.
2. Jacques Derrida. "Violence and metaphysics," *Writing and Difference*. Translated by Alan Bass, Chicago: The University of Chicago Press, 1978, 86.
3. *Ibid.*, 125.
4. Gilles Deleuze. *Difference and Repetition*. Translated by Paul Patton, New York: Columbia University Press, 1994, 51.
5. Derrida, *ibid.*, 80.
6. *Ibid.*
7. Emmanuel Levinas. "Is ontology fundamental?", in Adriaan T. Peperzak, Simon Critchley, and Robert Bernasconi (eds.), *Emmanuel Levinas; Basic Philosophical Writings*. Bloomington and Indianapolis: Indiana University Press, 1996, 9.

CHAPTER 5
The Vocation of Female Teachers in a Changing Society

Teachers and Nation-Building

The Zionist enterprise may be considered a model of the formative power of personal and collective consciousness. While being a condition for Zionist productivity, the formative power of private and collective consciousness is also one of its manifestations. This productivity is what I call educational violence. At a time of essential cultural change, the degree (but not the orientation) of educational violence is measured by its ability to produce a new conceptual apparatus, a new private and collective consciousness, and new conditions for an effective political and military struggle. In the present cultural reproduction, educational *violence* is tested by its ability to minimize, halt, or prevent this historical process. In each case the status of teachers dramatically differs. This is the situation in general, and historically it has been the Israeli one in particular, as will be shown.

In 1916 Leon Simon, one of the first Zionist educators, wrote:

> Among all the manifold branches of work that have to be undertaken by a national movement, there is none more vitally important than the work of education. This is true of a national movement among a people which is already concentrated, to a greater or less extent, on its own historic soil, but it is robbed of the possibility of full national development, or is in danger of losing its identity through the influences of a foreign culture stronger than its own. Education is, then, the very life-breath of a national movement. But of no national movement is this so emphatically true as of Zionism, which is an attempt to restore national life to a people cut off almost entirely from its ancestral land, scattered over the face of the earth, participating in every culture, speaking all languages, assimilated to all types of national life and thus in constant and ever-growing danger of being split up into fragments.[1]

Ne'emann wrote in 1902 that

> The history of the teachers federation is nothing but the history of Hebrew education and it is the history of the new settlement movement, the vision of redemption that motivated the *Hovevey Zion* to leave the Diaspora and come here. The social vision that created the labor movement is the vision that was active in

the hearts of the pioneering educators, a vision of establishing a Hebrew school in Palestine, realizing it, and bringing it to this point. Without this vision, it is unimaginable that one could understand education here and the vital role which the teacher has played in it. Whoever sees our organization as a strictly professional movement ignores the Israeli reality. . . .[2]

Even scholars like Rachel Alboim-Dror, who consider education to be the second or third national challenge, after immigration and settlement, acknowledge that

> education is supposed to serve the political aims of the national movement, and to function as a political instrument for social, economic, and cultural change. Education was especially supposed to supply workers for agriculture, workshops, and industry in order to change the structure of Jewish society's employment structure and cultivate "a new Jew."[3]

There are also scholars who distinguish (mistakenly, to my mind) politics, culture, and education, owing to their narrow concept of education, perceiving it as the pure practice of power/knowledge dialectics, yet who in the end agree that "a great part of the Zionist movement's budget was spent on financing educational services, amounting to 40 percent of the entire budget."[4]

The constitutive stand of these production practices, which in the narrower sense are generally called "good education," can be understood only in the context of certain, definite relations. The centrality of these practices is closely connected to the consciousness that will interpret and change these historical conditions. Therefore, in any critical reconstruction and deconstruction of nationalist education, one should begin any study of the stand of texts, teachers, and pupils by referring to the socio-cultural context of their representation and activation in the Israeli school arena. Here I do not refer to a certain dimension of Zionist education but to the productivity of its violence. After all, "nationalistic education is defined not by its content and not by its methods, but rather by its goals and achievements."[5]

There were no substantial changes in the goals of nationalist education in Israel between 1916 and 1953. In 1953 the aims of education were established in a special law. In it the human subject or the pupil is not mentioned at all. The law does not even refer to schools as places where children are supposed to learn or study.

In 1916 Simon explicitly defined the grand aim of Zionist education as "part of the colonization movement,"[6] and until the end of the 1970s the collective consciousness remained unchanged in this matter. In the last generation, however, important changes have been manifested in the technological, social, and cultural arena, and these have been of vital importance for the stand of male and female teachers, their political role, and their cultural, and social possibilities. To my mind, this is the context of the recent initiatives to change the law of national education. I will argue that it is wrong to disconnect the Zionist answer to the Jewish problem from the question of knowledge and the proper manipulations enacted for its production and distribution. The Zionist project can be seen as a reflection of collective identity of the Diaspora Jew, which was not unconnected to what one of the Zionist educators, Ernst Simon, called "Zionist antisemitism."[7]

The Jewish supposed transition from *galut* (Diaspora) to *geula* (redemption) was conditioned by essential change in concepts of knowledge and by the production of new bodies of knowledge as part of the constitution of a new meta-narrative, a unified collective consciousness, and a new collective identity. Texts and writers of constitutive texts played a role here no less important than the changing economic, social, and cultural conditions in the countries where Jews lived and within their own communities. Zionist educational and teaching practices were of extreme importance in the realization of the Zionist project, and according to my thesis this is the vantage point from which to view the traditional stand of the Zionist teacher. This study refers to a local historical development, but it also serves as a paradigm since the issue here is nothing other than the conditions and the ways in which private and collective consciousness was constructed. Teachers acted as central agents in the era of national formation while struggling amidst rapid changing and non-monolithic contexts. Jewish teachers had to create/restore a language and use it to build a new "Israeli"/"Hebrew" conceptual apparatus, new values, and new political and transcendental aims. The goal of the ideal teacher in the Zionist arena was to constitute the Zionist subject, to legitimize the productive forces of the constitutive *myths*, and to guarantee in all educational means the future of one meta-narrative, one collective memory,[8] one cluster of myths, a single legitimate ground for an effective collective act. Against the system's subjective point of view, one can say that the will to power or the degree of effectiveness of Zionist education was the foundation of the entire project.

In the Zionist arena, the link between education and teaching is manifested in the ability to form and inherit those dynamics that will form a different system: ideologically different, and unique in its social and cultural possibilities in terms of the reality of self-evidence, where dominant powers and logic will always be neglected by the human subjects that are manufactured by the Zionist system.[9] Ideally, it is an arena in which meta-narrative has absolute rule with no opposition. The essence of the educational practice as I reconstruct it here is also the essence of the sophists' education, as Socrates shows in *Protagoras*: rule over and mastery of the soul and its potentialities.[10] What Plato attributes to individuals (the sophist and his pupils) is, according to the philosophy of education presented here, ascribable to the collectives, the powers, and the conditions that produce and activate them and the individuals dwelling within each system in such a realm of self-evidence. The extraordinary character of the virtuous individual, the existential dimensions of subjectivity, and the undetermined possibilities of its spontaneity are part of reality, but not solely part of reality, and ultimately burst into reality from *beyond* its horizons which it transcends—yet, always, within history. While being the manifestation of *the totally other* it is always realized within the framework of historical developments and according to the unique and diverse spiritual possibilities of the arena in which they take place.

In its historical development, the Zionist meta-narrative had to struggle with considerable competition over the hegemonic formation of the Israeli system. Examples are to the battles over the Hebrew language in the new culture, over constituting the nature and aims of schools, and more.[11]

All the above was a special version of the open education: a life-and-death struggle between competing meta-narratives. It was a struggle over the nature, horizons, and potentialities of the new system. To destroy its rivals, the victorious meta-narrative had to be sufficiently violent: to be persistent and enduring, to be acceptable to conceptions of valid and relevant knowledge and also in its competence to marginalization, destruction, and seizure of other bodies and concepts of knowledge no less productive for the self-reproduction of the collective consciousness. Such consciousness would ensure the conquest of the land, the constitution of symbolic and political sovereignty, and the creation of conditions for visible violence, debarring armed and symbolic threats to the victory march of the Zionist project.

The philosophy of education presented here denotes the usual openness of education in the normalization processes that it produces in mental and institutional frameworks. This philosophy of education emphasizes the textual dimension of events and institutions, much as what Michel Foucault does in *Discipline and Punish*.[12] At the same time, this philosophy of education sees the historical dimension and the socio-cultural context as central to any critical reconstruction of the questions under study. This critical analysis is conceived as a political praxis that reflects, but at the same time might also disrupt, current power relations characterizing the normal and legitimate discourse in the Israeli educational arena in light of the utopia of an epistemic break and new, more human possibilities as foreseen by Jewish tradition and the Enlightenment's redemptive projects.

The Zionist movement took advantage of modernistic knowledge concepts and reproduced them for the realization of its own local national version of the modernistic liberation project. The tension between two competing orientations in the Enlightenment's project—between the erotic-universalistic and the violent-particularistic—is strongly present in the Zionist project as a specific violent-universalistic version of the Enlightenment's ideals.

As a cultural manifestation of modernity, the Enlightenment emphasized that the struggle for its ideals and the battle against formed the modernistic arena of self-evidence. Among these ideals are the autonomous subject, the historical progress of mankind, and the realization of reason as preconditions for improved general conditions and self-constitution of the subject as part of universal progress toward the good, the true, and the beautiful. Already in the Renaissance, in the writings of such thinkers as Bacon, Hobbes, and members of the Royal Society, knowledge was conceived as power.[13] In the late eighteenth century, the beginning of the nineteenth century, the Enlightenment presented knowledge as incubating a universalist emancipatory potential, not solely in an instrumentalist orientation as in the works of Bacon. According to the instrumentalist conception, "Human knowledge and human power meet in one, for where the cause is not known the effect cannot be produced."[14] Other Enlightenment thinkers approved scientific progress in a not entirely instrumental orientation, for example in the writing of Gotthold Lessing in *The Education of the Human Race*[15] and Kant in *Perpetual Peace*.[16] The French Revolution dramatically demonstrated the limitations and possibilities of political realization of these ideals, in addition to the dialectics between the commitment to truth and its historic realization, which usually emerges as an exceptionally developed version of the reality it challenged and rebelled against. The quest for power invaded erotic quest for Utopia, and erotic longing became domesticated as a regular inhabitant of everyday life. This was a vital part of the normalization process that enables the present post-modern totality of spiritless reality. In the current stage of the developmnt of self-evidence, the Israelis are locked in one of the systems that it has produced.

Concrete, material life-possibilities allowed the evolution of the ideals and utopian longings. However, conceptual possibilities ontologically precede the daily reality that frames their realization in concrete historical development and power relations. It is especially important to emphasize such ideals as universal liberation, true knowledge, and progress for framing the socio-cultural conditions that made possible the development of human educational progress. The schooling about which the Enlightenment thinkers speak has nothing to do with mere storage of "practical" knowledge, but it is obligated to *Bildung*, to the general and moral education of humanity as long as it is committed to truth and to transcendental values and aims[17] in the framework of an integrated universal meta-narrative. This belongs to the German division between *Vernunft* (reason), which is committed to truth and supreme objective values, and *Verstand* (rationality), which refers to the most sophisticated and fruitful subjective adjustment of goals and means regardless of objective truth and value of the given aims.

In modernity both these orientations had their manifestations: the one, in the tradition of Objective Reason, and the other in the tradition of Instrumental Rationality. Both these accompanied the development of Western tradition from the start, reflecting and shaping the changing social conditions, challenging and invading each other. It is of vital importance to emphasize that within the tradition of Objective Reason the conceptions of the possibilities of the autonomous subject as reasonable and independent, and as the ideal language possessor (with its symbolic and social possibilities) developed. This tradition also understood language as omnipotent and human beings as a reflection of its potential. These two dimensions of the Objective Reason tradition are manifested in the Greek word *logos*, which refers to the speech act, language, and reason.[18] In certain historical stages, like that of the Greek sophists, Instrumental Rationality had the upper hand, and in others, as in Christian medieval Europe, Objective Reason (in the form of the Catholic Church) realized in the political sphere the ontological essence of the concepts and myths of the realm of self-evidence. In the mid-nineteenth century the modernistic achivements manifested by scientific progress and political transformation to parliamentarian democracies were accompanied by a dramatic increase in the role of Instrumental Rationality and the bureaucratization of the public sphere, as Max Weber and Max Horkheimer showed.

In constituting the unique Zionist system, Zionism synthesized two different realms of self-evidence; it conduced an original synthesis between Jewish tradition and one of the central courses of modernity, namely national liberation. The connecting line was the universalist dimension, and it was an entirely new meta-narrative, including those dimensions that were supposed to make possible the synthesis between the theoretical and the practical, the religious and the philosophical and scientific, the temporal and the eternal.

The secular Zionist project also has included since its beginnings, an important *humanist* consciousness, both in its socialist and in its liberal versions. This is also true for the archaeology of Zionist knowledge. I do not intend to contrast this archaeology of knowledge with a positivistic reconstruction of historical "facts," but to complete and challenge this archaeology of Zionist knowledge (and knowledge about the Zionist self included) with the history of its political realization. Such a dialectic is the methodological aim of this study.

An anti-humanist and anti-reason stand has been a vital element of Zionism since the beginning of the historical success of the Zionist project and the essence of its materialization (conquering the territory, capitalizing on its wealth, and dictating its cultural identity). At the same time, the political realization of this Utopia constructed a challenge to reason, not only for the possibilities of realizing the ethical "I," and the flourishing of what Max Weber called *Zwekrationalitaet*, where the supreme yardstick is the national, ethnocentric, aim. Yet universal emancipatory attitudes were vital to the Zionist project, from the Jewish and the humanist tradition, being present in its secular and religious, as well as socialist and liberal versions. Of course, none of the versions was a monolith, and the same dialectic is present in the Enlightenment itself, as in the Jewish redemption tradition. Zionists like Ernst Simon and Martin Buber were conscious of this basic problem of Zionism. In today's cultural discourse, more and more people claim that there is no need to critically reconstruct the tension between national liberation and universal liberation, namely, the opposition between the emancipatorian and the repressive dimensions in the universal liberation vision of the humanistic project. Within the framework of postcolonial culture, critical thinkers like Homy Bhabah, Edward Said, Eric Hobsbaum, and Gilles Deleuse claim that this dilemma, being the preference of national liberation to disable, marginalize, and destroy the Other, is not a "problem" in humanist tradition but a manifestation of its colonialist essence. The tension between the two levels and the two dimensions of Zionism is present in the history and production of Zionist curricula, for example, in Zionist geography and Zionist historiography. This is so since "Nations, like narratives, lose their origins in the myths of time and only fully realize their horizons in the mind's eye," as Homi Bhabha puts it.

Conflicting Trends in Zionist Education

The formative figures of Zionist education organized the educational possibilities in accordance with their conception of knowledge and their understanding of the human subject. The curriculum, the preferred pedagogy, and the didactic were all consciously produced in accordance with the specific needs and as a manifestation of Zionist *Zwekrationalitaet*. One of the greatest figures in this field, Ben Zion Dinur, testifies explicitly to this.[19] The crystallization of Zionist educational success was realized in an era when modernist national European projects had already been established for more than two centuries. Zionism developed as an independent national identity, while Western European nationalism and humanism alike lost their youthful vitality, and new powers were forcing their way, constituting or rather destroying, the public sphere.[20]

The central figures in secular Zionism, who were all educated in Europe, were committed to the concept of knowledge that originated in the tradition of

Objective Reason. However, the local historical context of Zionism enforced the realization of the Zionist project through knowledge concepts belonging to the tradition of Instrumental Rationality, whose dominance in the second half of the twentieth century became almost total. The efficiency of instrumental knowledge is tested by its ability to appear as non-ideological or "neutral," with no real threat from the objects of its normalization practices on the one hand or from the bodies of knowledge and the "other" concepts of knowledge that are to be demolished, marginalized, or digested, on the other.[21] Normally, this dialectic was placed out of sight, and Zionist knowledge was conceived and represented as belonging to the tradition of Objective Reason, as humanist in nature, and as committed to a project with no conflict between national liberation and general human advancement, as in the case of Jefferson and the American Revolution or Mazzini and the Italian *Risorgimento*. This unreflective collective consciousness formed the paradigmatic Zionist narrative and its texts such as *Megilat Ha'atzema'utt* (Declaration of Independence).

This great secret of Zionist education has three main implications: first, it allowed and provided the productivity of the Israeli *Evil Industry* while being out of sight, without its agents being weakened by a bad conscience and semantic confusion. And so, for example, Arabs, being deprived of work is formalized in textbooks and the collective memory as the "struggle for Hebrew labor"[22] and Palestinians being deprived of their land termed "Judaization of the Galilee" or "redemption of the land," and so forth.[23]

The second implication is the assurance of the intellectual impotence of the Israeli public sphere. This was important for mainstream Zionist politics and for the stability of the institutionalization of the hegemonic ideology and the protection of its product: the Zionist subject or ideal of "the Israeli" as the "new Jew."

The third implication is the inability of the Zionist subject to deconstruct the circumstances and the practices by which his or her destiny is determined. It is hard to overestimate the importance of this for Zionist educational practice.

In Israel this was acknowledged by consistent humanists and radical antihumanists alike. Thinkers like Martin Buber, Hai Rot, and Ernst Simon felt uncomfortable with the Zionist formation, and they suggested an organized humanist and democratic counter-culture. Yet one has to keep in mind that even those radicals (and in the formative years of Israeli society to be a democrat was synonymous with being a radical) viewed themselves as Zionists and accepted the Zionist framework as a possible non-ethnocentric, humanist, and democratic arena. The consistent anti-humanist thinkers in the secular Zionist camp had much sharper fore: Uri Zvi Greenberg, Abba Achimeir, and

Yisrael Eldad are representative figures of this group. They wanted to educate Israeli youth of the pre-state period to be completely liberated from the quasi-humanistic chains typical of the central trend in secular pre-independence Israel. They did not confine themselves to the introduction of new bodies of knowledge, a eugenic attitude toward the body, and politicizing of the soul. They also demanded, by the same token, new knowledge concepts; they understood what was at stake, like in any essential educational manipulation in which power exists to enforce new concepts of (relevant and legitimate) knowledge and identities. These violences, they hoped, would constitute a real new Jew, "a hero, generous and cruel," in the words of Ze'ev Jabotinsky. At the same time, the very idea of Zionist education producing "a new Jew" was not an invention of the Israeli right or their inalienable possession. It had been a central Zionist idea from the time of *Hovevy Zion* and was most popular among the Zionist left. This idea also had concrete and specific manifestations in the history of Zionist education in Israel, as seen in the case of Ziegfrid Lehmann, the constitutive figure of the Ben Shemen youth village.[24]

The future of Israeli society and the current sickening of Zionism, as a presentation of the prosperity of the social-economic-militaristic construction of Zionism, was already established (though not ensured, since nothing can be "ensured" in history) before the institution of Zionist education, in the era that preceded the establishment of the Israeli state. This may be explained in the basic conflict in Zionist education between the opposing tendencies Objective Reason and Instrumental Rationality on the one hand and as a reflection of two competing tendencies in hegemonic Instrumental Rationality in Israel on the other. Here I will restrict myself to the evaluation of only one dimension, namely the evolution of the educational philosophy of Zionism and the special position in which the Hebrew teacher served.

In the era of the struggle for independence, the Hebrew teacher was a figure that is not remote from the centers of national charisma. Teachers were rewarded more with cultural capital than with economic dividends, yet step-by-step, that cultural capital became eroded. This trend is well documented in research.[25] According to my thesis, the historical decline in teacher's social status and cultural role (a process paralleled by the feminization of the profession) is basically explicable as part of the general transformation in the nature and in the practices of Zionist violence. This phenomenon should be understood as a reflection of the general change in the essence of Western knowledge and the possibilities and orientation of basic Western concepts and myths.

Female Teachers as Agents and Victims of the Zionist Project

Historically, Zionism did not lack male and female teachers. Zionism did not use exclusively male teachers, as it had female students in addition to male students. But even so, historically, the male teacher held the distinctive and formidable stand. This position gradually changed alongside Zionist economic and political accomplishments, its rapid decline, and spiritual aging. Aharon Bar-Adon describes the public image and social stand already in the first stages of the advancement of Zionism in Palestine at the turn of the century: "The number of Hebrew female teachers was small, and most of them were only assistant teachers or kindergarten workers (who were not considered real teachers). The attitude toward them was at the very least paternalistic, if not total mockery."[26] The Zionist utopian project, which by its nature represented the most violent nationalistic version of "reality principle," was also essentially paternalistic within the system it created. The women participating paid the required tribute to the prevailing newly constructed Zionist truths but did not succeed in changing their traditional status. "Even in utopias that speak highly about equality and praise radical changes in the social and family structure, the woman remains outside professional and public life," says Rachel Alboim-Dror, a leading historian of Israeli education.[27]

Rhetorically the Zionist project was committed to the Enlightenment's conception of knowledge and its representation as part of universal human liberation via progressive education and humanist establishment of the conditions for the advancement of humanity and the expansion of its human potentials. By the same token, production, representation, and distribution of knowledge in Israel/Palestine were part of the *struggle* for conquest of the land and production of the Zionist subject.[28] Victory in this battle demanded erasure of any essential separation between the new Jew as a farmer-warrior, struggling for the geographic territory that Zionism finally conquered, and the teacher, struggling for the exact shape and construction of the parameters of the collective identity, the language of its private and public consciousness, and the structure of the student's psyche and conceptual apparatus. These were the intellectual and moral dimensions of the mental space demarcating the conditions of subduing/producing the Zionist geographic horizons. The Hebrew teacher was primarily a special pioneer-warrior whose success in the daily struggle was a precondition for Zionism to have male and female pioneers, male and female commandos, male and female farmers/workers who "will dress the land with concrete dress," "purify," and "liberate" the land from its Palestinian Arab inhabitants. The latter still firmly claim that the land's identity was formed by *their* collective identity for the last 1,400 years. Other

Palestinian Arabs see themselves as descendants of the Canaanites, Hivites, and Jebuosites who formed the region's identity before the previous Jewish invasion. Despite these strategies of delegitimization of Zionism, the productivity of educational praxis is seen as part of the production process of Zionist and Palestinian normality: violence that produces the claims to the truth and their evaluation procedures, the Israeli and Palestinian realities, and their inevitable clash. From here springs the knowledge concept that materialized in the history of formal Zionist education. This is also the origin of the cultural rewards and the material gains of the teacher, of teacher-student relations, of concepts about legitimate relevant knowledge, social-cultural possibilities and limitations, and of the stand of the internal (the Jewish homosexual, woman, ultra-orthodox, etc.) and external (the Palestinian, the "goy" in general, the Diaspora Jew, etc.) Other.

This is the setting of the teachers within the Zionist project. Other factors also affected their earnings, such as economic prosperity or decline, wars, and the like. However, according to the thesis I present here, their essential status sprang from their stand in the Zionist project and the evolution of central concepts in the realm of self-evidence and the truths, values, and souls it produced. Basically, even at the highest point in Israeli idealism, the "teacher's stand was based primarily on intrinsic rewards, especially on prestigious rewards."[29] Jonathan Shapira summarizes the accepted mission of these poorly paid Hebrew teachers as nothing less than "to recreate the Hebrew people and its culture."[30] In his *Elite With No Followers*, he shows how paralleling the phenomenon of teachers as a cultural elite who joined the pioneers, as a social elite, Hebrew teachers suffered an inherent weakness in defending their independence and promoting their political strength and cultural rewards. The conscience of their great goal urged them to protect at least their institutional independence, if not their ideological autonomy; but their organization, their social status, and their influence on education worried the heads of the labor movement at that time (the leading political power in pre-independent Israel).[31] Already since the 1920s, in face of the labor movement's growing political hegemony, one observes a gradual but steady decline in the social standing and in the salaries of the teachers.[32]

The formation of a sovereign meta-narrative reflecting/serving the hegemonic Zionist ideology is also reflected in the "independent" performance of the teachers as an organization and as agents of forming the private and the collective consciousness. But the major political party, *Mapai*, did not allow even such a "derivation." Facing steady pressure and efficient maneuvers that brought about the collapse of major strikes in 1931 and 1932, "Teachers accepted the politicians' preeminence, and educated their pupils according to the Zionist values, in terms of the interpretation given to them by the heads of the *Mapai* party. They taught their pupils that the correct way to realize Zionism was pioneering settlement, that the *kibbutz* was the highest form of settlement, and that national capital would build the land in the proper manner for the realization of Zionism, not private capital controlled by the play of private interests," and so on.[33] In this way the symbolic power of hegemonic Zionist education was constituted, ensuring the fertility of the instruments of violent production that was directed to Zionist expansion and prosperity, inside and outside the system, to the collective, to the individual "self," and to the Others.

As one of the dimensions of violence, war is essentially masculine: it is one of the manifestations of what Freud called the "Reality Principle," which guarantees the styled instrumental practices and the constitution and progress of social-cultural space. Herbert Marcuse called the principle realized here the "Performative Principle," and he

> tried to identify certain basic trends in the instinctual structure of civilization and, particularly, to define the specific reality principle which has governed the progress of Western civilization. We designated this reality principle as the performance principle; and we attempt to show that domination and alienation, as derived from the prevalent social organization of labor, determined to a large extent the demands imposed upon the instincts by this reality principle.[34]

This principle is central to culture as a male manifestation. Feminization, in contrast, represents the principle which is opposed to that kind of culture and its progress, and from this point of view the woman was conceived by Freud as "opposition to culture."[35] The woman is the Other of the normal male culture, as "the Jew" is of traditional Christianity or "the Arab" is of the normalized Israeli. Yet the woman is also part of the ultimate condition of this culture and a central contributor to it.

While being the Other of male culture, the woman becomes an object and not the subject of culture.[36] She might internalize the constitutive myths of the system repressing her, while rebelling against this system and while operating as part of it to her advantage. A woman might fall in with the progress of the dominant male culture and share its "success," though sooner or later this will be revealed as her defeat, as a woman and as a human being.

In the history of Zionist education female teachers, like male teachers, functioned as an essential part of the struggle for the realization of Zionism. At their best they struggled "like men" for the formation of collective consciousness and the mental constitution of their pupils, in the setting of Zionist classrooms. I believe it is wrong to explain the special status enjoyed by male teachers, compared with female, within the narrow context of functional explanations. An explanation has to show an understanding of knowledge, and in a functional description no place exists for right or wrong or for knowledge or principles.

From a positivistic-functionalist point of view, one can demonstrate the status, the financial rewards, and the cultural capital of teachers as relatively high, compared with some other public service occupations in pre-independent secular Jewish society. One can point to the "fact" of higher education of Jewish males than of Jewish females, and give "explanations" about the reality of the male majority and the female minority in public educational organizations. These dimensions should not be ignored, but they should be included, evaluated, and deconstructed within a general theory aimed at penetrating the essence of the production procedures of Zionist truths. It should reconstruct the manipulation practices of its representation and distribution apparatuses. It also has to critically reconstruct the context of the pedagogical discourse and the ways in which it produced the Zionist subject. Such a thesis has to overcome traditional differences between modernist and post-modernist traditions of cultural and social critique. Therefore, I think, such a thesis should be a dialogue that deconstructs and evaluates the formative elements of the authorized "facts" that characterize the history of Zionist education. From this perspective, female and male teachers are evaluated as agents of repression but also as objects of formative manipulations. In this light, I ask the following questions concerning the constitutive and formative powers that established the stand and the change of female and male teachers in Israel at the end of the twentieth century.

The Change in Western Knowledge and the Feminization of the Teaching Profession in Israel

On the issue of education, two processes parallel the state of Israel's success: growing feminization of the teaching profession on the one hand and a steady decline in the status of teachers on the other. This may be understood within the context of the transformation in the stand of Western knowledge, technological developments, and the change in social and cultural structures and relations in the West and in secular Israel.

Instrumental Rationality's advancement manifested the interest of control and delimited the efficiency of its strategies operating in the private and public spheres, while minimizing the lines of division between the private and the public. The interpretative-critical interests proved decreasingly relevant to the reality taking shape in the second half of the twentieth century. This is especially true within the Israeli context. Along these lines one can reconstruct in the Israeli system two major trends, as follows.

The first is the traditional, idealistic trend, committed to the modernist ideals of national liberation and the construction of the new Jewish collective consciousness. This trend is totally obligated to certain legitimized bodies of knowledge, those of Objective Reason within the tradition of the concept of objective knowledge, and it is a warrior-repressive trend. But it is not a one-dimensional repressive trend in its essence, since it includes an anti-instrumental concept of knowledge. In its purest form it is patriarchal and hierarchical. Where there is room for female teachers in such a trend, they are supposed to act "like men" at their best, and normally in such a case they successfully reproduce the hegemonic ideology, or else they are forced to play the part of "women," professionally realizing themselves in their "womanly" aspects. For the system's well-being, this is necessary to guarantee the comforting, caring, and dormative dimensions of the marginal parts of society or the marginal elements of the warrior-male psyche. In this sense, at their best, women are supposed to perform publicly as nurses, teachers, kindergarten workers, and the like, that is, to function as an enhancement for reproduction of traditional "female" characteristics that ensure the permanence of political impotence among women, on the one hand, and the concrete appearance of social utopia on the other. Either way, in this context, women do not demand, nor can they try, to present the Others' perspective in the dominant meta-narrative. They are prevented from presenting their voice concerning the legitimized and accepted real bodies of knowledge and patriarchal power games as they relate to their own reality. They are prevented from legitimately presenting their opinions in the major debate about the yardsticks of knowledge and legitimization, as they are not represented there as bearers of a legitimate educational alternative, the alternative of the female "voice."

The second trend that has guided Israeli society's development springs from the successful violence of Zionist education. It includes the ability to symbolically protect and facilitate the expansion and prosperity of the Zionist project in its economic, technological, and organizational dimensions. In this sense, Israeli society has developed in an increasingly normal way, as in the current Western hegemonic trend. As in some Western societies, technological and economic progress has demanded the "democratization" of hegemonic knowledge. The advanced capitalistic marketing and distribution of knowledge, like any other commodity, has sterilized this knowledge of its antagonistic dimensions, as well as its reflective potential that characterized it in Western tradition,[37] especially within the tradition of Objective Reason.

The parameters within this new image of knowledge are performance, function, its efficiency, and productivity. Performance of this kind may be rationally examined only within a performative space,[38] and this too only as a function. The functionalist examination of knowledge and the functionalist critique of reality and their analysis of the ways that fertility and efficient function of knowledge are produced presuppose the present reality as the only legitimate and relevant point of reference. The present reality itself, even if it is perverted, is not conceived as deserving critical evaluation or deconstruction. According to this ideological philosophy of science, in principle the legitimacy and the omnipotence of present reality is an incontrovertible precondition, and only within the functionalist framework is there room for relevant theoretical work. Only within these limits is there meaning to studying "facts" and theories about these "facts." This is a conservative positivistic stand which, in my view, contrasts the main Jewish tradition and the essence of Enlightenment's humanism, as two manifestations of Objective Reason that are still very relevant, especially in face of the current success of functionalistic ideologies in science and education.

In its new, anti-erotic form, neutral to the utopian axis and to value commitments, the denial of spiritual autonomy and the refusal of Utopia become a precondition for the effective functioning of women and men as agents, as conformist/efficient producers/consumers. Advancement in social and economic competition is feasible only by the capitulation of narrower bodies of knowledge that are ever more precious and dear from the viewpoint of Instrumental Rationality. This process, which is increasingly stimulating and intensive in the second half of the twentieth century, allows a growing feminization of the teaching profession in the current educational market, paralleled by the deterioration of the social status and the reduction in economic rewards of teachers in advanced capitalism. Local capitalistic developments in local systems, as in Japan and Germany, modify this thesis but they do not negate its general validity, certainly not in the Israeli context. According to this thesis, there is a historical tendency which dictates that as a capitalistic educational institution includes more female teachers, the status of the institution will decline, and correspondingly, the cultural capital of its students and the economic rewards of its functionaries will decline as well.

According to the *Statistical Abstract of Israel*,[39] in 1948-1949 there were 4,153 teachers in elementary Hebrew schools, 2,328 (56%) of them women. In comparison, in 1992-1993 there were 40,373 teachers in the elementary educational institutions, 90.4% of them women. If, as is likely this trend continues, women will constitute close to 100% of the total teacher workforce in the very near future. In high schools the same trend is evident, though more modestly.

In 1992-1993, at all teacher-training institutions, there were 4,150 teachers, of whom 2,438 were women, 1,650 were men, and 62 were described by the Central Bureau of Statistics as "unknown." On the one hand, the data here, as in the other educational institutions, reflect women's social mobility. However, even from the statistical point of view the picture is far from marvelous. Even an uncritical analysis of the data shows that (while neglecting the "unknown" sex of 62 teachers) 568 of the teachers holding B.A. degrees were women, as compared with 261 men. Among the M.A. holders, 647 were men and 1,159 were women; as for Ph.D. holders, the ratio was 603 men to only 285 women. Here too one sees that the feminization process of the educational institutions is slower as the institutions involved are more prestigious. However, even the more prestigious institutions cannot effectively resist this trend, which is vividly present there as well, albeit in a more temperate form. I do not want to delve into this issue with its reactions and counter-reactions, involving greater understanding of the capitalistic opportunities of "improved" schooling in technologically advanced societies like Japan, and the influence it has on female and male teachers' status in these societies. Here I will direct my critical reconstruction solely to local Israeli conditions.

The stand of the Israeli female teacher is determined at a confluence of those capitalistic technological-social-cultural trends that have been reconstructed in this paper in their most general Western context. In today's Israel, the teaching profession is for most women a move up from lower social status and lower income professions—a profession, not a vocation. Even if in its present form the Israeli school is open for limited social integration from different socioeconomic backgrounds, today it functions as a much more efficient socialization instrument for female teachers. This success is rapidly losing ground as the trend develops. This opportunity to rise in social status is open to Jewish women of lower socioeconomic status, mainly from Arab countries (*Sepharadim*), and to Palestinian women, who gain the economic power and social status that enable them to gradually change the traditional structure of the Israeli Palestinian family and society.

The dominant social developments in Palestinian society in Israel are, in various aspects, different from those that characterize Jewish society in Israel, being slower and more moderate. This parallels the general reality of obstructed opportunities (as a collective, not as individuals) to obtain positions in the public service and to integrate in civic institutions and, to a lesser degree, in private organizations, in contrast to the typical Palestinian occupations like agriculture, construction, and motor mechanics. This reality is undergoing rapid change due to knowledge instrumentalization and "objective and neutral" performance criteria as the market's supreme criteria in post-Zionist

Israel. Nevertheless, this trend is taking place on the fringes of society and is very fragile and threatened by nationalistic clashes and crises ahead of us. A positivistic analysis of the occupational integrity of Palestinians in Israel (in the public sector) might conclude that the situation is far from dreadful.[40]

I do not accept the positivistic research and the functionalist analysis. The conclusion that Palestinians are well integrated in the public occupational market in the middle and in high posts is of more value in a study of the politics of positivistic statistical maneuvers and deserves critical deconstruction. Historically oriented research sensitive to the possibilities of critique of ideology (but not restricted to it) might draw different conclusions. Research that also attempts to study the issue from the victims' point of view and reconstructs of their marginalization, while establishing an unproblematic, "scientific" discourse on the issue, will probably result in a different picture.

A critical study might bring to light some improvement of the occupational situation of the Palestinians in Israel. By the same token, it might highlight their marginalization before, during, and after their educational development and their integration in the Israeli capitalistic system. This is an important part of the context in which the state educational institution has become the major factor in Israeli Palestinian's possibilities for social and cultural mobility. This is why the Israeli-Palestinian sector's educational system in Israel is more male-dominated than the Jewish sector's. In his research on social developments facing Palestinians in Israel, Palestinian sociologist Majid Al-Haj concludes that education has become the chief prestigious asset and has inherited the place traditionally held by land in Palestinian society in Israel.[41] However, technological progress and the enlargement of production, distribution, and service agencies in Israel have also had their influence on Palestinian society. The logic that these are only its manifestations also constitutes new concepts, myths, and values in Palestinian society which deconstruct and transform the old ones. This exerts its influence on the attraction of teaching occupations and on attitudes toward teaching, a profession that even in Israeli Palestinian society is experiencing a rapid feminization process.

The integration of Israeli Palestinians into the relatively prosperous economic development of Israeli society might be evaluated, at least partially, by the feminization process of teaching in Arab schools in Israel. According to the data I collected at the Arab Institution for Development of Educational Workers in Beit Berl,[42] in 1972, 70 students, 30 of whom were women and 40 were men, graduated. In 1981, 67 students graduated, 46 of them women and 21 men. In 1991, 60 Palestinians graduated the Institute, of whom 50 were women and 10 were men. By 1995 the ratio was 82 women to 9 men.

A positivistic study would refer to the data as a manifestation of Israeli Palestinian integration in middle-status positions in public institutions. Such an analysis would no doubt praise the number and percentage of female Palestinians obtaining positions as teachers. A critical deconstructivist would reconstruct the general context, the ideological orientation of the functionalist-positivist analysis. This kind of analysis would have to emphasize that the opportunities given to Israeli Palestinian and Jewish women in Israel are part of a process in which the knowledge they are transmitting is conceived as decreasingly relevant and rapidly losing its traditional status, and as no longer considered vital to any level of technological or economic advancement. This conclusion is increasingly valid even for the role and status of universities as research institutions.[43]

Men who head the social and cultural developments or are driven to its margins have seized the more competitive and prestigious occupations, in which today one can realize the productivity of chauvinist energy. In Israel these new spaces are closer to the significant developments of current capitalist society and are perceived as more prestigious and relevant, and accordingly provide men or "manly women" with greater rewards.

Traditionally, it was impossible to distinguish among four teaching dimensions: A) the teacher as an educator. B) the teacher as an agent of transmitting privileged bodies of knowledge. C) the teacher as a reproducer of concepts about knowledge that were essential parts of the realm of self-evidence and, therefore, were viewed as valid and as parameters for the validity of claims and claims about facts. D) the teacher as a repression agent in the service of hegemonic power focuses in existing power relations, commissioned to marginalize and destroy alternative concepts about relevant knowledge, self-interests, and identities. This last was intended to secure and *productively* activate the normalization practices of the existing system or its establishment. For example, teachers who presented the geography of Palestine/Israel were the vanguard for ensuring the successful mythicization of this knowledge and making it a vital part of the mental constitution of their pupils. They were the ones who ensured the self-evidence of geographical "facts" about Israel and the abolition of "Palestine" and Palestinian identity as "fact." Namely, they were the producers of the factuality of facts, not "just" their representatives. They were a vital element in the production of the Israeli subject and the Israeli system.

Within this meta-narrative, Israel was basically always *Eretz Israel*, not a mere territory about which the teacher introduced to his/her students parts of relevant information. *Eretz Israel* was much more than that: it was a grand transcendental *ideal*. Geography is suggested here just as an example for all traditional Zionist bodies of knowledge that were relevant (in secular Jewish Israeli society) until the last generation.

The Zionist success, in economic levels and in advancing the efficiency of symbolic production, representation, and distribution, also allowed dominant Western cultural processes to be realized in Israel. On the one hand, this was made possible by the relative security, prosperity, and self-esteem. On the other hand, the realization of these processes became necessary since they were part and parcel of Western capitalist developments, new technologies, and new concepts about knowledge. These provided the means for introducing and activating the new bodies of knowledge that stimulated Israeli industry and scientific knowledge. At least in the Israeli case, the two seemed inseparable: Zionism could not advance, institutionally, without making use of new bodies of knowledge and detaching them from the concept of knowledge that made them possible and incubated them and their social and other material manifestations. As a result of being involved in a permanent military, economic, and cultural struggle, both externally and internally, Zionism had to compensate for its inferiority in size and resources by developing technological and economic competence. The Zionist instrumental attitude and the Jewish educational system (along with massive foreign aid) made this process possible.

Part of the rationalization process of merchandise at this historical stage of capitalism was the reification of human relations. From a transcendental dimension, which has social relevance, knowledge became a thing with no *otherness*, no transcendental dimension, a mere commodity whose purchase has only one valid parameter: sheer practicality. As the crystallization of this evolution education, which once was conceived as a vocation, changed its aims and its social status. Teaching increasingly turned into the transmission of information and practical knowledge, a kind of marketing in mercantilist space, in a historical situation where knowledge was expected to be more and more "practical," "useful," and "efficient"—disconnected from any idealistic, moralistic, or aesthetic transcendent orientation. The logic of the market spilled over into the educational arena in one generation made it a vital element of a new culture industry. The erotic/idealistic educational dimension that Zionism saw as indispensable (and the bodies of knowledge conceived as the means for its incubation and flourishing, or even as being of equal value) has been eroding from the 1960s until today, when nothing much is left of it. The quintessential dimension of Israeliness in our days is *lo li'hyot frier* (not to be stooge by acting morally),[44] and it is vital as a manifestation of the current historical standing of knowledge in Israel and the possibilities still open for the teaching profession.

This is not to say that Zionist education was not instrumentally oriented from its very beginning, in the sense that bodies of knowledge which were declared legitimate and relevant at schools were always mobilized to serve the

Zionist project. The teacher's goal was to shape the young Zionist psyche according to Zionism's needs and to reproduce the hegemonic meta-narrative as a major dimension of the reality of self-evidence and its local system with as few impediments and challenges as possible. However, even traditional Zionist education was historically confronted with internal as well as external threats and challenges, and it has now been changed.

A century of secular Zionism also had to face the challenges of the remainders of Judaism, *galutiut*, as well as the humanist ideals of the Enlightenment and other representations of Objective Reason's tradition. However, as in other collectives, their realization in the Israeli system was marginal and abused.

The Vocation of Female Teachers in a Post-Zionist Israel

In the closing years of the twentieth century we faced a new stage in the development of Instrumental Rationality. In secular Israel we are facing such an instrumentalization of knowledge that there is no more living expression of the tradition of Objective Reason in its two local manifestations—traditional Judaism and the Enlightenment's ideals. In today's secular education there is practically no room for any ideals whatsoever, and it lacks any spirituality. But, while the present historical stand of knowledge might be seen as entirely analogous to the one common in other Western societies, current Israeli education has its unique features.

An important aspect of present Israeli secular education is that it is completely disconnected from Jewish tradition, and in this respect it is utterly ruthless, with no obligation to any collective transcendent or practical goal, and is really post-modern. By the same token, in the educational arena there is no vivid presence or even remnants of humanist ideals and basic concepts. This is different from other advanced capitalist societies like the Japanese, the Americans, or even the British, where traditions, while digested as part of the global culture industry, still have some relevance, as in the case of religion in America, and might become a focus of refusal, opposition, and critique against the new rational-instrumental realm of self-evidence. In the Israeli case, Instrumental Rationality does not face any challenge or resistance from the vast majority of society, which is perceived to be secular. At most, its hegemony creates uneasiness from what is understood as lack of personal (transcendental) goals or lack of spirit.

One should not underestimate uneasiness or other cracks in the general satisfaction, which guarantees and reproduces the prevailing hegemonic ideology with no need for censorship, secret agents, and other obvious normalization and repression apparatuses. In the current conditions prevailing in the range from gaity to gravity, conformity has the upper hand. This is why uneasiness, gravity, and unspoken anger are so important, I believe. Their bruteness presents the implicit demand for an alternative to sublimation and high cultural traditions that were sources of rebellion, refusal, and critique in earlier historical stages.

On the other hand, one should not overestimate the current role that these aspects play since they, as traditional utopian potentials, are regularly and systematically recruited to serve the hegemonic systems in the realm of self-evidence of "our" post-modern world. Uneasiness, anger, fright, and all kinds of "perverseness," as well as all kinds of alternative social institutionalization and intellectual opposition, are all forced to play the role set for them by the internal logic of the system. The only "aim" of this aimless system is to reflect and further the current realm of self-evidence and its basic concepts and symbolic/material potentialities. In this sense, today there is no more validity to traditional emancipatory concepts like repression, and there is no use for old versions of ideology critique that emphasize concepts like estrangement. Therefore, today's critical theory should not restrict itself to the negation of the present reality: it should combine this imperative with the negation of old optimistic-positive-utopianism.

Today's Western capitalistic systems are not irrational and repressive, as in Marx's thinking. Nor are they to be criticized and negated for not being rational and for creating estrangement. However, they are to be rejected because of the mode and the degree to which they have neutralized estrangement and because of their (instrumental) rationality and general efficiency. In this sense the system is not "repressive," and there are no rational social actions to confront here. Even ideology critique from a social-cultural libertarian instrument, has been reified by its enemies and devotees and has been transformed to an object of consumption, as spiritless transcendentalist dogma.

> The more total society becomes, the greater the reification of the mind and the more paradoxical its effort to escape reification and its own. Even the most extreme consciousness of doom threatens to degenerate into idle chatter. Culture criticism finds itself faced with the final stage of the dialectic of culture and barbarism.[45]

In such a reality, there are no values and ideals to educate for, in the traditional sense of the word: no value or aim has a transcendental and objective status from which it is possible to challenge current reality or struggle for a reasonable social consensus devoid of power manipulations. The power maneuvers of daily reality are the only space from which it is possible to judge the aims, limitations, and potentialities of this given reality. The systems within the horizons of the post-modern realm of self-evidence that are being formed in our era are perceived as developing contingently and are producing contingency as a prime element of collective consciousness, with no "aim," "foundation," or "meaning." This Western realm of self-evidence is establishing in the local Israeli system the current stand of knowledge and its agencies. It also acts as a main force dictating the stand of Israeli teachers, who have no relevance even as teachers, let alone educators.

Teachers are conceived by their students as having no part in relevant knowledge production, even as knowledge transmitters. Moreover, they are seen as having no real understanding of the knowledge that they are supposed to transmit to their students. More than any other dimension of vital importance is the general feeling that present-day school knowledge is outdated and irrelevant, and that the school itself does not serve and cannot serve its traditional adductive and schooling missions.

In our era, general education, especially in the "great books" tradition, is no longer conceived as having real value or as holding important patronizing-repressive value. In suspicion of apathy toward, or militant negation of the "great book" tradition, multiculturalists, feminists, post-modernists, and their mainstream functionalist rivals are united. The very possibility of preserving a living connection with this tradition is questioned[46] in an era in which fashion inherits the traditional place that objective truths and transcendent values once held. In the post-modern realm of self-evidence, there is less and less room for tradition at all, not only the hegemonic tradition. The school is a dinosaur from an era that no longer exists in the most advanced spaces of the Western public sphere. In the Israeli context, to the degree that school is still conceivable and its staff considered an agency transmiting a valid tradition and relevant bodies of knowledge, it is at the same time also generally understood as a repressive institution that obligates the acceptance of unwelcome "material" in unpleasant and depressing conditions.

The intellectual discourse, the theoretical stance in itself, and the reflective potentialities are deemed by the educational system, as by many teachers, more irrelevant than a threat or bothersome commitment. They have lost their relevance as they are conceived as not "practical" or target-oriented.[47] By the relevant parameters of present-day Instrumental Rationality that is dominant in most (but not all) Western systems, there is no room for intellectuals and no need for a critical theoretical/social stand, still less considering the role of intellectual teachers of the kind for whose development Henry Giroux is working.[48] In Israel the governmental secular school functions as a transitory stage and as the selection and reproduction instrument of the present social and ideological hegemonic hierarchies. In such schools only two aspects of education are still possible.

In such a schooling space, the role of the institution is to reproduce knowledge and to reduce it to constitutive myths of Zionism. Schooling should function as the grand protector of the basic concepts of traditional Zionism: concepts such as bravery, loyalty to the tribe, self-sacrifice for the tribe, and the like.

Today, after more than a century of Zionist education, the effectiveness of this kind of education is diminishing, reflecting the erosion of Zionist *Geist.* The same phenomenon may be seen from another angle, namely the successful penetration of the inner logic of the capitalist market as an explicit, legitimate, sole ruler, as a reflection of the new general realm of self-evidence, in which everything is commodity and the sole "value" is the market price. The year 1995-1996 was proclaimed officially, by then the (so-called leftist) Ministry of Education, as "The Year of the Industry," not in the Bolshevik tradition but in accord with the Reaganist-Thatcherite ideology of the supremacy of "the market." This was represented and praised as the supreme point of reference which, from a functionalist point of view, does not differ from the function of obsolete traditional truths from which transcendental aims were established and appropriate pedagogical means were deduced.

Current Israeli privatization of schools and fragmentation of curricula according to changing fashions and rotating needs of the local market ensure the validity of "excellence" in its performance, as preached by T.Q.M. experts and other, more up-to-date functionaries. However, it is wrong, I think, to restrict critique to these issues, which themselves are to be contextualized within the framework of the changing stand of Western knowledge and teachers as subjects and as objects, in and as part of its threat to change pedagogy, curriculum, and even school architecture.

The general developments reconstructed here have made possible the new orientation and the new possibilities and limitations of Israeli secular schools. Today, Israeli schools function as an effective educational apparatus only to the degree that they reproduce images and bodies of knowledge relevant to participating in myths of consumption like that of the luxurious car or villa. In the post-modern era that Israeli society has entered in recent years, the school can protect its relevance only by using culture heroes and sex stars (or as they are called in Israel, "blasts") like Michael Jackson, Madonna, Robert Maxwell, Shoul Eisenberg, and local figures of this kind. To attract clients, high schools are trying to open exotic and extravagant programs such as law studies for beginners, advertising, modeling, movie-making, and the like. Post-modernity is not seen in the same degree and manner in different localities; in some poor peripheral schools, old myths may still have some relevance, even for secular students, with some modifications. The post-modern condition to which I refer is much more extensive in the middle-class and yuppie social spaces, but even so, the death of the Zionist spirit is present everywhere, even if in different formations, as "the Israeli" devolves to various collective identities.

In such circumstances, the reproduction tendency of the system is trying to protect itself by utilizing the new heroes in the service of the dying gods. Such is the case in the way that the establishment treats the most popular Israeli pop singer, Aviv Geffen. The school is becoming a mere reflection of consumption mobility in the open market and is contributing its share in the reproduction and intensification of the developments that essentially it must to destroy, or else be destroyed by them.

Real education, the formation of the conscience, and the construction of the soul which guarantees the smooth regulation of men and women as efficient producers/consumers, as clever, cynical anti-intellectuals, is mainly realized outside of the formal schooling process. By its "nature," the current formal schooling space cannot return to the position and power it lost more than a generation ago. It is too fragile to become, again, an arena of reflection and mainly construction of one, ethnocentric, collective identity, with concepts about (relevant) knowledge, values, and interests. As the last election proved, Israeli society is dissolving into fractions and essentially different interest groups and ethnic identities competing inside and outside parliament over resources and powers on a strictly separatist and opportunist basis. Yet the establishment does not give up, and is probably still not even aware of the role the school really plays in current Israeli culture and society. The trend toward separation of lower socioeconomic levels of secular Jewish groups from the secular middle class, with its rapid atomization and extreme individualization, is well underway. While these developments gather momentum, the privatization of educational institutions and their market orientation is developed rapidly and "successfully," serving the competing developments. Basically, the secular educational system is still explicitly anti-pluralistic, so teachers are challenged with conflicting demands: on the one hand they are supposed to be relevant, "open," to acknowledge different backgrounds of their pupils and different potentials and areas of interest. On the other hand they are strictly committed to a unified curriculum, to the hegemonic interpretation, and to the Zionist jargon and myths. They are forced into anti-intellectualism, anti-humanism, and anti-democratic and real pluralist attitudes. As a result the school, as is generally recognized, does not train and prepare the inmates arrested in it for the real world outside its walls as long as it is a Zionist school. The real training for what is conceived as the pantheon of reality, namely the job market, occurs in institutions like universities, and especially in small, specific private training institutions. Two social justifications exist for operating schools under such conditions, very different from the justifications of the political elite's calculations and interests. One is to disarm young people, especially young males, of their potential revolutionary impulse in its sexual, emotional, and intellectual dimensions and to reproduce in their conscience other facets, including the most remote and elementary, in the service of the local system. The second justification is the activation of a preliminary social selection and hierarchy building, in which the reproduction of existing power relations in the market is possible.[49] This double function of schools in today's Israel is guaranteed by apparatuses so complex that their power is much more effective and penetrating than those which operated in previous stages of Zionist schools in Israel. All these developments place teachers in an impossible situation as people, as educators, and even as good teachers in the strict traditional sense of the word. The politically radical, intellectual, and emotional potentialities still open to teachers in Israel make Ivan Illitch's demand for abolishing schools a mere Utopia in the naive sense.[50]

Feminization and False Emancipation

In these circumstances, in which conformist-oriented "success" in market competition is the ideal, it is not surprising that the more competitive Israeli males, those with higher self-esteem, will act rationally, according to Instrumental Rationality and the prevailing fashion, and will act in line with the market imperative. Insofar as they are rational and possess adequate potential, they will not see the teaching profession as a suitable job for them; they will not even see education as a vocation. Therefore, teaching and education, while in the most recent stage of Israeli history having become irrelevant and disconnected from the prevailing myths of the present culture industry, have become a job for the weaker socioeconomic strata of society. Teaching increasingly has become an occupation for disadvantaged people and those deprived of opportunities to do something more socially appreciated than teaching. It also provides an opportunity for these people to appropriate a tool for compensating their anger and frustration about not being able to participate in the real battle. In other words, teaching has become a "womanish" occupation. This is the background for the current feminization of this profession.

This development would have been impossible without the structure of Israeli society as it is today in the systematic discrimination against Palestinian citizens of Israel, against the *sepharadim*, and against Jewish women in general, as part of the realization of the concrete Jewish orthodox *halacha* as an essential part of the legal system, given that the Jewish religion is the state's official religion.

Women's liberation from traditional and limiting ways of life has also been facilitated by their changing economic role at "home" and outside the "home." In the current social and cultural circumstances, women's liberation is not manifested solely at the legal level, for all its importance. It is impossible outside the context of the market, the political conditions of the market, and the power struggles of the financiers. At the same time, the system in which these are some of its universal commanding powers is determined by its concepts, myths, and spiritual possibilities and limitations, as a reflection of its realm of self-evidence. That is why most feminists and anti-feminists alike are missing the philosophical conditions of women's liberation. Moreover, the general accepted representations of current conditions serve to strengthen the misleading impression that women are being liberated or that women are about to be liberated on the grounds of present reforms and developments. This is so since it looks as if women are getting better jobs, leaving the confines of "home," harvesting political power along the way. In Israel the teaching profession enables many women to participate in the struggle for their liberation (or at least to make some advancement in this direction) without entering into jobs such as cleaning, agricultural work, low-level secretarial positions, or in which the work is physically hard, vacations are scarce, and social status (and political potential) is low and problematic.

In the Israeli system this trend takes different formations than might be evident in other systems. In Israel a handful of men still see themselves as courageous and talented, and even so decide on the teaching profession. There are still many middle-class women in teaching, and not a few of them are efficient and talented teachers in Israeli schools. Furthermore, there are also veteran teachers from the last generation, who still see teaching and education as a vocation, and even now they manage to resist cynicism and practicalism in the name of the old gods and their ancient ideals. Nevertheless, in today's Israel all these are a derivation or remnants of yesterday's world.

In terms of the hegemonic trend in Israeli society, it is reasonable to predict that fewer and fewer teachers will also be scholarship-oriented and possess general knowledge in the *Bildung* tradition, people with self-esteem and potential for success in the competition on the free market. The advancement of the market-oriented rationalization of Israeli educational institutions will probably ensure the strengthening of the feminization of schools. This trend itself will push/liberate ever lower and weaker socioeconomic level women into the profession. This is but a reflection of recent developments in the apparatuses of relevant-knowledge production at the turn of the century. This progress is ratified as well as paralleled by advancing hegemonic concepts of knowledge and the current hierarchies of present social formations.

One has to see the positive-productive dimension of this development and denote the importance of the historical chance for women's liberation. This is so since the advancing of lower-strata women and their entrance into such a formative system as education is important for their personal liberation, just as it is important for the entrance of marginalized voices and diverse traditions and knowledge.[51] This trend might also be considered important since for many Israeli women the teaching profession is just a necessary step before continuing their climb to a more respected profession and an improvement in their economic potential and social status.

To my mind this positive dimension should not be seen in an overly optimistic perspective. This is so since its critical reconstruction shows its vital contribution to the promotion of the order in the current Israeli system and its bestowal to the bettering of the closeness of the realm of self-evidence in which Instrumental Rationality prevails. This positive-productive diminution of teachers' work reflects and advances the process in which knowledge is transformed into bits of information,[52] women and men into spaces of urges that were planted there from outside with no internal control or reflection. The "self" and "self-identity" itself become one of the commodities that the market produces and distributes with no "aim" or "meaning." In such circumstances, human agents become statistical data controlled in a totally rational manner, in order to reproduce the system's dynamics and to further advance the rational control over "reality" and its "facts," including individual and collective identities, and knowledge and practices relating to it and reproducing it.

As in other spaces of today's capitalist rational control, the relative success of Israeli women in the teaching profession is determined by the degree and the specific character of their participation in the de-humanization processes of their lives and the lives of other people in the educational institutions in which they work. As female teachers, their work is evaluated and determined in accordance with the achievements in the era of destruction/production: blocking or preventing the spiritual autonomy of the pupils, sterilizing their symbolic space, and dissolving the languages, memories, and mentalities that in the past allowed identification with the primitive repression of Others, but also a degree of spiritual autonomy, struggle for transcendence, and the demand for a new and more humanistic historical stage. In other words, we are dealing here with teachers' contribution to *deportation* of thinking, within the framework of which it is possible to collectively work for dialogical communicative acts. At the same time, this is a positive and constructive contribution to the trivialization and in practice to the abolition of Jewish and humanist traditions for secular Jewish people.

Dialectically, these dimensions, which are so central to today's teachers' work, are part of the universal conditions for different expressive "voices" and different orientations. But under present conditions in the Israeli arena, such conditions are absent, due to radical critical reasoning and overcoming basic impediments of the system, which are at the same time also the foundations of the prevailing realm of self-evidence. Solidarity has become irrational and serious reflection a matter for bureaucrats or for non-mature types (philosophers, as once they were called).

The current bodies of knowledge, which are consumed by the new human being as an efficient producer/consumer, turn male and female teachers into agents of anti-humanistic dynamics. Their ability to internalize the logic of the normalization process and their acceptance of intellectual impotence is a precondition for survival, not to mention their success as teachers. In such circumstances, with some modifications, there is room for the traditional female characterization in current educational dynamics: immanent "receptivity" and passivity of the agents in the school arena—in the heart of a society which adores the ideal of "free competition"—make the feminization of the teaching profession a historic imperative.

Paralleling this process of feminization of the teaching profession and the decline of teachers' cultural and social status in Israel, more and more women are succeeding in entering the real battlefield: the open market. In today's Israeli society there is a parallel feminization of such professions as journalism, advertising, architecture, law, and communication. As a rule, the women competing with men under open competition conditions are those driven to see themselves as strong and competent enough not to descend to the teacher's status. Here there is no place for commitment to an ideal or responsibility to a discipline. It is strictly a preference of one particular lifestyle over another as a representation of self-esteem in the non-philosophical sense of the word. This is from each woman's own subjective perspective.

At the same time, an objective false libertarian conscience is being realized. This is so because the gay conscience of feminist liberation manifested here is unconcerned with and unconscious of the powers constructing reality, its representations, and its liberation. This liberation is conditioned by surrendering not only *the grand refusal*, but even the modest one to current reality. It is a liberation conditioned by women's surrendering their identity (determined as autonomously as possible under human conditions), and they are forced to surrender even their (repressed) traditional stand in opposition to hegemonic male-dominated culture.

In the mid-twentieth century, Theodor Adorno and Max Horkheimer could still nurture some hope for the female essence as an opposition to hegemonic surveillance logic in the current realm of self-understanding and the civilization identified by Freud's project. That is, since "the division of labor imposed on her by man brought her little that was worthwhile, she became the biological function, the image of nature, the subjugation of which constituted that civilization's title to fame."[53]

The Possibility of an Alternative Feminist Emancipatory Education in Israel

In the progressive male-dominated discourse, women were presented as an undistorted manifestation of unrestrained nature, or as an unperverted cultural realization of natural compassion and the capacity for love. At the same time, this discourse gave its share to male dominance in the public sphere and in the cultural discourse. This dominance is of the same family as the vulgar Domination Principle that they challenged. Yet by the same token the discourse about female essence—even in its appearances in male-dominated orientations—made possible the Utopia of a humane alternative to current reality, something *totally other* than the given. To my mind it is an essential issue, since this premise or this imperative of *the totally other* than the given is a precondition for a critical theory of society, radical political praxis, and counter-education.

The appearance of growing numbers of women liberating themselves from traditional restrictions does not necessarily represent counter-education and genuine liberation. My impression is that in the Israeli arena what is happening is first of all a refusal of "the grand refusal," as part of a refusal of anything "grand," transcendental, non-contingent, practical, and daily. From its very beginning, "refusal" was a male construct, where honor in the military sense was dominant. As a public posture and political act, "refusal" was not considered to be essentially female in the high-culture paradigmatic texts from Aristotle to Freud. This progressive discourse was essentially non-dialogical and did wonderfully without the active and equal participation of women. At the same time, it also made its contribution to disarming the political potential of women and taking part in such an education that ensured the internalization of repression by women as well as their identification with their repression and devotion to their repressors, which usually was called "love." And yet, as an internal Diaspora, the female "nature" that was historically constructed by these dynamics was offering and realizing a real space of otherness besides the

Domination Principle that male-dominated culture praised and developed. Under the surface of the dominant culture, an alternative was a living ideal and a concrete way of life. Even without idealizing these traditional ways of life among Jewish women as a community, and after considering the actual powers that forced them to be so peaceful and non-violent, on the one hand, and considering the violent expressions that were taking place and are still occurring in traditional communities of that sort, a female alternative is still evident here. This is an alternative that could and should be relevant both to females and males as human beings, an educational alternative that I refuse to surrender. The current popular identification with "strong women" and their entering male-dominated combat and the praise for them is a manifestation of the demolishing of a feminist-humane alternative. It is a surrender of the female as well as human utopia. It is the entrance ticket for women into the violent space of free competition and its promised "successes" at this historic stage. Israel does not differ in this respect.

I do not accept the Platonic or that kind of radical separatist feminism which praises naive essentialism, feminist or male essentialism included. The position I suggest might be seen as an advanced conservative understanding of women's essence and the political stand of women that is derived from it. It might be seen if I could disallow the entrance of women to the only real space where their practical liberation and self-constitution and ability to sound their own voice is possible. In addition, one might ask, why should women defend, develop, and fight for traditional female essences or alternatives, given the general acceptance of contingency in current liberal discourse? Why should women not constitute for themselves a new female identity, disconnected from the old historical stages? And does such a thing as "essence" and women's essence get realized in history?

I think that there is such a thing as woman's essence, just as there is such a thing as human essence. On an ontological and a historical level, this claim must be clarified. "The materialist concept of essence is a historical concept. Essence is conceived only as the essence of a particular 'appearance,' whose factual form is viewed with regard to what it is in itself and what it could be (but is not in fact). This relation, however, originates in history and changes history."[54] The ontological aspect of the female essence is derived from the dialogical essence of humankind.[55] The concept of dialogue implies two different competing essences building the realm where, if it is not distorted, they can realize themselves ideally. Utopically, men and women are the essential elements of the human dialogue. This dialogue is a historical event, and different stages and localities realize differently the essence of men and women. The distortion, the perversion of the dialogue or, as happened in the last century, the transformation of the dialogical track into a discursive, totally violent, historical way of human coexistence, is part of the realization of human potentialities. This is so since human essence is not determined one-dimensionally, and its utopic potential is complemented with a Tanathos striving, which is historically interwoven in complicated construction and balances. This means that human and feminist liberation is not determined as all positive utopists thought, and it implies that sometimes the distorted human dialogue or discourse might be seen as liberation and realization of the utopian imperative. It also implies that within the systems involved, it is impossible to determine or differentiate between a discourse and a dialogue, human perversion or human liberation. In saying this, I do not imply relativism, defeatism, and one-dimensional pessimism, but pessimistic utopianism.[56]

According to this theory, the female essence is evolving historically in certain natural and human conditions that are to be reconstructed, criticized, evaluated, and changed. However, this is only from outside the system, or as a transcendental dialectical deconstruction of it. The transcendental moment in the critical theory I suggest should be imbedded in an immanent critique, and its parameters, ideals, and goals should spring from the tradition of Objective Reason in its critical-humanistic orientation. The transcendental dimension should not replace the immanent, historical concreteness of this critical dialogue and political praxis. That is why the Utopian moment is so vital for such a critique or for such a deconstruction, since the potential and the otherness of "the given" situation is a precondition for a theoretical and political stand such as the one that I offer here.

The historic-ontological conception I suggest here is very different from those radical feminist essentialists and their conception of the unbridgeable gap between men and women.[57] It also differs strongly from those post-modernist feminists and their ideology of playing with construction and deconstruction of identities and the contingent transfer from the one to another,[58] to the point where there is no room for any certain identity at all.

Immanently, while not objectively, it is possible to reconstruct the historical conditions of a universal pragmatic that better suits the dialogue in which human essence and its potentialities will be better realized. These more human conditions are tested by the opportunities for developing the potentialities and the self-identity of women. However, in principle and in reality there are historical stages in which, given the current horizons of a particular system, there is no scope for more than one possibility for realizing women's essence or its distortion/perversion. In the current development in the Israeli system, within the framework of the present realm of self-evidence, the only open possibility is deconstruction of women's essence with no Utopian connected

Aufhebung, but with reproduction of the new mode disconnected from a foundation, essence, or goal. Postmodern discourse in the Israeli system is striving there, and the post-modern condition in the Israeli system makes the only rational way for the Israeli system.

Critical humanism rejects these dimensions of post-modernism and refuses the total deconstruction of women's essence and the parts of the dialogue which concern their historical production, local and diverse representations, distribution, and consumption—in light of their symbolic and material social context. The position suggested here demands that the female essence less passively represent current fashions and hegemonic dynamics and be more actively involved in the shaping of present reality. This moral imperative is ontologically derived from the concept of the dialogical existence of humanity in the world, as part of a concrete utopian obligation. This obligation is to the creation of new and more human modes of coexistence between men and women, between the historical moment and its utopian axis. Marx saw in men and women realizing non-repressive sexual relations the ultimate criterion for communism and the overcoming of the domination urge.[59] The liberation, realization, and development of potentialities that are invested in women's essence as anti-culture and the feminization of men are some of the central conditions for the Utopian fulfillment, namely life as art and the eroticization of world life, in Marcuse's thought.[60]

Here the issue at stake is the concrete social-cultural possibilities for such a change, its foundations, its *telos*, or the very possibility of having a non-contingent criterion for criticizing and evaluating the present. In each system a circular process necessarily reaffirms and reproduces the local manifestations of the realm of self-evidence, reproducing itself, its basic power relations, and its vital symbolic interactions. This is so since this is exactly what a system is for. In the present realm of self-evidence that the Israeli system reflects, the feminist movement is but a fragment of this existence, and challenging it is supposed to be the central element of feminism. Politically and theoretically, the question is raised as to what are the grounds for the demand for a liberation that is nothing but a new version of the same patriarchal, domination-oriented space that feminism is to transform or replace. Woman was traditionally the Other but not *the totally other* of the present culture and its realizations. *The totally other* remained transcendent and Utopian, and in its Objective Reason tradition, Western culture included the potential political possibility of negating the present and its treachery in the name of *the totally other*. In the new realm of self-evidence being constructed in our time, where there is no place for objective, transcendentalist, and universalistic concepts and criteria, and where there is no place for the Enlightenment's central concepts and radical speculative social critique, what might be the foundation, or at least the direction, for a humanistic feminist alternative?

The new, post-modern realm of self-evidence is not yet complete, and is, therefore, not yet completely closed. This is manifested by the relative openness of its systems, as they include vivid elements of the previous, modern realm of self-evidence. That is one of the reasons why in current Western culture, there are still revolutionary potentials that are relatively protected from daily power relations, as manifested in the soul and in tradition. Saying this does not amount to the claim that these germs are not a social-cultural construct that was historically developed. Given that in being, space and time merge, the argument made here is that the ontological dimension can be revealed only within the framework of historical horizons and concrete and diverse social contexts.

Three examples are suggested here to elaborate the critical potential still existing within the framework of the Enlightenment's humanist tradition. The first is connected to reason being the essential element of language and public discourse turning into a dialogue, as Habermas introduces it[61] in terms of Western democracies. The second is connected to the permanence of Western tradition, as various neo-conservatives understand it, from Ellen Bloom and David Hirsh to bourgeois liberal post-modernists like Richard Rorty. Finally, there is the uneasiness and the feeling of emptiness and alarm and fear that accompany current civilization's existence.

The permanence of the current realm of self-evidence reflects violent logic of traditional paternalism. It ensures the conditions for the fixation of women in space where, while being repressed, they protect their oppositional essence from the power relations, saving the potential and the ideal of a less repressive alternative, a more just and more human reality where love and solidarity are recognized and are accorded the proper place in the public sphere. Historically, it has to be said, the permanence of women's essence has exacted the price of even more efficient repression. In Western societies this is changing at the end of the twentieth century.

During this century, technological progress, the instrumentalization of knowledge, and the conceptual transformation have created major changes in local systems. This transformation of systems reflects the destruction of the modern realm of self-evidence. It facilitates the illusion of strong liberation or progress. For the first time in the history of Western societies, a real challenge to woman's essence and her human liberation potential has emerged. Within these conditions, new opportunities are opening for adjustment and integration in the main power struggles for women from the hegemonic groups. This is conditioned at the cost of their masculinization, that is, their functioning as "strong" and "successful" women. The essence of their masculinization is revealed in the term "muscle," which builds the masculine concept at the base of the only permitted way of life of the new woman. In positive Utopianism, there were visions of a synthesis between the "pleasure principle" and the "reality principle," a synthesis that Herbert Marcuse called "a new reality principle." Within this Utopia, humanity was to overcome the historical estrangement between culture and nature, the ought and the must, between male and female essences. In our time, it looks as if in the affluent groups of Western societies a reality is being constructed, one very similar to the Marxian Utopia of abolition of work and the Marcusian Utopian vision in which "the new reality principle" is realized. The annihilation of estrangement between essential female and male characteristics is not connected at all with the utopian synthesis; it is connected to the total collapse of the one and the all-penetrating power of the other. The masculine-domination logic is that of conquering the feminist alternative. This is but a reflection of the ways in which the *absence* of the utopian quest is manifested. In the absence of a Utopian axis and of a conceptual, and therefore also social-cultural, foundation, the very possibility of radical critique and democracy is being destroyed. What is conceived as the admirable liberation of women and successful entrance to the real power spaces is but a reflection of this evolution, which is just beginning. The feminization of the teaching profession is part of this evolution. Let us return to the Israeli system.

From an uncritical point of view, there is room for hope that the feminization of the teaching profession in Israel will contribute to social progress and will even contribute to the humanization of life at school and result in the reduction of aggressive aspects of schooling. From this point of view, there is also hope that woman's "voice"[62] will create in the much more feminist school arena a space for freer and more emancipatory development. Such a development should favor universal free evaluation and creation of knowledge, more of a dialogue, and better human relations at school. Such is the utopian vision of that kind of feminist pedagogy, that current historical conditions enable the struggle for its realization.[63] However, ontological conditions and historical developments create a fatal change in the stand of knowledge and invested potentialities in and around the practices and institutions of its production and distribution. It is naive and misleading to try to realize the nineteenth-century Utopian model in the context of present knowledge and in cultural conditions that sterilize the emancipatory potential of those utopias. Basically, these pedagogical utopias are sectorially oriented, and local, and not only anti-intellectual and anti-liberal, but even anti-libertarian.

One might have hoped that in Israel this process would give women the power that it has given feminists in some parts of the Western world, and would provide a new opportunity for feminist self-emancipation as part of a more general civic activism. Teachers as educators in Israeli schools could have been agents for real change, and the teaching profession could have become a counter-power focus politically, morally, aesthetically, and philosophically.

Yet these developments did not occur in Israel. At the present historical stage, such hopes of supporting women's liberation by using such potentialities of current power relations are doomed to fail. This is because the dehumanization process of society, which manifests itself through the all-penetrating logic of the market in the educational arena, the curriculum, the pedagogic practices, and school administration, is a process that by the same token has to demolish woman's "voice" and essence. It should be acknowledged that the feminization of the teaching profession in Israel does not promise liberation, but advanced manipulation under the logic of the Domination Principle. In the end, the common ground for major developments in woman's mobility within the Israeli system is the strengthening of existing dynamics and the Domination Principle.

The struggle for advancing toward an "ideal speech situation," about which Habermas speaks, includes the struggle for the formation of conditions and the challenging of threats and distortions of such a speech situation. As the major developments and central conditions of feminization of teaching in Israel demonstrate, we currently face the historical banishment of potential Israeli counter-education: the banishment of conditions for teachers' personality development as independent intellectual and social activists, with strong civic motivations and capacities, who educate and introduce possibilities of creating in school a kind of knowledge other than that introduced by the current Israeli culture industry. Today's Israeli teachers all manifest the advancement of the production of civic impotence and political neutrality, not to mention weakness and pessimism. To the degree that they show some strength, it is in the form of contrived optimism, manifesting the power to create truths, meanings, and collective consciousness. Namely, they act more or less effectively as repression agents in the service of the Israeli system. This is the same system that manipulates teachers and creates their false consciousness. Eventually, this is only one of the means by which the system reproduces itself. One of the manifestations of its strengths is to be seen in the teachers at schools, who have no interest even in this thesis, or any other thesis that refers to the essence of the change of knowledge and the current stand of teachers in Israeli society.

NOTES

1. Simon Leon. *Hebrew Education in Palestine*. London: The Zionist 1916, 1.
2. A. Ne'emann. "Hesegim vehasagot," *Sefer Hayovel Shel Histadrut Hamorim*. Tel Aviv (1902) 1955, 227, in: Ada Lumski-Feder and Reuven Kahane, *Dyucano Shel Hamore Bahevra Hayisraelit*, Jerusalem: Akademon 1988, 1 (Hebrew).
3. *Ibid.*, 3.
4. *Ibid.*
5. Simon Leon, *ibid.*, 1.
6. Simon Leon, *ibid.*, 12.
7. Ernst Simon. *Hamashber Batzionut Vehachinuch*. Jerusalem: Katon 1947, 36 (Hebrew).
8. Uri Ram. "Zionist historiography and the invention of modern Jewish nationhood: The case of Ben Zion Dinur," *History and Memory* 7: 1 (1995), 93.
9. Ilan Gur-Ze'ev. "Hama'avak al hashem—al yizuro shel hasubyekt hatziony besifere hageografia vehamoledet," *Davar*, 18.3.1994, 24 (Hebrew).
10. Plato. *Protagoras*. Oxford: Clarendon Press 1976.
11. Rachel Alboim-Dror. "Nashim bautopiot hatzioniot," *Kathedra* 66 (1990), 108 (Hebrew).
12. Michel Foucault. *Discipline and Punish; The Birth of the Prison*. Translated by Alan Sheridan, New York: Pantheon Books 1977.
13. Francis Bacon, "Nouvum Organum," in: *The Philosophical Works of Francis Bacon*, London: Routledge 1905, 259.
14. *Ibid.*
15. Gotthold Ephraim Lessing. *The Education of the Human Race*. Translated by F. M. Robinson, London: Anthroposophical Pub. C. 1927.
16. Imanuel Kant. *Perpetual Peace and Other Essays on Poitics, History, and Morals*. Translated by Ted Humphrey, Indianapolis and Cambridge: Bobbs-Merril Co. 1983.
17. Wilhelm von Humboldt. "Theorie der Bildung des Menschen," in: *Gesammelte Schriften*, I., Berlin 1968, 285.
18. Max Horkheimer. *Eclipse of Reason*. New York: Oxford University Press 1974, 6.
19. Ben Zion Dinur. *Arachim Uderachim—Beayot Chinuch Vetarbut Beisrael*, Tel Aviv: Urim 1958, 11-21 (Hebrew).
20. Juergen Habermas. "The public sphere," in: Steven Seidman (ed.), *Juergen Habermas on Society and Politics*. Boston: Beacon Press 1989, 236.
21. Pierre Bourdie and Jean-Claude Passeron. *Reproduction in Education, Society and Culture*. Translated by R. Nice, London: Sage 1977, 1-68.
22. Moshe Lifschitz. *Toldot Am Yisrael Badorot Ha'aharonim*, I. Tel Aviv: Or Am 1985, 60-72 (Hebrew).
23. Shlomo Horowitz. *Kitzur Toldot Yisrael Ba'et Ha'hadasha*, II. Haifa: Beit Hasefer Harealy 1977, 157 (Hebrew).
24. Ziegfrid Lehmann. *Ra'aion Vehagshama*. Tel Aviv: Tarbut Vehinuch 1962, 98 (Hebrew).
25. Edna Lumski-Feder and Reuven Kahane. *Dyukano Shel Hamore Bachevera Hayisraelit*. Jerusalem: Akademon 1c, 16c (Hebrew).

26 Ah'aron Bar-Adon. "Aa'imaot hameisdott' umenat helkan batehia ha'iverit behithavuta (1882-1914), in: *Lashon Veivrit* 3 (May 1990), 8 (Hebrew).
27 Alboim-Dror, *op. cit.*, 112.
28 Gur-Ze'ev, *op. cit.*, 24.
29 Lumski-Feder and Kahane, *ibid.*, 1c.
30 Yonathan Shapira. *Ilit Lelo Mamshichim.* Tel Aviv: Sifriat Hapoalim 1984, 66 (Hebrew).
31 *Ibid.*, 68.
32 *Ibid.*, 29.
33 *Ibid.*
34 Herbert Marcuse. *Eros and Civilization: A Philosophical Inquiry into Freud.* Boston: Beacon Press 1955, 129.
35 Sigmund Freud. *Civilization and its Discontents.* Translated by John Riviere, London: The Hograth Press 1968, 40.
36 Josephine. Donovan. *Feminist Theory.* New York: F. Ungar Pub. Co. 1991, 125.
37 A. Wellmer. "Reason, Utopia, and Enlightenment," in Richard Bernstein (ed.), *Habermas and Modernity.* Massachusetts: MIT Press 1985.
38 Jean Lyotard. *The Postmodern Condition: A Report on Knowledge.* Translated by F. Jamson, Manchester: Manchester University Press 1984, 47.
39 Halishka Hamercazit Lestatistika, *Shnaton Statisty Leyisrael*, 1994 (Hebrew).
40 D. Rabinovitz. "Maskilim o defukim," *Ha'aretz* (2.8.1995), 1b.
41 Majid Al-Haj. *Education, Empowerment, and Control: The Case of The Arabs in Israel.* Albany: State University of New York Press 1995.
42 The data were collected with the help of Dr. Nimer Ismair, a colleague and a friend to whom I am indebted.
43 Ilan Gur-Ze'ev. "The vocation of higher education: modern and postmodern rhetorics in the Israeli academia on strike," *Journal of Thought* 32: 2 (Summer 1997), 75-84.
44 Michael Feige and Louis Rudinger, "Tarbut hafreier vehazeut hayisraelit," *Alpayim: A Multidisciplinary Publication for Contemporary Thought and Literature*, 7 (1993), 118-136 (Hebrew).
45 Theodor Adorno. *Prisms.* Translated by Samuel and Shirry Weber, Boston: MIT Press 1981, 34.
46 Alan Bloom. *Giants and Dwarfs: Essays 1960-1990.* New York: Simon and Schuster 1990, 369.
47 Henry Giroux. *Teachers as Intellectuals.* New York: Bergin and Garvey 1988, 123.
48 *Ibid.*, 125-128.
49 Michel Apple. *Cultural and Economic Reproduction in Education.* London: Routledge and Kegan Paul 1982.
50 Ivan Illich. *Deschooling Society.* New York: Harper and Row 1971.
51 Rosemarie Tong. *Feminist Thought: A Comprehensive Introduction.* London: Unwin Hyman 1989, 224.
52 Lyotard, *op. cit.*
53 Max Horkheimer and Theodor Adorno. *Dialectic of Enlightenment.* Translated by John Cumming, New York: Herder and Herder 1972, 248.
54 Herbert Marcuse. *Negations; Essays in Critical Theory.* Translated by Jeremy Shapiro, Boston: Beacon Press 1968, 74.

55 Charles Taylor. *Multiculturalism and the Politics of Recognition.* New Jersey: Princeton Press, 32.
56 Ilan Gur-Ze'ev. *The Frankfurt School and the History of Pessimism.* Jerusalem: Magness Press 1996 (Hebrew).
57 Susan Brownmiller. *Against Our Will: Women and Rape.* New York: Simon and Schuster 1975. See also: Shulamith Firstone. *The Dialectic of Sex: The Case for Feminist Revolution.* London: J. Cape 1971.
58 William Tierney. *Building Communities of Difference: Higher Education in the Twenty-first Century,* Westport, CT: Bergin and Garvey 1993.
59 Karl Marx. *Early Texts.* Translated by David Mclelian, Oxford: Blackwell 1971.
60 Herbert Marcuse. *Eros and Civilization; op. cit.*
61 Juergen Habermas. *Der Philosophiche Diskurs der Moderne.* Frankfurt a.Main: Suhrkamp 1989, 433.
62 Caroll Gilligan. *In a Different Voice: Psychological Theory and Women's Development.* Cambridge: Harvard University Press 1982.
63 Sheila Ruth. *Issues in Feminism; An Introduction to Women's Studies.* Boston: Houghton Mifflin 1980, 15.

CHAPTER 6
The Vocation of Higher Education

The 1994 academic year in Israel was of great significance. For about three months all the universities in Israel were closed and all academic activitiy was paralyzed. Officially, the battle was fought over "the future of higher education in Israel," the stand of academics in Israeli society, and the place that the university occupies in Israeli society. Whether it was so or not, the context, if not the purpose and the content of this rhetoric, was to try and justify a 120 % rise in the Israeli academics' salaries.

This strike and its rhetoric gave rise to a rare public debate on the role of today's university in society and culture and the question of academic vocation or profession in the Israeli university. Since I consider these questions to be multicultural and historical-context oriented, I will consider the rhetoric of the academics on strike in light of the modern history of the university.

I intend to de-code some of the central symbols that were used by the mandarins of academia, and I will try to offer philosophical appreciation and a historical explanation for them. According to my thesis, in the study of the rhetorical manipulation practices of the Homo Academicus in Israel, we should not separate the symbolic battle from the political struggle, the text from its cultural and social contexts. The central problem here is the status of different discourses about knowledge.

Herewith two reconstructions will be presented: in the first one, the stand of scientific knowledge will be studied in the context of the producers of the scientific knowledge as part and parcel of the power apparatus and manipulations that produce the subjects that are supposed to use this knowledge but are not supposed to produce it. In the second reconstruction, the question of knowledge will appear in the context of the reproduction of Homo Academicus: the direct producers of knowledge and the eternal duplication of the academic apparatus. That is to say, the educational dimensions of the university as cultural reproduction, namely, an educational project.

I will analyze the rhetoric of the Israeli academics (synchronically and diachronically) in three categories: 1. Technocrats 2. Modernists 3. Post-modernists.

The academics' rhetoric played itself between two levels; on the first level, they demanded higher pay in the light of the liberal view, according to which the amount of one's deposit in his bank account symbolizes perfectly the market value and the use value of the commodity produced or distributed.

On the second level, they argued that their occupation is of a special kind in that it belongs to a privileged stand, beyond the daily power struggles. Accordingly, there is no way to judge the same judgment between the owners of knowledge and the simple players in the daily power struggles who use this knowledge (sometimes as "information"). Therefore, they argued, in order to symbolize the special status of pure knowledge (or metatheories, basic research, and so forth), there is a need to designate the permanent residents of the academic ivory tower in a manner that is uneven and unparalleled to their real political power as a pressure group in society striving for higher status and more political power and its economical benefits. Here, the main argument is based on the special stand of culture—and in it, the special stand of the erotic quest for *truth*—comparing technological progress, economic achievements, and social status that one can get from a styled and well-coded participation in the everyday social game of violence. One can uncover here the traditional Western arrogance as to the special stand of *praxis* compared to *poesis*, *vita contemplativa* compard to the *vita activa*. Of course, already in Plato's days the *Academia* as a realm for the quest for truth is also a political arena, but it is also a place in which its residents see themselves obliged to transcend themselves of it as a realm of self-evidence, which is also the place of social and symbolic power struggles that look for more and more power as their end. The Academia, as an ideal of a philosophical realm, is a special terra, an erotic locus for the quest for *aletheia* ("truth"), as concealment (Heidegger 1996, 130). For Plato, just in this place, where philosophy has the upper hand and develops a new praxis, there is a place for real *poesis*, and what we call today "technology." In the modern era, a separation developed between art and craft as using technology, "work" that gets an independent status as for the direct producers from the one side, and as for the special stand of praxis and its highest manifestation, philosophy, from the other side. In the postmodern discourse, I will try to show, parallel to the erosion in the traditional arrogance of Philosophy, the *poesis* swallows *praxis*, after its transformation to its opposite. This is crucial as to the concept of knowledge in general and especially as for the concept of academic knowledge and academic education.

In contrast to the postmodern vision, the modern concept of the division between high culture and popular culture follows the Greek concept of the supremacy of the moral-political activity of the farmer's or merchant's work. In its height, like in Marx's thought, we find the challenge of overcoming the division between intellectual creation and physical work—a kind of thought that denotes the centrality of this division on the humanistic tradition. Consequently, this concept has a special meaning for those whose main capital is the protecting, developing, and distributing of this knowledge and knowledge about knowledge (methodologies, traditions, epistemologies, and so on). As if these are not to be judged according to the criteria of the regular social power struggle, because there should not be a reduction of meta-knowledge and basic science to economic function and technological know-how and efficiency. Here is the substratum of the university mandarin arrogance, that, as living symbols, have been dead for so long. And yet, academia is one of the last strongholds of the Enlightenment and its defenders, while even there they have to protect themselvs from the postmodernist's attacks, from the one side, and from the technocratic-functionalist-pragmatist's threat, from the other side. No wonder that the striking academics were so confused as to the way they represented themselves in public—as "experts," or "the wise" intellectuals, "men of letters" who combine the praxis and poesis in their academic work ? The official images were distributed by a public relations office, and the academic image was sold like Coca-Cola drinks or jeans, fitting to candidates for the presidency.

This practice took place while many of them were becoming experts and technocrats. Their only exclusiveness lies in the fact that a central part of their work is practiced in academia, and nothing is in common between them and the idea of Vita Contemplativa, the Scholar idea, "Men of Letters" in the Geistreich, or a Scientist who is also an active and radical citizen of his community, a critic and re-evaluator of his cultural horizon and its traditions, who sees a great educational challenge in his/her academic practice as a vocation. But even so, they hold on to the rhetoric of modernism that views the status and other manifestations of cultural capital as disconnected and independent from their political weight. They pretend to see as self-understood that their positions and revenues should be undebatable, unchallenged like that of the supreme judges, the president or the chief of an archaic tribe, they pretend to still be what Max Weber called "Geistesaristokratie." But their public relations advisers did not tell them that an aristocracy does not go to battle for better salaries—at least not as an idea.

Like for the Greek philosophers and also for Kant, education was perceived as a practice of a human evasion from the jaws of brute nature and wild conditions (wildheit). "Maybe," he writes in *On Pedagogy*, "education will go on improving itself and every generation will advance, step by step, closer to the perfection of humanity. . . . it is exciting to imagine that human nature will be developed by education. . . . it opens for us a prospect of a vision of an happy humanity" (Kant, 1968, 13). This educational utopia was understood as conditioned by a moral solidarity and solidarity with all mankind (Kant, 1968, 22). Therefore, it had a revolutionary potential, a political project. This Kantian educational concept was a paradigmatic one for the Enlightenment. There is still no division here between "Giest" (the real spirit) and the scientific practice, between the philosopher and the scientist, between science and ethics, between the quest for truth and the social obligation. But as the critical dimension of the new philosophy started to apply its critical eros against itself and not just against tradition—its retreat from science started, then science started to be more and more dynamic and its system was reduced to specific and independent research programs.

Since the mid-19th century, academic work was starting to be evaluated less and less from the metaphysical view and the quest for truth; more and more it was evaluated by the standard of its contribution and relevance to technological advances and the pretension of its relevance to be utilized by the hegemonic social group's interests. As a byproduct, the status of the academic started to change: The ideal of the scholar, that its origin was in the absolutist era or even before, was exchanged with the ideal of the professional, the expert.

In the beginning of this century, Max Weber still could compare the vocation of the scientist in the academia to the emancipational-educational mission of the philosopher in Plato's *The Republic*, who was obliged to emancipate those kept prisoner in the darkness of the cave (Weber, 1930, 91). But Weber already was aware that while for the Enlightenment, science's image serves as an erotic way to emancipate man from religion and prejudice, in light of the technological and social developments of the late 19th century, people look for shelter from the scientific "freeze" and rationality. In the 20th century, science is no longer conceived of as a sure way to happiness (Weber, 1930, 21) and scientific work becomes a job, work as any other work. Weber was lecturing this thesis in the time of an end of the academic world of yesterday and before the definitive victory of the new era and the new politics of knowledge; the lecture was presented to the poetic revolutionaries like Gustav Landauer and Kurt Eisner in Muenchen, people who could have hoped to realize an anti-instrumental obligation to science, that in their mind should have and could have been turned to serve the "real interests" of free men and women, science as vocation, pacified praxis-poesis.

After that, not just the Soviet in Muenchen was defeated, but the very substratum of the utopia aroused. Today we turn back to this question as a translator's problem: How should one translate Weber's lecture/text "Wissenschaft als Beruf"—to mean science as a profession or science as a vocation?

Today there is no way to imagine science as vocation; this option is open either as an insane rambling or as an ironic gesture or as an unsophisticated manipulative rhetoric that looks for "more and more" power. That is so, as Raymond Aron wrote already in the fifties, "even those who yesterday could have been man of culture today turn to be a kind of experts; that is, for them science is not a vocation, but a profession" (Aron, 1962, 298). Parallel to this evolution, knowledge and its representations in the West are changing according to and as part of the cultural, social, and economic developments; knowledge turns to become information, and the place of traditional (speculative) thought is taken over by calculations and calculators. The centrality of the shift can be recognized not so much in the instrumental level as in the instrumentalization of thought itself and the human psyche that in the post-industrial era in the West is involved in a dramatic mutation worked out by its own victims. Here a special role is reserved for the development of the electronic communication system in the last two decades: A system whose objectives are the search for, storage of, production and distribution of information and information about information. I do not use here the term, "knowledge," and knowledge about information because in this context, there is no place for archaic ideals and terms, such as "knowledge," "truth," or "justice," but relevant and functional terms that are reducible to quantitative functions, such as "effectiveness," "expensive," and so forth.

> The nature of knowledge cannot survive unchanged within this context of general transformation. It can fit into the new channels, and become operational, only if learning is translated into quantities of information. We can predict that anything in the constituted body of knowledge that is not translatable in this way will be abandoned and that the direction of new research will be directed by the possibility of its eventual results being translatable into computer language. . . . along with the hegemony of computers comes a certain logic, and therefore a certain set of prescriptions determining which statements are accepted as "knowledge" statements. (Lyotard, 1991, 4)

In the second half of the 19th century, academic knowledge still was founded on a unified and coherent concept of knowledge. There was still a central role to the quest for "Bildung" and the cultural mandarins that were supposed to hold, protect, and advance "Bildung" were ensured a special status in society as supreme representatives of culture. In this era it is impossible to distinguish between the educational concept of "Bildung" and a certain concept of culture (Kultur) and the educational vocation of the university and its staff. This is well exemplified by John Henry Newman, who wrote in 1852 that the university is the supreme power that protects all knowledge and science, facts and principals (Newman, 1959, 135). In Germany, the prestigious stand of the

Homo Academicus was constituted in their special place in a special historical moment, when the traditional status of aristocracy had already vanished and the status of the businessman, in the American sense, was not yet firmly established (Ringer, 1969, 7).

This romantic image of knowledge and the cultural and social status of the academics who were attached to it has dramatically changed in the late 19th century. This turn has to be seen in light of the cultural, social, and economic developements of the period. In the 20th century, a differentiation has developed between the representation of the different bodies of knowledge, on one side, and the general change in the social stand of the academic, on the other side. A rapid erosion started of the unity of the self-evidence of the culture that in it, the academic elite had a special role alongside great outsiders as artists.

Parallel to these trends, inside academia dramatic changes were taking place when philosophy was gradually losing the supreme rule as the only legitimate interpreter of science's findings and as the irreplaceable guide of science and its goals. Research was fragmented into independent, private, professional activities which do not gather into a coherent whole (MacIntyre, 1990, 216). In 1953, when Martin Buber lectured in the Hebrew University, he said,

> 55 years ago, when I studied in the University of Liepzig, it was a kind of a natural completion of the work in the psychological lab of Wondt that I will take a biology course and to both of them I will add lesson in the psychiatric clinic. It did not wonder me at all that in the terminal exam in philosophy I was asked about the experiments that were taking place in the eggs of a certain marine creature. Today almost nothing is left of that kind of cooperation between the disciplines. The university of our days is no more a real "Universitas Literatum" since there is no more organic link between the different sciences and this is just one side of the same phenomenon, that today the university is no more "Universitas Magistrorum et Scolarium." This is so, since there is no more the partnership and collaboration of life and a quest between teachers and pupils that in past times gave the universities their glorious spirit. Even general education, that gives a general perspective of humanity, is eroding into different and unconnected bodies of knowledge. (Buber, 1984, 421-422)

Today this evolution comes finally to its end. It is supposed, even by the great humanists of our generation like Juergen Habermas, that in today's universities, there is no place for a general scientific perspective (Habermas, 1969, 57) and not even for a pretension to a cultural-moral-professional education or a protest or a "great refusal," a protest or critique by the intellectual, such that was so typical to the humanist tradition and the concepts of "Bildung," "Kultur," and their social obligations.

The Vocation of Higher Education 163

> Today the intellectuals are dying out since in the current praxis, there is no more need in their work, there is no use in their work, and their fate is that of the creatures and parts of animals of paleontologic times that did not succeed to adjust to their environment (Adorno, 1993, 266).

Alongside the development in which gradually classics and humanities were decentered to the margins of academic importance and relevance by the "practical" disciplines, today the victory march of Instrumental Rationality enters even the strongholds of the most excited and pious of natural scientists and other "practical" bodies of knowledge. Gradually, step by step, bigger and bigger parts of today's most practical and easily applicable bodies of knowledge are departing today from the university into semi-private institutions that serve or are controlled by multinational giant firms. Here the criteria for the pay of the staff are totally different from those that are relevant to the scientists who hold on to the university as an institution and academia as an idea, scientists who are exiled in the university with their total but unreflective devotion to the system of ideologies that serves and reflects the demands of technological progress but is not yet explicit and direct.

The post-modernists are attacking the modern Western structured university from the von Humboldt's style because of science's remnant metaphysical pretensions to truth and the terror of the philosophical shadow in academia (Derrida, 1986, 66). We can find special interest in Jacques Derrida's stand that wanted to "displace and to question the dominant model," a stand that materialized as an alternative university (with other French intellectuals), the "College International de Philosophy." From the post-modern point of view, the modernist model appears as a goal-oriented (Derrida, 1986, 66) technocratic reality that is opposing "fundamental" research which is not programmed as something to be used by state or civil society—medicine, army, industry and so on" (Derrida, 67).

Derrida attacks the current structure of the university and its dominant trends, not because the university of today gave up modernistic pretensions and obligations, but vice-versa—just because of the remnants of the Enlightenment's ideology in today's Western (most prestigious) universities. Therefore, it was of utmost importance for him to posit the post-modern alternative to the imperialistic trend inherent in the modernistic project (and the university as part of it) and its imminent striving for power that accompanies its scientific-philosophical quest and pretensions for universal truth and objectivity that comes to its supreme realization in technology. The institutionalization of the post-modern academic alternative to its modern Humboldtian model might be understood also as an improved modern project; a project in which the mission of the violent overtaking of the modernistic arrogance about the truth (or the legitimate way to realize the quest for truth or "objective findings of research" and so on) is in a fascinating dialectical confrontation with the Humboldtian pretension to truth and transcendence from everyday social power struggles in the Humboldtian-modeled modern university as an institutionalization of the scientific-philosophical pretension to real knowledge.

Lyotard ends the "foreword" to his *The Postmodern Condition* in an evaluation of "this post-modern moment that finds the university nearing what may be its end, while the Institute may just be beginning" (Lyotard, 1991, xxv). He concludes with a post-modern Utopia, an alternative to the modernist-oriented Utopias of the sixties and seventies of this century, an alternative Utopia about the acquisition, storage, and distribution of knowlege in a society that has new ethical formations and new moral horizons. "This sketches the outline of a politics that would respect both the desire for justice and the desire for the unknown" (Lyotard, 1991, 67).

The academic Utopia of another post-modernist, William G. Tierney, tries to combine the political activism of the Critical Theory orientation with Lyotard's and the post-modernistic obligation toward the difference in general. Central to Tierney's project is the recognition of instability and mutational—unpredicted and un-evaluated immanent fragmentation of reality that is to be understood as "reality," hyperreality. This concerns essences in general and sexual identities too. Therefore, he is for indefinite, non-monolithic sexual and cultural identities (Tierney, 1993, 63).

In new, alternative, post-modern academia he sees an important contribution to the overcoming of the class, cultural and sexual Others that are oppressed by their Western, modernist objective-truth seekers and his ideal academia is supposed to be a de-construction of their norms, ideals, and knowledge concept; Lesbian women, homosexuals, African-Americans, and other "Others" are supposed to become autonomous speech-communities in this post-modern Utopia (Tierney, 1993, 62), where love (agape) will flourish. The liberated academic is here supposed to be liberated from his old national tradition, like in the modernist Utopias, liberated men and women are supposed to become cosmopolitan citizens, and their educational mission will be the advancement of "cultural citizenship" (Tierney, 1993, 141) instead of a national citizenship. Here, in this post-modern Utopia, they will be liberated from *any* "identity" and their academic project will be liberated from any telos or even "a meaning" whatsoever, that always realizes itself in and as part of a "meta-narrative" that Tierney, as other conservative post-modernists, is obliged to deconstruct. The institutionalization of Tierney's conclusions obliges a different academia for lesbians, people of color, and other cultural "minorities" and others who will represent their own knowledge, different concepts about knowledge, different concepts about concepts of knowledge (meta-theories concerning their knowledge), different internal regulations in discourses that produce knowledge as a condition to a dialogue ("real dialogue"?), as an alternative to Western, modernistic concepts of phalogocentric dialogue, knowledge and the place of academia in (dominant) society. Here "anything goes," and there is no reason to attach a special importance to one meaning or value over others (Burbules, 1991, 396).

The postmodernistic conceptions of an alternative to the modern university vary, of course, but they are united in rejecting the modern, Humboldtian approach.

Humboldt, who formulated his concept of university in the beginning of the 19th century, was manifesting the optimism of the Enlightenment as a project and its educational pretensions (Habermas, 1969, 53). Likewise for Kant and Schiller, the modern university was supposed to be a realization of the ideal *Universitas*, a community. The Western, modern universiy was supposed to become an Academia: a common locus for common study and research among teachers and students, total freedom for research and rigorous obligation toward the students and academic standards and values. The university was supposed to be an erotic realm with Utopian visions toward knowledge: an academic free realm, where there is no conflict between Bildung and Kultur, where research is realized with no restraints whatsoever and with a social solidarity and obligations. There was a coherent image of scientific knowledge that united the "self" with "the world." Here there is a vision of no less than a "unification of [general] knowledge, wisdom and 'the good'" (von Humboldt, 1968, I., 284). Here the concept of science is that of a vocation (Beruf) and not that of science as a profession. Science as a vocation in Humboldt's thought, and in the thought of the Enlightenment's thinkers in general, was that which "constitutes the spirit" (von Humboldt, 1968, III., 220) parallel to its educating and constituting "personality," that their co-existence enables self-construction of the autonomous subject in a society in which science has universal emancipatory mission.

Approaching the end of the 20th century, an era that from different orientations and interests got the name of "post-industrial," "third wave," or "post-modern" era, the instrumentalization process of knowledge and knowledge's image has come to its peak, a state in which "people are but an 'Abfall' [useless reminder] of the machine" (Adorno, 1993, 275). In our era, we are witnessing a rapid qualitative change in knowledges and knowledge's images' stand and in its distribution strategies in light of the general technological, social, and cultural changes in the West. Parallel to these phenomena is the dramatic change in the concept of the subject, that turned out to be "one-dimensional" in Herbert Marcuse's terms. In this reality, a new kind of rationality is present, "an unrational rationality," in the terms of Adorno and Horkheimer. Foucault's and Derrida's (pessimistic) concept of "the end of man" is but a development of this perception of today's reality. Foucault, as a declared anti-humanist, witnessed himself in his great debt to Adorno, Horkheimer,and Marcuse, the great critics of modernism and Enlightenment who saw themselves as the last true diffenders of humanism who's Critical Theory is nothing but a humanist sruggle for the sake of whatever still remains of Enlightenment's tradition (Foucault, 1988, 26).

Since the Cartesian era in the West, a belief emerged not just in rationality but in universality, that in principle was supposed to be shared by all the human race. Here is the base for the academic educational pretension to produce and distribute knowledge that will formulate and discover universal truths for the benefit of all mankind. In the Enlightenment's concept of knowledge a special place is occupied by the call for the liberation of the oppressed, who are deprived of the chance of participating in the scientific adventure and its technological and economic fruits. Here, technological advancement is still understood as being supposed to be obliged to rationality and serve the needs of (rational and free) people. Today, the university takes part in the process of manipulating mankind to live, think, work, and struggle for the sake of technological progress and its autonomous needs.

Electronic communication, digital information production and transfer, information storage and its retrieval, are parts of an economic order that is not "open" and democratic like some of the technocrats and modernists want us to believe. Today in the West, control comes not just from the outside, as a manifestation of a "bad" attitude of a person, group, or class, but rather its utmost manifestation and power base is in the subject's inside, as part of his internal constitution.

The autonomous subject—as an idea and as a reality—that in Western culture could struggle in the nineteenth century for the realization of the idea, not just in the Western world, but as a global emancipatory (patronizing and oppressive) project, has already lost all its cultural relevance in the West. Culture itself has changed in Western society and images of (relevant) knowledge have changed. As part of this evolution, the place of the Homo Academicus has changed dramatically: The university has even lost its special stand as part of the production, duplication, and representation apparatus while science has become ideological and political. This trend has important implications for the "third world" humanists who struggle against internal and Western oppression in their societies. Under present conditions, can they offer an alternative that will be parallel to, if not part of, what "we" call the Enlightenment project?

In Israel this development also includes a drastic change in the special stand of knowledge, men of letters and education in Jewish tradition. This is the historical moment and cultural place where the rhetoric of the academics in Israel is functioning and in which it is being evaluated here.

On the instrumental level, an argument is brought up by the technocrats in the universities, according to which knowledge that is today produced, reproduced, and distributed in the academic realm, knowledge that is an applicable one by its nature—and therefore isn't higher than its market value—is the base, the ground for technological advancement and its specific applications like overcoming our Arab enemies and elevating the living standard of the general (Jewish) population.

In the rhetoric of Baje, a professor for administration and business in Tel-Aviv University, the aim of the strike is nothing but "to protect scientific and technological supremacy" over the neighboring nations and as a manifestation of loyalty to "the idea of Zionism" and "high living standard" (Baje, 1994, 1c). For Moshe Many, the former president of Tel-Aviv University, the academia is considered to function as a greenhouse for cultivation of the technologies needed by the army; therefore, the enemies of the striking staff are considered as nothing less than traitors. "Whoever harms the university is considered by me as a traitor" (Many, 1994, 2a). These are extreme manifestations of the instrumentalization of knowledge, that is evaluated in a diametrically opposite way to that of the 19th century modernism of Kant and von Humboldt's Utopia. The usual argument of the Israeli technocrats in academia, on this rhetorical level, is that academia is the locus for the production and distribution of the relevant knowledge for our civilization, knowledge that, to my mind, is reducible to technologies of controlling and oppressing nature and people, production of merchandise, and efficient manufacturing, distributing, and advertising of the culture industry and Israeli nationalism which is one of its local products. From this point of view, academia is nothing but one of the picks of everyday life that is dictated in our era by Thanatos. Some of the post-modernists, like Baudrillard, are ontologizing this coexistence and make it into one of basic concepts in their philosophical pessimism (Baudrillard, 1993, 149-151). The ego strives to function as Instrumental Rationality's foundation, as directed by Thanatos, the death strive that is manifested in the imminent violence of technological progress. "It looks as if the pleasure strive stands to serve the death strives" (Freud, 1988, IV., 137). The Israeli culture is a violent manifestation of this concept while stiving to control the representation apparatuses which will ensure the reception of an essentially different concept of its realities.

In the margins of the technocrat's rhetoric, we could also hear another kind of rhetoric, a rhetoric that also demands higher pay for the academics in the university, but as condition for the future of the ongoing discourse of humanity and the transformation and development of modern science. This is the Israeli humanist rhetoric that was quite dominant in and around the strike. This rhetoric reproduced Humboldt's and Newman's concept of the university and the implicit connection between Bildung and Kultur. This is the case, for example, in the articles of Ze'ev Sterenhel, one of Israel outstanding humanists, who dominates the humanist's discourse in Israel (Sterenhel, 1994, 4b), in the articles and interviews of Marsello Daskal, and those of Iron Ezrahi.

Ezrahi argues in a way that might be shared by conservatives who look for nothing but a flourishing capitalistic economy and "democratic" law and order. This is a stand according to which

> science is the modern and renovative engine of society and societies that are incapable of cultivating advanced scientific communities are marginalized to the edges of the international community and are made dependent on the scientific, educational and cultural centers that are outside. (Ezrahi, 1994, 4b)

Implicit here is the argument that higher pay for the academics is synonymous with the support of greater research opportunities for the university and at the same time is also a strengthening of the culture and its independence from social power games and foreign interests. Like Sterenhel, Ezrahi also emphasizes the academic dimension in its universal context: the struggle that goes on is for the possibility of a future free and open humanistic discourse in this world, a discourse that is supposed to be founded on academic freedom, which also produces standards for rational decisions between competing arguments that claim for validity. Implicit here is the concept that the struggle is for the future possibilities of the spirit ("Geist") by the protection of higher education and especially, the humanities as Bildung, the eternal arch-enemy of conservatism and repression. Both education and freedom are the foundations of democracy, and so the struggle for higher pay for the academics in the university is supposed to crystalize a heroic defense of the very possibility of future democracy and an open and free discourse in the best modernistic fashion.

The post-modernists in Israeli academia attack the stand of the modernistic position of those academics who see in the strike a struggle on behalf of the Enlightenment's tradition against conservatism and repression, and the modernist stand is represented as a repressive-conservative stand.

A special role was played in this rhetorical debate by Henry Wasermann from The Open University. He combined his attack on Sterenhel's stand in the strike and his crusade against the translation to Hebrew of a French Nazi writer, Selin, and his view of postmodernism as a sure way to fascism (Wassermann, 1994, 4b).

According to Wassermann, the typical modernistic arrogance of Sterenhel was manifested not only in his claim to be a just cultural censor, but also in his fierce defense of the interests and arguments of the strikers in academia. Of course, if Wassermann would have been more coherent as a postmodernist, he would have been forced to say that principally, he cannot pretend to be more correct as a postmodernist than a real modernist, and there is no way but a sophist, rhetorically based preference for his arguments over those of Sterenhel.

Adi Offir, a leading figure in the postmodern discourse in the Israeli academia and local culture, was quick to notate the naiveté of Israeli academics that their rhetoric represented them as if they really believe they are part of the Israeli elite, as part of "the crisis in the organization of Western postmodern knowledge" (Offir, 1994, 28). According to Offir, the duration of the strike should not be explained as a manifestation of their strength but as a reflection of Western academics in general—that they do not have much to lose and as a partial manifestation of academics' disconection with actual social and cultural discourse. This strike was a good example for a reflection on the scale of academics' disconnectedness and their cultural impotence; the knowledge they produce and their language has no relevance to the actual cultural discourse. "Mediocratic academia is a perfect instrument for maintaining the existing social order, and conservative social order as ours is a guarantee of the permanency of a mediocratic university" (Offir, 1994, 29). Offir regrets Israeli universities are not a locus of opposition and protest that can offer a new cultural discourse (Offir, 1994, 29). But Offir, the postmodernist—as Israel's academic modernists and Israel's leftists in general—does not develop this crucial issue as well as the general cultural situation in the West, according to which historically, there is no possibility for academia as a place of producing social criticism, refusal, and a new, different, cultural discourse.

Both the modernistic and the humanist-modernistic rhetorics of Israeli academics in the strike manifested to what extent Israeli academia did not become sanctury for cultural and social struggle and become irrelevant for utopical eros. Richard Rorty "is glad there are such sancturies" (Rorty, 1994, 20) in American colleges and universities but he regrets the American "left" is not more "broadly based, less self-involved and less jargon-ridden than our present one." In contrast to the Israeli academics' self image, Rorty represents American academia as relevant to the local cultural discourse and social critic. I believe the main difference is not in the nature of the Israeli academia, rather in the uncritical nature of Rorty's position.

I will offer a position which challenges that of the technocrats and which is located between that of the modernists and the postmodernists. I argue that in order to defend Enlightenment's ideals one should take very seriously the postmodernist critics on the modernist concept of knowledge and university images. Here I will try to evaluate some of the "romantic" knowledge images that were dominant in the modernistic rhetoric of the humanist defenders of the Israeli university.

According to Bourdiue, the university's field [and the academics therein reflect the power structure, while its function, selection, and indoctrination actively contribute to the reproduction of this same structure (Bourdieu, 1988, 41)]. From this point of view, in contrast to Offir's analysis of the Israeli academia on strike, it turns out to be that the Academia is very much relevant to the local culture, its production, reproduction, and distribution—as a repressive apparatus; the university is one of the main production apparatus of the control and repression apparatus. Today's university in Israel—and in the West in general—is a central production center for passions, specific bodies of knowledge, and useful political manipulation strategies that also include the production of the subject, that is, the sum total of passions, symbols, and consciousness that activates a person in the service of the self-reproduction of the system that he is thrown into. The knowledge that we speak about here is that of the overcoming of the subject's defense maneuvers and the tactics of breaking away from the control of the system. At its best, today the university offers the students, or at least pretends to offer them, opportunities to become residents of their traditions through meta-narratives in which the relevant symbols get their meanings. While they are producing in the university penetration practices of symbolic systems and more efficient modes of using knowledge, the aim is the production of the "normal"—conformist, cooperative—subject, his telos, and the strategies of gaining knowledge that enable establishing and legitimating the possibilities which are made to be open for the subject in the current self-evidence realm; that is to say, the production of the subject as an object for manipulation, the manipulation of the "autonomous subject" which is produced as part of a repressive system.

Some of the academics are very well aware of this dimension of academic work. Ironically enough they are more outspoken in the technocratic rhetoric then in the postmodernistic rhetoric in the Israeli academia at strike. As real positivists, they implicitly claim that if it is so, then it is only a legitimate act to demand that the "experts" who devote their lives to justifying, reproducing, and advancing the current power games in the society will translate their power into economic gains, political power, and symbols of higher social status. This is so in the name of Francis Bacon's 17th century scientific ideology according to which "science is power," that no one can doubt after Auschwitz and Hiroshima.

Both armies of Israeli modernists—the technocrats in the Israeli academy and to a lesser degree also the humanists of the Israeli university, argued—for the justification of a higher pay demand—parallel special stand of academic activity. This argument did not declare academic knowledge as "different" from practical practices and information, but vice-versa: knowledge that is produced and distributed in the university was first of all represented as of a great value to everyday life, as easily reducible to production, distribution, and purchasing practices.

Confronting the strike's results, parallel to the fast erosion of the arrogant academic claim for the quest of truth and universal happiness that traditionally was connected to it in the modernistic tradition, the obligation for social solidarity is eroding even faster. They gave their share of the instrumentalization of knowledge and knowledge's images in our society and brought it to an additional erosion in the cultural status of the Israeli academics.

The strike helped to push the university—while the university did not need any help since for so long it has been part of the culture industry—to the game of social power apparatus, especially to crystalize this trend. Now, more then ever, it is harder to keep alive, in an un-neurotic manner, the modernistic claim that the university is a locus of "otherness," the "Geistesreich" for "Men of letters," and the locus of the idea of truth and higher education as part of a universal social utopia and cultural redemption.

The three rhetorics of the strikers: the modernistic, the technocratic, and the post-modernistic have important implications and are relevant not just to the aim and possibilities of higher education in Israel.

All three rhetorics are manifesting that the Instrumental Rationality is victorious. This is an easy conclusion for the technocratic ideology which strives for power, efficiency, and pleasure.

The importance of the analysis of the strikers' rhetorics is by manifesting to what degree in academia today modernistic and postmodernistic ideologies are serving the same instrumental, spiritless trend.

The representatives of the academics in the Israeli strike of the university did not separate between the three levels of argumentation, and the bottom line is, that all three rhetorics were driven to the same economic, violent, instrumentalist vision that did not separate between practical knowledge (in the sense of *poesis*) and its use and basic science (in the sense of *poesis*), between traditionalism and rigid academic worship and erotic striving for freedom and truth in academia and its context, a striving that can take place in the old academic traditions and in the struggle against them, but not in the postmodern version.

The post-modern view of multicultural, equally legitimate narratives that struggle for local knowledge and different but equally legitimate strategies of representations of knowledge and images of knowledge is in an ever-fragmented processs with no love of "the good and the beautiful" —truth—and with no emancipatory project of liberating humanity, different societies, their traditions, and knowledge. As Tierney and other post-modernists show, the deconstruction of universal categories like "humankind," "love of truth," "women," and the ideal of "Academia," leads in the first step to ideals such as "African-American woman's knowledge" and special academies to develop and represent the difference between different cultural fields. In the second step it leads to the deconstruction of the very categories as "deconstruction," "knowledge," "emancipation," and "woman."

For Tierney, this is not a problem at all, since he is against one, permanent, stable, monolithic identity in sexuality as in any other field of human experience, for personalities as for academies. As for me, I can see in this postmodernistic analysis of the current state of higher education and in its alternative, an expected cooperation with the instrumental-positivistic tendencies. Both give up love of truth and the idea of an emancipated "Humanity," where different cultures and different representations of knowledge will be legitimate in an open, public, equal, and rational dialogue. We, all of us, have to be part of this dialogue that is possible if we can see as relevant the idea of Autonomous Subject and the possibilities of its realization. With no Autonomous Subject, there is no place and no partner for a dialogue because "love of truth," as love, has to be shared by equal partners or it is not a true love, not a real dialogue, and there is no chance for liberation.

The giving up of this tradition in post-industrial societies, or in "the post-modern era," opens the door for the tyranny of power of the convention that has many faces; the Instrumental Rationality can offer prosperity but not justice, pleasure but not happiness, technological progress but not wisdom, "freedom" but not freedom, objectives but not vocationalism and meaning.

In contrast to all of the modernistic academics and some of their post-modern colleagues in Israel that their rhetoric was analysed here I would like to argue that in Israel today, as in typical Western universities, there is no place in the Israeli universities for any of these hopes. But there is also no place in the Israeli universities for traditional Jewish love of truth, and, therefore, there is no striving for justice. These concepts and eros are still very much alive in the traditional Jewish *Yeshiva*, a total different kind of "academy."

The Enlightenment's experience in Judaism, to combine the traditional Jewish quest for truth and justice and love with Western humanistic "Bildung," has failed. Today we witness in Israel a total apartheid between the Yeshiva and the university, the quest for love and truth and the quest for instrumental-practical information that anachronistically is still called "knowledge." From a political point of view, in the Yeshiva of today it is not that the quest for truth is disconnected from the practical, political world—even the quest for love here is the love of God and, to a lesser degree, the love of Man, if he is a Jew.

We, Jews in Israel, have to revitalize humanistic Judaism like that of Herman Cohen, Albert Einstein, Martin Buber, and Max Horkheimer. This is our duty as Jews, as human beings, as humanists, as educators. The questions now are: "Can we contribute to the revival and development of Enlightenment's ideals in higher education in the present condition of the universities?" "Can we ignore the utopian visions of yesterday's Enlightenment concept of higher education as vocation and its revolutionary implications as political praxis?" "Can we ignore that social structures, political possibilities, and cultural tendencies in the West, such that they constitute this educational vocation of the Enlightenment, are totally irrelevant to today's condition?"

My answer is negative: This used to be the vocation of higher education in the modernistic West—at least as a regulative idea, a utopia that today has no place, since there is no relevance for utopia and meta-narrative in the postmodernistic West. It is part of liberation from their arrogance and their legitimation for violence of suppressing the voice of the Other, a liberation that includes also deconstruction of "position,"" tradition," and quest for the "truth," "justice," and "beauty," as well as "autonomous subject," "meaning," and "vocation."

And yet, deep in the basement of the Israeli university, the idea of academia and the Socratic eros for truth, justice, and beauty are still alive, as the Jew in exile/or in the *Yeshiva*/or in his powerful state, exiled from his Jewishness as exiled in history until universal redemption and overcoming of history. In Israel, as in "the West," maybe they are waiting for their awakening by Third World humanists, fundamentalists or post-colonialists, as part of a new revival, in higher education. The September 2001 attacks on the New York World Trade Center signal this openness and its new possibilities.

BIBLIOGRAPHY

Adorno, Theodor. *Myvhar Askolat Frankfurt*. Tel Aviv: Po'alim, 1993 (Hebrew).
Aron, Raymond. *The Opium of the Intellectuals*. New York: W. W. Norton, 1962.
Baje, Avra'am. "Heshbonot ketanim beshvita gedola," *Ha'aretz*, (8. 3. 1994).
Baudrillard, Jean. *The Transparency of Evil: Essays on Extreme Phenomena*. Translated by J. Benedict. London and New York: Verso, 1993.
Boirdiue, Pierre. *Homo Academicus*. Cambridge: Cambridge University Press, 1988.
Bourdiue, Pierre, and Passeron, Jean-Claude. *Reproduction in Education, Society and Culture*. London: Sage Publications, 1978.
Buber, Martin. *Teuda Viyeud*, II., Jerusalem: Hasifria Hatzionit, 1984 (Hebrew).
Burbules, Nicholas, and Rice, Susanne. "Dialogue across Differences: Continuing the Conversation," *Harvard Educational Review* 61, 4 (November 1991), 393-416.
Daskal, Marcello, "Mi Zarich Professorim?" *Ha'aretz* (11.2. 1994).
Derrida, Jacques. "On Colleges and Philosophy," *Postmodernism: Ica Documents*, London: Institute of Contemporary Art 1986, 4.
Ezrachi, Yaron. "A society which insists on going backwards," *Ha'aretz* (28.1.1994), 46 (in Hebrew).
Foucault, Michel. *Politics, Philosophy, Culture*. New York: Routledge, 1988.
Habermas, Juergen. *Protestbewegung und Hochschulreform*. Frankfurt a.M.: Suhrkamp, 1969.
Heidegger, Martin. "On the Essence of Truth," *Basic Writings*. London: Routledge 1996, 115-138.
Kant, Imanuel. "Ueber Pedagogik," *Bildungsphilosophie*, II. Frankfurt a.M: Akademische Verlagsgesellschaft, 1968.
Lyotard, J. F. *The Postmodern Condition*. Manchester: Manchester University Press 1991.
MacIntyre, Alasdair. *Three Rival Versions of Moral Enquiry*. Indiana: University of Notre Dame Press, 1990.
Many, M. "Mi shepogea bauniversitaot hu boged," *Ha'aretz* (21.3.1994)
Newman, C. J. *The Idea of a University*. New York: Holt, Rinehart and Winston, 1959.
Offir, Adi. "Zo lo universita, zo haltura," *Shishi* (3.5.1994).
Ringer, Fritz. *The Decline of the German Mandarins*. Cambridge: Harvard University Press, 1969.
Rorty, Richard. "The Unpatriotic Academy," *The New York Times Op-Ed*, (13.2.1994).
Sterenhel, Ze'ev. "Nemerim shel neyar," *Ha'aretz* (28.1.1994).

Tierney, William. *Building Communities of Difference—Higher Education in the Twenty-First Century.* Westpoint: Bergin and Garvey, 1993.

Von Humboldt, Wilhelm. "Antritsrede in der Berliner Akademie der Wissenschaften," *Gesammelte Schriften*, III. Berlin: 1968.

Von Humboldt, Wilhelm. "Theorie der Bildung des Menschen," *Gesammelte Schriften*, I. Berlin: 1968.

Wassermann, Henry. "A Doubtful Assertion," *Ha'aretz* (23. 2. 1994), 46 (in Hebrew).

Weber, Max. *Wissenschaft als Beruf.* Muenchen und Leipzig: Duncker und Humboldt, 1930.

CHAPTER 7
Multiculturalism and Education in Israel

As in the case of other versions of normalizing education, which is devoted to the construction of collectives and the reproduction of their realm of self-evidence, the destruction of diversity and the negation of the external and internal Other was traditionally a central target for Zionist education. Now, after four generations, the origins are disclosed of the symbolic violence of Zionist normalizing education, which enhanced the commitment to Israel, knowledge, and the successful realization of the Zionist secular project on its two fronts. On these two fronts Zionist normalizing education was committed to a successful "external" and "internal" *colonization* of the Jewish soul and of the Palestinian land, which was conceived as an impure, perverse, or at least unattainable arena, whose purification is a matter of life and death for Zionism.[1] By the same token Zionist education conceived itself as a decolonizing power: as a cultural struggle for the undoing of a historical perversion. It saw itself as a historical *Tikun* (putting things back in their natural sacred order). As such it had to include all required (justified) acts of counter-violence. In its secular and religious versions Zionism did not conceive itself as aggressive even when occupied at the height of violent cultural, social, economic, and military battles.[2] The justification of Zionist violence within the framework of secularized political theology allowed an effective denial of its very existence. The violence of normalizing education and the violences of its agents in the public sphere became invisible through the effective control of the representation apparatuses.[3] Thus Zionist violence became either unrecognized as such, invisible or explicit as a holy violence, which actually maintains or strives for real, true, *peace*.[4]

For all their diversity, secular Zionist movements worked up their educational projects within the framework of secularized political theology.[5] The "un-natural" conquest of the Jewish free instincts, consciousness, and possibilities of national sovereignty by the formative powers of the Diaspora demanded counter-normalization: purification through strife of the collective soul and the constitution of the "new Jew" at all costs.[6] Within the same framework and with no less devotion, the taking of the motherland by Others was conceived as an act of unjustified violence which brutally imparted Other, strange, inauthentic, identity to the land, replacing the authentic, Jewish, one. When some aspects of the Palestinian identity of the land were conceived positively it was always part of romantic orientalism within which Jewish sources and forefathers were conceived as the foundation of everything worthy in the Palestinians. This kind of orientalism is very far from the colonialist one, which is suggested by Edward Said and his followers.[7] Confronting these two fronts with secularized political theology, the educational colonization of Zionism was remote from the typical colonialist enterprise in the current postcolonial sense. It was, however, colonialist in a much deeper sense, in its essence: it was colonialist-oriented in the sense that characterizes all versions of normalizing education.

The Zionist project contained conflicting demands for revolution on the one hand, and for undoing a historical perversion (*lehahazir atara leyoshna*) on the other. On both fronts Zionist education was confronted with the question of colonization, namely overcoming diversity, as a life-and-death matter.[8]

From its beginning the success of the Zionist project was conditioned by its ability to overcome the diversities of Jewish histories and identities, and the interests of diverse Jewish communities, as citizens of "their" countries and as residents of the universe. Zionist education was committed to a violent subjectification of a new individual and collective identity:[9] the "new Jew." It had to silence differences and construct a unified, unique, and coherent narrative which would destroy or swallow local and diverse Jewish histories, identities, knowledge, interests, and ideals that were unproductive to the Zionist project or even negate or explicitly threaten it.[10] Such were many powerful Jewish socialist groups as the Bund,[11] certain Jewish secular and religious liberals, and most of the religious orthodox establishment of Eastern Europe.[12] Certainly, the normalizing Zionist educational project has been vivid and effective, yet for all its productive violence it has had only very limited success in destroying diverse Jewish identities and ideologies which were competing for influence within the pre–World War II Jewish world. On the psychic-cultural front, Zionists remained a minority group until the Holocaust.[13] This is due to the historical events and the political situatedness of the project. But whence comes this potential of the situatedness of normalizing education? It comes from its "never totally abandoned" rival, the human Spirit, or from infinity as realized in the openness of Being,[14] which makes counter-education an immanent open possibility, regardless of the efficiency of the hegemonic normalizing education.

The constitution of the hegemonic historical narrative that would serve the Zionist goals demanded coherence and uniqueness in the hegemonic narrative.

This was achieved by teleological frameworks for history teaching and received titles such as "from Diaspora to salvation," or "Holocaust and emancipation."[15] The historical sequence was established on the ruins of local, diverse memories, which represented the otherness of the Others and allowed the reconstitution of their diverse identities, narratives, interests, and their alternative normalizing education, their violences, and their own commitment to colonize and destroy their Others and their otherness.

The construction of such a sequence within a teleological narrative realized the secularization of Jewish political theology as a principal and systematic destruction of multicultural reality. It was targeted at saving from the pervasive, daily, and "marginal," the "essential" "truth" about the Jewish *hidden* imperative mission in history. This attitude is very explicit in the words of David Ben-Gurion, when concerning "the uniqueness and the aim of the State of Israel" he started by saying:

> The Jewish nation is not solely a unified national and political entity. It contains within itself a special will: a Spiritual-moral will, and it has inhabited a historical vision throughout the existence of the Jewish people.[16]

Zionist historiography remained within a theological framework, yet it was secularized. As such it presented a setting for deciphering global reality and allowed an understanding of the Jewish return to history, confronting its power play, on the one hand, and an understanding of its special requirements as Jewish history on the other. According to hegemonic trends in Zionist historiography, Jewish history in Diaspora had to be represented as essentially a history of tragedies, miseries, discrimination, and destruction.[17] Zionist historians like Ben-Zion Dinur were quick to write the appropriate textbooks, even when knowing that oppressed practically in normal times, Jewish life in the different countries was relatively bearable, or even prosperous, in the context of the time and the place. Still, Jews were almost always the Other for the Christians, and to some degree for the Muslims too, for most of their history, and the evil inflicted on them structurally, systematically, and explicitly was real and endured many centuries. During that time their attitudes to the Land of Israel and to God were not to be separated and were part and parcel of Jewish identity and Jewish religion. The saying "next year in Jerusalem" was a constitutive element in their construction as Jews even when the reference was to a heavenly Jerusalem.

The essentialistic orientation of Zionist historiography was committed to the representation of the essential, hidden, common fate and mission, amid and above the apparent differences in the various Jewish histories. The essential, fundamental, common, hidden, denominator was supposed to be the relevant and the central element.[18] The philosophical essentialism, which was successfully translated into an aggressive political ethnocentrism, made possible within Zionist political theology the creation of an educational telos: "the new Jew." In this sense, there is a fundamentally common ground between diverse Zionist projects as the socialists ideals of *halutz* (Zionist pioneer), *Sabra* (Israeli-born Jew), and the *hayal yisraeli* (Israeli soldier), and the revisionist mission of the political right to give birth to "a imposing, generous, and cruel" Israeli "race." The *had nes* (having a sole banner)[19] of Ze'ev Jabotinsky and his disciples and Ben-Gurion's *mamlachtiut* (state-ness),[20] for all their important differences, were ultimately united in their commitment to enact the necessary efficient educational violence that would give birth to a new Jewish "race" on the ruins of rich Jewish diversity, plurality, and differences. Only on its ruins or by its capitulation to a united Zionist narrative was the "essential," hidden, Jewish goal supposed to be realized as an Israeli spiritual, social, and political alternative to Jewish mentality, existence, and missions in the Diaspora.

After a century of Zionism and over half a century of existence of the State of Israel the multicultural issue remains central to education in Israel and to the critique of Israeli normalizing education. Today Zionist educational vitality has been eroded and the internal and external violence of Israel is founded on a new sets of myths, represents an entirely different reality, and it aims at goals very different from those of the founding fathers.

In today's Israel the discourse among the various communities and among the different cultures is explicitly violent.[21] Accordingly, the equilibrium of the diverse possibilities and limitations, and their nature, is determined by visible, direct, and brutal manifestations of power between the rival ideologies and collectives. And yet the violence within each of the rival collectives and social-cultural projects remains invisible and nameless.

The current Israeli arena is caught up between two seemingly opposing trends. The first is that of globalization and the constitution of a one-dimensional reality. Here are manifested the *Ashkenazi* middle-class integration within world capitalism, advanced technological adaptations, and the changes in the stance of knowledge, which allow this development and reflect its realization. Among these changes one should mention the freeways of transporting, storing, distributing, and consuming of electronic information, which is not halted by any national borders, censorship, or non-commercial dimension.[22] Within these global developments the instrumentalization of knowledge[23] has immense importance for the identities, the possibilities, and the limitations of the users and agents of this global system. They are both its agents and victims, and as such play a vital part in current capitalist advancement. Today it seems irrational to dispute the inner logic of the Internet[24] or the laws of the capitalist markets, and modernists, post-modernists, and pre-modernists are all conditioned by the fate of capitalism and the realization of Instrumental Rationality. This process opens up new possibilities[25] and new realities of diversity, pluralism, and individualism, yet all these are to be realized only within the conditions set up by this *meaninglessness.*

This trend meets another ethnocentrist and ultra-religious nationalist. In the local post-modern reality we face a mutual nurturing of the "spiritual" closure of the world of myths, such as that of Rabbi Kadduri, "the doyen of the kabbalists" and a man of magic, abracadabra, and political manipulations, and the meaningless one-dimensionality of the world of mass-media representations of myths and culture heroes, such as the billionaire (international arms-dealer) Shaul Eisenberg or a new model of Mercedes-Benz cars. Together they function as central pillars of the Israeli culture industry from which many groups and cultures are still excluded. Neither of these cultural arenas has room for autonomous subjects, for reflection, for transcendence, or for democracy. Myth is successfully manipulated to control present "Jerusalem" and "Tel-Aviv," pre-modernity and post-modernity. One can even show the common ground and similarities between these different organs of controlling symbols, myths, and peoples' identities, knowledge, and political limitations. In some cases there is a structural resemblance in rituals, the recollection of "spirits," "mystery," and miracles. Within the Israeli culture industry there is an important semblance between their modes of distribution and commodity-like consumption. They are united in their destruction of the autonomy and uniqueness of the individual. In the two arenas "spiritual" success is founded on external, supra-rational, and anti-humanistic control, which in itself is a commodity, like any other commodity in the advanced capitalistic market.

The integration of the pre-modern (and anti-modern) and the post-modern mystifications of reality is an important and fruitful part of Israel's Evil Industry. It is manifested in the control, representation, and consumption of attitudes to the Palestinians and to the constitution of a more peaceful reality, or in the attitude to weak social groups who yearn for solidarity, acknowledgment, equality, and, yes, their own hegemony and homogeneity, "harmony," "justice," or "peace." In Israel the call of the marginalized for "justice" or "peace" is no less violent than the hegemonic one. This is a competition between rival violences, and it is because normalizing education is equally effective in all collective producing networks. The question of justice or the possibility of struggling for good in a non-violent manner or as a human stance toward the world which is not a mere representation of meaningless power relations (which produce meanings, subjects, values, yardsticks, and counter-violence) is here very central. It should be answered in the context of the *possibility* of counter-education, which is not a mere representation of counter-violence. In the meantime we should further develop the articulation of the reasons for the abandonment of humanistic messianic-oriented, anti-violent Judaism as a possible counter-educational stance in Israel. One of the reasons is that the principle of control is the ultimate ruler in Israel's social arena, where the instrumentalization of knowledge, capitalism, and the consciousness-external-control of militarist, economic, political, and symbolic violence are the supreme yardstick and goal.

In current conditions there is a historical shift, in which the production and reproduction of myths, control of knowledge, identity, consciousness, and political limitations are moving from the purview of political-ideological organizations to the province of more advanced powers which are less transparent to critique, resistance, and alternative. The very possibility and importance of a critical theory of society is being challenged by humanists and progressive thinkers influenced by Ulric Beck and the "second modernity" idea,[26] together with post-modern thinkers influenced by Heidegger and Derrida. Actual education (in the sense of the production and the control of the conceptual apparatus, knowledge, consciousness, and possibilities for social function) is being transformed within a higher level of sophistication. Not the teacher at school nor the family is the most relevant agent of consciousness, constitution, and control.[27] Today the violence of the logic of the system's regulations, laws, and fashions is the most relevant educational component. Fast capitalism replaces knowledge constitution with positivist representation now projected into technique itself.[28] The *victims* of the system become its greatest admirers and its most productive and loyal *agents*. This is clearly manifested in mass media: the previous stage of the culture industry assumed and demanded the passivity of the subject; the present stage demands the active participation of the subject. Consequently, instead of a culture industry rooted in the totalizing logic of central broadcasting, reified reproducible aesthetic experiences, and the passive acceptance of media-born values and needs, the current historical moment demands a (false) individual craft production, Internet communication, self-made and home-made video editing, and virtual creations, which give an illusion of decentralized media communication and individual and group self-constitution.[29] The self-regulation and the dynamics within the conflicting/complementary Israeli networks are regulated by non-foundations and "needs of the market," with no transparent center of interests, "aim," or "meaning." By the participation of its victims it penetrates via mass media and other routes into the psyche and consciousness of individuals and collectives and determines their social structured possibilities, limitations, and aims.

The ethnocentric religious-nationalistic trend is essentially different from the trend of capitalist globalization and the invasion of Instrumental Rationality (and its technological, economic, and cultural manifestations) to all levels and dimensions of life. However the ethnocentrist ultra-religious-nationalism is joining forces locally and temporarily with the trend of almost total instrumentalization of the human world. The current Israeli synthesis between the two trends is paralleled by the constitution of a rapid cultural and social cantonization and political disintegration while the Israeli institutional frameworks are preserved, only to consume this "Leviathan" from within. Within this trend independent educational organs such as *Ma'ayan hahinukh hatorani*, *Hahinuch ha'atzma'i*, and the state-religious network take advantage of current possibilities: possibilities opened for them in the era of the demolition of the secular Zionist spirit in order to efficiently introduce self-propagated (Jewish) "values" and "Spirit,"[30] which eventually will ensure the ("peaceful") constitution of a Jewish theocracy.[31] Some trends within this Jewish telos are promising/demanding successful control of the Arab world or even the entire terrestrial sphere, which will efficiently purify the internal Jewish world and will protect it from an external liberal spirit or other Western threats.

The crisis of modernity and the threats of the economic and technological possibilities of modernity's successes function in the current situation as a highly effective educational fuel for the constitution and strengthening of anti-modern trends and for the formation of an authoritative, anti-democratic, anti-humanist education which is aimed at a pure, total, "Spirituality" as a philosophical and political alternative to the current order of things. As part of the crisis of modernity the new post-modern conditions redistribute capital and casually help the marginalized (while deepening their dependence), in parallel to the disintegration of the welfare state. The educational vision of Jewish theocracy should be opposed by the reality where hundreds of thousands of foreign workers live beyond the humane parameters of Israeli social services, human rights, human respect, and public debate. This is without mentioning the hundreds of thousands of Palestinian workers, who are either permitted to work in Israel under discriminating conditions, are systematically humiliated and oppressed, or are refused work at all, even under discriminating conditions. They are left with no resources in their territories, which for three decades were systematically prevented from developing any independent economic capacities. This was to promote to their function as a cheap labor force and captive Israeli market and as an living space for devoted Jewish settlers who are today's pioneers, rebuilding and protecting what they truly believe is their homeland as the realization of the Zionist political theology. They struggle against what they see as Palestinian colonization under difficult existential, political, and economic conditions, and manifest the power of normalizing education in a manner that challenges the simplistic implementation of the anti-Western orientalistic theory.

The crisis of modernity is reflected beside and within this project. It is also present in the reactions of the religious sector to the secular sector and its identity, daily life, aims, and education. Within this process religious education, even the state religious-educational network, attacks the "Western" ideals and establishments of the state, without encountering any serious resistance. So not only are humanism, individualism, and pluralism assaulted, but even the courts, especially the Israeli High Court of Justice. At the same time some of these forces use post-modern communications media and traditional techniques to praise idolatrous rituals, namely magic practices for killing hated people (*pulsa denura*), such as those worked prior to the actual murder of the late premier Yitzhak Rabin. Rabbinical and popular religious ("kabbalistic") witchcraft for personal good fortune and for collective political success is spreading rapidly. The reaction to the crisis of modernity, as we already asserted, is not restricted to those sections of Israeli society that were brought or were manipulated to emigrate overnight from a pre-modern society to a modern society in an era of crisis. However, large parts of those groups are manipulated by an educational and political system to join a bona-fide, anti-modernistic alternative in the form of a Jewish theocracy. Politically and educationally this project is realized by the use of the economic, administrative, and political organs of the state in order to replace them with a non-democratic, anti-humanistic spiritual entity which is beyond the world of politics, transcends history, and enters the realm of redemption. This orthodox Jewish reaction includes vicious rejection of conservative and reformist Judaism. It is paralleled by an Islamic fundamentalist renaissance around and within Israel, which strives to realize its own negation of humanism. For the realization of its totalistic spiritual alternative to the crisis of modernity it seeks to establish a Muslim theocracy that will redeem Palestine, and ultimately the Arab world and the entire world. Both versions of theocracy are united in their ethnocentricity and violent educational theory and praxis on the one hand, and by their acceptance of capitalism and Western technology on the other. We hold that the issue of multicultural reality and the multicultural discourse are to be challenged by acknowledging and facing these trends.

The Israeli state-education network constantly denies the multicultural nature of the Israeli arena, even when the very justification of the Israeliness of this arena is questioned. Today, in face of the dissolution of the secular Zionist

Spirit, this is allowed mainly by indifference, ignorance, and dogmatism regarding the new, instrumental-oriented functionalist attitudes in most dimensions and levels of life. The hegemonic state educational network thereby perpetuates the ideological rhetoric of "melting pot" and "Israel's unity," while actually representing and serving new interests, such as those of Israel's industrialists' association and the international fashions disseminated by the mass media.

Multiculturalism and education are currently deemed important in two contexts. The first is their being a threat to the very survival of a public sphere and civil society or to the very existence of the State of Israel as a Zionist modern project. The second is cultural diversity in the internal Israeli arena.[32]

In this chapter we refer mainly to the first context, namely to the possibility of the constitution of a free, rational, and open public sphere where everyone is permitted/obliged to participate in the construction of the rules of the public discourse, of decision making concerning the needs of individuals and groups and the ways of attending, developing, and changing identities, interests, and possibilities for coexistence within and between different groups. Education for creating, taking part, developing, and changing the public sphere and its discourses is the central issue here. In this context education in the public sphere is totally neglected in Israel. The importance of this issue is denoted by the Israeli secular reality, where humanist traditions have been deeply eroded as the price of Zionist success on the one hand, and by pluralism enhanced by the rapid technological, economic, social, cultural, and mental changes, on the other.

Today's Jewish Israeli society is subject to a dynamic cultural and political cantonization. It is sharpened by growing ethnocentrism, cultural and political closure, and abandonment of commitment to any kind of common good or shared denominator such as a grand narrative, a constitution, or civil codes accepted by all.[33] This trend reflects a hardening refusal to build or acknowledge common ground with Others and their otherness, even partially, temporarily, or contingently. It is paralleled by refusal of most groups to acknowledge the legitimacy of any rules, regulations, and aims of the discourse in the public sphere, though destroying the very possibility of a public sphere which reflects and builds consensus and understandings amid differences and diversity. This reality is very different from the one imagined by some optimist post-modernist thinkers, who believe in the radical democratic potentials of contingency, difference, and ethnocentrism as an alternative to the liberal Western model.[34]

Within a network in which such dynamics are growing stronger, democracy is not a value and the state's law or any inter-collective or supra-collectivist responsibility is not accepted as worthy of defending, enhancing, or realizing. Even informal general laws of the public sphere, what is sometimes called tact, or the fulfillment of the pragmatics of democratic discourse, are conceived at best as a useful tactic, manipulation, or an unfortunate temporary surrender to unpleasant, and illegitimate, historical situation in order to overcome it. Such an attitude is not foreign to any group in Israeli society today. However, among certain groups it becomes ideological, and is being explicitly declared, for example, among ultra-religious Palestinians and Jews of diverse sectors. However, as a non-ideologically formalized reality, namely as a collective mentality, today it is the most widespread characteristic of most "Israelis." This common mentality of lawlessness and abandonment of human responsibility toward the Other is manifested in the Israeli ideal of not being a *freier*.[35] The main separatist groups, namely the Palestinians, the *Mizrahi* Jews, most of the Jewish immigrants from the Asiatic regions of the former Soviet Union Asian areas, and the foreign workers, suffer from some common unfortunate conditions. All of them are demographically rapidly growing groups, living geographically in the periphery, with a relatively low level of income, poor educational opportunities, and the highest unemployment rate. As such they are relatively easily manipulated by the Israeli system in general and politically by the ultra-religious and the extreme right, as shown by the results of the last general elections.[36]

Counter-education, which is committed to the constitution and transcendence of an humanist-oriented public sphere, must challenge this reality not solely on an intellectual level of consciousness-raising but also as a political issue of actual conditions of life. This must be part of its struggle for the constitution of a democratic public sphere where different and conflicting identities, interests, and views are not violently destroyed. Instead, they are expressed, discussed, and crossed or (at least partially) changed for the good of everyone, not for the "general good" as expressed by the strongest. Here the ethical "I" and its commitment to the otherness, to openness, to infinity of a human transcendence is met by the presence of the moral "I." The presence of the *abyss* between the moral "I" (and rational fulfillment of responsibilities toward the otherness within the "I") and the ethical "I" and the otherness as a threat enables space for hope. Hope opens us to the light of Utopia. Within the framework of the moral "I" this is a Utopia where relative freedom, equality, and openness are realized as a rational and solidarian way of life. Counter-education must realize this project as a concrete Utopia, and as such it is not only a regulative idea: it is also part of the actual praxis of negation and transcendence from the current order of things.[37]

Counter-education negates idealism, yet it does not negate all forms of general theories, universalism, and transcendence. At the same time it acknowledges the vitality of diversity, the legitimacy of differences, and the importance of contradictions and disagreements. This is part of its concept of dialogue,[38] its acknowledgment of the Other, the centrality of solidarity, the potentials of love, and the possibilities of mutual action between and amid differences, or at least their universal pragmatics. These are also the concern of education for multiculturalism and for peace, which is very relevant to the Israel/Palestinian reality and to the prospects of transcendence from the bloody cycle into which the Jewish and the Palestinian national liberation movements have been drawn. This concept, however, should not be conceived as a wonder cure. Because of its importance, and in light of its internal problems and challenges, education for multiculturalism deserves some critical remarks. But first we have to do some preparatory work concerning the concepts of multiculturalism and of education.

We claim that one should differentiate multicultural education from education for multiculturalism. These are projects with different propositions, goals, challenges, and practices.

Multicultural education implies the possibility and the imperative to accept the otherness of the different culture, to use the different as a impulse for change within it and outside it, in order to develop better, together within endless diversity the human potentials and possibilities. However, it is not rare that the adorers of multicultural education, who passionately debate all forms of Western ethnocentrism and philosophical essentialism, are drawn to an essentialism quite close to the kind they have attacked. At times this philosophical position is approximated to an advanced version of ethnocentrism. Many of these proponents of multicultural education start by attacking European, Western, or Israeli-*Ashkenazi* ethnocentrism, and end by defending within an essentialist framework the uniqueness, authenticity, or "special interests and ways" of their culture, which is conceived as supreme to the point of a claim of incommensurability. Even when the claim of incommensurability is not raised it is implicitly assumed in view of the absence of any common foundation, framework, common meta-narrative, ideals of the common good, or even agreements on the rules governing present disagreements and on procedures for reaching partial/temporary agreements.[39] According to this claim, there is no real meeting point between differences, especially between their unique culture or group and Others, who are fundamentally different or inferior.

This claim has many implications. For example, there are different sets of morality, namely "ours" and "theirs," not noticing, as Homi Bhabha does, that any attempt to frame the problem of identity leads inevitably to being caught athwart the frame, at once inside and outside.[40] Difference here is held as central in all versions of post-modernism, but only to end up as a commitment to homogeneity among the chosen ones and as justifying rejection of moral commitment to, and love of, the others beyond the border of difference. This line of thought has two seemingly opposing manifestations in the collective and in the individual context. Note that acknowledgment of the centrality of difference is also valid between individuals and even within the individual herself. There it culminates in the concept of eternal and contingent changing of identity. At its peak it ends up in solipsism, abandonment of the subject as some-one, becoming some-thing, part of the thingness of the world of objects. In all cases this line of thought is committed to violent education.

In the absence of dialogue, or willingness to ignore or accept the educational violence of the hegemonic group, when it does not directly commit violence against the Other, it is always on the edge of collective or individual suicide. This is to be seen in the case of the Manson Family and other such instances. Even before entering this stage multicultural education is on the edge of producing a kind of recognition in the centrality of diversity and essential difference, which produces or legitimates rejection of self-critique and easy sinking into an ethnocentric self-evidence while building high walls against a possible invasion of other cultures. Any other subject or culture is here conceived as violent, threatening, and dangerous, not to be satisfied unless it destroys or swallows "us." The local culture, therefore, is conceived as living in constant battle, and it must use every moment and all means to destroy or fend off all its internal and external enemies. This is the historic line that enabled some Fascist thinkers to look to Nietzsche's philosophy for justification of their violent ethnocentricity. In the Israeli context we may mention thinkers such as Abba Ahimeir, Ya'akov Klachkin, and Uri Zvi Greenberg. Multicultural education, however, has many important critical achievements. These include its attacks on nationalism, its critique of the violent practices and manipulations of national curricula enforced on marginalized groups and cultures, and the importance it ascribes to resisting such non-dialogical manifestations of normalizing education.

Today there are many adorers of the different versions of multicultural education, who struggle individually or collectively over its realization. Among many individuals and many groups such as homosexuals, African-Americans, Latin-Americans, and Native Americans, multicultural education is seen as a desirable alternative to traditional mainstream Western education. It is seen as an alternative to Western education and its pretension to introduce universal valid knowledge and values and personal development, which are fundamentally Western and ultimately serve the interests of the hegemonic groups within this ethnocentrist project. For all the importance of this critique, which has many achievements, we see it as a problematic stand. As will be shown, the ideology of multicultural education makes it more difficult for counter-education to defend humanism within the framework of multicultural reality.

Multicultural education claims to reveal the repressive elements, contradictions, and injustice on which the ethnocentrism of traditional Western education is founded as part of its commitment to conquer other cultures and societies. Backed by many post-modern critics and much politically correct rhetoric, the disciples of multicultural education, for all their differences, share a common ground. They are united in their effort to abolish the traditional division between high culture and popular culture, between Western rational-scientific and non-Western cultures, which are devoid of any written history and are less advanced from a technological point of view. Within the collectivist version of multicultural education, the legitimacy of marginal cultures, and in many cases also the incommensurability of cultures, are emphasized. Sometimes the value of diversity will be praised out of this acknowledgment. Sometimes, out of concepts such as the primacy of diversity and the irreducibility of difference, marginal cultures, esoteric art, scandalous philosophy, or perverse sexual practices—as seen from the center—are praised, and actually preferred to the hegemonic, the centered, the respectable, and the "normal."

Multicultural education leads hence to the concrete political and moral acts. Within it, education is realized as restoring to the discriminated, repressed, and controlled their dignity, and it tries to empower the marginalized, silenced, and oppressed. It is realized in social action for change. This kind of education is a political deed. Since it explicitly rejects any general theory, philosophical foundations, or meta-narrative (except the general theory of resisting any general theories) it is directed solely by practical success and pragmatic arguments, without philosophical justifications of its actions and rhetoric. There is, however, an important moral imperative of struggling on the side of the oppressed in this kind of education, accompanied by philosophical problems. These, being unaddressed, make possible its development into individual or collective philosophical, educational, and political terror, or suicide, which are but two manifestations of the same phenomenon of education as violence.

Multicultural education has no serious manifestation in Israel. It is fragmentarily echoed here or there within the rhetoric of intellectuals who represent different oppressed, marginalized, and controlled groups, who seek an alternative to the present order. But in Israel there is no conscious and direct representation of the individualist version of multicultural education, which favors "permanent revolution" of the body and psyche of the human being. In Israel there is no ideological framework for articulating the actuality of individuals moving rapidly from one identity into another, replacing ways of life, consciousness, fashions, intersubjectivity, and places with no telos, interest, or "meaning."[41] In Western countries, where there is such a philosophical or ideological framework, it is the intellectuals who introduce these conceptual frameworks, not the individuals practicing individualistic multiculturalism. In Israel, philosophical and ideological discourse of this kind is still absent. However, there is a presence in the Israeli arena of collectivist-oriented multicultural education in two main models.

The weaker version of the two is the kind of multicultural education that is influenced by liberal and especially post-modern conceptions. One of its manifestations is a group of *Mizrahi* intellectuals who are committed to challenging the *Ashkenazi* Zionist establishment and its ideology of "Israeliness," "melting pot,"[42] and the necessary and justified oppression of groups as Palestinians, women, and especially *Mizrahi* Jews. The last, it is alleged, were brought to Israel to serve as low-paid workers and guardians of the Zionist project when its colonization effort proved to be successful. Even if it was not intentionally planned, they served structural needs of the system. Shlomo Fisher is right when he claims that the differences in rhythm and nature of meeting modernity and its crisis constitutes a central element in the current Israeli multicultural crisis.[43] Today there is a trend among some young *Mizrahi* intellectuals to acknowledge the differences among different feminists, along ethnic, cultural, sexual, and other lines. There is a great emphasis, for example, on the uniqueness of *Mizrahi* feminists, and their being patronized and manipulated by *Ashkenazi* liberal feminists,[44] in parallel to the situation of colored and white liberal middle class feminists in the United Sates. One of these groups is *Hakeshet Hademokratit* (Democratic Rainbow) and its effect is very limited, especially among the *Mizrahi* Jews whom it claims to represent and emancipate. Another example is an educational network with a similar orientation, which is called *Kedma* (Eastwards). In it, *Mizrahi* pupils are supposed to be liberated, to get back their "voice" which was silenced by the hegemonic ideology, to study their forgotten history, and to reformulate their identity in conditions free of the hegemonic ideology and most of the establishment's enforced curricula. In reality, this project is far from turning into a success story. The strongest version of multicultural education now present in Israel is the collectivist-oriented, which is not oppositional to hegemonic Israeli ethnocentrism but is in itself one of its most violent manifestations.

This kind of multicultural education rejects inter-cultural dialogue, seeing it as a necessarily dangerous entry for foreign cultural innovation. Like all versions of normalizing education, and in common with multicultural education, ethnocentric views of multiculturalism regard free and open discourse between cultures and within cultures as immanently violent. This view is not necessarily wrong nor should it become a principal rejection of dialogue. What halts the prospects of dialogue within the collectivist versions of multicultural education is its explicit identification with symbolic violence. It conceives itself as immanently violent. Within it there is no willingness to be open to a comparative cultural study of the kind that must displace our horizons in the resulting fusions.[45] As a strong version of multicultural education it arrogantly closes its ears to any call for dialogue.

Dialogue must be free, and it is realized between (at least potentially) worthy yet unequal partners who cannot reach their telos or aim without a genuine partnership with the other partner to their joint Odyssey. Practically, we must remember, the call for dialogue always suspends self-evidence and interrupts history from the outside. It always enters unexpectedly. In Walter Benjamin's thought, "messianic time"[46] *bursts* into "now time."[47] It is not the product of normalizing education nor the production and control of hegemonic power relations. It is a trace of *the totally other*. It connects our present and our potential for being other than directed to the not-yet-existing, which determines the human as a subject and not a mere object.[48] It opens the door to a non-dogmatic sense of "difference," as in the case of essentialist ethnocentrist and individualistic multiculturalism, and it is also distinguished from the liberal "pluralistic" version, which is marked by a unity of identity of one social group against the other.[49] That which *calls* for dialogue calls for transcendence from the self-evident and from violently produced and maintained normality, and it might be responded, abandoned, or co-opted. But it is always a concrete possibility within conditions of oppression, discrimination, and erasing collective memories, identities, and cultures by powers that make possible the perpetuation of the hegemonic self-evident. Dialogue, however, might be struggled for, and partially even become an (always temporary) alternative, non-violent way of life, where love and the commitment to challenge injustice are not contrasted with being exiled within the production of the hegemonic quests, values, and truths.

Multicultural education is not really committed to dialogue. But we should be aware that even the demand for dialogue is not safe from being drawn into a violent discourse and into normalizing educational practices. There is a permanent, immanent, danger that the critique on cultural oppression will develop into an ethnocentrist project of the marginalized and the oppressed. Too common is the phenomenon of resistance to the reproduction of hegemonic self-evidence, which culminates in an uncritical and even dogmatic reproduction of the marginalized self-evidence of the oppressed.[50] Normally the oppressed are liberated from their oppressors only to replace the hegemonic self-evidence and its educational violence with another, which ultimately aims to become itself the hegemonic, the oppressor.[51] In our mind there is no essential difference between the self-evidence of the oppressed and the self-evidence of their oppressors. Self-evidence and injustice are what make the difference between differences, not the difference in itself. Collectivism and ethnocentrism are the best partners and devoted companions of self-evidence. They and their immanent internal and external violences are the rivals of counter-education. Multicultural education, however, fails to see it.

Another weakness of collectivist-oriented multicultural education is its fierce anti-intellectualism. Here the critique of the hegemonic Western high culture ends up too often in total negation of high culture, of the quest for transcendence from the common and from the self-evident. This occurs in the service of ethnocentrism and out of hate toward any manifestation of free Spirit. This is in the name of hatred that was constituted by the violence of normalizing education. This is how the members of marginalized groups are re-enslaved with ever-more efficient chains. This process ensures their impotence for genuine critique and dialogue, determining their position as objects for manipulations, control, and oppression, even as members of the ruling group should their violence be more effective than the evils inflicted on them by their current oppressors. This hatred of real struggle over transcendence, by the hard way of reflection and overcoming ethnocentrism and self-evidence, is the real foundation of the present-day shrines and saints' cults. These have become a prosperous industry on an unprecedented scale amidst a pre-modern high-tech society in the name of celebrating multi-culturalism and justified by "proven" "spiritual" experiences and actual medical, economic, and political successes.

Education for multiculturalism is something very different. It is currently being developed within different conceptual frameworks and within other social contexts than multicultural education in both its individualist and collectivist-oriented versions. Multicultural education is being developed, as we asserted, mainly within the post-modern and the ethnocentric frameworks. Education for multiculturalism, by contrast, is mainly developed within the different versions of Critical Pedagogy and in the liberal and democratic traditions. In the current educational discourse both are highly influenced by post-modernism and they are committed to central post-modern critiques on the Enlightenment and the very tradition which gave birth to education for multiculturalism.

The two versions of education for multiculturalism share a harsh critique of modern education, yet in contrast to the stand of multicultural education here there is no room for total negation of Enlightenment and humanism, nor of the special place among the different cultures occupied by the ideal of emancipation of humanity.

The liberal version of education for multiculturalism implicitly assigns this kind of education to reforming the present order, improving it, while identifying or even justifying capitalism, parliamentarian democratic and current bourgeois anti-utopianism.[52] Critical Pedagogy's version of education for multiculturalism negates capitalism[53] altogether, criticizes the present "democratic" order,[54] and it is explicitly anti-bourgeoisie. Yet neither version is genuinely revolutionary and the two share the abandonment of the claim for *the totally other*, the quest for transcendence, and the overcoming of the self-evident as the entry for a dialogical alternative to all oppressive versions of normalizing education.

A central principle of education for multiculturalism claims that it is important to acknowledge that, in principle, no one culture is higher than others. Accordingly, there is no way to justify social and political hierarchies which oppress other groups and cultures, pushing them to the margins of social activity, cultural possibilities, and political power. Both versions of education for multiculturalism emphasize the need for openness to other cultures and self-critique as a precondition for a more free and democratic condition.[55] Practically they are united in the call for dialogue between equals as a precondition for bettering our world.

Education for multiculturalism contains simultaneously both moderate ethnocentrism and anti-ethnocentrism. In this issue Richard Rorty's position is paradigmatic. On the one hand, Rorty refuses to relinquish the Western tradition, bourgeois well-being, liberalism, and democracy. He is even willing to fight for its right to exist and he openly declares that Western democracy is superior to all its alternatives. By the same token Rorty abandons the pretension to be able to constitute a principal justification (as well as the need for such a justification) of Western culture or democracy's supremacy. All his arguments are pragmatic and ethnocentrist. But this is a moderate ethnocentrism, which in contrast to the total negation of ethnocentrism by multicultural education does not result in his assuming that his group incubates the absolute truth. Yet according to Rorty

> a belief can still regulate action, can still be thought worth dying for, among people who are quite aware that this belief is caused by nothing deeper than contingent historical circumstance.[56]

This is why as an ironist he does not ascribe to his version of education permission for counter-violence, which will search for ways to enforce itself on the Other and redeem or educate those who are still living in the dark. Quite the contrary, Rorty's moderate ethnocentrism enables him to invite Western culture to open windows for a dialogue with other cultures. He urges Western culture to educate for the acceptance not only of the Other but also of the otherness of the Other as a desirable addressee and in a certain sense even a partner, as part of an ongoing development of democracy and an intercultural discourse. It is precisely as a proud liberal and democrat that Rorty emphasizes diversity, skepticism, irony, and critique.

This version of education for multiculturalism is not without its problems, as one can see in the works of thinkers whose work is more directed to the school arena than Rorty's. Biku Parech, as an example, articulates specific and very precise plans for multicultural schools in the United States, in the Netherlands, and in other places where we encounter examples of schools actually practicing education for multiculturalism. In Parech's programs we are presented with plans for students of different cultures studying together. Within this framework the students are not urged to neglect their identity, knowledge, and interests. They are encouraged, however, to be interested in the identity, knowledge, and needs of the others. Here he refers to different kinds of clothing, diets, and histories not merely as exotic knowledge, values, and manners but as an integral way of life common to all members of a school which educates for multiculturalism. In contrast to multicultural education, this version of education for multiculturalism has an explicit commitment to actual communality and acknowledgment of the legitimacy of the Other and her otherness. The legitimacy (not just the relevance) of the otherness of the Other is conceived as the starting point for a dialogue and self-elevation.

However, we have to remember that ultimately this version of education for multiculturalism is liberal-oriented. As such the limits of liberalism, or of Western high culture, constitute the horizon of its tolerance. This is the source of the coherence and of the immanent weakness of the liberal version of education for multiculturalism: anyone too different from the requirements of liberal-oriented standards of coexistence will fail to receive an entrance ticket. So the question of violence and counter-violence, oppression, and reproducing the self-evidence returns through the back door, while the well-being of the capitalist order and the Western kind of democracy will remain the ultimate guards of this door.

Both education for multiculturalism and multicultural education have much relevance to the Israeli context, as an acute multicultural actuality. According to the hegemonic Israeli ideology, the state educational network is responsible for the constitution of a collective consciousness and coherent ethnocentric national identity (for the Jews, or at least for secular Jews). This project is aimed at a successful change of the identity of the region, purifying the land of its Palestinian identity, and the Jews of the Diaspora mentality that took hold of them. This is quite explicit even in the law of state education (1953), which not by chance was articulated at the same time and by the same minister of education (Ben-Zion Dinur) as the law of the Holocaust commemoration. While being targeted at the constitution, protection, and reproduction of the Zionist realm of self-evidence, the 1953 Israeli law of state education acknowledges Others and their right to difference, especially if they are Jews. It treats different Others differently. Accordingly, religious Jews have not only the right to separate and independent educational networks, they are also entitled to state funds to protect their otherness. Palestinians are directed to the state educational network, with special controls and compulsory studies in Jewish history and culture, which substantially eliminate possible manifestations of national Palestinian identity, rights, sufferings, and aspirations. They can avoid this educational network only by entering a variety of elite Christian private schools centered on Christian theology and where there is not much room for Palestinian separate national or cultural identity or political aspirations.

The Israeli antinomy here is that while the "secular" state educational system has no room for cultural diversity or political alternatives to the hegemonic Zionist ones, it is committed to the legitimacy of other Jewish, non-Zionist, non-democratic, and anti-humanist educational alternatives. At the same time, beyond the borders of the state educational system, where actual multicultural education is realized, there is no room for dialogue or for the acknowledgment of the legitimacy of difference. Most versions of Israeli Jewish educational systems are united in their rejection of dialogue with the Other, and generally actualize extreme ethnocentrism and ultra-nationalism in their most arrogant manifestations. The Others are seen here as babes who were lost and tempted (*tinok shenifta*) or, if not Jews, they are accordingly seen as not really human, or at least as ultimately incapable of anything except supporting or observing the realization of a Jewish telos which is fundamentally beyond their potential. This is because only a Jew is a fully realized human being: *Ein umot ha'olam keruim adam*.[57]

We do not aver that this is the only possible interpretation of Judaism, and in fact we should speak of "Judaisms" or different traditions within Judaism, not of a monolithic "Judaism." Many Jewish traditions contain important universalistic and humanist potentials and it is an important source for counter-education and for the struggle for emancipation. However, in Israel today, the hegemonic orthodox Jewish religious educational trends (which apply to a minority in world Jewry) are dogmatic, ethnocentric, anti-democratic, and potentially violent. Within this context there is no room for education for multiculturalism, but for the denial of the Other, for destruction, and for being victorious over the others' truths, memories, values, and interests even if in a non-direct and "peaceful," namely invisible, normalizing educational violence.

Education for multiculturalism might be seen by some liberals and humanists as an educational theory and practice whose realization might be of great importance for Israel, as long as the state exists and reproduces its central power relations, even before its transformation into a fundamentalist Sparta. It might be seen as the right solution for the liberals' bad conscience for the cultural toll inflicted on *Mizrahi* Jews, women, Palestinians, foreign workers, and others. On the positive side, fewer and fewer liberals are able even to stand alongside Richard Rorty and present themselves as proud liberals; more and more of them are swept up by the "harder" versions of post-modernism. They abandon the Enlightenment's universalistic ideals and its commitment to educate within an emancipatory Western framework for a more just, free, and rational human existence. Today many of these former liberal intellectuals and educators favor education for multiculturalism as a humanist alternative and as a manifestation of moderate liberalism, which might still be held and justified. This is their way to defend the special status of Western culture and its latest cultural imperialism, which attracts so many of today's most brilliant third world intellectuals. We argue, however, that education for multiculturalism, in its critical and in its liberal versions, is far from being unproblematic.

The Israeli context might serve as a valuable test case for some of the principal weaknesses of the liberal version of education for multiculturalism. The liberal conception of multiculturalism implies the transfiguration of discourse into a dialogue between and within different cultures, narratives, passions, and interests. This assumption is common to all its representatives, from Habermas to Rorty, and they are not genuinely critical of this conception. Thinkers who are more critical of multiculturalism, such as Foucault, reject the Utopia of non-violent communication on which this conception is founded. The optimists' conception implies that an important precondition for education for multiculturalism is acceptance by the parties involved of some general rules and at least one common goal. The commonest rules accepted by all participants are those for presenting and regulating assertions, disagreements, and movements toward a non-violent consensus about each of these. Another precondition must be common assertions and practices concerning the legitimacy of the Others' participation. All the rest might be elaborated, developed, agreed, or disagreed within the pragmatics of this kind of communication, which Habermas claims to be universal; ultimately Rorty shares this positive liberal Utopia. We have here two claims. According to the first, this positive Utopia is groundless. It is invalidated both logically and historically. Logically, we hold, a certain party might be an active partner to such a multicultural discourse while accepting its minimal set of agreed or realized regulations but without sharing even a single common aim with the other parties. Even the very existence or progress of the discourse must not be accepted by all participants. A party might take part in such a discourse in order to destroy it and its explicit common goal. Historically, this is not an uncommon situation, as the Israeli example shows.

In the Israeli context there is no common ground for a non-violent public sphere, namely no real public sphere in a genuine civil society and surely no liberal tradition and commitment to pluralism. Different degrees of aggressive ethnocentrisms characterize most contesting collectives, systems, and networks. There is also no general acknowledgment in the legitimacy of the Other or agreement concerning the rules and conditions of entering the multicultural dialogue and the mutual development within the dialogical framework. It is possible to oppose this claim by asserting that it is refuted by the actual democratic process within the Israeli system. Others might agree, at least partially, with our reconstruction, and yet claim that it is still justified to make the necessary efforts and implement education for peaceful multiculturalism, at least in one educational arena, which is still the biggest: in the "secular" part of the state educational network. According to this claim, within this framework liberal and humanistic-oriented principles and practices prevail, even in pedagogic and didactical levels. Here it is possible to educate for integration of, and respect for, Others, their cultural values, and their knowledge, as part of an educational process which will eventually change education itself and ultimately will better the Israeli public sphere and advance the prospects of a civil society. Israeli democratic optimists will assert that this is the best way, and maybe the only way, to guarantee a genuine future democracy in Israeli society. This optimism has been defeated by the history of Israeli education and by the current reality of Israeli society, even in its secular part. Ethnocentrism characterizes even its most advanced liberal versions, as manifested by the development of a new, secular, humanist-oriented educational network which is explicitly Zionist and implicitly middle-class *Ashkenazi* and looks for preservation of a dying culture of a small elitist sect in a special reservation.[58] There, from its elitist and segregated fortress, it is committed to realize education for pluralism, humanism, and democracy.[59]

In other Israeli arenas it is even less likely to expect education for multiculturalism to be realized. This claim must be broadened: multiculturalism, democracy, and an open, free, and rational public sphere are impossible in current Israel. This is because it cannot fit into one of the four major trends of this arena. Education for multiculturalism cannot be accepted within the secular political theology, which uses all means to repress, control, detain, destroy, or obliterate the Other. Education for multiculturalism cannot accept its integration into a project, which strives to establish a Jewish or Muslim theocracy. Such a project cannot but become totalistic, negating diversity and heterogeneous public life, and receiving its legitimacy directly from God or his Holy Scriptures. As manifested by the Israeli example in principle, education for multiculturalism might also be tolerated by the major modern trends in Israel: Instrumental Rationality and its technological-economical-social manifestations on the one hand, and the post-modern alternative on the other. Ultimately both acknowledge the Other merely as a consumer/producer. They are united in their conservatism, which either is unable or refuses to transform the present order. As such it cannot develop a genuine education for multiculturalism as a new, more humane, order. This is a brief conclusion to a complicated historical refutation of the optimism about education for multiculturalism. Education for multiculturalism might be refuted, however, on a principal level, and we think this is the main issue, which is overlooked by the good-will optimists who are devoted to the new magic. Here we refer to the essence of education itself as a main obstacle before successful education for multiculturalism.

What is the *essence* of education and what quest does it respond to? The essence of education is violence. The abandonment of the call for its overcoming enables being drawn into the quest for the formation, control, and reproduction of the conceptual apparatus, the psyche, the consciousness, the possibilities and limitations of human subjects and collectives as part of their normalization, standardization, and closure. The violent "external" formation of the subject and her/his transformation into an object of care, control, and emancipation improves the subjectification of the subject. Namely it enhances the production and enforcement of "her" subjectivity, constituting the "I" and as such manifests the not-I, which guarantees the unlimited adjustment of the subject to "his" or "her" invisible normalization forces. As such the subject is expected to function as an agent of the reproduction of the existing order and as one who contributes to the effort of establishing a firewall. That is, blocking the possibilities of an essential change in the prevailing realm of self-evidence in all its economic, social, and cultural and psychic manifestations.[60]

Counter-education introduces a humanistic-oriented alternative to normalizing education. It is always a "trouble maker," "unproductive," and it strives to overcome not only hegemonic violence but violence as such. It can never be institutionalized or articulated as an effective dogma. This is why throughout history, normalizing education prevails, even if it constantly has to ensure the production of effective violence, which will destroy all external and internal life alternatives. Accordingly, education cannot but be repressive, and the emancipatory ideal invested in education for multiculturalism can, if at all, be seriously addressed solely by counter-education. The normalizing essence of education is especially expressed within multicultural education. To a certain degree this kind of education is already practiced in Israel, even quite intensely.

In Israel of today many Jewish religious groups and sects enjoy various degrees of political, social, and ideological autonomy. These religious groups are united by their rejection of the hegemonic and the traditional Western values, ideals, passions, knowledge, and images of knowledge, and they are all committed to a successful avoidance of the political aims of the hegemonic groups. For groups such as *Neturei Karta*, and others which educate within frameworks such as *Ma'ayan Hahinukh Hatorani, Hahinukh Ha'atzmai,* and the like, marginal knowledge not only stands at the center of the educational project, it is actually the only relevant knowledge conceived as true knowledge. At the same time they conceive all other knowledge and educational systems as dangerous rivals, to be treated as sinners, ignorant of truth and worthy values, or both. They see their own images of knowledge and yardsticks as the only valid ones, while perceiving themselves as responsible for the fate of all other Jewish groups and individuals. Other groups have the same attitude toward their Others. This is why rival normalizing educational projects in Israel cannot avoid a life-and-death struggle with each other.

By their violence and animosity these groups acknowledge and empower each other. However, they are all united against the hegemonic state educational network and its ideology, and against the current power relations, in order to constitute a reality where there will be no heteronomy: no room for cultural alternatives, for difference or dialogue between and within cultures. This is the heart of the educational-political struggle, which determines the Israeli agenda, while the secular majority is not yet sensible to the issue of education and multiculturalism. Only lately have we taken the first steps to acknowledging the multicultural actuality, whose Israeliness until recently was not questioned at all. The possibility of a humanistic-oriented educational alternative is by no means being raised as reclaiming the universal emancipatory project. It is far from an attempt to regain and reconstitute the center in such a manner that education for multiculturalism will be presented as a general option. It is more of an additional fragmented, separatist, version of multicultural education as a struggle of all against all.

The absence of (even a minimal set of) agreed rules for non-violent consensus, even if only temporary and marginal, characterizes not only the theory of multicultural education; it is at the same time a major element of the Israeli multicultural actuality. This reality and the absence of a genuine public sphere is intended to justify the obligation of the hegemonic establishments and trends to establish themselves mainly on direct violence (army, police, strategic economic control based on ethnicity, cultural interests, and so on) and on manipulative rhetoric aimed at the implementation of a general program in conditions of fragmentation and disagreement. This actuality makes the current system highly vulnerable, especially as it careers toward an explicit violent national collision with its Palestinian population within and outside the State of Israel.

However, it is exactly this actuality which opens the way for an alternative humanist education. Such an alternative, if it wants to struggle for the realization of its potentials, must acknowledge its post-modern actuality, where pre-modern and anti-modern educational alternative are growing stronger and are about to gain the upper hand and conquer the center from its margins. It has to present an explicit agenda of education for a non-peaceful multicultural reality or of life within an endemic multicultural crisis. The counter-education we suggest goes beyond the traditional humanist educational projects, yet is not to be separated from the tradition of the Enlightenment and critical philosophy. A place like Israel is a place where the relevance of counter-education might be seen with special clarity. However, according to its essence, counter-education cannot offer counter-violence and halt the triumph of multicultural education in Israel. Multicultural education demolishes the vitality and potentialities of general education and opens the way for its conquering of the power centers which will ensure that there will be no danger of successful education for multiculturalism and for multicultural actuality. This is how multicultural education accomplishes its immanent telos coherently and how its violent essence is realized. However, multicultural education in Israel is a self-defeating project.

Multicultural education which realizes itself and conquers the power centers of the Israeli cultural arenas, networks, and dynamics, loyal to its essence, cannot but go on to colonize the neighboring arenas on national, ethnic, gender, religious, class, cultural, and psychic levels. This project has no limits, and it has to grow and extend its borders until the final "victory" or "redemption." At the same time it grows old, domesticated, and instrumentalized and determines its destruction or replacement by a more vivid idealistic-oriented educational and political alternative. Even if this kind of multicultural education isolates itself as a Jewish theocracy, awaiting the advent of the Messiah, refrains from a military, economic, or cultural assault against its neighbors, and is available for open discourse with its neighbors, it will be attacked by its neighbors, consistent with their own normalizing education and its colonizing imperative. This is because as a Jewish theocracy it cannot but be ethnocentric, and it can realize itself only by internal colonization, including discrimination of its Others, such as Jewish liberals, Palestinian nationalists, or politically oriented feminists. It is not impossible to predict that in the case of the rise of a Jewish theocracy, or even in the persistence of the present asymmetry within the Jewish state, the Palestinians will counter this structural violence with explicit violence. In such a case, total conflict with the Arab Middle East is a likely scenario. Alongside its commitment to Instrumental Rationality, Western individuality, and freedom, this external colonizing attitude will most probably guarantee the downfall of the State of Israel.

History, however, is not deterministic, and even in a post-modern era the human subject has potential autonomy and responsibility for the Other. On the one hand, nothing and no one can totally deprive the human being. On the other hand, the human being cannot liberate herself/himself. The commitment for liberation is not the manifestation of free will, it is determined by something totally other. In a certain sense freedom is the one to choose the human who will commit herself or himself for counter-education in many, unexpected, sometime dangerous ways. The current dominant trends in Israel might make a turn, change, or suddenly be cut off by something totally other than the current actuality. Then new possibilities will open. But even before this moment comes, the issues of education and multiculturalism are already knocking at the door, and we should know on what side of the barricade we should be. It means, among other things, that we should also be ready to realize counter-education in a non-peaceful multicultural reality as a concrete way of life.

NOTES

1. But even in the 1920s, during the period of the second wave of immigration (*ha'aliya hashniya*) there was a more moderate, or functionalistic-positivistic attitude. See: Yoram Bar-Gal, *Moledet and Geography in Hundred Years of Zionist Education*. Tel Aviv: Am Oved 1993, 55-57.
2. Uri Ben-Eliezer. *The Emergence of Israeli Militarism 1936-1956*. Tel Aviv: Dvir 1995, 137-140 (in Hebrew).
3. Stuart Hall. "Introduction," in Stuart Hall (ed.), *Representation; Cultural Representations and Signifying Practices*. London: Sage Publications 1997, 1-11.
4. Ilan Gur-Ze'ev. "Philosophy of peace education in a post-modern era," a keynote address at the August 2000 INPE Sidney conference.
5. Amnon Raz-Krakotzkin. *The National Narration of Exile, Zionist Historiography and Medieval Jewry*, Doctoral dissertation, Haifa 1996, 70 (in Hebrew).
6. Oz Almog. *The Sabra: A Profile*. Tel Aviv: Am Oved 1997, 127-128.
7. Edward Said. *Orientalism*. New York: Pantheon Books 1978.
8. Ze'ev Jabotinsky. "Shir Beitar," in: Beitar Israel, Department of Education, *Main Chapters in the History of the Revolt*. Tel Aviv 1963, 7.
9. Ernesto Laclau. *New Reflections on the Revolution of Our Time*. London: Verso, 33.
10. Uri Ram. "Zionist historiography and the invention of modern Jewish nationhood: The case of Ben Zion Dinur," *History and Memory* 7: 1 (1995).
11. Levi Kantor. *100 Years of Struggle 1865-1965: Jewish Workers in Czarist and Soviet Russia*. Tel Aviv: Yahard 1969, 73 (in Hebrew).
12. Shalom Razabi. "Anti-Zionism and messianic anxiety," *Zionism* 20, Tel-Aviv 1996, 80 (in Hebrew).
13. Benjamin Beit-Hallahmi. *Original Sins: Reflections on the History of Zionism and Israel*. New York: Olive Branch Press 1993, 180.
14. Emmanuel Levinas. "Philosophy and infinity," in *Collected Philosophical papers*. Translated by Alphonso Lingis, Lancaster: Martinus Nijhoff Publishers 1987, 47-60.
15. Ruth Firer. *Agents of Holocaust Lesson*. Tel-Aviv: Hakibbutz Hameuhad 1989 (in Hebrew).
16. David Ben-Gurion. *The Restored State of Israel*. Tel Aviv: Am Oved 1975, 1.
17. Yoram Bar-Gal. *Homeland and Geography in a Century of Zionist Education*. Tel Aviv: Am Oved 1993 (in Hebrew).
18. Dan Diner. "Cumulative contingency: Historicizing legitimacy in Israeli discourse," *History and Memory* 7: 1 (Spring/Summer 1995), 152.
19. "Prior to anything else—a Zionist monism... and I am looking for youth which has in its palace only one conviction, no more, the youth which does not need more and which will be proud of it and praise it more than other beliefs. God first created the nation; all which helps its regeneration—is sacred, all which disturbs it—is sinful, anyone who interferes is black, black is his conviction, black are his banners." In: Moshe Bella (ed.), *The World of Jabotinsky*, Tel Aviv: Defusim 1972, 233.
20. David Ben-Gurion. "The eternity of Israel," *Stars and Earth*, 130.
21. Even if normally it is not a direct military use of force. On the nature of symbolic and non-mediated power see: Ilan Gur-Ze'ev, "Total Quality Management and Power/Knowledge Dialectics in the Israeli Army," *Journal of Thought* (Spring 1997), 9-11.

22 Juergen Habermas. *Der Philosophische Diskurs der Moderne.* Frankfurt a.Main: Suhrkamp 1988, 136.
23 Zigmunt Bauman. *Postmodern Ethics.* Oxford: Blackwell 1993, 232.
24 Here we do not accept the optimism of Timothy Luke, who believes Critical Theory of the cyberspace can do the trick. See: Timothy W. Luke, *Screens of Power: Ideology, Domination, and Resistance in Informational Society.* Chicago: University of Illinois Press 1989, 46.
25 As will be shown, this claim does not share the theoretical framework of critical optimists such as Henry Giroux, Peter McLaren, and Kathleen Weiler, who ultimately accept post-modern orientations toward the current "democratization of knowledge and the emancipatory potentials of popular art." See: Peter McLaren, *Critical Pedagogy and Predatory Culture: Oppositional Politics in a Postmodern Era.* London and New York: Routledge. Henry Giroux. *Teachers as Intellectuals: Toward a Critical Pedagogy of Learning.* New York and London: Bergin & Garvey 1988, 74-85.
26 Nathan Shneider. "The feature of loosing direction," *Israeli Sociology* 1: 2 (1999), 451-459.
27 We do not mean that traditionally they were not also part of the system and its agents. Our assertion refers to the historical shift where teachers and parents are smoothly integrated to the system and are primarily its agents, and even as such they lose their traditional special place and become agents of lesser importance.
28 Ben Agger. *A Critical Theory of Public Life: Knowledge, Discourse and Politics in an Age of Decline.* London and New York: The Falmer Press 1991, 77.
29 Timothy W. Luke. *Social Theory and Modernity.* London and New Delhi: Sage Publications 1990, 175.
30 On a secular humanist critique on the current state's education of Jewish values and on the "administration for value education" see: Joseph Goel, "The administration for education for values—the next battlefield," *Free Judaism* 10 (December 1996), 10.
31 On the religious parties' commitment to constitute a Jewish theocracy see: Gershon Weiler, *Jewish Theocracy.* Tel Aviv: Am Oved 1976, 212.
32 Arnon Soffer. "Israel Arabs in readiness for autonomy: The case of the Galilee," *Studies in the Geography of Israel* 13 (1992), 198-209 (in Hebrew).
33 Arnon Soffer. "The implications of geographic-demographic analyses," paper for the conference on "Multiculturalism in Israel," Gordon College, Haifa 23 December 1997.
34 Ernesto Laclau. "Introduction," in Ernesto Laclau (ed.), *The Making of Political Identities.* London and New York: Verso, 5.
35 Luis Runiger and Michael Fage. "The *freier* culture and Israeli identity," *Alpayim* 7 (1993), 136 (in Hebrew).
36 As non-Jews the foreign workers are discriminated and treated under such conditions which prevent their becoming a target for party power games and manipulations since they are even not recognized as a political subject. Culturally they are unrecognized and totally ignored.
37 Ilan Gur-Ze'ev. "Introduction," in Ilan Gur-Ze'ev (ed.), *Conflicting Philosophies of Education in Israel/Palestine.* Dordrecht: Kluwer, 2000, 1-6.

38 Ilan Gur-Ze'ev. "Toward a non-repressive critical pedagogy," *Educational Theory* 48: 4, 463-486.
39 Yael Tamir. *Liberal Nationalism*. Princeton, New Jersey: Princeton University Press 1993.
40 Homi Bhabha. "Interrogating identity," *Document* 6 (1987), 5.
41 Homi Bhabha. "Culture's in-between," in Stuart Hall and Paul Du Gay (eds.), *Questions of Cultural Identity*. London: Sage Publications 1996, 59.
42 Zvi Zameret. *The Days of the Melting Pot*. Sde Boker 1993, 2 (in Hebrew).
43 Shlomo Fisher. "Two models of modernization: On analyzing the *edot* (ethnic groups) in Israel," *Theory and Criticism* 1 (Summer 1991), 1-22 (in Hebrew).
44 Viki Shiran. "Oriental women and others," *Mizad Sheni* 5-6 (October 1996), 26-28 (in Hebrew).
45 Charles Taylor. *Multiculturalism and the Politics of Recognition*. Princeton, New Jersey: Princeton University Press 1992, 73.
46 Walter Benjamin. "Ueber den Begriff der Geschichte," *Gesammelte Schriften*, Frankfurt a. Main: Suhrkamp 1980, 1.2, 703.
47 *Ibid.*, 701.
48 Ilan Gur-Ze'ev, Jan Mascheelein, and Nigel Blake. "Reflection," a paper presented at the Oxford conference, 2-5 April 1998, Oxford.
49 Teresa Ebert. "Political semiosis in/of American cultural studies," *The American Journal of Semiotics* 8: 1-2 (1991), 117.
50 Ilan Gur-Ze'ev. "Toward a non-repressive critical pedagogy," *ibid*.
51 Max Horkheimer. "Kritische Theorie gestern und heute," *Gesammelte Schriften* 8 Frankfurt a.Main: Suhrkamp 1985, 346.
52 Michel Walzer. "Education, democratic citizenship and multiculturalism," *Journal of Philosophy of Education* 29: 2 (1995), 188.
53 Peter McLaren. *Revolutionary Multiculturalism: Pedagogies of Dissent for the New Millennium*, Oxford 1997, 209.
54 *Ibid.*, 295.
55 For the critical attitude of this trend see Peter McLaren, *ibid.*, 297. For a representation of a liberal attitude see Walter Feinberg, "Liberalism and the aims of multicultural education," *Journal of Philosophy of Education* 29: 2 (1995), 203-216.
56 Richard Rorty. *Philosophy and the Mirror of Nature*. Princeton: Princeton University Press 1979, 189.
57 Pesahim 61, 1.
58 Ilan Gur-Ze'ev. "A well-fortified secular reservation," *Ha'aretz* (26 November 1996), 26 (in Hebrew).
59 Nimrod Aloni. "Education for the defense of democracy," *Hed Hachinuch* (June 1997), 6-7 (in Hebrew).
60 Ilan Gur-Ze'ev, *ibid.*

CHAPTER 8
Literacy, Education, and Violence: The Israeli Example

Literacy and Violence

In contrast to the mainstream literacy discourse in Israel we would like to introduce the individual's writing and reading capacities—in all their levels—as part of a struggle; a symbolic struggle between and within speech communities, their histories, images of knowledge, and their interests. According to our claim, the individual is not to be conceived but within the totality in which he/she is raised; it is a framework of which he/she is an agent, a constitutor, and a rebel. In this sense reading and writing are to be understood as a cultural and social process, reflection, and precondition. As such it is a struggle over authority to represent reality and to analyze symbols and their references; it is a *struggle* over the authority and capacity to tell the other's story, the control of its representation, interpretation, censorship, and destruction. It is a struggle that, while symbolic, is also part of total war/creation that is realized in its psychic, cultural, social and economical implications. This totality is composed of elements that have no "foundation" nor a telos for its history that constitutes its essences[1] while colliding with and creating realities.

What is at stake here is the *colonization* of the subject and the effort to liberate and conquer the psyche of the individual, with his/her acceptance, against his/her will, or by producing these elements of resistance and collaboration as part of the subject's normalization and its function as an object. This is the starting point of dialogue, but also the beginning of its opposite—discourse. In discourse the Other and his/her self-consciousness and "authentic" symbolic power; this becomes an integral part of the "self," while being part of its constitution in the "self" that meets itself always in relation to the others, that becomes for him/her "zones of control or of abandonment, or recollection and of forgetting, of force or of dependence, of exclusiveness or of sharing."[2]

Dialogue and Discourse

In dialogue the recognition of the Other is realized. This recognition refers to his/her knowledge and interests, a recognition that is immanently Utopian.[3] As long as it is truthful to its utopian nature, dialogue appears as the negation of discourse; dialogue attacks discourse as a storm that bursts in from the outside, brought in on the winds of the "hope principle." Within the framework of concrete political power games, hope can succeed and have the upper hand. This is, however, at the cost of its transformation into its opposite: its being drawn into a discourse that it was committed to replace. The immanent conflict between discourse and dialogue takes part in creating and dissolving texts, subjects, and social realities. The dialectics between them takes a central role in creating the human totality while being one of its manifestations.

The dialogical text is essentially Utopian; this is because within its horizons human ontology is being realized and challenged, and since only a real human society will be able to constitute an ideal speech situation which is a precondition for dialogue as a positive alternative. Such a social condition is immanently transcendent and absent, beyond human horizons. But already the very presence of its absence, as a negation within oppressive reality, constitutes new possibilities, transcending the current realm of self-evidence, by being the messenger on behalf of "the grand refusal." According to Edward Said, the reality of power and authority—as well as the resistance of men and women and social movements to orthodox authoritarianism—is the reality that enables the existence of texts, which strive for their critics' attention.[4] That is why every text reflects the lack of understanding or, in other words, the presence of the power to produce "the truth," the absence of the recognition of the falsity of the literary violence. In this sense, according to Said, texts are power systems that are constituted by the hegemonic culture and always at a certain human cost,[5] a cost that enables people to function normally in "their" own realm of self-evidence.

A non-violent literary work should start with facing the *polemos* in its Heraclitic sense, as a life-and-death struggle between the official and the marginalized knowledge and its production, distribution, and consumption. This is a struggle over self identity and the identity of the Other.[6] Through its false and "authentic" designation, human beings constitutes themselves as symbols, while delineating themselves within various formative technologies.[7] "The human beings in whom destiny becomes form are split into two fundamentally different parts: the ordinary human being standing in the midst of a real life is turned suddenly, in a single instant, into a symbol, the vector of a supra-personal, historical necessity."[8]

However, today, at the beginning of the twenty-first century, in opposition to the nineteenth century it is impossible to make clear distinction between the "normal" and "the great person." It is impossible to maintain the separation between "authentic" and nonauthentic, emancipation and oppression, elimination and its overcoming. It is not only that naiveté and arrogance have been dissolved, paralleling the transformation of the conceptual arena and the technological and social changes within it: even human mission or the possibility of transcendence has been banished from the historical reality and a new one has been formed, in which there is no place for tragedy, nor for concrete utopia.

This victory has not destroyed myth paralleling its destruction of exaltation, yet it has made irrelevant the Utopia of the tradition of Objective Reason. The new realm of self-evidence that has not yet arrived but, in the distance, its galloping can already be heard by those with sharp hearing and is the one to be credited for this victory. Yet this victory might still be challenged, since nothing is totally or eternally determined. Under these circumstances it is of vital importance to develop a competence to centralize the official history, and to develop new strategies of marginalizing and distracting the Others' collective memory, identity, and voice. This is the historical mission of today's schools and teachers, which normally perform as agents of oppression, rationalization, and normalization.[9]

The productivity of literacy's violence creates the very possibility of writing and publishing textbooks that will be used in the schooling process, the nature of the curriculum, the official didactic, and the ability/need to represent as irrelevant the knowledge that is developed in the collective memory of rival speech communities. This is one of the major ways of reproducing, expanding, and re-routing power, paralleling the increasingly effective colonization of the students' consciousness and the production and reproduction of their identity. The knowledge here referred to is of various kinds and levels. Yet what is of immense importance here is the image of knowledge and its concepts.[10] The more effectively the hegemonic knowledge colonizes the self of the students and constitutes their mental constitution, conceptual apparatus, consciousness, and skills for successful social function, the less its violence is visible, detectable, and challenged. In this way violence presents/hides itself and is empowered, tough manipulation apparatuses that work through hegemonic social and cultural networks that are dynamic and in constant development. The effectiveness of the hegemonic system reproductions is determined by its efficacy in leaving violence in obscure shadow and the question of being as irrelevant.

The discourse or, in other words, the literary struggle, is understood by Bourdieu as a struggle over the constitution of identity, over human lives as the life of a self-conscious subject who is aware of her/his legitimate interests, power, and hope.[11] Yet this position is too committed to foundationalism, and we are interested in introducing a utopian-dialogical stand as a starting-point for critique of the discourse and resistance to its socio-cultural context. Regarding this project the understanding of Jan Masschelein of the relationship between language, the autonomy of the subject, and socio-political praxis is much more relevant.

According to the thesis here introduced, discourse cannot be understood solely within the framework of power/knowledge dialectics since it is also a manifestation of the current reality's potential for change and the possibilities of discrepancy from it. Ironically, it is within the horizons of discourse that *the totally other* appears; as such, it appears in the image of "the hope principle." With the hope principle's presence as impetus, the resistance and refusal that illuminate the fallacy of present reality is possible. Yet, the historical presence of *hope* draws it into the process of empowering and advancing the current order of things and the language that shields and hides it. This is also the hidden curriculum of the literacy industry.

Central Trends in Today's Literacy

The power/right to read and write a text, is basically a reflection of power relations and the symbolic dynamics that produce the legitimacy of activating the prohibitions, confiscations, classifications, and deportations over the subjects of the written or verbal text, over the legitimate forms of interpretation. These and other manifestations of this sort are incarcerated within the inner logic of the local system. As authority, it always shows up as aimless, anonymous, and meaningless—practically hiding the interests, apparatuses, pre-assumption, and manipulation practices while encoding in secret codes its ways of controlling, representing, and distribution of its special objects; objects that conceive themselves as subjects: and sometimes even as autonomous subjects.

Like other systems of the current realm of self-evidence, the Israeli system represents a conflict between the world where the autonomous subject has been conceived as desirable and possible, and the characters of the age which accepts its own decline as a cheerful and exciting experience.[12]

Knowledge, and its possible interpretation and advancement, includes knowledge about self-identity. Here, literacy is revealed in all its richness: as a struggle over the identity, as a struggle over the possibilities and the limits of the subject as a possessor of her/his own life, identity, and as the sovereign of consciousness, interests, powers, and hopes, while being constituted as a reflection of their negation.

The strongest power in the human world realizes itself in symbolic interchange and practices that concern the ability and the right to read and write certain texts, as well as in the production, reproduction, and the advancement of executing the prohibition, the hope, the expropriation, and control of the objects and subjects of these linguistic entities, their essences and realizations in society. Such a concept of literacy is realized in the Critical Pedagogy of Paulo Freire and Henry Giroux.

According to Giroux, literacy, in its broadest sense, is committed to the empowering of human beings by synthesizing pedagogical skills and critical competence. But more than that, literacy is understood to be a central element in challenging hegemonic practices and theories of the constitution of gender, class, race, and subjective identities as socio-historical constructs. In this instance, literacy becomes a central pedagogical and political mechanism for the constitution of the ideological conditions and the social practices that are committed to the development of social movements and subjective possibilities that are aimed at a radical democracy and the struggles on its behalf.[13] While being progressive we have to criticize and negate Girouxian mechanistic literary concept and praxis. One of the central weaknesses of this literary theory is its limited concept of political power; it does not ask for the essence of politics and it does not refer to the being that constitutes social power networks and operates within it as power.

In our mind, these are the central issues that concern literacy, and not the ones that are denoted in Israeli hegemonic educational discourse. First some hegemonic definitions of literacy will be introduced. We will not develop the definitions and their critique, nor the central trends in current literacy: their elaboration will restrict itself to aim of preparation work for the critique of literacy in Israel today.

In 1971 a special UNESCO commitee introduced the following definition of literacy: "A person is literate when he has acquired the essential knowledge and skills which enable him to engage in all those activities in which literacy is required for effective functioning in his group or community."[14] This definition well reflects the functionalist trend in literacy.

Functionalist literacy has three main dimensions: fix minimalist yardsticks for determining the reading competence, according to the demands of the labor market; precise measurement, quantification, and standardization of the individual's competence that is classified and examined in opposition to her/his human essence and reduced into her/his narrowest and most abstract instrumental and functionalist "meaning", and the advancement of the synthesis between the achievements of the person examined in the literacy test and her/his chances of effectively serving the requirements of the job that is the point of reference in the case specifically referred to.[15] "The actual competence, the skills of the individual, are emphasized, and always in a given context. The functionalist literacy was developed by the American army in accordance with the experience of the Second World War; it indicated that the poor performance of American soldiers in their missions was connected to their reading/writing performance. When determining functionalist literacy the American Army referred to the capacity to conceive instructions needed for the successful fulfillment of basic military functions and tasks. . . a fifth-grade reading level."[16]

In accordance with its multicultural sensitivity and the commitment to contribute to the disadvantaged and marginalized, the definition of the commitee appointed by UNESCO is broader in the sense that it does not solely concentrate in the reading and writing competence. However, its orientation is as functionalist: here too the individual's literacy is determined according to the effectiveness of her/his function in regions of meaning and status production.

Within the framework of this conception there is another popular trend that does not even refer to the efficiency of the individual's function and is solely concerned with the formal years of schooling. This is the case in the CAAE's definition.[17] This trend is very much alive even today, with the adjustments needed in reply to changing conditions. It is important to assert that some of the current multicultural alternatives are as repressive as this one; it manifests Instrumental Rationality and current needs of the market. In the United States, the language of literacy is connected to popular forms of the liberal and the right-wing rhetoric. Here literacy is reduced to a functionalist perspective that reflects, serves, and is part of an ideology and economic interests that aim at manipulating the poor, the minorities, and the disadvantaged to be swept by the logic of unity, namely, be drowned into the dominant cultural tradition.[18]

Central Trends in Israeli Literacy (A)

In Israel, too, the distribution of literacy as a relevant product pays tribute to excellence, professionalism, and social success,[19] and other aspects of conformist consciousness, a consciousness that is always the right and the relevant one, from the hegemonian discourse point of view. In the era of the end of meaning, the rapid-advanced manipulation strategies of the literacy myth in Israel serve the existing order of things as follows:

A. By cutting discourse into tiny parts of literacy, parts such as lingual literacy, computer literacy, media literacy, cultural literacy, Critical Literacy, moral literacy, and aesthetic literacy;[20] as if all these might be classified into a meaningful general category. This fragmentation is very important for the production of a discipline where technocrats are cultivated in and by independent spaces that are segregated and fortified against any possibility of foreign experts, infiltrating from neighboring regions of truth production. Naturally, not less important is the immunization of all aspects of literacy from possible critique concerning the philosophic-hermeneutic axioms of the current system.

B. Even when the centrality of "cultural literacy" is emphasized, there is a regular neglect of the socio-cultural context in which this discourse is framed, and a failure to acknowledge that discourse is a bonafide political process; it is not surprising that the interests which this discourse is serving or struggling against are not elaborated. The systematic avoidance of conceptual analysis that will refer to concepts such as meaning, text, and truth is also not unimportant. Central to this kind of literacy is the neglectness of challenging the practices of the production of the reader by texts and the interpretive strategies to which she/he is exposed to and activated by, as well as their positioning in the socio-cultural context.

C. As a theory, literacy is distributed within the new discourse as a tool, a mere instrument. In our mind this is to be seen as a meaningful political contribution to the further instrumentalization of knowledge and the strengthening of the impotency of those for whom knowledge distribution is their profession.

A non-instrumentalist orientation will acknowledge the dialogue that we are. It will denote that we are positioned and mostly produced within the framework of a text that is not to be totally separated from the socio-cultural context that infiltrates it and produces it for its own sake. Such an understanding demands a philosophical commitment that is inseparable from political activism, a stance that does not serve the new needs of the market that the new literacy is committed to serve. Herewith, the reconstruction of the new discipline and its new experts will be accompanied by showing how the experts themselves are being created as part of the production of both the new field and the need for it. According to the thesis here presented, literacy is aimed at the production of critical impotency, and enhancement of the imposition of the relevant desires, skills, and socio-cultural products of the discourse in every one of the discourse's agents. As such, she/he will be an efficient producer/consumer; as a unproblematic and productive citizen and, while acting for its own "success," will ensure the realization of the system's logic and its reproduction. It is of vital importance that literacy should produce a cheerful *false* consciousness that will be conservative enough to abandon "the grand refusal," on the one hand, and the claim for reflection, transcendence, and essential social change, on the other.

D. One of the most effective marketing strategies in distributing today's literacy is the elimination of the historical evolution and the historicity of every philosophical-hermeneutical discussion. In this light, it is also of vital importance to neutralize the relevancy of ideology critique of texts. This is because this orientation might introduce the demand to criticize the stance of literacy as a new ideological element as well as a repressive apparatus.

The problematics with which the new discipline is dealing are not represented by its experts as philosophical but, rather, as practical: as a field of research that might be supported by a functionalist theory and neutral praxis, with no attention to the history of the interpretative tradition into which the new literacy would such as to join, or the tradition it wants to overtake. Accordingly, the inventors of the new literacy feel free to avoid analyzing the meaning of the pretension to produce skills and practices for constituting, revealing, or destroying meanings in Western society today, the end of the twentieth century. They disregard questions such as "What is a text in our era and arena"; "What are its borders (if it has them)"; "What are the ontological relations between a text, its author, and its addressee as a dialogical issue"; "What is still the possible textual understanding in our era—concerning the institutionalized education and the counter-educational alternative"; and "What are the legitimate and illegitimate forms of production, the encoding and decoding of texts, readers, authors, and interpreters, in a changing context"?

Beyond the professional functionalist jargon, beyond the good will and creativity of the well-intentioned experts who are today developing, brightly, the new literacy, blooms a new cooperation with the present order of things, and new tools for its advancement are developed. To a certain degree, this is because the efficiency of the inner-colonization strategies in the system has grown to such a degree that illiteracy has become a threat to the present economic order.[21] Another reason is the need for new strategies for the self-reproduction of the current realm of self-evidence and the clearing-concealing advent of being itself,[22] that for that matter uses traditions, social forces, and technological progress that block the unmediated appearance of the dialogical essence of human beings and the world.

Central Trends in Israeli Literacy (B)

Consciously, or unconsciously, the production of the new field fits perfectly and strengthens the visions of Israeli figures such as Steff Wertheimer, Shimshon Shoshani, Ehud Barak, and Benjamin ("Bibi") Netanyahu. The technocratic rhetoric of advanced technology and successful industry as well as the bureaucratic, academic, and current relevant political rhetoric are taking part in the same trend, albeit from different interests, jargons, and perspectives. They all share a discourse that is relevant, up-to-date, and effective; one which reflects an important dimension of current Western economy of repression/production. This trend is not challenged but, rather, is strengthened, even when in the Israeli academic knowledge industry literacy is produced under labels and explicit goals such as "advancing critique," "multi-dimensional thinking." From time to time it even happens that literacy is introduced in its broadest contexts and explicitly introduced as something that refers to more than simply reading and writing competence.

One might find a good example in the work of Zvia Walden. She represents literacy as something which is not merely technical that refers to reading and writing.[23] Walden explicitly rejects the "mythical" notion "according to which reading is a technical and not a way of life." However, at the same time she attacks intellectual treatment of the issue of language; in her mind it is nothing but an obscure game that refers to manifold cultural messages, instead of reintroducing writing and reading to the context of developmental processes and the introduction of tools for well-defined and controlled abilities for evaluating the progress of learning.[24] In the Israeli context, the texts of Hezi Brosh[25] and Shoshana Fulman are typical of the general trend.

For Shoshana Fulman, literacy is but a synonym for traditional reading and writing teaching in a functionalist and instrumental framework.[26] For Amikam Marbach, "Exactly because the origin of *orianut* (literacy) is *orita* (the Jewish religious law), it is important to connect it first of all with the concept of learning. In the more precise context of excellent *academic* literacy as learning, which we try to develop in our college, in our mind, it is important to identify it with *excellent learning*, that is founded on the research process: the definition of the aim and the need for information, identification of the information, the selection of the relevant information, its appropriation, organization, communication and production."[27] Even in its humanistic-emancipatory most sophisticated and advances forms, the Israeli literacy industry is not totally disconnected from its commitment to the instrumental-functionalist orientation, as manifested in the work of Rachel Hertz-Lazarowitz.

Hertz-Lazarowitz's conception of literacy is derived from her general understanding of communal learning, which is realized within the framework of her highly respected project called *Elash*. The system she developed synthesizes communal teaching procedures with the construction of reading, writing, speaking, listening, and language-understanding processes within a socio-creative learning process that attempts to become meaningful for the child.[28] This project, perhaps the most advanced in the Israeli context, tries to see literacy in its socio-cultural contexts, while positioning in the center the students, their active involvement, the improvement of their self-esteem, and their social integration. However, with all its importance, in our mind, this system, which is founded on the American CIRC (Cooperative Integrated Reading and Composition), does not transcend and overcome the obstacle that Hertz-Lazarowitz is committed to overcome.

The literacy that is introduced within this system is supposed to be founded on the speech community as the source of knowledge, and of the constitution and support for the literacy process.[29] In that, it reflects the influence of American democratic and radical pedagogies[30] as different from the hegemonic conceptions of literacy worldwide and in Israel. In opposition to these trends in her work, Hertz-Lazarowitz is very sensitive to cultural and social dimensions of teaching/constituting language and identity. However, in the last resort, it is but a most advanced mode of instrumentalist-functionalist orientation.

No real opposition and different speech communities are treated here; and neither the critique nor the development of their real political interests as part of a violent discourse are treated in this project. The project does not refer to their collective memories, and their abolished and unrecognized rights by the hegemonic group are the target of this learning process: the process refers to the reading competence of politically neutral creatures, that in the language of this project are called "weak groups." The teaching materials and the texts are all taken from the normal curriculum and are not directed against the hidden project of hegemonic education as normalization violence that calls for counter-education: basically, the process aims at nothing more than improving the level of the students' achievements in school and in life, according to the hegemonic expectations.

The instrumental orientation of this schooling process is revealed when it is shown that within its framework even the denotation of social relations in the discourse, around and within texts, is ultimately revealed to be another instrument for promoting the academic achievements of the students in accordance with the hegemonic expectations: the more a group of students improves its so-called positive-social behavior the better is the chance that its members will be involved in a "high quality learning process," and the more a group is supposed to improve its learning and produce better learning achievements.[31] Hertz-Lazarowitz even suggests teaching "intersubjective skills" as early as possible—before the teacher (he/she and no one else!) enacts the cooperative group learning, namely, as a preparatory stage for successful learning. In this progressive and emancipatory teaching, even the relation to "the other" and to the self-esteem become an instrument for promoting "achievements" that the hegemonic ideology determines as such. A critical reading of the specific programs of this version of literacy reveals in detail to what degree it reproduces the power/knowledge relationship and the given hierarchies in hegemonic culture, as part and parcel of realizing this concept of literacy within the groups' interactions. This is so to a degree that one of the students is appointed to the post of "the 'watchman'" of time who is in control of 'the good words'—trying to empower students and strengthen the positive aspects that are in the group."[32] In our mind, the idea of the "watchman" of the time and the control of "the good words" of the others is to support weak groups and the encouragement of those who did not reveal, or those who were weakened to the degree of losing their ability to defend, develop, and express their identity. As a principle, and not only as a literacy practice for young students, this is an important humanistic idea, and it is important to see this project in this light. However, in the current Israeli socio-cultural context, taking in mind the real economic, social, cultural, and emotional trends, this concept of literacy is to be seen as being at the same level as the Panopticon and the development of the status of knowledge, as analyzed by Michel Foucault.

The Panopticon as an architectural form and as an idea was constituted toward the end of the eighteenth century, in order to secure institutionally (in schools, jails, and hospitals) the student/prisoner/patient as an object of inspection and control. The transparency of the human space and its rational control were meant to prevent evils,[33] as part of the production of the modern French citizen. In the new literacy the system is no longer satisfied with towers and inspectors and with explicit regulations of external centralized control (which are easily to be acknowledged, criticized, and resisted), as in the case of the Panopticon: from now on the normalization/repression process is supposed to be fully and subtly internalized. Now the system's rationality is supposed to evolve from within the controlled inmates themselves, namely, students who are taught "live skills" and "intersubjective capacities"[34] in an anti-dialogical manner, skills such as flexibility that are needed for the efficient reproduction of the system, in which other capacities, needs, and knowledge are irrational, irrelevant, and do not promise "success" as in this project. Yet, there is still a need for a watchman who will guard "good words"—only that in contrast with the classical Panopticon, in today's sophisticated Panopticon the watchman is one of the inmates themselves, that the literacy that he/she will purchase, with that of the others, will pay its fair share to the withdrawal of the demand for dialogue, to *the totally other* and for the constitution of motivations, perspectives, and goals for struggle and resistance to the current order. One of the manifestations of the banality of our tragedy is to be seen in that we have reached a historical stage in which ignorance and illiteracy have become for many groups the last base to protect their historical memory and collective identity. The omnipotent penetration possibilities of mass communication and educational and teaching strategies—electronic and cooperative such as the one that Hertz-Lazarowitz is introducing—are aimed at normalizing and fully controlling even these potential oppositions by enclosing them as an integral element of the system.

There is an ideological base to the claim according to which one should differentiate between acquiring reading skills and intersubjective capabilities and the capacity to criticize, decode, and decipher high culture texts and the socio-cultural sphere in general. This claim is shared by all instrumental tendencies. This separation is common to all the literacy projects in Israel, as reflected in the proceedings of the *SCRIPT* conference that were published in Volume 11 of the Israeli literacy journal, *Helkat Lashon*. This claim is valid also concerning the local constructivist tendencies in Israeli literacy, such as the one developed by Michal Zelermeier,[35] who sees her work as a developed Critical Literacy, and in other work, such as that done by Freema Elbaz, who tries to recollect the voices and stories of teachers and give them hope.[36] These works have contributed meaningful educational gains. Yet they are not critical enough; they are domesticated critiques. After all, the present order of things is their foundation and telos, and basically they serve the current power hierarchies and hegemonies.

An Alternative View of Israeli Literacy

In opposition to the literacy as activated in Israel, we claim that basically literacy is philosophical; literacy is a reflective glimpse at the utopian dialogue that we are—or to the discourse that blocks the dialogue or the struggle over the possibility of the dialogue which we could have realized in a reasoned reality. By the same token, literacy is a political practice, and a moment of socio-cultural critique. In the concept of dialogue that we introduce, we refer to the kind of fusion of horizons that is actualized in cultivating authenticity and conceptualization potentials as Charles Taylor suggests within the framework of his project of discursive understanding,[37] which is not very far from what Nicholas Burbules develops in his pedagogical project.[38] In both cases, understanding is not a revelation of absolute, eternal, and objective truth, but rather a product of understanding which is always a socio-cultural and historical discursive intersubjective process.

In our opinion, in this context language should be used in its broadest sense. As such, language not only contains the words we use, but also other expressive modes, as mediated by art, sport, and love. We claim that the acquisition of a language and the realization of the writing and reading competence, let alone a dialogical self-constitution or a struggle over the possibility of a critical dialogical fusion of horizons, is always framed within a concrete socio-cultural context, reproduces or challenges a certain tradition, and is a product of certain power apparatuses that determine who will learn, what is to be learned, who will not learn, as well as who will be the teacher, what pedagogy and what language will be permitted, encouraged, or restricted and which histories are forbidden to the sight of the students who learn to read.[39] However, at the same time, language might be much more than that. Even cognitive development and the psychological conditions for the acquisition of lower and higher reading capabilities are basically philosophical issues and a political praxis which are to be understood in the context of ideology critique and in the context of concrete conditions for inter-cultural discourses and for different truth productions within the framework of each rival system.[40]

In its present mode, the literacy discourse in Israel neglects these dimensions, even in projects that have been explicitly emancipated from the ideology of the supremacy of the expert (except, of course, the expert for literacy);[41] even Eli Kuziminsky is apparently not aware that the teaching of reading and writing is always possible as part of a death and life struggle between rival histories, identities, and interests of different systems and groups and within them, as he is also indifferent to the utopia of a dialogical struggle within each speech community and between speech communities, and to the dialectics between pessimism and utopia in literacy per se.

The theory and practice of teaching/learning and the writing/reading of texts as here mentioned emphasize the need to challenge the successes of hegemonic, as well as marginalized power apparatuses which are present in the schooling process and in education in general. It denotes the special role that these manipulations have on securing the impotency, the conservative outlook, and the productivity of subjects that function as objects of their systems. In opposition to this reality, the theory here introduced suggests a different concept of subject, autonomy, knowledge, schooling, and cultural reproduction. This Critical Theory conceives differently the process of schooling in general and the school arena in particular: here the school is conceived first of all as a space that is structurally committed to determine the *limits* of the legitimate discourse and the quest for the truth; in addition, it strategically operates to produce and control the reflection, resistance, and refusal as well as the introduction of alternative capabilities, bodies of knowledge, images of knowledge, and political order. The normal school is where the violence of education executes its productive potential by activating its apparatuses for producing and controlling human subjects that will reflect, protect, and expand the current realm of self-evidence. In this sense the literacy industries serve the system and its truths, and as such are undefeatable. Here, Michel Foucault's position is of special relevance: Truth, in this context, is not something to be revealed and acquired, but rather a bond of regulations according to which the truth is separated from the false, and certain effects of power are attributed to the truth.[42] Or, as he says elsewhere: "'Truth' is to be understood as a system of ordered procedures for the production, regulation, distribution, circulation and operation of statements."[43]

In a discursive context, when the issue is texts' understanding or the ability/encouragement/prohibition of texts' writing, what we are facing is an interpretative struggle; a struggle in which a subject might realize its (potential) autonomy and constitute herself/himself, while activating her/his self-consciousness. The other possibility, which is more likely, is that the subject will enter this struggle while realizing *another* self-consciousness, and in her/his struggle will realize the power, the character, and the targets of the repressive power that produced her/him; and plays with it in the most possible productive way. Normally, these two alternatives are dialectically connected, and they are closely linked to the possibility of a successful normalization in which education secures the individual's indifference to the call of being, and will not struggle furiously against the restraints on his/her self-constituted identity and the world's articulation within an ongoing dialogue. Some examples will be introduced to connect this claim to the Israeli context.

In Israel literacy should treat, in parallel, the issue of the competence and the issue of justice, of philosophy, and of political praxis. It should be implemented as action research that will treat the right and the competence of Jewish students from Morocco to read and write their history as independent from the Zionist narrative, but also to change it, as well as to transcend themselves from this collective identity, knowledge, and interests, toward a non-repressive realm of self-evidence that will transcend its participants within a negative utopia. Another example is the real possibilities and right of the sons of four hundred destroyed Palestinian villages to re-map Israeli/Palestinian historiography, and tell the currently forbidden story of their lost communities, as part of their struggle over memory, language, and texts that enable and represent counter-memory and hope. However, this literacy is also in constant danger of replacing one realm of self-evidence with another and the literacy that is non-repressive should enable the individual to overcome such a progressive literacy and transcend herself/himself within the framework of negative utopianism and the impetus of *hope*, on the one hand, and the *call* of the potentials of the dialogical human essence to be realized, on the other. However, literacy as counter-education that negates every sort of self-evidence and is committed to overcome every obstacle to transcendence and dialogue does not have to ignore the achievements of Critical Pedagogy as reflected in the literacy of Freire and Giroux. In the Israeli context, it should take seriously the examples of the Morocco Jews and the re-mapping of their language, identity, and future together with their Palestinian partners/enemies/victims and their part in the dialogue.

The theory and practice of the literacy introduced here should tackle the presence of manipulation apparatuses in the schooling space, on the one hand, and the brutal fact of the constitution of the subject as an agent of the system and as an object, on the other. This is of vital importance for understanding the possibilities of the emancipation of teachers and students. In the absence of a critical reconstructionist emancipatory interest in literacy, the instrumental or the abstract-interpretationist projects will reproduce the current power relations of the system and its realm of self-evidence. In the absence of a critical-emancipatory treatment of the issue of power/knowledge acquisition to read/write, it is of no use speaking about understanding a text or teaching to write—unless as another manifestation of the presence of the control practices of the system. In Israel, even the first level of Critical Literacy has not yet been reached. Within the framework of this kind of literacy one can treat the issue of the Palestinians' texts, that were already mentioned, or the feminist issue, if we mention another one. Yet, again, the central issue here is the status, the possibilities, and limitations of the subject: the possibilities for a human intersubjectivity within which she/he can realize herself/himself as an autonomous subject in a reasoned dialogue. In the school arena we refer here to the students' possibilities to regain sovereignty and solidarity, power and language, knowledge and telos. In a word, to constitute herself/himself as an *autonomous* subject within a dialogical coexistence with the Other, the partner, the lover.

In opposition to the common assumptions in Israeli literacy discourse, we say that the individual acquires writing and intersubjective structures and syntax only within the networks of power games within and between different speech communities and traditions. Yet the individual is not a mere manifestation of the context that he/she normally reflects and serves, even as a rebel. This is since the hope principle[44] manifests itself in the human potential for transcendence through reflection on the self-evidence[45] and for dialogical elevation through self-constitution in a counter-education of a solidarian, dialogical, and self-critical speech community. The realization of the subject's autonomy is a Utopia, yet the struggle over its realization, or the very possibility of such a struggle, enables human beings to be more than mere manifestations of meaningless power games.

A Short Critical History of Literacy

At the beginning of the modern era, literacy was conceived as a splendid personal quality. Whoever was blessed with this quality and the possibility of its cultivation was conceived as one whose way to truth and redemption is paved. Literacy, here, was conceived basically as a moral quality. The official patronage over the interpretative power of texts—and the Holy Scriptures before any other text—was, naturally, the Church. However, in general, an individual who was conceived as blessed with this benefit was not only regarded as educated, but also as a good and moral person, or as the messenger of the devils. To a certain degree one can understand the Protestants' revolt against Catholicism as a manifestation of literacy's violence in action. The struggle was over the answer to the question of who has the interpretative sovereignty; What are the criteiria for a correct interpretative diction? What are the theological and political meanings of a lack of consensus in understanding a holy text? What are the limits of a Holy Scripture? and so forth. According to the conceptions common in Protestantism, personal attachment to the text might improve the soul and strengthen belief, with no major need for clergy's mediation. This theme is clearly emphasized in Luther's *Letter to the German Nobles* (1520).[46]

In many aspects, literacy in the modern era has developed under the umbrella of hermeneutics. In other words, it is impossible to understand the current discourse on literacy unless it is understood as part of the hermeneutic tradition. In the last generation, while continuing its traditional theological orientation as revealing the truth in the Holy Scriptures, it continued its development in three different trends and under different titles. One should mention titles such as the status of language, textuality, philosophical hermeneutics, literary criticism, and literacy.

In his work *On the Education of the Human Race*, Gotthold Ephraim Lessing presents the history of human education through three texts which represent three stages, in which humanity develops suitable different reading strategies. And, in parallel, different possibilities for salvation are brought to the world. That which provided humanity with the progress of the three stages and the three progressive stages of the correct reading of the word is that which secured the adjustment of the human being's needs to the level of the Scriptures of the time. According to this conception, the correct reading is the key for salvation and is shaped by revelation.[47] The Old Testament is conceived here as a historically childish textbook, suited for educating a childish nation.[48] As the historical readers of this text, the Jews were educated to the degree that they could take the burden of educating other people.[49] According to Lessing, the New Testament and its suitable reading strategies make up the second historical textbook of humanity, which is at a high level, when compared with its predecessor.[50] It is similar to what happened in the education of humanity in its second stage, that replaced the Jewish religion by Jesus Christ and the Old Testament with the New Testament, with the entire set of reading strategies, way of life, and the pattern to salvation and transcendence, it is suggested by Lessing that the third stage has been opened and with it new human possibilities are actual. The special context of the new book constitutes its uniqueness: Humanity can relinquish, gradually, the New Testament since humanity faces a new revelation. In the new revelation humanity is educated in an enlightened way and finally reaches maturity. In its third stage of education, since it reached its maturity, humanity needs no dogma or authoritative teacher. Reason, according to Lessing, can offer the needed literacy competence to such a degree that there is no need to abandon totally the holy texts of the past if one is emancipated from dogmatism and false fate. In its maturity literacy can provide humanity with relevance of the Scriptures, even without a naive belief in the historicity of Jesus[51] and the supposed validity of old interpretations. As one of the paradigmatic representatives of the Enlightenment, Lessing understood that the time had come for a new education freed of authoritative interpretation strategies in the spirit of the new book. Such a book is unique in that it is not introduced to humanity by an omnipotent writer. This book has not been written, and humanity itself has to write, read, and interpret this unique volume. However, one should notice that what we are facing here is not an early postmodern version of "the death of the writer" ideology, but rather the opposite. What we face is religiosity that still transforms reasoned humanity into a divine entity and the book that it will write into a new gospel.

In its narrower sense, nineteenth century literacy was bonded to the service of national ideologies. This is the peak of an educational development which started with the introduction of printing in the West, a process paralleled by the recognition of the nation as the sovereign, and of its responsibility for the welfare of the entire population. Within the framework of this project there is a commitment for the mass teaching of reading and writing as the pathway to general education, well-being, and happiness[52] to the degree that they are a manifestation of reason. They are an object for de-codification, inspection, and control, as Foucault shows in his critique of the Panopticon, and they are conceived as powerful instruments for socio-cultural control and capitalist expansionism.

With the gradual erosion of the old realm of self-evidence, the construction of consensus (namely, the possibility of control with minimum waste of direct repressive energies) has become more dependent on the effectiveness of symbolic manipulations. This is an education that uses the masses of new readers as objects for internalizing effective symbols, and productive desires, constituting a useful conceptual apparatus. In special institutionalized spaces, experts were trained for this mission by the system, in order to deliver to the normalized masses the symbolic energy that would secure their productivity as servants and agents of the system and its elites. The control, activation, and selection of the collective consciousness were from now on determined by the new status of literacy and in the expansion of literacy into ever larger levels of society.[53] Paralleling the formation of more effective and deeper-penetrating strategies of control, selection, censorship, and reproduction, the seventeenth century also introduced potential emancipatory changes with the widespread written text. As shown in the research of Davis, the widespread phenomenon of printing was accompanied by the demolition of traditional monopolies over knowledge and its distribution, and new possibilities for new knowledge and speculations entered human reality.[54]

Since the beginning of the twentieth century, especially since its second half, people in the West were not educated in light of the autonomous subject's ideal; people are not conceived seriously in light of the Enlightenment's ideals as autonomous; as ideal rational individuals they are capable of deciphering truths from traditional beliefs as well as new texts. Ideally they are also creators, in the form of objective writers of texts that are illuminating and potentially transcending. Today, the modern Eros that manifested itself in a claim for truth, self-constitution of a reflective subject, and happiness by a kind of education that since the era of Kant and von Humboldt to that of Max Weber, Sigmund Freud, and Theodor Adorno was called *Bildung*[55] has been totally eroded. In the era of "the death of the subject,"[56] there is no more room for such an arrogant conception of knowledge, and with it was dissolved the concrete potential for dialogue and the rescue of the real meaning of humanity realizing itself; with it disappeared the concrete possibility for non-manipulative reading of texts, within which potential dialogues are to be realized, or struggled for.

In important parts of current postmodern discourse, both the text's interpreters and the people whom the texts are supposed to manipulate, are conceived as constituted by the symbols of a reality which is nothing but a supreme text, with no objective foundations and transcendental horizons: a text in which signifiers refer merely to other signifiers, with no objective point of reference: simulacra of simulacra, copies with no origin, or reality. Simulacra as iper-realia are, according to Baudrillard, a manifestation of post-modern reality's power.[57] However, in contrast to Baudrillard's one-dimensional pessimism, other postmodern de-constructions have a Utopian axis, in contrast to its objection; Western meta-narratives are deconstructed, and with them also the repressive elements of the quests for truth and the commitment for human solidarity within the framework of a humanistic emancipatory project and its general theories with their special status. In this development the traditional claim to reveal the true meaning of a text was also deconstructed. Most of the postmodern thinkers devoted themselves to the mission of revealing the manipulation hidden by the self-evidence of a true or objective meaning in the text and in its claim for universal validity. In parallel to the postmodern celebration of Foucault's declaration about the end of the subject, Barthes's declaration about the death of the writer[58] is celebrated as well. All this is in order to save the fragmentary, the chaotic, and the local: to save them from the immanent repression of the totalitarianism of the central concepts that govern truth regions (that when constituted were equipped with a sound metaphysical anchor). In the past the original author was considered one of the manifestations of this "anchor," as a point of reference; the author was considered as a locus of the original intention and a junction of the authentic meanings of the text. Accordingly, qualified and authoritative interpreters are the text's interpreters. The post-modern *escape* from this trap is presented very similarly to the modern positive utopianism against which it rebels.

Today, the attitude toward the text is determined by the effort of reconstructing the author's original intention as a rich container of assumptions that enable the positive utopianism in literacy: reaching true, objective, and changeless knowledge, as well as enabling rational subjects to overcome their ignorance or solipsisms and to transcend themselves by creating a dialogue between the writer and the reader who is qualified to reconstruct the original intentions of the writer.[59]

In its second stage of development, this modern tradition is represented/elevated by ideology critique. The transcendence from the realm of self-evidence and the demand for essential change in reality are part of its understanding of the autonomy of the subject as a locus of reason and potential transformation, normally conceived in a rather optimistic and naive fashion. In the postmodern discourse, an important shift has taken place, toward the acceptance of the supremacy of the text over the writer and reader. This is in the cost of extreme relativism in which reality itself is a construct of a game between texts and apparatuses that create/shape/represent this textuality. Baudrillard understands current reality as a meta-reality[60] in which symbols are real and even quests and human acts are conditioned and directed by the symbolic system and function as mere simulacra, as are all other commodities.[61] In such a world there is no place for metaphysics or for ideology critique.[62]

The historical sensitivity of the time shifted its attention to the presence and power of the new prayer. The secular prayer of the post-modern era is very similar to what in Judaism is called *tefilat hayachid* (the prayer of the individual) in the mass society's desert. By the same token it is also the prayer of the masses: as individuals and groups are controlled by the violence of contingent fashions that manipulate them. This prayer is not styled, and formally it does not have a conventional version: it is a prayer from the heart that represents the reality of the quest for redemption and the need for care in an era that Baudrillard calls "after the end of the orgy"[63] of modernism and the ideals of the Enlightenment. The traditional quest for redemption and the suitable organization of the soul for such a stance are being transformed in our era. They are presented as Eros in the service of Thanatos. The traditional object of prayers calling and the quest for God's divine approval or revealing of the objective truth or the Absolute, have been transformed into a mere striving for power which is represented in commodities in a world where even their signifiers are mere commodities. This reality conceives itself as an anti-transcendentalist, as the final one. Daily examples are to be seen in the sport industry, the clown's status at birthday parties, electronic games in which even happiness and laughter are totally built-in and controlled, in virtual reality's pornography, and so forth.

Postmodern discourse has many trends, some of which try to justify alternative ethics and a non-foundationalist and unrepressive emancipatory project not committed to the abandonment of reason. In our mind, Zigmunt Bauman's project exemplifies this trend.[64] Within the framework of such a project the critique of texts and the conditions for a dialogue between different texts within a culture and between different cultures are not as foundational, arrogant, and optimistic as that exemplified by the projects of Schleiermacher and Dilthey. Yet this is a post-modern trend that did not really disconnect itself from an Enlightenment project, as one can see in the work of Foucault. These works should be recognized as important especially for those of us who are still humanists. For such people, it is important to connect such works as Foucault's and those of Adorno, Habermas, Jamson, and Freire. Within the framework of this critical tradition, textuality is presented as the central question of the potential dialogue that we are. This critical tradition introduces the possibility of writing, censoring, interpreting, forced oblivion, and the distribution of bodies of knowledge and images of knowledge in opposition to the hegemonic instrumentalist-functionalist ideology, and beyond the current division between ethnocentristic pluralism and universalism. Within this tradition, rational critique of texts is part of the critique of reason and one of the potentials for reason's realization into a concrete way of life. It is part of the problematization of the self and its evidences; part of its re-articulation in face of meaninglessness where the ethical "I" has no words yet its very presence of its abyss promises hope. Hope which is not directed toward anything specific yet enables the reality of the moral "I" as a partner for deconstructing normalizing education and its "normalities," "truths," and other demons. It enables the kind of estrangement that will overcome oblivion of the human mission by enabling the attention to the call of *the totally other*, of transcendence into the dialogue that we are. This is the kind of critical and dialogical literacy; and that in Israeli literacy discourse is not even positioned as a relevant theoretical position to disapprove.

Herewith we will attempt to show to what an extent and at what cost the Israeli discourse on literacy refuses to acknowledge both the post-modern and the Enlightenment's traditions. Special attention will receive the philosophical and the political unacknowledged relevancy of these traditions for today's literacy and the endowment of a critical Eros in our era. As a first step we will denote the socio-cultural conditions and the images of knowledge that enable the current tremendous success of the hegemonic trend in Israel.

Bibism, Coca-Cola, and Literacy in Israel

Historically, the founding assumptions and goals of Israeli education were formed as a bona fide manifestation of modernism. The urgent need of socialists, liberals, and religious groups of new bodies of knowledge that would serve the national project has formed knowledge images and meta-narratives that have met these interests. Since 1967 there has been a strong pragmatist-functionalist tendency which is anti-idealist, anti-solidarian, technocratic-oriented, and assumed neutral toward the political context. Within its context even the recently arrived constructivist attitudes have found themselves a comfortable accommodation. In Israel, a unique historical junction has been constituted between the modern national-instrumentalist attitude, with both its socialist and liberal wings, and the anti-idealism of instrumentalist functionalism. This unification blooms within the framework of economic liberalism which, to some degree, attracts even the religious nationalists of Israel, whose final aim is nothing less than a full-scale Jewish theocracy in Great Israel.

In Israel as a local arena of a current Western realm of self-evidence, knowledge is no longer evaluated in categories such as those common in the tradition of Objective Reason: promoting fulfillment of the cosmic telos or betraying it, patriotic-not-patriotic, true-false, beautiful-ugly, and so forth, have been replaced by performative and functionalist yardsticks such as efficient-inefficient, high rating-low rating, fashionable-not-fashionable; the difference lies in the abandonment of the absolute, transcendental, and all-encompassing rational-moral categories. In Israel, the shift from absolute categories to non-foundationalist, local, temporary, and contingent ones is paralleled by another shift: one from the imperative of self-sacrifice for the collective as a manifestation of an idealist and utopian commitment to a different commitment—to the subjectivity of the individual. Under these conditions this individual is not a persona, has no essence and self-constitution capabilities, but rather the opposite: instead of realizing human potentialities and their development, this individual is realized as a manifestation of the omnipotence of the system, which produces him/her as a productive production/consumption unit, with no transcendental horizon. This shift does not manifest itself directly and positively. Bibi Netanyahu exemplifies it.

The function of Bibi's image might be a good example for the way in which the new functionalist-instrumental trend is reproduced and advances rapidly in line of a Thatcherist economic vision and postmodern attitude toward the media (and itself as one of its signs), while marketing himself in a traditional idealist-ethnocentrist rhetoric. In a sense, the prime minister's career, or Bibism, is part and parcel of traditional Zionism as a local manifestation of modernity. As such, it reflects apparatuses, practices, and conceptual possibilities that melted the Zionist constitutive myths and took over its energies for the sake of the most extreme and narrowest of all subjective quests and transformed it into part of its own power. Bibism represents not only a certain level of literacy competence of Bibi's voters; it also represents the effectiveness and the nature of knowledge representation and the extent of control of knowledge representation in Israel. In Bibism, as in a post-modern situation in which various historical spaces coexist simultaneously, a unique merging has triumphed: the effectiveness of amulets, abracadabra, and the curses of Rabbi Kaduri or Rabbi Joseph, combined with the advertisements and propaganda experts who explicitly declared their selling of Bibi's image in the way they sell "Coca-Cola."

From a critical-dialogical literacy point of view, the writing of the text, that its interpretation was "democratically" decided in the 1996 Israeli elections, its ideology-critique, its deconstruction or uncritical approval, acceptance or disapproval, is a bona fide educational issue. The success of the Zionist project and the nature of the educational manipulations of traditional mainstream Zionism made Bibism possible, even inevitable.

It is impossible to separate the control of the symbolic world (that is manifested in the successful revival of the Hebrew language) from the constitution and control of a new Jewish identity. It is impossible to make a division between it and the control of this identity's means of conquest of reality to the degree that it will be "correct" and "just," from the utopian Zionist point of view. In other words, the status of the Hebrew language is not to be separated from the mental and consciousness production of its agents that are also its objects. Here we can see with special clarity the inner logic of discourse as a negation of dialogue in concrete terms: Zionism is a project in which the politics of the discourse and its violent products—in symbolic as well as in material and military manifestations—which create/enable its rival and its violence/counterviolence. In this arena the roles and practices are exemplified very clearly, since the tragedy of participating collectives and their very existence supplies endless shocking testimonies to what discourse is all about.

The possibility of writing, interpretation, re-writing, and realizing texts into an alternative cultural/social/military reality was an inevitable stage in the development of Israel's literacy, before it reached the stage in which it grew rapidly old, was weakened, and needed the help of counter-Poisson in the form of the new literacy that is the hegemonic one in the Israel of today. The history of literacy in Israel should be critically reconstructed. Here we will indicate only some of its central characteristics.

The Politics of Israeli Literacy

In the 1950s, Ben Zion Dinur, the minister of education, was explicit regarding the aim of the Israeli curriculum:

> the Jewish thought of past generations, from the times of Jewish martyrdom to the days of the renewal of our ties with the country, as a connection that is tied and woven with a new vision of its views and in the real feeling of the

motherland's essence. . . . This should enables us to invite the new growing generation to take part in some dimensions of the development of the ideal of our project and its realization. The integration between the study of such texts in the new Israeli history will not only deepen the understanding of Jewish history, but also will enable us to transfer to the students all the ethos of our empowering for the sake of reconstitution of our nation and its improvement; The student will live through all our struggles for independence, a history of bravery and courage.

In one of the first general managers of the Ministry of Education's circulars, in the first days of Israel's independence, it was explicitly declared that the knowledge that promised the new collective identity and the conceptual needs of the construction of the New Jew, according to the requirements of the national project:

The teacher's duty is to emphasize for his pupils the epochs, deeds and figures in which the national will for life was exemplified in the strongest way. . . total devotion and bravery, martyrdom and the love of Israel, the commitment to Zion and faith in redemption.[He has to] sow in their hearts feelings of admiration for the great Jewish figures, its saints and its heroes.[65]

In light of the erosion of the Zionist spirit by local manifestations of Instrumental Rationality and its pragmatism, as reconstructed before, the official paper of the general manager of the Ministry of Education from 1989 was doomed to failure in its attempt to reproduce the Zionist spirit of the system and the reproduction of the traditional Zionist subject as in the case of Bibism here, too, the traditional Zionist rhetoric can hope to be considered relevant only at the high cost of being integrated within the framework of an instrumental-oriented text which explicitly claims to be anti-idealist and professional.

In a 1989 text, the literacy ideology of the political and bureaucratic administration of Israeli education still manifests the traditional naive relationship toward Zionist education, toward language, and the rhetoric concerning the constitution of the Zionist subject and Palestinian as his/her Other counterpoint.

It is no wonder that the explicit aim of the Israeli educational administration is (a) "to pass on the knowledge about the aims of the Hebrew language's revival and its place in the Zionist project and to give the people the feeling of taking part in the continuing development of our language. (b) to present the importance of our language in the cultivation of our national and cultural identity. . . to cultivate educated citizens who have a special sensitivity for the Hebrew language. . . . In its being the national language of the Jews. . . ."[66] In light of our critical historical reconstruction we can claim that here is a trend that reflects a defensive attempt to protect the traditional Zionist cultural capital by developing new linguistic strategies as a gateway to the realm of sacred

Zionist myths. It is to be seen as a reaction to the changing cultural horizons and the constitution of an anti-idealist and anti-solidarian secular Jewish society. This consciousness, which degenerates the Zionist Spirit, could have been developed only as a by-product of the Zionist success. Committed to the aim of preserving the relevancy of this fundationalist conservativism, even an institution such as the State's educational system acknowledged that it has to adjust itself to the pragmatist rhetoric of the day. It did so as a manifestation of two conflicting trends. First and foremost, in order to conserve the Zionist constitutive myths and to resist the changing social context and its pressures for the reorganization of the modern schooling model, and the growing need for constituting a complete fresh to this leviathan. As part of the other trend, as part of the new power networks, it used the traditional myths, symbols, and narratives in the service of the new truth regions and desires, fears, and hopes, which had very little in common between them and the ideal of "the new Jew" as produced by traditional Zionist education.

This development can be seen even in official documents of the Ministry of Education. In one of the circulations of the general manager of the Ministry of Education from 1991, the Ministry of Education is officially adopting literacy. As we see it this is to be understood as part of its unofficial but vivid instrumentalist orientation. One should pay attention to the fact that the adoption of literacy as a magic formula for the rescue of Zionist education took place at the time of the right-wing government, even before the victory of the left-center coalition in the 1992 elections, forces generally considered less ethnocentrist and sometimes even post-Zionist. In 1996 even the religious-nationalist party, *Mafdall*, which politically is committed to ultra-nationalist positions, accepted the new literacy into its sectarian educational system. If our thesis has some ground, then one should not wonder that, in the official publication of the general manager of the Ministry of Education, Zevulun Orlev, a nominee of the *Mafdall*, literacy has been integrated with "education for excellence." It is a manifestation of the measures taken for defending the ethnocentric Zionist narrative. We read, "School has an important role in exposing the child to the written culture with all its richness. . . and in constituting a positive attitude toward this culture."[67] To a reader not familiar with the Israeli ethnocentrism we should note that in such a context, when an official refers to the "richness of culture," he/she refers to the Jewish culture, as represented by the hegemonic ideology, and when a representative of the religious-nationalist party refers to "culture" he (it would probably be a male) would refer to the interpretation approved by the party's Rabbis. As is common in academic research that is supplied to the official educational discourse and practice, in the rhetoric of the general manager too, literacy is conceived as a neutral tool aimed at strengthening the reading and writing abilities of students.[68] Ultimately this power is used in the service of a fruitful meeting between the canonical texts and the conclusions that will ensure the destruction of the student's uniqueness as a persona, her/his will and potentials for free and critical/creative thinking. The birthmarks of the functionalist-orientation literacy are present here too. It exemplified in the same document that pronounces its official acceptance, by the specific instructions directed to the teachers (in issues such as strategies to the listening to the radio, watching television, and so forth).[69]

This trend is to be seen even in new trends within the national-religious educational system. It is an occasion where the general manager Shimshon Shoshani and the director of the State National-Religion educational network, Matti Dagan, can cooperate today (1996) and join forces as if they are not committed to opposing educational aims (theocracy, on the one hand, and secular and liberal democracy, on the other) that one cannot prevail without the total destruction of its rival. One might presume that in the education of pre-*yeshiva* pupils, the Nationalist-Religious party's education would emphasize traditional Jewish talmudic hermeneutics. However, it does not do this but, in elementary and high school education, it hails the new literacy.

Within this framework the treatment of language does not refer in any way to the absolute truth of the world being created by God in a word and the place of words and meanings in it. It is even ready to accept uncritically the most vulgar version of instrumentalist literacy as a skill development, as presented by UNESCO and the American army.[70] How should one understand this use of literacy in pre-*yeshiva* class, on the one hand, and the rigor of talmudic traditionalist Jewish literacy that is re-produced in the *Yeshiva* with no change whatsoever, on the other? According to our thesis, this situation should be understood in light of the current content of the instrumental methods assembled to protect one of the most orthodox educational attitudes in Israel. It is a kind of compromise with modernity, on behalf of pre-modern commitments by post-modern media. Yet this compromise with modernity reflects a total refusal to compromise with Enlightenment and humanism. In the concrete contextual level, our explanation refers to the fact that the vast majority of the students in the State Nationalist-Religious system are traditionalists and of *Sepharadi* origin. The majority of them come from a relatively low socioeconomic level of society. Therefore, it is an additional problem for the *Ashkenazi* religious elite to digest this group of students into the educational traditions of the *Ashkenazi yeshivot* (Jewish traditional studying institutions where students live as a community that studies nothing but religious texts).

One condition for the successful reception of literacy in the present Israeli secular society is the apparently temporary conjunction of opposing forces. In the one axis we see the triumph of the ultra religious-nationalist and the fundamentalist's force, gaining more and more influence, confidence, and agents. In the other axis we see the representatives of secular Israel, economically affluent and spiritually and politically exhausted, looking for an alternative solidarity and public sphere that will overcome the losts of the traditional, mainly imagined, solidarity that was inevitable, as a side effect of local capitalistic success. The economic liberalism of Steff Wertheimer is one of the most relevant educational alternatives which reflects this trend.

Literacy, Industry, and the Zionist Renaissance

Steff Wertheimer is considered by many as one of Israel's well-intentioned industrialists. He is also considered as a herald of the new Zionism. His economic ideology contains central educational chapters whose political implications are explicit. He combines the educational meaning of the constitutive myth of traditional Zionism, *Tel Hai*, with a new *Teffen* community myth and its industrial park.[71] These are central themes in his alternative Zionist ideology, which also includes a critical evaluation of knowledge, within a theoretical framework that might recall the positivistic eschatology of Saint Simon.

In Wertheimer's teaching, creativity is the quintessence.[72] Industry, for him, should be subordinated to creativity, and not vise versa:

> Economics comes after creativity.... Therefore, we should unite all capabilities, qualities, knowledge, powers, and soul's energies together—in order to reach the right order of priorities, the one that finally will lead us into independence, into real freedom, into honorable work, into a Western quality of life.[73]

Wertheimer's ideology is interesting first of all because it manifests a conjunction of revolutionary conservatism with an accurate reflection of the most advanced aspect of changing reality. His Utopianism reflects the erosion of the relevance of traditional Israeli myths, namely, the degeneration of Zionism as an relevant ideology, and the constitution of an economic, social, and cultural reality in which Instrumental Rationality has the upper hand. However, Instrumental Rationality appears here in an extremely conservative nationalist orientation. In opposition to the majority of the other capitalist representatives of Instrumental Rationality in the context of advanced capitalism, in Wertheimer's teaching the acquisition principle is bona fide idealistic. However, Wertheimer sees himself as the heir to the founder of

Literacy, Education, and Violence: The Israeli Example

Zionism, Theodor Herzl, and as the grand restorer of secular Zionism. As such, he claims to present an educational alternative. Even the title of one of his publications reflects this message:

> *A New Israel on the Horizon: If You will Really Want Economic Independence—it is Not a Legend.* In one of his articles he compares between two capitals: Jerusalem and Teffen, as two equally important axes in the history of the Jewish people: "Jerusalem, the capital of Israel is chosen to be the flagship of Israel, of the return of the people to Zion, the capital of all the Jewish people. Yet, Jerusalem is focused on the past.[74]

Wertheimer tried to see in the Hebrew University in Jerusalem a change in direction—yet he was disillusioned:

> In our naivity we believed that the campus of the university, Givat Ram, will be an idealistic challenge, by representing the change in the direction of Jerusalem's development. Namely, that *Beit Hinuch* (the house of education) will provide a home for practical activities and targets, and will contribute to the planning of the new road for Jerusalem's future. But something different happened, and the university resisted the practical orientation and preferred to stay in its ivory tower.

As an awesome idealist and one of the richest people in Israel, Wertheimer erected a new capital for Israel. He founded the new capital in an uninhabited place in Galilee, at a place called Teffen. Now, the call for national revival comes out of Teffen:

> In Teffen, that is in Galilee, there is a small area of few square kilometers and some thousand workers which export about $200,000,000 annually. Israel's capital exports less. Something here is wrong, something is illogical. The flagship does not only lead with its flag, it should also protect itself. The flagship of Israel should proudly lead the merchandise of the country to the world's markets. It should contain in its storehouses fifty times more than it exports today—and only then will it become the real capital of Israel.[75]

Implicitly, until that time or in the absence of such a trend, Teffen becomes the real Jerusalem, and from Teffen comes the call we should accept and educate others accordingly. This is to be seen in the religious—such as architecture, in the artistic self-representation and the special synthesis between art and industry, and in missionary—such as educational programs for the workers and for invited Israelis from the not-yet saved Israel.

The educational impotency of the Israeli system and the infiltration of the new myths and concepts of knowledge lead the educational bureaucracy—that partly operates already according to the new instrumentalist parameters—to look for saviors of all kinds and in all fields of education. This is reflected in the system's disarray: from the introduction to schools of military and industrial managing systems to the integration of media and literacy. There is a growing awareness of the anomaly and split between the official's rhetoric and the pedagogical commitments of schools and the real possibilities in the changed reality. The pragmatc trend and the instrumentalist images of knowledge celebrate their victory within the secular state's educational system. This trend is stronger than bombastic declarations and heavily financed new conservative programs introduced by changing governments and education ministers. Nevertheless, this development is much more explicit outside the formal schooling system.

Literacy as Castration

The way in which academic literacy research has been accepted by the political establishment should in itself put a question mark on the new medicine. The critique of the theory underlying the present hegemonic Israeli literacy reveals its supposed critical dimension as an agency for the process of modern society's drowning in the one-dimensionality of the newly formed realm of self-evidence. In this sense it is a new kind of surrendering to myth. Within this background, literacy, in its present form, can flourish and say "yes" to those who praise it and direct to it their own quest for salvation. This kind of salvation is a special kind of intellectual nirvana, *castration*. The castration complex functions as a central idea and practice in the psychic construction of the individual, in the disciplining of any society and in controlling and developing of all cultures. Sigmund Freud places this issue as central in the formation of a human society:

> It is our suspicion that during the human family's primeval period castration used actually to be carried out by a jealous and cruel father upon growing boys, and that circumcision. . . fear of castration is one of the commonest and strongest motives for repression and thus for the formation of neuroses.[76]

The Freudian analysis of culture's origin, the tackling with the fear of castration, and the realization of the quests directed against the primordial father is useful for the understanding of the ways in which groups tackle the "primordial father" of the post-modern age, the system that contains both one-dimensionality and huge diversity.

One of the central manifestations of this encounter is that of groups that were already castrated of their historical memory lost their "voice" and have no language to formulate their loss or their needs. Many times, as in the case of the non-religious *Sephardi* Jews in Israel, they have to use the language of their perpetuators in order to pronounce rage and anger. These groups lost their traditional realm of self-evidence, yet were not received as equal partners to the new, civic realm of self-evidence that remained alien and uninviting. The loyalty and conscience that prohibits the murder of the "father" in their lost tradition joined the prohibition in the new space: authoritarianism of one realm of self-evidence demanded the negation of the authoritarianism of the new realm of self-evidence (the Jewish state, respecting the law and its representatives or rules, the hegemonic Zionist narrative, and so forth). This is a vital element in the blocking of any potential force of a non-repressive literacy as a struggle over de-coding and meaning formations, as we shall show. What we are facing here is not so much the tackling of fear of the punishment (castration as signifying it in the most general way), as the very legitimacy of rebelling, of being freed of authority, without a "father," as philosophically analyzed by Plato and Nietzsche, who basically see the free spirit and rebellion as a manly issue. For Freud, "What makes hatred of the father unacceptable is *fear* of the father; castration is terrible, whether as a punishment or as the price of love."[77] The heuristic power of this metaphor is due to the violent, "manly" nature of discourse, as opposed to dialogue. And it shows to what a degree, within the framework of literacy, the counter-reaction manifests the same logic that constitutes its operation.

The sexual context of castration and the fear of it is an educational event. An event that contains bona fide political implications. It is an educational event in the sense that it refers to the shaping and controlling of the soul and the consciousness within the framework of Eros's realization. In organizing the disciplining of the self-consciousness of the Other, castration functions as a constant threat, one that is basically sufficient to guarantee the conformity of the oppressed or their animosity to anyone who is shown as a potential castrator. It is of vital importance to emphasize that castration is both an act of execution and an act of creation. It kills the self of the man and as well as his oppressor's self-reproduction potency. This is manifested in the traditional function of the unique. The castration act roots out, yet it also plants. It denotes a meaningful lesson, educating its executioner, his object, and their spectators. This metaphor might help us to represent the manly, repressive, phallocentric nature of Western culture. Its success is so immense that even the rebelling text cannot enact its meaning without using its words and syntax. The possibility of deviation, of creating a new language and a new syntax, is the mission of today's literacy, if it is to pinpoint the possibility of *the totally other* and transcendence, instead of reflecting and serving the current order of things.

Our use of the castration metaphor does not refer to an act done at a specific moment by a certain individual, but rather to a series of acts of ongoing normality; it refers to the system's process of institutional selection, marginalization, centralization, constitution, and control of private and collective consciousness. This violent process is normally called education. It is aimed at rooting out individuals and collectives of their memory and history; it takes their voice and castrates their reflective potential by controlling the content and limitations of their consciousness so that they will devote themselves to disable themselves from self-constitution and the critical development of their identity and cultural heritage. As such, they are not the owners of "their" own self-consciousness and they are unable to enter into a dialogue with the Other. This is a pre-condition for their false consciousness.

In Hegel's "Dialectics of the Master and the Slave" one can see how the education of the Other includes not only his/her castration, but also distracts the self-consciousness of the castrator himself. The self-consciousness cannot avoid an educational life-and-death struggle. It is committed to the destruction of the other self-consciousness and to the castration of the Other's selfhood in order to reach itself.[78]

In the present cultural stage in the West, the castration act is not enacted in explicit public ceremonies, but rather in sublimated and vague violent roots, that rationally and cynically use the contribution of the victim's own body and soul's energies: it uses the originality, creativity, hopes, anger, and hate of young people that are specially trained for their mission by the system. In the era when Critical Theorists such as Horkheimer[79] and Bauman[80] show to what a degree there is no place for an autonomous subject, there is no place for a life-and-death struggle between different self-consciousness: in the absence of an autonomous subject, even as an ideal, the repressor also is not a persona, and no person, group, or class is responsible for the repression. The inner logic of the system is "responsible" for it in "a totally administered world."[81] The system reproduces itself by its objects: educating them, normalizing them, rationally castrating them, systematically, invisibly in a process that at the same time also fertilizes them.

The "primordial father" was murdered by his "sons," yet they could not really emancipate themselves from authoritarianism, and their "father" is reproduced in their very act of liberation, as well as their later worldview, their knowledge image, their attitude toward "a woman" as a metaphor for any passive object to be at its peak of repression—fertilized to reproduce their own image. In this sense human history only in its post-modern era starts its second stage of development. In this second stage the "father" is reproduced as an external, non-personal, classless, and non-political power, that is omnipotent also in its infiltration capacities to the most subjective and deep psychic dimensions, activating them as his embryo. The post-modern system gives its agents the possibility of realizing their eroticism (their "own," in their mind), as part of the production and re-production of the system. In the postmodern era, or in the era of the dissolving of alienation's consciousness, the struggle between the "master" and the "slave" has not come to an end. However, the current pleasure production also creates images of restlessness and quests for alternatives. Most of the "alternatives" are parts of the same system that they are supposed to overcome. This reality activates different parts of the system, as conservatives in the ruling group, and parts of the bureaucracy, especially the middle-class bureaucracy that in the service of their types with the political elite and the sinking narrative look for new, creative solutions. This is where the philosophical dimension of literacy is so important.

Critical Philosophies and Literacy in Israel

The literacy discourse that has been reconstructed here is basically an Israeli liberalist-oriented reaction to the new economic, social, and cultural trends, while neglecting three other important possibilities. The first is that of Critical Theory. In Israeli literacy discourse there is a systematic neglect of its conception of texts and ideology-critique and its elaboration of the relations between text and historical context. It goes without saying that totally unmentioned are Critical Theory's critique of the competence of understanding writing/reading or refusal to hegemonic texts and their power networks, as well as the possibility of the struggle over the realization of the claim for critical dialogue, refusal, and resistance, as formulated in the works of Adorno, Horkheimer, and Habermas. The Critical Pedagogy of educational thinkers such as Paulo Freire was strongly influenced by these thinkers[82] and constituted an important alternative literacy which was further developed by eminent students such as Henry Giroux.[83] The literacy marketed today in Israel is obliged to neglect Critical Literacy or, at least, to discredit its legitimacy or relevancy. This does not prevent the constructivist literacy version from adopting parts of Critical Literacy's rhetoric. Critical Literacy might become a progressive element and empower intellectual capacities of Israelis which will overcome some of the manipulations of the Israeli education. However, Critical literacy too, in its feminist, multiculturalist, and post-colonialist versions, is manipulative, inhales positive utopianism, and is basically anti-philosophical.[84] It is a dialogical Critical Literacy, which we suggest. It is part of a reformed Critical Theory and a new Critical Pedagogy that has yet to be constructed.[85]

The second possibility neglected by the hegemonic literacy discourse in Israel is the post-modern one. The postmodern orientation emphasizes language as a region in which within its horizons power apparatuses produce the subject, her/his conceptual possibilities, truths, historical memories, identity, and voice. The production of the private and collective identities enables and restricts their voice and determines their possibilities to write and read texts. However, even from the postmodern perspective, the conclusion does not have to be that there is no sense it speaking about the world represented, only that all representational acts of something are at the same time both the representation of power and its realization. The literacy that is possible within this framework does not refer to truth, but rather to the possibility of pinpointing the production of truths by specific apparatuses in the regions that border the concepts of the critical thinkers and the possibilities of their de-construction. The aim of such a literacy denotes or reconstructs the characters of these zones of truth production, as in the case of the jail, the school, or hospitals, as shown in the work of Michel Foucault, in order to cast light on the marginal and the hidden. In most postmodern works this does not intend to constitute a base for transformative intervention, historical change, and hope. When hope is represented within the framework of this context, it is a concept of hope which differs substantively from the hope principle that is central to Critical Theory. These dividing lines between Critical Theory's project and the critique of postmodernism is very often too crude. Quite often; in the last generation, the dividing lines between the critical project and the postmodern one, especially between the postmodern one and the multi-culturalist one, are too brute, and practically they merge into new, interesting literacy projects, as that developed recently by Henry Giroux.

The multicultural literacy concept concentrates its attack on the cultural monolith of canonical Western knowledge. It searches for the traces of the relations between language and the politics of the difference of writing, reading, interpreting, representing, and distributing of texts, meanings, and truths. These traces are supposed to be connected to the hegemonic power of Western reproduction of knowledge, interests, and hierarchies, which gives privileges to the current Western hegemony. This is done by ignoring, manipulating, or downplaying non-Western texts, identities, and interests, marginalizing them or castrating them. According to the multicultural ideology's concept literacy is a product of power relations between cultures and within groups, groups that are committed to the reproduction of their culture, their memory, and their voice. From this point of view the business of literacy is the struggle over collective identities and it is definitely not a neutral, professional issue that should occupy experts. With different points emphasized, such a literacy fits sometimes into the postmodernist framework and at other times into the post-colonialist project, as in the works of Edward

Said,[86] Homi Bhabah,[87] and Richard Yang.[88] The presentation of that kind of literacy is a great threat to the Israeli system. It threatens to revolutionize the fragile cultural coexistence in Israel, which while facing rapid cultural and political cantonization, is trying to look for an even more effective "unification" medicine—within a strengthening ethnocentric orientation. Such a literacy, which is committed to reveal the politics of voice, texts, identities, and power, is an arch-enemy of the present hegemony. For the marginalized groups, such as the Palestinians, such a literacy is problematic too: while it might be an effective weapon against the Zionist cultural oppression, it also endangers the authoritative, anti-humanistic, and anti-democratic tendencies dominating the internal hierarchies of the Palestinian people in Israel.

The feminist literacy in its most radical version views through the framework of the man/woman historical struggle the issue of texts, the possibilities of constructing identities by constitutive texts, as well as the marginalization of identities and the elimination of potential representation, education, and realization of identities. Historical patriarchal control over women's concrete conditions and their representation, as well as their role in the public sphere and hegemonic culture, is here criticized and treated as a political weapon for resistance and liberation. According to this ideology, the decision about the literacy to be chosen is a political one; it is part of this historical struggle between men and women.

According to the feminist literacy, the hegemonic education, which defends and reproduces the patriarchal language and the political structure that reflects and serves it, as well as the counter-education which is suggested by the feminists, is not merely a theory: it is a synthesis of political praxis and theoretical discourse. Of vital importance here is the claim that this project is to be defended and developed basically in accordance with gender politics and its requirements, that is, it is basically a pragmatist orientation, where the will to power always has the last say. Thinkers such as Elizabeth Ellsworth attack the hegemonic language of the hegemonic curriculum as part of their general attack on manly culture and its emancipatory rhetoric.[89] They show how in the name of categories such as justice, equality, and freedom—which serve the manly interests of the ruling groups—women are systematically oppressed. Many feminist literacy thinkers are very critical of Critical Literacy.[90] Gor and Ellsworth join forces in attacking paternalist dimensions in Critical Pedagogy and its Critical Literacy, as in the case of Paulo Freire and Henry Giroux. Ellsworth particularly criticizes the reproduction of patriarchal power relations in the texts and in the text's critique that is developed in the critical discourse. According to Ellsworth, critical thinkers manifest these patriarchal power relations by emphasizing the theoretical dimension, speaking on "empowering," "dialogue," "critique," and "texts critique," while building in classes new hierarchies, selections, and control apparatuses that aggressively eliminate some of the voices seen as problematic in the "emancipatory" discourse.[91]

The implicit aim of literacy's hegemonic educational ideology is the castration of the revolutionary potential of these alternative literacies. The very recognition of the legitimacy of these alternatives endangers the existence of the Zionist state. It goes without saying that a general change in education, in accordance with one of these three neglected versions of literacy, is a danger that the Israeli system will do all it can to avoid.

By the same token, it is important to add that no one of these versions is presenting a real dialogue, a viable alternative to the castration process of hegemonic education and its preferable literacy. They are only suggesting a counter-castration, not counter-education. This is because all these strategies are incurably optimistic and arrogant, on the one hand, and praise (counter) violence, on the other. A non-repressive literacy is possible. However, it is determined by the possibility of a non-violent Critical Pedagogy which is impossible without a radical reformulation of Critical Theory, in accordance with the changing reality and eternal philosophical *aporia*.

In the meantime, the future of Israeli new literacy as manufactured today by its culture industry is secure. It looks as though, in the very near future, the students at teaching colleges will be taught the practices of literacy. It will enable them and their teachers to feel slightly better, even if, and maybe because they do not read and write their own text, history, identity, and truths. The oblivion of an erotic struggle over meaning and change in actual life will probably integrate with the neglect of the political and philosophical dimensions of education. Their oblivion is a condition for their function as good teachers, to the degree that they are efficient agents of the system's reproduction and productive agents of enhancing violence and its invisibility. By that we do not mean that such teachers will be totally impotent, politically incorrect, and inefficient. On the contrary, a central part of the efficiency of the Israeli evil industry is conditioned by the good intentions, inspiration, and talent of these teachers who are devoted to the production of the Zionist subject in increasingly difficult conditions.

NOTES

1. Ilan Gur-Ze'ev. "The politics of literacy production in the Israeli Culture Industy," *Davar* (21 October 1994), 21 (in Hebrew).
2. Homi Bhabah. *The Location of Culture*. London: Routledge 1994, 149.
3. Ilan Gur-Ze'ev. *The Frankfurt School and the History of Pessimism*. Jerusalem 1996, 12 (in Hebrew).
4. Edward Said. *The World, the Text, and the Critic*. Cambridge: Harvard University Press 1983, 5.
5. *Ibid.*, 53.
6. Micahel Apple. *Ideology and Curriculum*. London: Routledge & K. Paul 1979, 7.
7. Michel Foucault. *Power/Knowledge; Selected Interviews and Other Writings 1972-1977*. Translated by Gordon Colin, Marchall Leo, and others, Brighton, Sussex: Harvester Press 1980, 18.
8. Georg Lukacs. *Soul and Form*. Translated by Anna Bostock, Cambridge: MIT Press 1974, 172.
9. Michel Foucault. *Power/Knowledge; Selected Interviews and Other Writings 1972-1977*. Translated by Colin Gordon and others, New York: Harvester Press 1980, 148.
10. Giroux 1989, 144.
11. Pierre Bourdie and Jean-Claude Passeron. *Reproduction in Education, Society and Culture*. London: Sage Publications 1978, 19.
12. Walter Benjamin. "Das Kunstwerk im Zeitalter seiner technischer Reproduzierbarkeit," *Gesammelte Schriften* 1.2 Frankfurt a.Main: Suhrkamp 1980, 508.
13. Giroux 1987, 6.
14. Carnis 1977, 44.
15. de Castel, S. Luke, and D. MacLennan, "On defining literacy," in: de Castel, S. Luke, *Literacy, Society, and Schooling*. Cambridge: Cambridge University Press 1986, 9.
16. *Ibid.*, 169
17. Carins 1977, 44.
18. Giroux 1986, 2.
19. Timothy Rush, Alden J. Moe, and Rebecca L. Storlie. *Occupational Literacy Education*. Newark: International Reading Association 1988, 11.
20. Nimrod Aloni. "What is literacy and what is to do with it in teacher's colleges," *Mazav A'ynianim* 2 (1994), 4 (in Hebrew).
21. Paulo Freire. *The Politics of Education; Culture, Power and Education*, Massachusetts: Bergin & Garvey 1987, XI.
22. Martin Heidegger. "Letter on Humanism," *Basic Writings*, Oxford 1996, 230.
23. Zvia Walden, in: Nimrod Aloni, "What is literacy," 4.
24. Walden 1991, 61 (in Hebrew).
25. Brosh 1989.
26. Soshana Folman. "Teaching writing-reading skills in classroom," *Melilot*, Beit Berl: Beit Berl 1993, 117-130.
27. Amikam Marbach, in: Nimrod Aloni "What is literacy," 4.
28. Rachel Hertz-Lazarowitz and others, "Literacy in collective learning: an Israeli beginning," *Helkat Lashon* 11-12 (1993), 6 (in Hebrew).
29. *Ibid.*, 9.

30 Henry Giroux. *Teachers as Intellectuals*. New York: Bergin & Garvey 1988, 158.
31 Rachel Hertz-Lazarowitz, *op. cit.* 11.
32 *Ibid.*, 12.
33 Michel Foucault. *Power/Knowledge*, 153.
34 Martin Buber. *The Knowledge of Man*. Translated by Maurice Friedman, New York: Harper & Row 1965, 86.
35 Michal Zelermeier. "Thinking while acting: literacy teachers' professional development as an example for a possible change in professional conceptions," *Golda Meir Institute for Society and Work Research* 51 (1990), 3 (in Hebrew).
    Michal Zelermeier. "Teachers' development toward reflective teaching and writing: an action research," *Teaching and Teacher Education* 6: 4 (1990), 338.
36 Freema Elbaz. "Hope, attentativeness, and caring for difference: the moral voice in teaching," *Teaching and Teacher Education* 8: 5-6 (1992), 421.
    Freema Elbaz, "Research on teachers' knowledge: the evolution of a discourse," *Journal of Curriculum Studies* 23: 1 (1991), 299.
37 Charles Taylor. *Philosophy and the Human Sciences*. New York 1995, 118.
38 Nicholas Burbules. *Dialogue in Teaching*. New York 1993.
39 Micahel Apple. *Ideology and Curriculum*. London 1979, 7.
40 Ruth Linn and Ilan Gur-Ze'ev. "Holocaust as metaphor: the Arab and Israeli use of the same symbol," *Metaphor and Symbolic Activity* 11: 3 (1997), 199.
41 Eli Kuzuminsky. "Reading as literacy and as skill," *Helkat Lashon* 11-12 (1993), 32 (in Hebrew).
42 Michel Foucault. *Power/Knowledge*, 132.
43 *Ibid.*, 133.
44 Ernst Bloch. *Das Prinzip Hoffnung*. Frankfurt a.M.: Suhrkamp 1959.
45 Ilan Gur-Ze'ev. *The Frankfurt School and the History of Pessimism*. Jerusalem: Magnes 1996, 12 (in Hebrew).
46 Martin Luther. *An den Christlichen Adel Deutcher Nation*. Stuttgart 1962, 16.
47 Gotthold Ephraim Lessing. *The Education of the Human Race*. Translated by F. W. Robertson, London: Anthroposophical Pub. C. 1927, 15.
48 *Ibid.*, 9.
49 *Ibid.*, 11.
50 *Ibid.*, 20.
51 *Ibid.*, 23.
52 Richard Venezy and others (eds.). *Toward Defining Literacy*. Newark: International Reading Association 1992, 3.
53 Luke 1988, 164.
54 N. Davis. "Society and culture in early modern France," in: de Castel S. and A. Luke, *Literacy, Society, and Schooling*. Cambridge: Cambridge University Press 1975, 16.
55 Max Weber. *Wissenschaft als Beruf*. Muenchen 1930, 21.
56 Michel Foucault. *The Order of Things: An Archeology of the Human Sciences*. London 1970, 308.
57 Jean Baudrillard. *Simulacra and Simulation*. Translated by Sheila Faria Giaser, Ann Arbor: University of Michigan Press 1994, 4.
58 Ronald Barth. "The Death of the Subject," in: *Image-Music-Text*. Translated by S. Heath, New York 1977, 143.

59 Friedrich Schleiermacher. *Hermeneutik*. Heidelberg: C. Winter 1959, 32.
60 Jean Baudrillard. *Symbolic Exchange and Death*. Translated by G. Hamilton, London: Sage Publications 1993, 63.
61 Francois Jean Lyotard. *The Postmodern Condition; A Report on Knowledge*. Translated by G. Benington, Manchester: Manchester University Press 1991, 23.
62 Michel Foucault. *Power/Knowledge*, 118.
63 Jean Baudrillard. *The Transparency of Evil*. Translated by J. Benedict, London: Verso 1993, 3.
64 Zigmunt Bauman. *Postmodern Ethics*. Oxford: Blackwell 1996.
65 Ministry of Education, *Circular of the General Manager of the Ministry of Education*, "School activities for strengthening Israeli-Jewish consciousness" (September 20, 1957), 21 (in Hebrew).
66 Ministry of Education, *Circular of the General Manager of the Ministry of Education*, "Introduction" (June 20, 1989), 3-25 (in Hebrew).
67 Minstry of Education, *Circular of the General Manager of the Ministry of Education* (December 20, 1991), 20 (in Hebrew).
68 *Ibid.*, 21.
69 *Ibid.*
70 Dagan 1991, 7.
71 Steff Wertheimer. "Tel-Hai garden followes Teffen," *The Industrials*, 21 (1992), 34 (in Hebrew).
72 Steff Wertheimer, *A New Israel in the Horizon: If You will really want Economical Independence—It will not be a Dream*. Tel-Aviv 1989, 27 (in Hebrew).
73 *Ibid.*
74 Steff Wertheimer. "Tel-Hai garden follows Teffen," 30.
75 *Ibid..*
76 Sigmund Freud. "Anxiety and instinctual life," *The Standard Edition of the Complete Psychological Works of Sigmund Freud* XXII. Translated by James Strachey, London: Hogarth Press 1971, 86.
77 Sigmund Freud. "Dostoevsky and parricide," *The Standard Edition of the Complete Psychological Works of Sigmund Freud* XXI. Translated by James Strachey, London: Hogarth Press 1961, 184.
78 G. W. F. Hegel. *The Phenomenology of Mind*. Translated by J. B. Baillie, New York and London: Harper and Row 1967, 229.
79 Max Horkheimer, "Zum Begriff der Vernunft," *Gesammelte Schriften* 7, Frankfurt a.M., 1985, 27.
80 Zygmunt Bauman. *Life in Fragments*. Oxford: Blackwell 1995, 41.
81 Max Horkheimer. *Dawn & Decline: Notes 1926-1931 and 1950-1969*. New York: Seabury Press 1978, 159.
82 Paulo Freire and Donaldo Macedo. *Literacy; Reading the Word and Reading the World*. London 1987.
83 Henry Giroux. *Border Crossings*. New York and London 1992.
84 Ilan Gur-Ze'ev. "Toward a more pressive critical pedagogy," *Educational Theory* 48: 4 (Fall 1998), 463-486.
85 *Ibid.*
86 Edward Said. "Yeats and decolonization," in: Terry Eagelton, Frederik Jameson and Edward Said (eds.), *Nationalism, Colonialism, and Literature*. Minneapolis: University of Minnesota Press 1990, 71.

87 Homi Bhabha. *Nation and Narration.* 1990, 36.
88 Robert Young. *White Mythologies; Writing History and the West.* London 1990, 133.
89 Elizabeth Ellsworth. "Educational films against Critical Pedagogy," *Journal of Education* 169: 3 (1987), 33.
90 Gor 1992, 6.
91 Elizabeth Ellsworth. "Why doesn't it feel empowering? Working through the repressive myths of Critical Pedagogy," *Harvard Educational Review* 59: 3 (August 1989), 304.

CHAPTER 9
The Philosophical Revolution in the Israeli Army

Violence is a plurality which manifests the realization of the principle of individuation. There are many and different violences. They make possible, constitute, control, and limit human intersubjectivity, most of which normally are effective enough to secure their invisibility.[1] Normalizing education is only one kind of violence which is fundamentally symbolic and, therefore, it is also political. As such it makes possible direct violence, which loses its invisibility, yet if it is efficient enough it can guarantee its legitimacy, divinity, "unavoidability," or even its humanistic appeal. Even if not all normalizing education culminates into militarism, there is no successful military project disconnected from normalizing education. Nor is there a durable and vivid collective that is not determined by normalizing education, which produces its ethnocentrism and its commitment to negate the otherness of its Others.[2] Traditionally most versions of Diaspora Judaism, or most "Judaisms," negated violence in the sense of entering into the historical power games. Within this tradition Jewish Messianism always carried the potential of anti-ethnocentrism and anti-dogmatism, and normally persisted in its anti-violent and anti-political political theology. These concepts were introduced and reproduced by Jewish efficient normalizing education which were secured by the invisibility of its violences, yet always it also had the potential of challenging these violences and overcoming its commitment to closure, exclusion, and dogmatism. All this has changed with the appearance of Zionism as a secular political theology. Direct violence and even militarism of various kinds became explicitly inseparable from normalizing Zionist education.

Since the first steps of its development in the Middle East, Israeli society has not only held violence as a precondition for fulfilling the Zionist idea but as one of its essential, constitutive, dimensions. As in the case of the constitution of any national existence, this is the precondition for the development of collective identity and the existence of the new Jewish being, in opposition to historic Judaism and the Arab identity, and within the ruins of the villages, memories, and aspirations of the Palestinians, who became the "real Jews" for many secular Israelis.

Zionist-Jewish violence has many manifestations: historical memory, devotion, funding, international support, a caring Diaspora, and a prosperous economy. These have been translated to military force too.

Since the beginning of Zionism and through the growth of the Jewish state, the Israeli army has not been only a defense instrument, a military organization that follows orders and realizes them automatically with no general considerations and with no social obligations. On the one hand, social dedication and national consciousness did not turn the Israeli army into a threatening organization that directly influenced the establishment of the nation in a praetorian tradition. It has not been an organization that interferes constantly and extensively in political life, and from time to time carries out a *putsch*. "The military has no incentive to intervene in political and social matters in a manner pernicious to democratic norms." Yet on the other hand, traditionally the Israeli army has never been neutral about the grand national tasks;[3] it was one of the essential components in realizing the hegemony of Zionist ideology, in shaping Israeli society, and in educating its members. While being a reflection of the process of the militarization of Israeli society it was a component of the nation building. Uri Ben-Eliezer calls this phenomenon "a non-praetorian militarism"[4] and even suggests that it was the state army that constituted the Israeli nation.[5]

It is possible for women and men to replace one ideology by another: aggressive symbolic exchange is part and parcel of their existence. At the same time this aggressive symbolic exchange is also a struggle that has its social, economic, national, and military representations. The *polemos* is immanent to the ideological struggle. This is true among the inhabitants of a certain collective and among representatives of different collectives and their related ideologies. But as changes are possible in this life-and-death battle, it is impossible to depart from one realm of common self-evidence to another. This is so since in their ideal stance, realms of common self-evidence are closed and totally strange to each other. Realms of common self-evidence are daily reproduced, not so much by battalions of educators and armies, but much more by countless acts, strife, truths, and value manifestations in concrete, temporary, and sometime microscopic human arenas which ensure the invisibility of the violences which ground and perpetuate the self-evidence. Invisibility, peace of mind, and political stability or peace are one of the manifestations of the power of their violence, since they create the preconditions for the aggression that constitutes and controls men and women who are fighting in the name of "their" collectives, truths, values, and sacred rights and needs.

While human beings are creations of the violence of "their" normalizing education in their respected arenas (and sometime they participate in and are disciplined by some conflicting normalizing educational systems), they themselves are also the agents who re-produce, reform, and destroy the normalizing apparatuses that govern them, restraining them and enriching their potentials of self-realization. Men and women as subjects and objects of metaphysical violence and of the horizons of their positioning in the world are also the agents of human violence, acknowledged as enemies to rise against. They are both victims and victimizers. As such they manifest in their very collective existence the Spirit's cunning,[6] which manifests itself through the creative violence of rival normalizing educational apparatuses which manipulate their servants who struggle against each other and against themselves. At the same time there is still more in the human, which is made possible by the openness of being, by infinity, which allows both normalizing education and the transcendence by counter-education. Not every case of erosion of realm of self-evidence and not any case of normalizing education that is being dissolved, manifests, however, the constitution of counter-education and new human possibilities. As the history of the philosophy of education in the Israeli army shows, it is very far from that. At the same time history shows that no realm of self-evidence and no social order is eternal: normalizing educational systems develop, grow old, and die of senility or are destroyed by aggressive young systems that collide with them. The historical moments of a system's death can become a rare moment of revelation of the violences which ground and protect the realm of self-evidence and the *Same*[7] it is committed to reproduce. It opens new possibilities for reflection and transcendence as part of counter-education.[8]

Conceptually and historically, it turned out that a self-constitution like that which the Zionist project promised was not possible except through the fertilization of a Palestinian national identity and the collision with it. This collision was a vital element in the determination of the special character of the Palestinian uprising and its development in the last hundred years. In the service of Spirit's cunning, the two antagonists manifest and orchestrate their ideologies, each being nothing but a necessary secretion of their common death economy.

This is a struggle in an arena that is common but not mutual for the adversaries that activate their violence against each other as part of the way to create, present, and sophisticate their own consciousness, identities, and collective symbolic and other power apparatus. This ideological effort also includes securing control over the horizon, as over the cultural, social, economic, and political potentials. Using this apparatus and potentials allows the reproduction and advancement of the Israeli system against its Arab rivals and especially against its Palestinian challenges. These possibilities are orchestrated through the struggle against the constitution of the Other's collective self-conscious and identity, and even against the very existence of the other as Other. This otherness determines the horizon and negates the selfhood of the national consciousness that demands the correlation between collective self-consciousness and the borders and identity of "its" geographical/symbolic horizon. This logic is enforced by the categorical imperative of the self-constitution of each collective identity as a national, cultural, and social entity through the elimination of the Other's power in all its manifestations: destroying the otherness of the Other as well as the otherness within oneself; destroying the potential for an existential, moral, philosophical, and political rebellion, destroying the impetus for revealing and manifesting the otherness in its manifestation as special interests, historical memory, and other cultural, social, and military dimensions of power. The determined blindness/pre-determined/manipulated-contingent "view" of the rival parties is very productive and constitutes their conception of the service they are obliged to give to "their" collectives, ways of life, or intersubjective networks. The ideologies are a deviant of the normalizing systems and are not to be simply reduced to an outcome of economic-social conditions. As such, they manifest the vitality of realm of common self-evidence and its power over human freedom as self-imposed duties within a dialogical, reflective coexistence.

In Western modernistic tradition the struggle against the "exterior" Other is parallel to a combat against the "internal" Other: a struggle for control of the borders of the speech community, for governing the interests, educational practices, and the legitimacy of the maintenance and reproduction of the private and social body. This discursive play includes symbolic and practical violence, violence that is concerned with the constitution of the legitimate goals of the human subjects who are jailed in their Platonic "caves." This play also contains an inevitable conflict over the ability to control and operate the foci of social and cultural capital, over the capability to determine the dominant collective identity and the ability to marginalize deviating identities, as it includes the appropriating of the social and cultural capital and determining its borders. In each network of Platonic "caves" the determining power in this struggle is manifested in the ability to construct the legitimate interpretation-representation apparatus of socially relevant knowledge for each speech community; this is a life-and-death fight over the character of the educator as an executioner, judge, healer, interpreter, hero, or sophisticated producer-consumer (or a certain combination of these). This struggle is not to be limited to the horizons of legitimating the judgment of the Other and producing practices for the continuation of the "external" fight against him: we are dealing here with total war about the birth, recollection, and murder of knowledge which produces/eliminates human beings, their emotions, identities, and enemies.

This struggle has an "internal" social face: a struggle over self-identity and collective consciousness of each speech community, a struggle over dominance in one's speech community, its enemies, ways of their representation, and practical treatment. This is a struggle over open possibilities of appropriating the reconstruction, interpretation, and facing of the Other's voice and his history. Its power/knowledge dialectics is the battle over the Other's *locus*, which by the same token is a struggle over his identity's place, symbolically and, therefore, also practically.

This process, which formulates the specific attributes of the system's ideologies, is fertilized through its contact with agents of rival ideologies; for its part, this process fertilizes its agent's internal world, their jargon, the images of their "enemies," and the required violence that is accepted as relevant and legitimate in a specific historical stage.

The Israeli-Palestinian case is a reflection of a general social-cultural development that transforms the present coexistence between the rival modern intersubjective networks. Our aim should be to reconstruct and challenge the ways by which the various processes of global capitalism (which is one of the central representations of Instrumental Rationality) reflects new constructs of the link between Spirit, the traditional Western realm of common self-evidence, and local social-cultural networks. It is important to try and see how the present development of modernity and the evolution of post-modern conditions bring about the consciousness that will see itself as obligated to new military and educational theories and to new forms of violence: this is in accordance with current technological and administrative needs. In this chapter this general problematic will be evaluated in a specific context, that of the national conflict between Israelis and Palestinians, and in an even more specific context, that of the current revolution in the Philosophy of education in the IDF (Israel Defense Forces).

There is no essential difference between the violence of the educators and the violence of the military. Especially since the French revolution, the army has been totally impotent without sufficient power of its constitutive ideology in the system it serves and manifests. The reproduction of knowledge and images of knowledge is, therefore, vital to the livelihood of the invisible tyranny of the system over its agents/servants/victims. This is principally clear in times of rapid disintegration of a seemingly stable, self-confident realm of common self-evidence. The history of education in the Israeli army reflects it with a special clarity. This is so since the violent coexistence with Israel's Arab neighbors re-vitalized the modernistic dimensions of the Zionist ideology, while the Israeli economy as a Western developed economy reflects the gathering forces of a post-modern social and cultural condition.

In his book *Samson*,[9] Ze'ev Jabotinsky presented the ideal of the new Jew in the Zionist revisionism in light of the spiritual Samson:

> Tell them in my name two things, the first one is this: Iron. Let them in-build in the iron everything they have: their money and Sinn, their oil and flocks, wives and daughters. Everything should be in-builded in the iron. There is nothing more precious than iron... and the second thing they would not understand, but they have to hurry and understand it. The second thing is a king.

Positioning himself as the educator of the new generation, Jabotinsky committed himself to the realization of the Samson's legend by developing, enhancing, and defending myths which will function as rich suggestive energy's symbols, which will enhance the progressing Israeli consciousness. Within half a century revisionist Zionism succeeded in making good use of Trumpeldor's death. In the revisionist ideology the functioning of Trumpeldor's myth acquired its full meaning in the slogan (which was related to his last words, spoken before his heroic death in battle): "It is great to die for your country." The execution of Shlomo Ben Yosef (who was caught with two other members of *Beitar* shooting and throwing hand grenades at an Arab bus in 1938 "in retaliation" against Palestinian attacks) became another constitutive educational myth for the entire *Yishuu* In this case, as in the case of present Palestinian *Hamas* violence, which is directed against the very existence of Jewish sovereign life in Israel, the rich diversity of the human life is composed and swallowed by and for the national myth industry. Following the myth of Trumpeldor the educational message is very clear in the convicted Ben Yosef's last declaration, "I sacrifice my life joyfully." It is worthy of note that not the "external" violence, namely killing randomly innocent Palestinians, was praised as the internalization of violence but the willingness, even desire, for self-sacrifice. It was not the value of hating the Palestinians that was so appreciated as the violence that was directed toward the reflective I, the self-sacrifice as an assault against the possibilities of transcending from the Zionist normalizing education. The violence against the Palestinians was important in three respects: as a manifestation of self-sacrifice, which is also an educational act; as a pragmatically justifiable resistance; and as an unavoidable retaliation which is a morally justifiably defensive act. These are only two examples out of many that manifest the ways by which the Zionist education created and used symbols, constituting the Zionist subject as an object for manipulation rather than becoming a subject who challenges normalizing education and the given order of things. As a normalized subject she was made to abandon her potential and imperative of overcoming the order which constitutes her. She was directed to become an agent of the given order of things by negating the otherness of the Other and the otherness within herself as part of her constitution as a war machine. The Zionist choice of violence might be seen as a utopian one, yet fundamentally it is the great refusal to hope, an anti-Jewish refusal of utopia central to which is the struggle for *the totally other* than the given and the transcendence already within daily life as represented by the idea of the Sabbath.

Jabotinsky's educational activity, which created or vitalized many of the central myths of the revisionist movement and the *Yishuv* in general, was directed to create what he called a new-old Jewish "race" who is genuinely "grand, generous, and fierce." One of his first military initiatives, the establishment of a Jewish battalion that fought as part of the British army against the Turks and the Germans on the Palestine front in the First World War, was part of the Zionist consensus of those days which functioned also as an important educational myth. The articulations of Jabotinsky contributed to this spirit of militarism, which overcame his liberal temper. He writes about the Jewish battalion:

> The vision of the birth of the first Hebrew army. I envisioned it in the form of a sudden burst of a free will, voluntarism which will sweep like a Godly storm over all Jewish Diasporas; Those whose sacrifice was not accepted feel unfortunate, disappointed, the fortunate ones sing joyful songs and play the cymbals.[10]

Abba Ahimeir, the leader of *Brit Habirionim* ("the covenant of the outlaws") and one of the great admirers of Jabotinsky, was concerned with the educational aim of *Beitar* (1928):

> *Tel Hai!*—the leaflet of Beitar's central headquarters in Erez Israel—will strip the vegetarian thoughts of the Buberianism and the Borochovism and will show them naked—we will present the nakedness of the defeatism that is inbuilt in the foundation of Zionist policy. *Tell Hai* will try to bring to the youth the ideas that were preached in the end of the 19th century and in the beginning of the 20th century by Yalag in "between the lion's teeth" and "Zidkijah in the prison," Berdizevski in "in front of Apollo's statue," Shneor in "in the eve of," and Jacob Hacohen, the poet of the "Birionim." The thoughts on the healthy nationalism, namely, the views on Jewish policy as they were presented by the greatest of our cultural renaissance—not just for mere talking were presented. *Tell Hai* of Beitar will strive to give the Hebrew youth a gentleman's and citizen's education. Instead of the mob will appear the public, instead of the hachsternick the knight, instead of the "comrade"—the citizen, instead of dust-man—the battalion.[11]

In the first appearance of *Habirion* (17 April 1932), it is explicitly declared that the Hebrew soldier is the new educator for the people, and the educators are selected from the history of Jewish military heroism: "Our teachers and educators will be Yohanan of Gush Halav, El'azar Ben Yair of Metzada, David

Hare'uveni, and Sarah Aharonson." Special attention is devoted to self-sacrificing heroes; heroes who internalize the violence they intend to execute against the Other. This acceptance of violence is explicit in Ahimeir's "The Third Stage" (18 October 1935): "Zionism," he writes in his article, "is not a matter of self well-being. Zionism is an altar that one should climb into, and there one should be a burnt-offering."[12] He demands "Zionism of self-sacrifice"[13] that will constitute the future Jewish state. In that state Ahimeir dreams to see a spiritual army:

> The future Israeli army will have to be a conscious army, like the Caliph Omar's Muslim army, which overran the Near East and North Africa. Our ideal has to be Cromwell's army in the days of the English revolution. In this army, the hands never abandoned the gun or the bible. The more the army knows what it is struggling for, the higher will rise its enthusiasm and fanaticism. Our army will not be a mechanical army nor an army of robots.[14]

These themes correspond historically and thematically to the cultural tendencies that preceded the victory of Nazi ideology and revealed the relevancy of creative violence and the commitment to the destruction of the otherness of the Other. This was manifested in Ernst Juenger and the conception of war as the supreme life experience,[15] which constitutes, bloodily, the new Tower of Babylon, creating the myth of the nation and the individual who loses herself within it. This pessimist heroism is of vital importance for this kind of collectivist utopianism. For Juenger the brevity and the model example at war, the heroic death in battle, became an ideal. The collective struggle, war itself and for itself, became a supreme ideal: "being killed for something you believe in—this is the greatest self-realization," even if this sacrifice is founded on error. This is because, according to Juenger, "The thing in itself does not count at all; the commitment is to totality." According to this view "the world and fantasy are one and the same, and even if a man is killed for a wrong thing, at least he became a hero."[16] Israeli tendencies parallel to European fascism were not manifested solely in the Hebrew national thought of the late 1920, the 1930s, and the 1940s, but also in the uniforms, symbols, and rhetoric of youth movements such as *Beitar* and political movements such as *Brit Habirionim* and the Revisionist Zionists.

From a positivist point of view, these were marginal tendencies in the Israeli public of the 1930s and the 1940s. Such a view is regularly conceptualized into a popular claim according to which one should distinguish the Israeli "right" and "left" conceptions of violence as essentially different. The protagonists of the claim of a fundamentally different conception of violence in the Zionist left and right could point to outstanding moments of general national violent ecstasy in the Israeli public, such as the 1982 war in

Lebanon, the "War for the Peace of Galilee," as it is generally called in Israel. We do not look for such argumentation, but prefer argumentation centered on a general theory of knowledge. Here we are much more interested in unveiling the violence of the hegemonic production and representation of ecstasy, in the well-intentioned nursing of violence, and its production and re-production as a regulative idea in the Israeli collective consciousness and its collapse into the new post-modern condition and the new post-modern realms of self-evidence within a McDonald'sized reality. A forgetful clash flourishes here between the fluid, contingent, hybrid, ecstatic construction/deconstruction of post-modern "individual" Jewish identities and their modernistic oriented multi-dimensional oppression of the Palestinians, ornamented by pre-modern modes of justification.[17]

The formation of the state of Israel in 1948 introduced a new setting for the internal disagreement concerning the status and the orientation of the army in the rapidly forming Israeli society and culture. The controversies between Socialist Zionism headed by Ben-Gurion and anti-Socialist Zionism headed by Jabotinsky's epigons developed considerably within the framework of the national consensus.

What in the Israeli *epos* is called "The War of Independence" offers a clear presentation of the Ben-Gurionist conception of violence. At a conference of his party, *Mapai*, on 6 January 1948, he declared that "these days *hochmat yisrael* (Israel's wisdom, Jewish philosophy) is the wisdom of war" and that "the war is not only the supreme examination of power, but also of the will to life." This was put forth not as part of the Jewish conception of the stand of (Jewish) man in the world, as part of a militaristic philosophy of history, but vice versa, as its conscious negation:

> This philosophy is an abomination for Judaism as we understand and, as I conceive, the wise men of Israel and its prophets did. We need the craft of war since we do not have any other choice—since it was forced on us. . . it is a must that we will undertake the burden of war and manifest a will to win. And we will undertake it precisely because war for us is not a goal for its sake, and we see in war a terrible and damned thing. We are forced into war only because of a compulsory situation—and war and victory are but an apparatus to something else, and this "something" is what will give us the advantage our enemies and the adorers of immortality are lacking: a vision of life, vision of independence, liberty, equality and freedom—to the Jewish nation and to all the world's people.[18]

The prophetic jargon does not reflect a one-dimensional utopia in Ben-Gurion and in the other Israeli socialist leaders of the time. This is to be seen in Ben-Gurion's militaristic politics and thinking. This dialectic has special transparence in the thinking of Yitzhak Tabenkin, one of the leaders of an important socialist faction and the Israeli *kibbutzim*. Tabenkin preached militaristic solutions for all of Israel's challenges in an anti-militaristic jargon that had long-standing educational fertility "education for war means fighting for something that is the opposite of war"; and elsewhere, "education for war in the face of pacifism is a war for a world without wars."[19]

In this light, on 31 May 1948 the declaration was made by Israel's provisional government of the formation of *zva hahagana leysrael* (Israel Defense Forces, IDF). Explicitly, the declaration of the establishment of the IDF was grounded on an antithesis to the Jabotinskian conception of violence. The constitution of the IDF is presented in the constitutive text as part of an evolutionary realization of the prophet's spirit of a totally peaceful reality.[20] Noticeable in this vision is a moral commitment and a broad anti-functionalist conception of the duties and aims of the Jewish soldier. In this respect Ben-Gurion, Jabotinsky, and Abba Ahimeir all contributed, each in his way, to a kind of normalizing education which made possible the success of the Zionist project. This attitude stands in severe contradiction to the current IDF military philosophy.

In Ben-Gurion's farewell letter to the IDF (7 November 1953), the educational duties of the army are declared "to be a melting pot for the Jews coming from all Diaspora, gathering together at the homeland from all the world's corners, being the formative force for a united nation, rooted in her rich heritage from her past and the vision of her prophetic future."[21] This was stated in face of a reality where "most of our people are from a Jewish point of view nothing but dust." The traditional modernistic educational ethos of forming an ideal, alternative collective through styled and well-disciplined organizational violence should not necessarily be reduced to a mere melting-pot ideology. Implicitly, here we are confronted with the conception of the realization of the idea of the *Sabra* and the production of the new Jewish subject as an anti-militarist pioneer-warrior who applies his power to master and fertilize the space that will became *Eretz Israel*, the land of Israel. This creative aggression will constitute the new reality while creating the new Jew as a *halutz* in such a strength that will enable him to be purified of any remnants of the Diaspora mentality. This conception of the relation to the land as a constructed homeland stays in opposition to the Palestinian notion of homeland as Mauten, which is conceived as a formative element of the Palestinian innerness.[22]

Those who are interested in dividing "leftist Zionism" from "right-oriented Zionism" will probably denote this Ben-Gurionist orientation as the most significant dimension in thoughts on violence in the philosophy of prominent political/educational David Ben-Gurion, Yitzhak Tabenkin, Yitzhak Sadeh, Meir Yahari, and Natan Altermann. Normally they will hold that it separates these "leftist" Zionists from the conception of violence of their right-wing counterparts, in the philosophy of Ze'ev Jabotinsky, Aba Ahimeir, and Israel Eldad. We would not agree. We negate this conception on two levels of argumentation. First, we will claim that declared anti-militarism is not necessarily a negation of violence; we will claim that the Ben-Gurionist anti-militarism is rooted merely in a different ideal of violence, not in an essential different praxis. The violence conception of the Zionist left is grounded in an ideal of violence that avoids direct, heroic confrontation and looks for a praxis that will paralyze its victims in such a way that it will avoid using military means, except in very rare cases. The conceptions of "conquering labor" (from the Palestinians working for the British government or other Jewish settlers), "Judaization of the country," and other central Zionist conceptions unite the Zionist "left" and "right" in such a way that makes the construction of the differences problematic if not completely futile.

The "left's" conception of violence was the basis for the articulation of the self-conception of the IDF and its traditional educational project. Here we should not look just for the reconstruction of Zionist ideology of violence as part of an explanation for its violent co-existence with its Palestinian Other. We have to look for the reconstruction of the violences of the hegemonic order; the theory and practice of the violence of the IDF has to be seen as one of the manifestations of the manipulations of a specific normalizing educational system that enslaves its objects (the Zionist subject and its Palestinian addressee). By struggling, fulfilling, and defending the realization of central concepts of the ruling Zionist ideology as "conquering the land" and "Judaizing the country" by agencies such as The Jewish National Fund and its manipulations,[23] the school system, youth movements, literacy, and art, the subject becomes an object of the manipulations of the system, she becomes something instead of some-one. The same principles are realized today in the Palestinian normalizing education. There too education is directed by the "concern for national identity."[24] There too the visible violence hides the fundamental inner violence within the collective that grounds its ethnocentrism and its commitment to destroy the otherness of the Israeli Other. There too visible violence is produced as counter-violence. There too it is a productive element of the hegemonic normalizing education, and fulfills itself as a manifestation of the current realm of common self-evidence. Therefore, it is impossible to divide this violence against the Palestinian Other and the violence toward the "Zionized" land from other violences such as structural unemployment, social selections, and their unchallenged justifications, established uncontested representations of history and present in textbooks, school celebrations, religious rituals, and other manners of assurance of establishing the consciousness that reproduces the current hegemonic order and its realm of self-evidence by destroying the Other's memory, history, and other material possessions. This is how education works normally and the Israeli and Palestinian normalization practices are of no exception. It is valid concerning both its symbolic and direct institutionalized power in the form of the army. Therefore, it is no coincidence that the IDF has traditionally had such a great educational mission. Even today, after the great evolution that we will reconstruct in what follows, the IDF is one of the greatest publishing houses in Israel, publishing "non-military" texts, functioning as the greatest educational force in Israel.

It was Ben-Gurion who formulated the basic concepts, the limits, and the declared aims of the IDF, to which the army is explicitly committed even today. According to Ben-Gurion

> All Israeli education should be directed to the aim of raising a generation of pioneers. These pioneers should be educated to see the greatest mission in rebuilding the country's desolation overcoming nature's powers in the land, in the sea and in the air and creating in the homeland an economy, society and culture. . . to totally destroy the gaps between the different communities and exiles, and elevating men and women that serve in its ranks. . . to the promising peak that awaits us.[25]

Ben-Gurion understood the nation building of the Israelis as part of a general war: against uncivilized nature (namely a non-Zionist and still not technologically advanced locus), against uncivilized Arabs in Palestine/Israel, and against the still not nationalistically united Jewish population that had to face grand challenges. The IDF had to function as a giant school[26] to melt down and then reintegrate the separate Jewish communities and traditions into a new, united, Jewish narrative, a collective and creative power: the Israeli subject. This ambitious normalizing education was viewed as a traditional anti-militaristic attitude of Zionist socialism whose pioneer-warrior ideal was the outcome of brutal conditions and not of a militaristic utopia which came true.

This conception was common in the main discourse in Israeli culture. To the left of it there was a noticeable critique of the ever-growing militarization of Israeli culture and its economy of symbols; to the right of it was the persistent Jabotinsky-Ahimeir call to see the imposing task in what Jabotinsky called "dying—or conquering the mountain" as a way of life.[27] For Ahimeir it was even more, the very purpose of life, as it was for Ernst Juenger at about the same time, to see humanity striving to build the Tower of Babel with blood[28] and the military struggle as the king of human feelings.[29] The Zionist hegemonic representation of Trumpeldor's dying words "It is good to die for our country" is different from Ahimeir's, for in the hegemonic (socialist)

Zionist rhetoric being killed in battle was not an aim in itself, although it was praised. For Juenger heroism in the battlefield and dying a hero was a supreme ideal since the collective struggle, war, was the greatest ideal: "Being killed for something you believe in is the greatest fulfilling," even if it is a sacrifice for a mistake. This is so since "the thing is nothing and the commitment is everything" and "the fantasy and the world are one, and the one who dies for a mistake still is a hero. . ."[30] For our following reconstruction, concerning the relevant ideals and developments in the Israeli army, it is worth mentioning Juenger's polarization between the *Arbeiter* (workingman) and the *Waldgaenger* (forest traveler), the writer, the individual, the *Fuerer*, to whom the "forest" is a place of freedom. The opposite is to be said about "the technical principle" as manifested in the enslaved modern collective, which has lost the *Mythos* and *Mysterien* of mother-land, lost original powers that strive for danger and heroic death. Ahimeir demanded the spiritualization of sacred/conquering violence, in which total obedience to the ruler/commander and the will for self-sacrifice will be praised. "Our movement," he writes about *Beitar*, "is not a flock, it is a battalion."[31]

This concept is represented in Uri Zvi Grinberg's poem "There Is One Truth and Not Two," which should be seen as one of the better representations of *Beitar*'s philosophy of education:

> Your forefathers thought: a land is not to be bought by money / one is buying the tilled soil and brandish in it a pick-axe. And I say: money does not buy a land / and with the pick-axe one also digs and buries his dead. . . and a day will come when from Egypt's river to the Euphrates / and from the sea till beyond Moab my men will climb / and they will call my enemies to the last battle, and blood will be shed to determine who will be the only one who masters here.[32]

As we have seen in Ernst Juenger, Uri Zvi Grinberg likewise demands the unification of violence and myth, sword and writing-feather: ". . . poetry and sword. Not this one without the other!"[33] Total (secular) devotion was an uncompromising educational demand among the socialist pioneers in Israel, the *haluzim*. As one of them wrote

> We have to create a new living religion, religion of devotion, we will set before us grand ideals and we will sacrifice ourselves for them. . . I am striving. . . for great devotion to a living religion that has a supreme vision, devotion to the point of asceticism and sacrifice, which will enable us to change ourselves.[34]

Uri-Zvi Grinberg, Abba Ahimeir, Ze'ev Jabotinsky, Menahem Begin, David Ben-Gurion, Ya'akov Hazan, and Natan Altermann understood, like Ernst Juenger, that a nation's life is in need of myths, creative symbols energetic enough to spur the nation's soul to a life-and-death struggle. This is the foundation of their educational philosophy, as for their current Palestinian counterparts, who's work is understood by Edward Said as matching the Zionist narrative with a rival, counter-narrative.[35] The fruitfulness of this manipulation goes beyond the practical needs of the collective and its hegemonic interests or groups. It relates to the heart of human's inhuman existence in face of meaninglessness and in the presence of the absence of God. Nietzsche knew it,[36] and Heidegger knew it,[37] but current Western culture has forgotten it. In face of the annihilation of absolute values, objective truths, and the actual social and cultural possibility of a self-creating subject that could have restored life to the Enlightenment. Western culture sinks into aimless desires of mere life as the prospect of life. The object swallows the subject in a post-modern culture industry as a grand *pleasure machine*.[38]

Ultimately, the Zionist philosophy of education was based on a modernistic realm of self-evidence and collective ethnocentrism that produced a human commitment to retain sets of values, knowledge-images, and bodies of knowledge that did not totally obey parameters as profit-loss, efficiency-inefficiency, practical-unpractical, but on the contrary, made them possible and negated them.[39] The presence of these was vital to the collective *telos* of the Zionist order. This philosophy of education included suitable theoretical means for the grounding of appropriate manipulations for making possible the Zionist subject's acceptance of military service's superiority as a vocation and not as a profession. It emphasized modesty, striving for honor, bravery, and total devotion to the Zionist narrative's supreme ideals, including a vivid radical interpretation of Judaism as a secular-socialist project. Until the late 1970s there were no marked cracks visible in the Israeli order, and these ideals still had real vitality: to state it generally, there was a consistency between the hegemonic Israeli philosophy of education and that of the IDF as an integral part of Israeli society and the modernistic meta-narrative that formulates it.

Since the 1967 war, more especially since the early 1980s, the ideological part of Israeli ethnocentrism started to show cracks.[40] Certain social groups, in which we can pinpoint middle-class representatives such as senior bureaucrats, technicians, young merchants, and generally the economically better-off, as well as those in free professions and others, grasped the sense of the collapse of the traditional realm of common self-evidence and its local (Zionist) modernistic order and the evolution of a new, post-modernistic realm of common self-evidence coming into being.[41] The popular reception of images, symbols, and desires denoted this evolution, which eroded both what was traditionally called (Western) high culture and the *halutz-Sabra* ideology. The images of wealth and power transmitted by television series like *Dynasty* and *Dallas* became very relevant. Traditional mythological figures and Zionist culture heroes, like A. D. Gordon, Josef Trumpeldor, and Meir Har-Zion, were openly rejected as irrelevant, to be replaced by figures like Michael Jackson, Madonna, and their Israeli local models. The culture industry of globalizing capitalism introduced new myths, drives, and violences which almost completely destroyed the constitutive Zionist myths. Post-modern conditions forced their way into the collective heart of the middle class.

The Zionist philosophy of education produced a unique order, in which there exists a total heroic commitment to values and knowledge concepts, which did not obey such parameters as the aforementioned profit-loss, efficiency-inefficiency, practical-unpractical. As part of advancing capitalism, these were naturally present in the Zionist arena, especially among the middle class, but they were secondary to high culture and the collective ideals and myths, which were vivid and fertile, especially in times of crisis and military conflicts, and the hegemonic educational ideology purposed to overcome them. The active presence of these myths, desires, fears, hopes, and concepts was vital to the *telos* of the Zionist project, which understood the individual and collective Zionist reality in the still nonexistent, in *the totally other*. This philosophy of education included relevant theoretical means for the constitution of the necessary effective educational manipulations.[42] They were indispensable to ensure acceptance and identification with it. In other words, they were vital for the production of the Zionist subject as a violence focus. They included, naturally, accepting military service as a vocation and not as a profession. They also included the expression of personal modesty, national honor, and the presentation of heroism and devotion to modernism's grand ideals as presented by the dominant Zionist narrative. Until the late 1970s, traditional Zionist myths were generally still alive, and were able to produce the ("internal" and external") required amounts of violence that were accepted as "needed" by the reality of coexistence with the Arab world and the Palestinian population. At that time this was still possible, because sufficient correlation existed between the philosophy of education in the IDF and the suggestive power of the hegemonic Zionist meta-narrative and its standing in central concepts of modernity.

But for a generation by now, the socialist and (political) liberal ideals of modernity have become problematized and even irrelevant in the Israeli order. In that same period the traditional cultural, social, and political elite of the labor movement, and its top level, the representatives of the kibbutzim, have entirely lost their self-confidence, and their socioeconomic power focuses as well.[43]

As elsewhere in the West, the new elites in Israel were also part and parcel of modernity; the new cultural and technocratic groups reproduced the traditional Zionist jargon. They represented modernity's weariness in the form of functionalist "pragmatism."

Parallel to the dying (atheist) Zionist myths, ultra-religious, and ultra-nationalist alternatives emerged.[44] This nationalistic religiosity inherited the aggressiveness and vitality of such traditional Zionist myths as the socialist farmer-warrior (*halutz*) and the Jewish fascist gentleman-soldier as a knight who represents *hadar*, Jewish chivalry.[45] The military concept of the new religious ultra-nationalistic alternative has many roots, but a special role is played here by the impact of the thought of Rabbi Zvi Yehuda Hakohen Kook. Continuing from Rabbi Avraham Zvi Hakohen Kook, he synthesized the religiosity of the Torah, Israel, and Erez Israel under a divine project[46] in which secular history becomes a part of a grand teleological divine history. The state of Israel, under such a conception, becomes a vital element of the cosmic revelation of God, and the military aggression of the IDF becomes part of worshipping the Lord, that is, holy violence.[47] This conception was observed already in the religious-poetic glorification of violence in the poetry of Uri Zvi Grinberg, a former culture hero of the Israeli political right. In "Memorial Vision to the Tribes of Israel" he writes:

> There are none so perfect for mastery as Jews, there are none so gracious as they... no one will fit more than they to boast the crown of world-ruling. There is no other mountain in the world but Mount Moriah to climb up to Jerusalem. There is no one but us to herald the tidings of the future on Mount Moriah to the peoples and to the world, to grant a new religion of yearning and new everlasting expressions to man[48]

The social milieu of Uri Zvi Grinberg's writing was basically secular, and his thought, like that of Ahimeir, was gradually abandoned even by the Israeli extreme right. Grinberg himself was conscious of the increasing irrelevance of his philosophy for Israelis of the 1967 generation and he ceased writing about the new religion of heroism. The cult of tragic Jewish heroism came to an end, colliding with the new civic religion that had started to develop in Israel since the 1950s. But the rhetoric of mysticism of violence did not die out. Instead, it has become transformed under the new conditions. Jewish heroism and sacred violence has been re-vitalized from a particular trend in Jewish religious thinking in Israel, some factions of which, like that of Rabbi Meir Kahane, returned to Grinberg's ideas and re-fertilized them.[49] The next step, the assassination of premier Yitzhak Rabin as a traitor, who "gave away" the land of Israel to the enemy, was quite natural, following the historical development of this intellectual tradition.

This conception is heralded by a vivid growing minority in Israeli society. Over the last twenty years there has been a constant change in the social-cultural formation of the army: as many of the kibbutz youth are less interested in idealistic life orientation and individual self-sacrifice in all its forms. As part of this trend they refrained from a military career as an ideal, especially in the "special units." Their traditional role in the army is gradually being taken over by religious ultra-nationalists who see themselves as Rabbi Kook's disciples. Is the fate of Israeli society going to be similar to that of Iran? We think that the presence of capitalism and high tech and the succesful distribution of its inner logic within the larger part of Israeli society as well as the relative affluent economy establish a challenge to the religious fundamentalism in Israel which was spared from the Iranians and many other Third World fundamentalist revivals. It might create an important transformation in the religious sector during the coming future. The basic conditions are so different between Iran and Israel that it is hard to take it as a realistic option even in face of a demographically and politically fast-growing alternative among Jews and Palestinians in Israel and Palestine. But that does not mean that the essence of the Iranian transformation will not manifest itself in the Israeli arena in various manners: the erosion of the current realm of common self-evidence has to be manifested in total transformation of the current Israeli multicultural order and its being succeeded by a new, fundamental, homogeneous system.

Ironically, the dialectic that we are reconstructing between the relations of the Israeli political elite (whose jargon is still basically traditional modernist-nationalistic) and the army (between the traditional ideological trends and the new, "neutral," professionalism-functionalist conceptual developments) took place in a very special situation: the expanding Palestinian uprising (the *Intifada*), which challenged the relative comfort of the Israeli repression of the Palestinian population, shook Israeli collective self-confidence and has now culminated in a new violent social-political situation that is called "the peace process," which will inevitably give birth to new forms of national violent clashes within Israel and between Palestine and Israel.[50]

In Israel of today, the apparent triumph of Instrumental Rationality within the framework of the positivistic ideology and its "anti-ideological" preformative conclusions matches the current situation in the West, where national conflicts are becoming less explicit, adjusting themselves to the rhetoric and the imperatives of globalizing capitalism and to the logic of the new technological developments and their social re-adjustments. In the new reality, collective solidarity is diminishing, and the visible confrontation with the Other is being minimized. One of the original peculiarities of the Israeli reality is that in it, parallel to the direct military/social/economic/symbolic confrontation with the Palestinians (who produce counter-ideological responses), a new collective consciousness is forming in Israeli society. It is anti-collectivist, pragmatic, functionalistic, and "neutral" on values and collective solidarity and aims.[51] This Western spirit of our generation has found very fertile ground in secular Israeli society since the 1980s. In Israeli society of the 1990s this ideology is gathering momentum and is attracting ever greater numbers of people in Israeli (secular-Jewish) society, who have grown tired of Zionist idealism and collectivism, basically from the Enlightenment's entire project. This essentially modernistic trend is adopting another "neutral" orientation: a post-modernistic rejection of the entire Western realm of self-evidence. In some cases the two orientations are united.

The ideal of the Israeli has not transformed itself—it was undramatically demolished and deconstructed by the new myths, symbolic exchange, and interests which were called on by the success of Zionism. It is from the ideal of a straightforward, plain, and honest farmer-soldier, a *Sabra* (a Jewish Zionist native of Israel) who is a *hevreman* (active, solidarian figure), into the ideal of a "professional" who is the opposite of the *hevreman*: he is an anti-solidarian, he is to be praised for not being a *freier*,[52] for being a successful commander, a wealthy stockbroker, for being unbeatable, if only he were not disturbed by "troubling" morality and legalism. The last generation faced the death of the traditional Zionist myths and symbols that negated intellectualism, rejected political liberalism and humanism, and refused democratic public codes, standards, and values in favor of *dugri* talking,[53] *hevreman* behavior and ethnocentric solidarity.

In the new explicit multicultural Israeli context, pre-modern, modern, and post-modern collective consciousness are constituted which are united in one point: the struggle with the otherness of the Arab Other. Within this context the strife with the Palestinians and actually with the entire Arab world is going to be decided by the "professionalism," "excellence," and efficiency of the holy trinity of Israeli army, economy, and education.[54] Under the new conditions, when direct visible national violence is not setting the agenda, the arguments for the reproduction of the conflict in military terms are becoming more and more pragmatic and formal, less and less offensive toward the outside world and the Palestinians. This, while combining the post-modern violences with the modernistic ones while still being committed; the pre-modern myths and symbols such as the religious rights of tombs of holy figures and other manifestations of *Tanatus*. At the same time, even in days when the Israeli police does not shoot the Palestinians and the Zionist planted forests are not set on fire by Palestinians who simultaneously try "riots," "terror," and mini civil war, the hatred and fear of the Other continue to gather momentum even under the layer of functionalist rhetoric of dreadful everyday life.

This dialectical contradiction does not terminate in the Israeli arena as a modernistic order, between its obligation to realize national ideals at any cost and its attraction to neutrality and practical orientation. Basically, these are both perfect manifestations of the violent (local) collision between two systems, modernity and post-modernity. This is one of the central aspects of the current phase of the Israeli/Palestinian engaging violences.

The postmodern discourse is grounded in post-modern conditions. It reflects and confronts the supremacy of Instrumental Rationality that Max Horkheimer, Theodor Adorno, and Juergen Habermas reconstruct in their critique. In the present phase, Instrumental Rationality in Israel has no internal rivals but religious fundamentalism and ultra-nationalistic religiosity (which, in part, is willing to cooperate with the pragmatic trends), post-modernists, who do not constitute a separate political force in the narrow meaning of the term, and traditional humanists like liberals and Marxists, who are of no challenge whatsoever.

Israeli society is currently experiencing a low stage of modernistic national conflict, but its structures of reproduction promise ever stronger and more visible violences against the imperatives of its post-modern dimensions. The representation of the national violence and its creative myths and powers are characterized by a combination of the most primitive and the most sophisticated manifestations of violence. This contradiction is a real challenge to educators and intellectuals but even to field officers who have to decide how to respond to a "mob" of fearless children and women who run against the Israeli soldiers or police and against their fire ready to pay any cost for the liberation of the land or for giving voice to the anger of being uprooted from their land and daily humiliated, discriminated, and marginalized.

The Israeli disorientation does not express abandoning ethnocentrism and it is being spread in all parts and levels of public life. There is a need for a medicine for the disorientation, not only for a solution to the practical challenges of control, oppression, and maintaining military supremacy. And so even in the Israeli army. This is part of the context for its reception of the T.Q.M in the Israeli army.

Total Quality Management (TQM) is a management strategy to organize production and delivery of merchandise in an age when the ideal of an autonomous subject is fading, the use value of a product is eroding, and basically what remains of it in the market is its distribution value. Within this context it represent "quality" as synonym to efficient "fitness" as the ultimate goal that is abstracted of any defendable value. It is not just a fashioned managerial/organizational theory, it is a (fashioned) reflection of the new status of the human being and the present evolution of Instrumental Rationality and its violence. The adorers of TQM speak of it as "brain power and human energy"[55] as a condition for "survival"[56] in an essentially total reality, where what Darwin called "fitness" is determined by naturalized omnipotence of laws of the unconscious market. This management strategy is based on the assumption that "in order to survive in the market it is necessary to bring about a rapid essential improvement in qualities, while reducing expenses." This is so according to the most recent educational material of the IDF, which is part of a new trend to reconstruct the Israeli army in accordance with the principles of the new strategy.[57] We should see in it a reflection of a much deeper and more essential change: it shows how little difference exists in developed capitalism between the economy of death production and the production of other commodities, since human life and human relations become totally reified and abstract. Therefore, to that extent such a common organizational strategy suits so well the present capitalist production in all its manifestations.

In the last two years, the leading managers of the IDF have adopted TQM not only as a substratum to reorganize Israel's military forces, but also as the foundation for the constitution of a new educational philosophy for the production of the Jewish soldier. This revolution in the collective Israeli self-consciousness and the Zionist philosophy of power is viewed as a simple, minuscule organizational change; but this revolution (and the general indifference to it in the Israeli public) is of utmost philosophical and political importance.

In July 1992, a change in command took place in the Israeli navy, and Rear-Admiral Ami Ayalon became the commander. The general climate, the IDF chief-of-staff's policy, and the new navy commander's attitude reflected the dominant tendencies in the most advanced parts of Israeli and Western societies in general. The TQM was also adopted by other IDF arms, such as the air force. In his inaugural programmatic speech, Admiral Ayalon said:

> 1. In the IDF we ought to adopt advanced organizational strategies that will enable us to make the most out of the present resources we have. 2. The improvement has to include all the navy's units, while marking out especially the combat units; an improvement in the combat units will guarantee an immediate and direct improvement in the navy's goals. 3. *The educational philosophy must be constituted in accordance with the requirements of the organizational and managerial needs.* This is to be implemented rigorously according to the definition of leading qualifications and leadership philosophy in the army as constructs of TQM's ideology.[58]

One has to acknowledge the American influence. We should take into account the close working relations between the American army and the IDF. Since the American army adopted the new myth, it was but rational that the Israeli army, which operates American weaponry, methods, and standards, would also adopt the TQM. A deeper analysis must consider the current development in advanced capitalism and Western societies of which Israel is a part. A comparison of the ideal of the *Sabra* and the Jewish soldier in Israel, as commander and leader/hero/*hevreman* of his unit in the history of the IDF, with Israel's current culture highlights the extent of the contemporary revolution. The IDF officer, particularly in "special units" and the air force, was traditionally represented as the supreme Israeli; he was accepted as a symbol of honesty, devotion to collective ideals and present existence, an idealist at his best. These qualities, as mentioned in Ben-Gurion's speech cited earlier, were understood as the main source of Israel's power. This guaranteed Israel's violence as legitimate and even as a part of a holy war for existence/expansionism. In Judaism this was traditionally understood not as existence for its sake, but existence as part of fulfilling a cosmic mission, as being *or lagoyim* (a light to the nations) and universal redemption. The Zionist (secular) version of redemption was reduced to ever more national-materialist expansionism. The obligation of the traditional IDF commander was to the entire Jewish past, to the recent Holocaust, to guaranteeing present national emancipation, and to future global redemption within traditional Zionist ideology. Secularist leaders of Israel, like the late Ben-Gurion, revitalized traditional religious Jewish conceptions in constructing and legitimizing the mainstream ethnocentrism of Zionist ideology and its violence.

Today's IDF conception of the Jewish commander in Israel's army understands him as a part and a reflection of advanced capitalism; as an ideal "professional" producer of efficient violence, whose aggression has no holiness or essence whatsoever, but efficient "quality."

In official IDF educational publications the commander is conceptualized as a professional servicing his clients: "An external client is the one who utilizes a product or a service that is offered by the organization. For an example: the clients of the *Bahad 1* (IDF officers' course) are the combat units. The clients of the dockyard are the commanders of the warships and the control stations. The clients of Central Command are the fortified outposts."[59] It is stated there that TQM (implicitly in the IDF) is not a mere technique but "a world view."[60] In a lecture "Excellence in the Israeli Army" given in Haifa University (1 May 1995), Admiral Ayalon (at that time the commander of the Israeli navy) spoke of training troops and preparations to war in terms of "input" and on the next war as the "output."[61] The performative principle was introduced at the conference as the only criterion valid for the evaluation of a commander's behavior. Pragmatism, like behaviorism, is not new, but in the current context one has to understand that one is facing nothing less than an educational revolution. This revolution is to be understood as part of Instrumental Rationality's evolution within the framework of a broader theory of knowledge. This revolution holds not just for the conception of the soldier or for empowering efficiency of military violence: it reflects a deeper and more general change. It is no less than what Marx called "revolution."[62] It is a manifestation of what we show here as the erosion of the present realm of common self-evidence.

Under the new conception of life, violence is transformed. "Only what is countable exists!" says a new IDF educational publication.[63] The dichotomy that Ernst Juenger and Martin Heidegger drew between the mechanistic/rational/controlled and the mystic/"forest traveler"/author/Fuerer, a dichotomy that is to be seen in the thought of Abba Ahimeir and Uri Zvi Grinberg, disappeared. There is no more grounding in the IDF's current philosophy of violence for such distinctions: Instrumental Rationality is the guide to living in a reality of uncertainty; violence is rationalized and becomes part of general social normality. There is no longer room for heroism and mystery or "real truth" in violence or for holy violence even when the clash with the Palestinians centers around issues such as the legitimate claim for relations to, and right on, the Mount of the Temple/al Akxa, since the anti-metaphysical totalization of violence leaves no room for mystery, truth, or any kind of otherness.

In the fantastic world of "the new global order," the political elites are reducing the financial and rhetorical support traditionally offered to the generals and the army as an exclusive part of the ethnocentric order. Under these advanced capitalistic circumstances, Instrumental Rationality can reflect and join forces for the production of the new human being, a man who will be immanently prevented from being an authentic Israeli. This is so because the ideal *Sabra* is a typical cultural myth of modernity[64] and was invented under social conditions that are disintegrating in a productive way into a new realm of self-evidence. In this sense, it is possible to show how the improvement and strengthening of the IDF under new organizational theories, which herald the future realm of self-evidence (and its systems), in practice contribute to the destruction of the Zionist state. The destruction of the Zionist state is certain, but the demolishing of the State of Israel and the IDF is definitely less certain; even under such conditions the bureaucratic structure might hold on, but not so its spiritual essence. Under post-modernistic conditions, the new Israeli personality will not be able to be a real Zionist and "a good" Israeli; he will not join efforts to make the desert bloom or to Judaize the land. More than that, in principle he will not be a *hevreman* or a *halutz* or a patriot, and with no present or potential living national myths, the protection and development of the present order of hegemony and structural, and at times, also direct and visible oppression, are impossible.

Some attributes of the women and men of the future realm of self-evidence are already to be seen in the most advanced parts of the present order. As an individualistic monad, its relation to the public sphere is no longer based on commitment to ideals of solidarity and myths of self-sacrifice, but on an education that at its best produces a temporal, individualistic-anarchist readiness to joint plots. This, one might say, is nothing new for human nature, nor for intellectual fashions like the nihilism of Max Stirner. But at the current historical stage, these phenomena have unique characterizations, as one of the manifestations of a post-modernistic order and the dying of the entire Western modern realm of self-evidence. Even the pure yuppies, though stripped of absolute and objective values and any *telos*, still leave room for values and principles, for resistance and neutrality as a revolt against the idealistic past. For the "X generation" this stand is accepted with disgust. Work, especially hard work, whether for one's self or for something or someone else, is no longer considered a value, not even a value to be rejected. "Success" is accepted, if it comes with no effort, but it is not desired. That which the "X generation" represents does not hate anything or anyone, nor does it love anything or anyone. It lost one of the main characteristics of the Western realm of self-evidence: it lost its *Eros*.

In the 1990s it was harder than ever to separate *Eros* from *Tanatus*, globalizing capitalism's violences from its militaristic manifestations, because of the success of the internalization of this violence, as can be seen in the "X generation" phenomenon, the virtual reality practices, and endless other manifestations of the dying out of the Western realm of self-evidence.

The Jewish modern national movement, Zionism, reflected general trends in the emancipatory/colonialist orientation of modernity. Jewish force was not just an instrument guaranteeing independence after two thousand years; the Israeli army became a *symbol* and an active force that was central to the Zionist spirit and reality.

This was part of the evil-production in/of the Israeli order. As part and parcel of this order the IDF's educational philosophy spared no effort to represent and re-produce its myths as something of common self-evidence. Of course, in real life there was enough room for personal ambitions and intrigues as well as for refusal for self-sacrifice, for modesty, and double play. Belief in the central symbols and myths of Zionist ideology was central to the IDF's pedagogical practice and educational theory, and it was unthinkable to detach combat and operational instruction from the obligation to the grand aims and central myths of Zionist ideology.[65] But as the Western realm of self-evidence and the dominant ideology in the Israeli ethnocentrism became eroded, the vividness of general modernist central concepts, symbols, and myths was lost. While staying within the framework of modernity, functionalist-instrumental-positivistic conceptions took the upper hand, and Instrumental Rationality came to rule, with objective reason proving no match whatsoever. This also had its impact on the army.

A modernist army is supposed to be a perfect instrumental organization: its products are not quantitative by functionalist yardsticks, since ideal success—victory, deterring the enemy, empowering collective vigorous spirit, and so forth—cannot be reduced into quantity or, in any case, it is unreasonable to evaluate them basically in input-output terms. Until the latest stage of its development, the IDF, as part of modernist Israel, was organized and understood itself as part of the historic Zionist project, its ideals and realities.

As Israeli society developed and the Israeli economy became wholly integrated into the most advanced leading economic trends and its parallel technological advancements, the IDF was also forced to integrate into the cultural and psychological dimensions of this trend. As a bureaucratic, administrative, and technologically highly advanced economic organization, the army adopted new technologies and their immanent logic. Consequently, the IDF blended with the aimless development of the new technologies and the rationality of decaying/victorious modernity; it became part of what it wanted to enslave, to make use as a mere instrument. But Instrumental Rationality does not permit such a freedom. An ever greater gap opened in the army between the constitutive national-modernistic ideals of Zionism and the practical interests of an aimless, bureaucratic-neutral ever-growing, and strengthening organization.

The army, especially at the level of high posts, suffered and integrated late modernistic and anti-modernistic influences. An ever-greater applicability has emerged between the inner logic and the needs of high capitalistic production and the needs of technological dimensions of the old-style death economy on the one hand, and the ideological obligations to the hegemonic Zionist ideals on the other.

The army as a violence-production machine against "external" targets was always a part of the ethnocentric order as a focus of violence, internalizing in the psyche and in the consciousness of its carriers (the pretended "subject") the realm of self-evidence; it was part of the educational project, producing "subjects" as objects that would re-produce the hegemonic realm of self-evidence. The military violence was to secure the cummunalitability of what turned out to be, in the case of success, "self-understood" truths. But as this production started to produce "individuals" with no soul, no *Eros*, and no God, their market value changed parallel to the changes in their military economy and technologies of killing. Inevitably, this trend is becoming relevant to the current struggle between Palestinians and Israelis.

The struggle over the legitimacy of different images of knowledge parallels the struggle over the legitimate strategies of producing the Zionist subject and the Palestinian subject and the legitimacy of their violences; this is a combat that is to be reduced to a struggle over sources of power to control land and knowledge about the land, the legitimate procedures of producing and enabling the subject's consciousness, producing and re-producing legitimate history and censured/forbidden histories, memories, and interests of the Other—an Other whose power and who's legitimacy as to be destroyed by all means. This is in order to ensure the safe production of a subject who will be ready to live, and especially to die for the Zionist space as "homeland." Azmi Bishara writes on this subject from a postmodern-Palestinian perspective,[66] but he neglects the brutal existential "fact": the subject, the Zionist subject included, is mainly a manifestation of the realm of self-evidence and the normalization processes which serves and *hides* its violences. Even his rebellion is recruited for the progress, safety, and permanency of the hegemonic order, "his" educational system that in late modernity is regularly called the "fatherland." This is an embedded network of systems that embodies forces and concepts which manipulate other "subjects" to re-produce it by "educating," "protecting," and empowering new "subjects" who will struggle against the representatives of rival systems. The hegemonic order has to ensure (through the "subjects" who are its carriers) material, psychological, and spiritual conditions. Finally, under the conditions of a technologically advanced society at the end of the twentieth century, the project is to succeed primarily by ensuring the right consciousness, drives, quest for pleasure, but also fears and limitations on self-reflection.

This is why currently the focus of violence has to be primarily internal, educational, assuming that for the time being the Palestinians in Israel and in Palestine did not yet open a full scale rebellion/war. The modern, Zionist, realm of self-evidence was intended to supply the hegemonic order with sufficient symbolic energy to control and develop the required practices of producing subjects' consciousness. Yet these are challenged by the very powers brought about by the victory of Zionism and the post-modern conditions which reflect its "success." This energy was traditionally sufficient to ensure the intellectual impotence of the repressor; a productive impotence that ensures his permanent desire to eliminate/control the Other as an agent of "his" normalizing educational system and its re-producer, in the service of the current realm of self-evidence that has no *telos*, meaning, or foundation, but just limits, the limits of the current horizons. The current horizons are determined by the vividness of the foundation myths, symbols, concepts, and desires which constitute standard subjects who are currently produced in the existing networks that combat each other. The entire energy of what was traditionally called "education" is nothing but a vast effort to camouflage this process and ensure human *impetus* for productive violence. This is the concrete context of emancipatory ideals of modernity, including its political liberalism and orthodox Marxist versions.

The Western modern realm of self-evidence is being eroded by its own success, and its current bourgeois systems are holding on through its organizational-bureaucratic structures, while losing its founding myth's vividness. The bourgeois world is being transformed into something quite different, most often referred to as post-modernity. What remains of it for the youth is pure aggressiveness with no *Eros*. Instrumental Rationality that is immanent to its success is not a *substratum*; it can guarantee "progress" but not powerful or meaningful life[67] of the normalizing educational system—in contrast to ancient Christianity, early capitalism, and other historical realms of self-evidence in the history of Judeo-Christian civilization.

Under these conditions the post-modern discourse had, in the last generation, great victories even among its Israeli enemies. The hegemonic force under current conditions is still economic liberalism, combined with bureaucratic practices and positivist orientations. There is no real rival to present conventionalism, an attitude toward the representation of reality which was completely abandoned by Spirit. The modernist (ideal of the) subject who is struggling, or who is categorically required to struggle for the emancipation of humanity in light of solidarity with humankind, was transfigured into an individual who lost his individuality, who is no longer an autonomous subject, and for whom autonomy, freedom, and solidarity have lost their relevance, even as regulative ideas. He has adjusted to the new post-modern conditions and has become an object that is manipulated by mass-production desires and is totally controlled by the stimulus of power and joyousness as a regular, cheap product of the culture industry. These tendencies are prospering in current Israeli society, especially among the elite of Jewish secular groups, and they are entering even into the Israeli army. Here they are joining forces with the oppressive dimensions of remaining modernist-bureaucratic tendencies.

It seems that today the technocratic dimension of Instrumental Rationality has the upper hand in the IDF orientation. Under these conditions "professionalism" is represented as the highest "value," and discussions are going forward on rewording the most efficient functionaries and analysis of commander-soldier relations in terms of "industrial tranquility." At the same time, more and more money is invested in an educational offensive aimed at re-producing traditional heroism, military battle sagas in museums, exhibitions, and publications; but by now these are consumed and produced as obsolete folklore, and not as vivid myths for the emerging elites in Israel's society. Not the hero in battle but the *expert* at the control room is praised as the supreme "successful" aggressor with whom to identify. One manifestation of the new stage in the erosion of the modernistic emancipatory *Eros* of Israeli society may be seen in the formal acceptance of the TQM organizational system as the theoretical-practical framework of the IDF. Even PUM, the IDF command and staff college, is organized according to the new fashion, and the educational orientation of the entire Israeli army derives from it, according to the "objective," "neutral" requirements of organizing the forces in light of the TQM. However, TQM is not to be reduced merely to an organizational method; it is a new fashion, reflecting a new way of life, a new "set of values": anti-ideological, anti-values, purely instrumental, neutral, and sterile violence. A characteristic is that even TQM as a "way of life" and as a theory is judged according to its performance (in an aimless society whose goals do not transcend the given reality). Accordingly, after two years of TQM dominance in the IDF, the army changed its attitude to the system. The new policy accepts TQM locally, "where it works," other organizational theories "where they perform better than TQM," and a combination of different organizational theories "where it proves to be more efficient," according to Admiral Ayalon (1 May 1995). Each unit in the IDF is conceived as "a closed market" that has to find the production methods that accord with its "desired" output more efficiently. This is a new version of pluralism that is so popular in today's cultural discourse and the special success it has enjoyed under the title "multiculturalism." The "pluralism" that is worshipped today in the IDF does not reject TQM's ideology; it develops it according to its inner logic and generalizes it as empty abstraction. As a cultural phenomenon it is a "pluralism" of *nothingness*.

The IDF's acceptance of TQM was not accompanied by discussions of its philosophical and educational implications. It is typical that the discussions were held after acceptance of TQM and from its orientation. The yardstick for this crucial decision was purely performative: would the Jewish soldier be more of an expert, and would the IDF's aggression be more "effective while economically worthwhile," and so forth. The decision was not affected by considerations of relations to traditional Zionist values and the emancipation of humanity and the Jewish role in it.

Some will rejoice in the face of the current tendency in Israeli society and in the IDF. It is not unrealistic that the new IDF education, which represents the neutrality of the bureaucratic-functionalist orientation toward knowledge, will join the neutrality of post-modernistic philosophy of knowledge. Current technological developments, especially in electronics and knowledge production, storage, and delivery construct a new status of knowledge and produce a new kind of subject. This post-modern, post-industrial production and consumption, which Lyotard describes in *The postmodern condition,* is extreme relevant to the transformation of the army's essence as representative of the hegemonic order. While accepting new technologies and possibilities (like virtual reality) for training and for combat and reaching top efficiency, the violence of the IDF becomes explicitly Spiritless, careless to its constitutive ideals, myths, and enemies. The neutrality of modernity's presently most relevant version is that of a bureaucratic-functionalist view of knowledge, which presupposes the subject as an abstract. The neutrality of post-modern philosophy, which emphasizes the end of the subject and the irrelevancy of modernity's ideals of self as an autonomous, reflective, and solidarian entity, might join productivity of bureaucratic violence that is immanently colonialist.

While different from modernity's twin bother, the emancipation project that was committed to direct educational violence, the power that the bureaucratic trend uses is much more "objective," less "aggressive," and of supreme non-ideological efficiency, colonizing the oppressor and the oppressed alike; it is the voice of Instrumental Rationality's efficiency and reality that sometimes joins with political liberalism's jargon but always with economic liberalism's praxis, and it is conservative by its nature. In Israel the transformation of emancipatory violence to mainly bureaucratic rational uses of power has special transparency. Therefore, the change in education in general and in the army's education in particular is enlightened in a way that can also show clearly the margins of this phenomenon: post-modernist tendencies are making their way into the army on the one hand, and an ultra-nationalistic religious alternative to secular traditional Zionism is gradually building its foundation in the army on the other. But undoubtedly, the traditional mainstream in the IDF is losing ground.

The TQM's introduction to the IDF in general and the restructuring of its educational philosophy and pedagogical practices in accordance with the requirements of TQM and other organizational theories of its ilk reflect a post-Zionist condition.

In itself, the death of the Zionist Spirit is not a death sentence on Zionism as a bureaucratic-organizational entity. Continuing development in its technological sphere and permanent strengthening of the IDF are a realistic possibility. However, education toward "specialization" and ever-growing expertise via "efficiency" of neutral military experts can ensure the assembly of a spiritless violence machine. As the heroes of present day positivism, interests can operate as a ground for ever more efficient use of organized violence, and the Israeli war machine is today in its best condition since its formation. We doubt the future of such a lifeless nation-building organized/killing machine even within the framework of the horizons of the present order. Yet we think of the army as a site of *normalizing* violence, not the original source of violence.

It represents the violence between rival normalizing educational systems that share and represent *polemos*, an anti-dialogical relation between different elements of the present realm of self-evidence. But, since the present realm of self-evidence is dying out, the fate of its manifestations is determined. Therefore, the introduction of TQM is entirely justified, as part of manifesting the power of transformation, as an interlude to a requiem for Zionism, which by the same token is the voice of further advancement in the Israeli violence machine. In the next war with the Arab states that will come, it is unlikely but not unimaginable that the IDF will emerge again as the winner. But it may be that on the crucial day, the constitutive symbols and myths of Zionism will not be vivid enough to ensure the required violence produced out of faith in "our" "truth" and "justice"—illusions that are demanded by organized killing machines such as armies. But even so, the voice of the winners will never be the voice of the real victor.

In both cases, the victor will be the aimless diversity that is giving birth to transformations in the present realm of self-evidence and activation of rival normalizing educational systems and their representative's changing war practices. As the Israeli example shows, the death of the military spirit does not mean the death of metaphysical violence, nor does it promise a decline of the violence of normalizing education. Much more, it represents the arrival of a new, more vivid and efficient normalizing education and the beginning of a formation of a new realm of self-evidence. Facing this reality is the starting point for any possible counter-education.

NOTES

1. Ilan Gur-Ze'ev. "Philosophy of peace education in a post-modern era" (keynote address at the International Network of Philosophers of Education), *Philosophy of Education in the New Millennium—Conference Proceedings*, Sydney 2000, 121-125.
2. Ilan Gur-Ze'ev. "Toward a non-repressive critical pedagogy," *Educational Theory*, 48: 4 (1998), 463-486.
3. In this sense the Israeli army (IDF) is not an exception, regarding agricultural settlements, developing the country's infrastructure and educational tasks, in both industrialized and Third World societies. See: Azarya, Victor and Kimmerling, Baruch, "New immigrants in the Israeli armed forces," *Armed Forces and Society*, 6: 3 (Spring 1980), 455.
4. Uri Ben-Eliezer. *Derech hakavenet: hivazeruto shel hamilitarism hayisraeli* [Through the gun-sights: The creation of Israeli militarism], Tel Aviv: Dvir 1995, 26.
5. *Ibid.*, 285-291.
6. This is to be seen in two models, one exemplified by St. Augustine, Hegel, and Marx, and one by Philipp Mainlaender and Jean Baudrillard.
7. Emmanuel Levinas. *Collected Philosophical Papers*. Translated by Alphonso Lingis, Dordrecht 1987, 55.
8. Ilan Gur-Ze'ev, Jan Masschelein, and Nigel Blake. "Reflection, reflectivity and counter-education," *Studies in Philosophy and Education*, 20: 3 (2001), 93-106.
9. Ze'ev Jabotinsky. *Shimshon*. Translated by B. Kropniek. Tel Aviv: Tabersky 1930.
10. Ze'ev Jabotinsky. *Autobiography*. Jerusalem: H. Jabotinsky 1958, 177.
11. Abba Ahimeir. *Berit Habirionim*, 3, Tel Aviv: Hava'ad 1972.
12. *Ibid.*, 47.
13. *Ibid.*, 89.
14. *Ibid.*, 92.
15. Ernst Juenger. *Der Kampf als Inneres Erlebnis*. Berlin: Mittler 1929, 5.
16. *Ibid.*, 110.
17. Ilan Gur-Ze'ev. "Introduction," in Ilan Gur-Ze'ev (ed.), *Conflicting Philosophies of Education in Israel/Palestine*. Dordrecht: Kluwer 2000, 1-6.
18. David Ben-Gurion. *Zava Uvitachon* [Army and security], Tel Aviv: Maarachot 1955, 26.
19. Yitshak Tabenkin. "Beit hasefer vehamilhama" [School and war], *Devarim* 3 113, in Uri Ben-Eliezer, *Derech*, 93.
20. David Ben-Gurion. *Zava*, 36.
21. *Ibid.*, 27.
22. Hisham Sharabi. *Jafa—An Aroma of a City* 1991, 15.
23. Yoram Bar-Gal. *An Agent of Zionist Propaganda—The Jewish National Fund 1924-1947*. Jerusalem 1999.
24. Non-Governmental Palestinian Education Institutes, "Palestinian educational vision," Ramallah 1994, 3.
25. David Ben Gurion, *ibid.*, 363-364.
26. David Ben-Gurion. "The *Mapai* political comity 24 July 1952," in Uri Ben-Eliezer, *Derekh*, 289.
27. Ze'ev Jabotinsky. *Shirim* [Poems], Jerusalem: H. Jabotinsky 1947, 205.
28. Ernst Juenger. *Der Kampf als Inneres Erlebnis*. Berlin: Mittler 1929, 5.

29 *Ibid.*
30 *Ibid.*, 110.
31 Abba Ahimeir. *Berit*, 93.
32 Uri Zvi Grinberg. *Sefer Hakitrug Vehaemuna* [A book of indictment and belief]. Jerusalem: Sadan 1937.
33 *Ibid.*, 264.
34 T. David. *Bamivechan* (March 1942). 12.
35 Edward Said. *After the Last Sky.* London and Boston: Farber and Farber 1986, 106.
36 "And now mythless man remains eternally hungering amid the past, and digs and grabs roots, though he have to dig for them even among the remotest antiquities. . . what does all this point to, if not to the loss of myth, the loss of the mythical home, the mythical maternal bosom?" Nietzsche, Friedrich, "The birth of the tragedy" in: *The Philosophy of Nietzsche.* New York: Vintage Books 1937, 327.
37 Martin Heiddeger. "Helderlin Erde und Himmel," in: *Erlaeuterungen zu Hoelderlins Dichtung.* Frankfurt a.M.: Vittorio Klostermann 1971, 179.
38 Ilan Gur-Ze'ev. "Critical education in cyberspace?", *Educational Philosophy and Theory* 32: 2 (2000), 227-228.
39 Herbert Marcuse. *One Dimensional Man*, London: Routledge and Kegan Paul 1968. Max Horkheimer, *Gesammelte Schriften*, 7. Frankfurt a.M. 1985, 56-57.
40 Uri Ram. "Zionism and post-Zionism," in Yechiam Weitz (ed.), *Between Vision and Revisionism: Zionist Historiography.* Jerusalem: Merkaz Zalman Shazar 1997 (in Hebrew).
41 These trends in Israeli society are parallel to Western social and cultural evolution in post-modern reality, as reconstructed by Lyotard and Jameson.
42 According to Adir Cohen, even cradle songs were composed to foster "pleasure with the Hebrew language, a sense of mission, commitment to struggle, and conquest." The songs "articulated to the youngster the miseries of the [Jewish] nation, the persecutions it had suffered at the hands of other peoples, its wanderings in the world, the endless catastrophes it had experienced; they nurtured the hope and belief in redemption and in the conquest and building of the land by its Jewish sons who would return to it." Cohen, Adir, "To awaken or to go to sleep: Education and indoctrination through cradlesongs," in *Changes in Children's Literature.* Haifa 1988, 16 (in Hebrew).
43 Eliezer Ben-Rafael. "Dynamics of social stratification in kibbutzim," in Ernest Krausz (ed.), *The Sociology of the Kibbutz.* New Brunswick: Transaction Books, 1983, 202.
44 Raphael Mergui & Philippe Simmonet. *Israel's Ayatollahs; Meir Kahana and the Far Right in Israel.* London: SAQI Books 1987, 121-135.
45 On the decline of the *halutz* as an Israeli cultural hero parallel to the inflation in representation of the Israeli pioneers in local museums, see Aviv, Aviva, *Hahevra haysraelit* [Israeli society], Tel Aviv: IDF Publications 1990, 23-26; Shafir, G. *Land, Labor and the Origins of the Israeli-Palestinian Conflict, 1882-1914*, Cambridge 1993; Firer Ruth, "Alyiato unfilato shell hamytos hahalutzi" [The rise and fall of the pioneering myth], in: *Kivunim* 23 (1984), 23-25. On the *hadar* ideology see Jabotinsky Ze'ev, *Ha'uma* 3: 9 (1964), 177-178.
46 On Kook's unification of *Eretz Israel, Am Israel* and *Torah* see Hakohen Kook, Abraham Isaac, *Igrot hara'aya* [Evidential letters], 1. Jerusalem 1962, 313.

47 On holy violence in Kook's thinking, see Hakohen Kook, Abraham Isaac, *Seder Tefila Im Perush* [The order of prayers with commentary], Vol. 1 Jerusalem 1984, 706. On Zionist violence as part of religious redemption in Zvi Yehuda Hakohen Kook's thought and its relation to the philosophy of Rabi Meir Kahane and ultra-religious-nationalistic thought in Israel, see Yovel, Yirmiyahu, "Masihach gam lo yavo" [But the Messiah will not come], *Politica*, 3 (1985), 16; another rather political manifestation of it can be seen in the religious justification to the assassination of prime minister Yitshak Rabin.

48 Uri Zvi Grinberg. *Rehovot Hanahar* [Streets of the river]. Jerusalem: Schocken 1968, 265.

49 Raphael Mergui and Philippe Simmonet, *Israel's Ayatollahs: Meir Kahane and the Far Right in Israel*; and Daniel Breslauer, *Meir Kahane; Ideologue, Hero, Thinker*, Lewinston/Quinsston 1986.

50 Ilan Gur-Ze'ev, "Introduction," *ibid*.

51 On the disintegration of solidarity in Israeli society in parallel to the advance of Instrumental Rationality, see Uri Ram, *The Changing Agenda of Israeli Sociology: Theory, Ideology, and Identity*. State University of New York Press 1995, 15.

52 On the centrality of the [not being a] *freier* as a current Israeli ideal, see Runiger, Luis & Fayge, Michael, "Tarbut hafreier vehazehut hayisraelit" [The *freier* culture and Israeli identity], *Alpayim*, 7, (1993), 136.

53 The *dugri* way of using the language was part of the grand Zionist project of constructing a new Jew by negating the Jewish tradition that constituted the typical Jew in the Diaspora. In her study of the *dugri* way of communication, Tamar Katriel rightly notes that "traditionally, Jews recognized the value of using speech adroitly, since it was the only 'weapon' at their disposal." This negation is to be seen as part of a positive, productive conquest of the land of Israel, overcoming the Palestinian collective identity, and building a new collective identity for Jews as Israelis, namely as *Sabras* and *halutzim*. Our interest is to denote this positive linguistic power of transformation as part of and made possible by violent social practices. This violence against the Palestinians and Jewish tradition was internalized in the Hebrew language and is to be seen as the substratum of *dugri* speech. See: Katriel, Tamar, *Talking Straight: Dugri Speech in Israeli Sabra Culture*, Cambridge 1986. On the Israeli value system's connection to its militarism, see Kimmerling, Baruch, "Between the primordial and the civil definitions of the collective identity" 286-282, in Cohen, Erik, Lissak, Moshe, and Almagor, Uri (eds.), *Comparative Social Dynamics*, Boulder: Westview 1985.

54 This is to be seen in the current change of jargon and concrete orientations of central figures in Israeli society, such as prime minister Ehud Barak, until 1995 the IDF Chief of Staff, some senior generals presently serving in the navy and air force, rectors of Israeli universities, the director general of the ministry of education, Dr. Shimshon Shoshany, and the head of a leading Israeli corporation, Stef Werttheim. This tendency is becoming dominant and it is reflected in studies and research work that use TQM jargon, which standardizes their writing style on military, business, and academic-educational issues. See the entire issue of *Iyyunim Betechnologia*, 19, 1-2 ; *Davar -Hinuch Aher* (7 Feb. 1995), and *Maarachot* (1994).

55 Steve Cohen and Roland Brand. *Total Quality Management in Government: A Practical Guide for the Real World*. San Francisco: Jossey-Bass 1993, 9.

56 *Ibid.*
57 [Israeli] Navy, Department of Behavioral Sciences, *TQM/TQL: Principles*, 1., n.d. 2.
58 Col. Azran Kokhavi. "Embarrassment in the organization: Advanced managing systems, jugglery of commanders—or a realizable formula for constant improvement?" Paper submitted to Dr. Ilan Gur-Ze'ev at Haifa University, September 1994, 2 (in Hebrew).
59 *Ibid.*, 5.
60 *Ibid.*, 7.
61 Rear-Adm. Ami Ayalon. "Excellence in the Israeli army," lecture to the School of Education, Haifa University, conference on "Excellence in army, school, and academia," Haifa, 15 May 1995.
62 Karl Marx. "Socialism, democracy, and revolution," in *On Revolution*. New York: 1971, 21
63 [Israeli] Navy, Department of Behavioral Sciences, *TQM/TQL: Implementation*, 5, n.d. 15.
64 On the production of the *Sabra* as an Israeli ideal, see Shapira, Anita, *Land and Power: The Zionist Resort to Force, 1881-1948*, translated by William Templer, New York: Oxford University Press 1992, 365.
65 Yitzhak Kashti and Anat Rimon-Or. "Security, identity and education," in Ilan Gur-Ze'ev (ed.), *Modernity, Pstmodernity and Education*. Tel-Aviv: Romot 1999, 165-196.
66 Azmi Bishara. "Bein makom lemerchav" [Between place and space], *Studio* 37 (1992), 6-9.
67 Max Horkheimer & Theodor Adorno. *Dialectics of Enlightenment*. Translated by John Cumming, New York: Herder and Herder 1972.

CHAPTER 10
Humanistic-Oriented Education in Context

The forces which raise the banner of emancipation in Israel today are currently involved in a bitter struggle; there are many determined enemies to the humanist educational project which is determined to change and even transform the prevailing order, on the one hand, and much competition among the oppositional forces to the current hegemony about the justified and unique ownership of progressivism, on the other. Most Israeli humanists are blind to the ambivalent stand of their battle; some of them are fighting in the name of conservative emancipatory conceptions, ignoring an entire tradition which called into question the concept of emancipation, as well as changes in the technological, social, and cultural contexts—a discourse which rendered archaic the naive conception of progress. Not only do they not see to what a degree their discourse is anachronistic, they are even blind to what an extent their position in the Zionist sphere is anti-humanistic, according to the standards of the traditional emancipatory project to which they are indebted. Here we will try to elucidate the position of the "enlightened" educator as a representative of the "progressive Israeli forces." Special attention will be paid to the philosophical context of their political praxis.

In Israel today some well-intentioned humanists try to engage the changing actuality on three educational fronts. On such fronts dangerous educational forces are conceived as endangering the Zionist system, which, on so many occasions, they are proud to challenge and to criticize.

1. *Nihilism, in its different local versions, which threatens the optimistic view on the Israeli society's future.* The best-known theme, which accompanies the struggle against nihilism, is the protection of the country's youth from various dangers. Practically, the alleged threats on the physical health and the good manners of the young people endanger first and foremost the secular hegemonic group's economic position, its symbolic capital, and the prospects of its socio-cultural and political reproduction. Fundamentally, the sources of the struggle of this group against the dangers of nihilism, in its various versions, are not to be found in any deep or rich spiritual struggle. The reason is political: it challenges the current cynicism and

neutrality toward the critique of the supreme national goals and the subjectivist alternative. This last trend refrains from critique and from taking its share in the public debate. In its own way it cooperates with the negative trends of the hegemonic political establishment and serves the dominant cultural trends in the secular Israeli society. The efforts of a "progressive" opposition are, however, not merely negative: the ultimate goal is to protect society from being drawn into an anarchist, unproductive, way of life; that is, a situation in which increase of drug use, mindless violence, and so forth are an integral part. All these elements are the object of an educational effort for the abolition of the dangerous "perversion" and for giving it a bad name. As such, this educational effort is seen as part of the current order of things.

2. *Religious repentance and joining in various sects.* The declared ideological pluralism of the "progressive" forces exhibit little sympathy or tolerance toward competing cultural alternatives such as the Jewish ultra-orthodox *Neturei Karta* sect, which are committed to constitute or preserve spiritual autonomy. The ideological or spiritual autonomy of the members of various Jewish groups and sects include, and promote, neutrality or actual rejection of the educational/political efforts to challenge fundamental trends in the Israeli center as the prolonged occupation and oppression of the Palestinian people, discrimination against women, widening social inequality, and so on. This kind of "spiritual" autonomy amounts to a successful alternative to the "progressive" message concerning the remapping of Israeli culture; it aims at restructuring Israeli society, its collective identity—or rather identities, and firmly resists any hegemonian framework such as the "Israeli," which was constructed by Zionism and lasted for no more than three generations. The reconstructionists among the Israeli "progressivists," however, do not direct their symbolic and political efforts directly against the other oppositional forces which constitute or conserve their unique spiritual autonomy. The "progressivists" perform solely in the secular arena.

3. *Ultra-nationalism* aspires, by means of faith in miracles and unlimited aggressiveness, to overcome any obstacle which limits the horizons of the Zionist order and its critique. Here, too, the "progressive" forces commonly cooperate with the long meandering arms of the establishment, often becoming the establishment itself, as can be seen in academic and judiciary examples. This claim does not exclude, of course, the claim according to which oppositional forces, marginalized elements, and oppressed cultural alternatives are all essential elements of the network that produces the possibilities and limitations of the discourse, the psyche, and the political reality.

When struggling on the nationalistic and other fronts, the representatives of Israeli humanism raise almost as a standard the ideals of the Enlightenment as a progressive alternative to the anti-humanism which has been successfully realized in Israeli ethnocentrism. As will be suggested, their project is part of the Evil actuality which should be negated by all aspects of the psyche, the mind, and the body. What should today's educator do when she/he tries to fight the trap in which current "progressive," "enlightened," or "humanist" education is caught?

The "enlightened" educator is challenged both in the negative and in the positive dimensions of the term. In the negative dimension, namely, in Critical Education, there are two fronts: a) The critique of the consensus. b) The critique of the trends, practices, and power relations which challenge the consensus, constitute it, and change it in accordance to the alternative to which they are committed.

A. *The critique of the consensus* is quite problematic for the "enlightened" educator. Suppose the educator we refer to is a teacher at school. How, then, could she or he bring about enlightened education, given the concrete conditions within which such a teacher can work in the Israel of today? It seems to us that the only teacher who is tolerated by the system must actually function as a positive part of the establishment's apparatus, which are accountable on the production of young women and men who will become "positive" productive, cooperative, and easy to manipulate, who fundamentally identify with the system and will serve the hegemonic ideology, protect and reproduce it for a future that is colored in the colors of the present. In the state educational network, in contrast to the religious-state educational network and other, totally independent, educational networks, teachers' cooperation with the oppression of the system is maintained without direct censorship, discrimination, and threats. Other, more effective and "democratic" ways ensure the reproduction of the hegemonic ideologies and the present order.

Along the line, from national studies (*sheurei moledet*) to botany and mathematics, studies in Israel have been traditionally structured to fulfill the aim of reproducing symbols, power-relations, and ideological systems[1] in the service of nation building. Within this educational tradition the future "normal" citizen was placed in a position from which he or she will enthusiastically support the existing Zionist and capitalist order. Even after the death of the Zionist Spirit things have not fundamentally changed in this respect. Education which directly or indirectly, but fundamentally, clashes with the present order is a risk that the established groups and the hegemonic ideology cannot tolerate. In the historical development of Israel into a rapidly technologically advancing capitalist society, a significant shift of values, myths, identities, and self-consciousness has occurred, yet the educational oppressive inner logic has not changed. Traditional centralized establishment and the market's logic join forces and cooperate on one level, while acting as historical rivals which have to fight a death-and-life struggle, on the other.[2] The traditional Zionist idealism, which is practically secularized political theology, and Instrumental Rationality, with its anti-idealism, subjectivism, and relativism, are bitter enemies. Yet in the Israeli arena, at present, they join forces against alternative ideologies, ways of life, and educational philosophies. In the "secular" section of Jewish society the hegemonic education protects itself from actual and potential oppositional educators by realizing various "democratic," "non-violent" strategies:

1. Being very insistent on having a monstrous curriculum, rich in unnecessary and/or outdated studies to an extent which will exhaust most of the time, the physical resources and the intellectual potential of normal students and teachers.
2. A balanced amount of false pluralism and tolerance toward marginalized knowledge, identities, and interests, in a way which will lead to their domesticated representation or their quiet destruction. This is to ensure that these alternatives will neither challenge nor threaten the self-evident, the ignorance, and the ethnocentric moral of which the Israeli state educational system is committed to serve and reproduce.
3. Local hindering of any version of radical education: The stress, frustration, and enmity among the school's staff and colleagues' lack of solidarity and refusal for cooperation will do miracles. It is reasonable to presume that they alone might cause any potential enlightened Israeli teacher to internalize the ideological repression and refrain from being simply rejected from the school. Normally the system will deal with such potential rebels, even unconsciously, by representing/making them as desperate, lacking self-esteem/arrogant, or perverse. Making her/him be seen as deserving compassion or dynamic restraint to bring her/him back in line, but never as a serious challenge with whom the system has to enter into a dialogue.
4. In rare cases potentially dangerous educators are to be neutralized by being promoted into high bureaucratic positions in the system or directed for success in the private business sector. These, too, contribute to the successful efforts of the system to select and control its agents and to sterilize the potential challenging educators.
5. Today's most effective instrument is the inner logic and the dominant trends in the social and cultural contexts. If we restrict our example to the

schooling system in its narrowest meaning, then we have to recognize that today the children themselves, both at school and of it, reproduce the conservative attitude and the repressive myths and control apparatuses, to serve as a most effective wall against "enlightened" education. This shows how effective is the educational system, in the broadest sense of the concept.

6. In rare cases, the system is allowed to officially reject an "enlightened" educator, which in the current situation is almost always more of a bother than a threat to the system. Such a reaction is today totally unnecessary. It will be carried out with some restlessness and only in the most extreme and unusual cases, reflecting the failure of all the apparatuses structurally responsible for the elimination for "professional reasons" and for "non-political motivations" the views of an "enlightened" educator prevailing within the system. This is how the "enlightened" educator is structurally positioned in Israel today, as long as he/she intends to realize in a positive manner a radical alternative within the system. As we shall see, even graver is the condition of the "enlightened" educator who is committed to a negative realization of her/his alternative while competing with other marginalized oppositions to the hegemonic education.

B. *The critique of tendencies which erode the consensus* constitute many different realms of self-evidence and alternatives to the traditional Zionist hegemonic ideology, creating its own challenges to the "enlightened" educator. Five main elements determine her/his capacities to compete with other alternatives.
1. The ontological situation, situated in its current historical setting.
2. Today's major technological, cultural, social, and cultural trends, which presently constitute the context of any possible "enlightened" education. The conceptual and material possibilities and limitations are embedded within and by these development. As we shall see, these are the concrete starting-points of any critical humanist education, which we call counter-education.
3. The circumstances enforced by the hegemonic groups and the cultural reproduction and social control apparatuses. These not only determine the possibilities and limitations of the "enlightened" educator but also influence the possibilities of other educational alternatives. For some, and to a certain degree for all of them, these restraints make up an important part of the prospects of the alternatives. Their hardships increase their relevance, showing that their critique, fears, and allegations are not groundless. As we have tried to show elsewhere,[3] in Israel today "enlightened" education is to be considered between the oppositions

which are weakened and successfully marginalized by today's central global and local developments. This is in contrast to the fortunes of other oppositional voices, as the ultra-religious, ultra-nationalist alternative in today's Israel.
4. In contrast to other alternative educators, today's "enlightened" educators have no optimistic prospect, and they are uneasy and suffer from a troubled conscience. Their status is especially problematic. This is partly because rhetorically the hegemonic state education is also committed to—at least some of—the values and ideals to which the "enlightened" educators aspire. They find it hard to distance themselves from established ideals admired by the hegemonic ideology such as pluralism, critique, and autonomy. This is a source of additional difficulties in positioning themselves as a clear-cut alternative to the centered group and its explicit ideals, on the one hand, and makes it harder to compete with rival alternatives, on the other.
5. More than any other component, the stand, possibilities, and limitations of today's "enlightened" educators are determined by their own project, its goals, contradictions, and potentials. However, all these are historically constructed and find their concrete content within their social and cultural settings. To the degree that this project is self-determined, it is possible to find out what is the inherent problematic of their humanist stand. Together with other distractions and limitations within current reality, this position places the humanist educators in their present miserable conditions.

The urgency of a positive humanist educational alternative is hard to deny, in the face of growing hedonistic indifference and active nihilism, on the one hand, and ultra-orthodox nationalism and its galloping theocracy, on the other. It is very tempting to offer a magic remedy: a positive critical and humanist-oriented alternative to the growing dogmatism, mythical manipulative rituals, and aggressive ethnocentrism in today's Israel. This positive humanist attempt strives for an educational tradition which is committed to universal values, for recognition of "the natural, inalienable, and sacred rights of man"[4] and "the truths to be self-evident, that all Men are created equal."[5] Present-day humanist education of this kind[6] is committed to emphasizing the centrality of the spiritual autonomy of the individual, in opposition to the current erosion of the individuality by the omnipotent mass media and other power apparatuses and manipulators of oppression. Such an educational project demands solidarity with the sufferings of Others and emphasizes philosophical eros and social activism. The actual position of present-day's humanist education is, however, very problematic.

On the one hand, to avoid failing in their mission, these educators are compelled to present a clear, positive, and convincing humanist alternative, so that they might give it a chance against competing cultural alternatives. On the other hand, under present conditions, if and when this positive mission is accomplished, it would be seen only as a self-defeating project. Ironically, today, humanist educators have to decide: to remain educators and realize their version of education by all available means, become "enlightened." They cannot be both successful educators and enlightened: if they pursue positively and convincingly a dogmatic, or at least unproblematic, humanism they would not be really enlightened. If they introduce humanist education as problematic in a non-positive and manipulative manner, which would reveal today's humanism as problematic, without clear-cut and definite answers then, under current conditions, they would probably risk being received as unconvincing, outdated, and irrelevant. More seriously, the risk of being accepted as "educators" and humanism accepted as an educational alternative, would become a fiasco amid the prevailing racism, instrumentalism, and religious fundamentalism in the Israel of today.

The ideals of the Enlightenment and the fundamental concepts of modernity have suffered turmoil, self-contradiction, and dramatic transformations. In the face of technological, economic, social, conceptual, and emotional developments their current postmodern critique is a success story, and one can follow Michel Foucault and justly acknowledge the death of the potentially autonomous subject.[7] Yet it is still possible to pursue other ways, as shown within the Habermasian project. However, today it is impossible to ignore the richness of the problematic, violence, naiveté, and arrogance which are immanent to the Enlightenment project. As one of the central representatives of the Enlightenment, Kant defined the uniqueness of the Enlightenment in its being the first era that acknowledged its own problematic and self-defeating potential.[8] It is important that the "enlightened" educator, striving to find the ways to open the hearts of people and transform them into disciples of the humanistic ideals and concepts of the Enlightenment, should be stupid and ignorant, or at least dogmatic. Such characteristics might help them defend their naive beliefs in their humanist alternative as a bright future. As long as "enlightened" educators do not acknowledge the immanent crisis of Enlightenment and remain deaf to the terrible cost of modern attempts to revolutionize reality by realizing Enlightenment's ideals at all costs during the last two centuries, they are definitely not enlightened educators. They represent the diametrical opposite of the Enlightenment's slogan *sapere aude* (be brave and use your own reason). Some of the "enlightened" educators did face the rumor about the dissolving of the Enlightenment's tradition but, in face of it, they held on to the uncritical perpetuation of these ideals and conceptions. In Israel this phenomenon takes place within a context of growing ultra-orthodox religious and political renaissance which "demands" a secular response at a time when secularism has no *Spirit* and cannot find the collective energy and the concepts to introduce a real challenge. The only realistic responses are various traditional humanist educational programs which are widely respected and generally left to decay and die. The "enlightened" educators are trapped in an impossible situation: if they will shed light and propagate the terrible secret of the Enlightnment's fortune, it would be unrealistic to prospect their success in the admission of others to these ideas and ideals. The devotion to the final aim seduces many "enlightened" educators to hide the contradictions and violence within the Enlightenment and the crisis of humanism. When confronted with their strategic attitude they promise that immediately after the successful plantation of the humanist cause they will unveil the sad and hard truth about the crisis of the ideals of the Enlightenment and humanist education. This would be done, naturally, they continue, in a careful way and with moderate amounts of truth-revealing. *"De omnibus dubitandum"* (question everything) promised themselves humanist educators in the late eighteenth century when they tried to realize their enlightened project. Today the "enlightened" educators in Israel desperately try to change the old and the new anti-humanist dogmas equipped with out-of-date, partly irrelevant, dogmas and orientations of their own. To soothe their conscience they offer relaxation pills of the cheapest sort: "There is no alternative", "It is the most effective method in the face of harsh alternatives"; and so on. "It is prohibited to leave the educational field open to the influence of anti-humanist trends," they say,[9] since both the hegemonic educational repressive and its alternatives are freed of the burden of such a problematic message as that of the realization of the Enlightenment's ideals in an ethnocentrism state amid a military or national conflict.

As will be shown, the main difference between "enlightened" educators and their rivals will be nothing more than that subjectively "enlightened" educators feel they hold the truth while the others are mistaken and mislead others. The "enlightened" educators manifest the same attitude as that of the anti-humanist educators. In certain aspects the rivals of the "enlightened" education manifest much more honesty. Those newly convinced of the truths of ultra-orthodoxy in Israel (Hozer b'teshuva) face Instrumental Rationality, nihilism, and the exile of Reason as a threat and they, at least, manifest genuine quest for transcendence from the current realm of self-evidence, and sincerely strive for human beings, transcendence to the source of truth as the only madness which is relevant for them.

The nihilist who witnesses the cold logical-mechanistic "tail" left behind by the gods after their disappearance is creating a new self and a new world. The truth which is used by them is not positivistic, one which is subject to a syllogism and empirical testing such as being smelled, weighted, measured, and so forth. It differs totally also from the "truth" of the cynic, since it is artistically created, conceived, and realized. This truth does not pretend to refer to any objective reality, which stays like a cold corpse with no breath; their truths are symbols, which are given to the world and become real because of their power to activate them as such in reality. The nihilist, as the first human being in Eden, gives things their proper names and constitutes by that their reality and the forms of the world and its meaning. The nihilists' spirit is yet ecstatic from the experience of being cast out from Eden, while they are well-informed of the death of the God who exiled them. Life as a dynamic and artistic creation offers them a certain kind of "coming back home," not of the kind of being adjusted to or domesticated in the world but rather pressing the eternal resistance in face of the absence of Spirit. Today's cynics are "liberated" even from this kind of despairing emancipation, and they are content in contingent, temporal, and non-essentialist victories. They react to the current human trend of ever-growing readjustment to the prevailing realm of self-evidence. They refuse to be satisfied with developing intelligent strategies to have the upper hand within this context, without being worried about its purpose, meaning, or their responsibility. The bottom depths of responsibility, ignorance, and loneliness are avoided and successfully ignored. In today's secular arena this trend is the most influential educational power. This too is a manifestation of Instrumental Rationality and the essence of being.

In contrast to most other alternatives to the hegemonic education, today's "enlightened" educators do not call for a dangerous "life on the edge." They have a lot in common with the cynic: their hidden conservatism. They will not explicitly spell out the demands which would endanger their well-being, as this would not really challenge the present order of things. They express willingness for a continued human dependence on the current world of facts. The differences are that the "enlightened" educators feel responsibility for their fellow human, maintain a determined stance toward reality, and are committed to change.

The foundations of the Enlightenment's educational project were its uncompromising demands for the realization of the potential autonomy of the subject, disenchantment, and the overcoming of the oppressive dependence on the teacher, on tradition, or on fear.[10] The "enlightened" educators who activate the more didactically/politically effective manipulations on their students betray the supreme ideals of Enlightenment.[11] In so doing they connect themselves as another link in the long chain of educational positions, which include Christian missionaries, Jewish *Mahsirim B'teshuva*, and other soul hunters. Is it possible, however, that today there is no other practical educational route for the cause of humanism, and it cannot be delivered unless by deception, temptation, and manipulation? Could it be that coherent enlightened education leads to immanent impotency and has no chance of becoming a realistic alternative within the present circumstances? My answer is definite: "enlightened" education cannot become enlightened. And, of course, it cannot transform enlightened ideas and challenge its repressive dimensions. This understanding is shared by some educators whose understanding does not drive them to abandon the Utopian project of human emancipation.

From all lost educators my choice falls on those who wander within a darkened world, struggling for autonomy and emancipation. With those who have lost the humanist fate in human beings and the Enlightenment's devotion to reason, without losing their hunger for truth and their thirst for love, with those who see themselves as pessimists and do not know to what degree they are still Utopists, with those I would like to open a dialogue about Socrates. Those are the ones to whom I send my invitation to participate in a symposium on the issue of the possibility of enlightened education under present-day conditions.

The Philosophy of Socrates, like that of the sophists, was born at the dawning of the classical Greek Polis and amid political deterioration and deep soico-cultural crisis. Within this context the appearance of the sophists was not unexpected. It was a reflection and catalyst of the rapid transformation of the Greek arena: traditional Greek culture could not reproduce itself un-tackled and continue to serve as a standard for truth. The honor of the gods and the self-evidence of the law were impossible to reproduce and fulfill their traditional rule within a growing circle of sophists and ambitious well-educated young people who hoped to find in the sophists' teaching the key to success and excellence.

The acknowledgment of the absence of an absolute and objective truth was the starting point of the sophists' project. Nevertheless they presented themselves as excellent teachers, as we can see in the *Eudemus, Gorgias,* and *Protagoras.* The essence of the sophists' project lay in acknowledging the impossibility of conceiving objective *truth*, on the one hand, and the educational praxis derived from this acknowledgment, on the other.

Protagoras's teaching as manifested in the *Theaetetus* 161c and as supported by Sextus asserted that "man (*ho anthropos*) becomes the criterion of the things that are; for everything that seems to men (*tois* anthropois), actually is; and what seems to no man, is not."[12] He also claimed that it is possible to teach both the *techne politike* (the art of politics) and *dike* (justice).[13] Protagoras asserted that in the absence of these, social life, the political gathering of human beings, was impossible. The teaching of these vital elements, he claimed, was his special expertise.[14] The relation of the sophists' educational project to politics has two levels. The first one is that declared by the sophist. The second is that which the sophist hides. Later we will try to reveal it. There is no agreement among the interpreters and scholars whether Protagoras really meant that it is not beyond the limits of his competence to teach these two levels. Here we will not enter into this discourse but will restrict ourselves to Protagoras's commitment/pretension to teach the *arete*, excellence, to his students.[15]

The sophist's education equips the pupil with a powerful weapon: the power of efficiently manipulating the language, which is also the persuasive power which enables the movement from manipulating to the actual constitution of the Other,[16] by destruction or exile of her otherness. The eristic education of the sophists had two roots: introduction of assertions for or against a certain thesis; and the introduction of a series of questions, which was supposed to destroy the rival by leading him to contradict himself and into a position of self-refutation. The bad name the sophistic eristic got during the ages represents more the brilliant career of their rivals than their own position. The sophists themselves were the ones who called their method eristics.[17] Philosophically it was committed to victory at all (rhetorical) costs.[18] Their method implies the realization of the subject by successfully destroying the Others' autonomy, eliminating the subjectivity of the Other as an independent subject, and the nullification of the otherness of the Other.

The sophist is a teacher whose argument is the negation of the Socratic dialectics which is committed to reveal the truth. The sophist, in contrast to the Socratic educator, directs his pupil to enslave and destroy his fellow human, as an alternative to the Socratic dialogue, which is morally directed for educating the other to reveal by herself/himself and in herself/himself the truth as something that is always not-yet-given.

It is as though the sophist's teaching restricts itself to delivering to the pupil nothing but methods and cultivating nothing but skills. This kind of teaching might be seen as though it were neutral toward the issues of values and the aims of education. This is because he teaches how to reach success to anyone willing to pay enough. Personal success in the Greek world at that time was generally conceived as being realized in the public sphere, especially in the political arena: at court in the army, and in the *agora*. The sophist equipped those who were ready to buy success in the political arena with the history of poetry, linguistics, and general education but, more than anything else, the "clients" received competence in rhetoric, the science of brainwashing, or the secrets of controlling the consciousness of the other. Despite their explicit declarations, sophists such as Gorgias introduced in their students first of all values and goals and not solely methods. At the same time the sophists were critical of certain traditional elements of their culture and introduced their pupils to the art of negating the hegemonic realm of self-evidence. In that sense they were "enlightened" educators.

As the representative of the progressive forces against the conservatives of his time, the sophist had an important educational message; he educated for the emancipation from earlier convictions and old values which had been proven to be unworthy. As the one who cultivated future successful politicians, the sophist taught his students to become enlightened efficient deceivers, who could live simultaneously in two parallel worlds. One is the world of the future politician, namely, the arena where the relations between the teacher and his pupil are revealed and realized. The second is the arena of the future relations between the politician and his audience. Depicting some of the characteristics of these worlds within which the future successful citizen dwells might help us to learn something valuable about the essential elements of the relations between teacher and student.

At first glance we might get the impression that the relations between the sophist and his pupil are founded on honesty. The sophist shares with his pupil the bitter acknowledgment of the bankruptcy of their tradition and its disintegration, which includes the idea of objective truth. The sophist does not pretend to teach his pupil the truth, which he does not know, which he like any other human being, will never know. He pretends, however, to act as an honest merchant: he offers to exchange for high payment and glory among the better ones his knowledge concerning ways of becoming a successful politician. He definitely pretends to be capable of teaching methods of manipulating the future political rivals of his student as well as bettering him.[19] The sophist also promises the student the power of governing his future audience in such a way that they will be overwhelmed and convinced, or at least will have to surrender their different views and potential autonomous stance, and admit that he, and only he, is right and should lead.

One might claim that between the politician and his listeners the structural relations are different. First and foremost, the politician, as the sophist's successful student, must deceive his audience concerning the very foundations of the relations between them. Contrary to the sophist, who offered the would-be politician his services as an honest merchant, who is concerned primarily with his own well-being, the politician is committed to appear in front of his audience as one who is motivated by devotion to something beyond his personal well-being, be it his devotion to God, tradition, justice, or the fortunes of his community.

The sophist's success is determined by his ability to appear as he really is: a teacher for efficient deception, a marketer of successful maneuvers for defeating the rival by rhetorical means, while being neutral to the quest for truth or even despising it. The success of the student of this kind, namely the politician, is conditioned exactly in his competence to appear as what he is not. It is untenable that the politician will systematically tell his audience the truth concerning the foundations of their mutual relations: that for him they are merely an object for manipulation, for his private purposes. Only within this framework, his rhetoric concerns "justice," "truth," and so forth. The politician who will bring to his audience the word about the death of objective truth and disillusion concerning the absoluteness of their values will abandon the very source of his powerful manipulations. This illusion is the spring of common self-evidence, which rules in the respected speech community. It concerns the possibility of reaching a consensus on the basis of a kind of discourse founded on the "objective" yardsticks.

The promised manipulative potential of the politician is basically founded on concealing an important secret: the secret which is reserved to the level of relations between him and the people whom he has not committed to this widely accepted objective truth. Then, and only then, is the stage opened for the knowledge which he purchased from the sophist and to the activation of his skills to convince his naive audience by efficiently manipulating the "shared" self-evidence, truths, and values. It is not solely, nor even mainly, the rhetorical tools which he obtained from the sophist, but rather the values which were transferred to the would-be politician by the sophist, which guarantee his success. The full richness of the educational implication of a sophist's project is here revealed: the sophist is first of all an educator. Only secondly is he a teacher; the power of his teaching is revealed and measured by the advantage he enjoys over his audience. We have already showed that the advantage the politician has over his audience is, ideally, the product of his engagement with the sophist. Now we have to complete our reconstruction by noting two elements in the would-be politician's project.

1. The rhetorical modes of the future-politician, who has becomes the sophist's student, enable him an unlimited arena for his maneuverings, compared with that of his rival politicians and within the crowd he is committed to manipulate. The group is always determined by certain horizons and symbolic limitations and possibilities. These, of course, are well-known to the politician—knowledge which is a pre-condition for controlling the audience by governing the interpretations and the representations of their symbols, identity, and knowledge about the world, about knowledge and about the self. The symbolic world treated by the

instrumental-oriented rhetoric of the sophists and their students contains constructed realities such as the self, family, myths, arts, religion, and science. This world surrounds their students' being, constitutes their "reality" and self. As a good student of the sophist the politician knows how to play on those symbols which still contain enough vitality to be included in the realm of self-evidence among his speech community members. This objective relevancy is ignored by the politician. In order to preserve his manipulative potential, however, he will hide the fact that for him this or that symbol has lost its status as something self-evident and he will pretend that it is a valuable self-evident thing for him, and he accepts it as the truth. It is exactly the use, or rather misuse, of these "truths" which enables the constitution of a consensus which reflects the beliefs and interests of the politicians. Since in practice the ideal politician is nothing but a deceiver and he is committed to the prevailing values, truths, and myths only as a camouflage, it turns out that he is the only free person on earth, in the sense that he is the only one not ruled by the prevailing realm of self-evidence, and as such is free to choose the most appropriate of all rhetorical acts and human intersubjectivity. For Heraclitus the concept of *polemos*, meant a life-or-death struggle, which is immanent to the cosmic order (fragment 53). The art of *polemos* which the sophist teaches as rhetoric is nothing less than a death-and-life struggle for the ideal politician as a full person, secured by the surrendering of the other. The discursive argumentation as *polemos* within this context has existential and ontological dimensions. The sophists' education as targeted for self-improvement and excellence and for polemic empowerment continues and transforms the Heraclitian conception of the battle as inseparable from justice.[20] It is but one example of the inherent violence of normalizing education.

2. The argumentative advantage held by the ideal politician is founded on his moral emancipation. Here too, the centrality of the sophist's education is revealed. The sophist is the one constituting the moral freedom of his student, the would-be politician. Logically, before the sophist distributes to his student the rhetoric competence he must change his horizons, liberating him from the prevailing realm of self-evidence. He is obliged to share with his pupil the consciousness of the *collapse* of the traditional values and truths. Only then is the arena opened to richer and more effective manipulative rhetorical maneuvers for the politician, but not before paying dearly to the sophist, his emancipator. This is a precondition for the acceptance of the methods and pre-positions of the sophist; they will result in possible victories for the ideal politician. This is the case if his pupil becomes his student only if he was emancipated, at

least partially, even earlier. This notion led him to knock at the door of the sophist and to ask for his and not for someone else's teaching.

The relationship between the ideal politician and his audience is fundamentally a battle against an enemy. The audience, as a collective, is an object and not a subject. It is an object consisting of people whose personae should be destroyed. As Others their otherness should be *broken* and eliminated or absorbed by any violence which may be needed for this vital goal. Here we will treat only rhetorical violence, while remembering that it is not the only aspect of the practice which is aimed at destroying the otherness of the Other. The debate and the speech manifest the symbolic violence to which we will refer as representatives of that kind of consensus, which the sophist trains his pupil to create. The common ground of the debate and the speech is their commitment to convince the Other, namely, to replace his or her manifestations of autonomy and uniqueness with those which represent the unique power of the rhetor, and finally of rhetoric itself. A debate might certainly reflect an immanent aspect of every human being. However, for the normalized person the debate reflects a partial and undetermined part of life. In contrast, for the Greek politician it is an essential element for his being.

It is necessary to deal with some aspects of the weapons of the ideal Greek politician in order to better our reflection on the issue of his enslavement to his commitment to enslave the others. It will help us also to reflect on the ways in which he guarantees his suffering as part of the context which enables and activates the misery of others. For the speech, as for the debate, victory not truth is the ultimate goal. This is its essence. It is inherently violent in the sense of subverting one to the other's rhetoric in the form of consensus. The *polemos*, which culminates into a consensus, serves the ideal politician as chains with which he bonds other people to his goals, beliefs, bonds and horizons, which detach them from their persona, from their uniqueness and potential sovereignty. Both the debate and the speech activate a philosophical stand. According to this philosophy, the Other is nothing but a stranger, a rival, and an object for manipulation. The meaning of others and of their very existence is for the ideal politician the possibility to enslave them. This is because their value as objects is derived from their potential for the constitution of the ideal politician as a free subject. The ideal politician is a free subject by the successful negation of the subjectivity of other subjects, swallowing their freedom. From our understanding of the concept of the human subject, practically he by doing so negates his own humanity. Ironically, by destroying the otherness of the Other he plays as an *agent* of the system, which activates him as a mere object for manipulation, in order to ensure its reproduction.

Essentially the ideal politician cannot be self-reflective. For the sophists, as for Hegel, freedom refers to the essential relation between freedom and (liberated) thought but at the same time also to property. For the sophists the control of the mind of Others has been the most valuable capital, the key for material, political, and emotional gains.

Contrary to his self-understanding he is totally dependent on his audience, as Don Juan is dependent on the women he is committed to conquer; in order to become himself, Don Juan is *obliged* to negate and destroy the humanity of the woman as a person in herself and for herself. Conquering a woman who is a persona in herself and for herself is a condition for becoming a persona in himself and for himself. However, Don Juan cannot be satisfied with his victory which is merely empty and endless repetition. He is ever obliged to aim for the next object, which as such cannot offer the conqueror his quested subjectivity. Therefore, he must conquer the next not-yet-conquered woman, until the last woman on earth is destroyed. As a real Don Juan he cannot be satisfied with "a good" or "suitable" woman, whoever she may be. And after each affair he is even more thirsty for more exciting experiences, each one emptier than before. To the degree that his need for the next victory is unsatisfied, his dissatisfaction grows, as does his desire for something bigger, stronger, and totally different from himself. Don Juan who really succeeds must be the most miserable and enslaved person in the world. In contrast, the women he met and those he did not encounter are freer and potentially happier: they can hope for love. As what they are they are potential rebels who will struggle against the normalizing education and the violence of the prevailing order of things. If not today then maybe tomorrow; if not in reality than at least in principle. Don Juan, as such, is unable to free himself and he must pursue, realize himself in a way that culminates in self-destruction. This is the basic position of the ideal politician.

The ideal politician, as such, is unable to free himself from his audience, from the *polemos*, from the commitment to realize himself by destroying the Others. The ideal politician is less capable than anyone else of searching for truth or beauty and justice. This is because success and not truth is his goal and his yardstick; principally he cannot fulfill his quest for more and more power of the collected subjectivities he has conquered and taken over for the Others. He is, as in the Nietzschean example, drinking sea water in order to end his thirst. The freedom from morality handed over to him by the sophist allows him endless argumentative possibilities for conquering other human subjects by using rhetorical manipulations. But this is at the cost of becoming enslaved to this quest for victories. becoming lonely. But by the same token he becomes enslaved to an omnipotent power which has no meaning and aim, but only futile self-repetition within human discourse.[21]

We tried to draw some lines to describe the ideal Greek politician and his world, in order to learn something about the relations between the sophist, as an "enlightened" teacher and his pupil. The framework of the picture we have drawn was that the sophist equips his student with philosophical foundations and morality as well as with methods suitable for effective deception of people, gaining control over them and taking advantage of them, on the one hand. Between him and his pupil, on the other, he pretends to remain within the framework of honest and free trade agreement between free rational subjects. This characterization of the "enlightened" educator would remain incomplete if we did not critically reconstruct the relationship between the sophist and his pupil in light of what we have seen of the connection between the politician and the crowd.

An ideal politician successful in the Greek world of that period was the full-grown fruit of the successful sophist. This fruit can help us learn something valuable of the tree and its roots. Until now we have taken it for granted that the link between the sophist and the would-be politician are a manifestation of free and rational coexistence between two emancipated adults. We have shown that the young man who was maturing became more and not less free than ordinary people. But was his freedom stolen by the sophist or was the pupil deprived of his freedom from the moment his Greek education started to normalize him? We think the answer should be dialectical and refer to the historical situation in Greek culture of that age: the only culture was the issue of autonomy as it became central and the struggle over it became possible. In any case, from the moment the pupil fell into the net of the sophist, he was ready to abandon his freedom and forget that it was stolen from him while he was convinced that he was advancing toward a new form of liberty. So far as the sophist is concerned it is vital that the student be deprived of his will for real freedom. This is in order to ensure he does not choose anything but that serving the sophist's project. Until he met the sophist he could have become a Diogenes, Pythagoras, or Alexander the Great. As a disciple of the sophist, the student has to choose between a political career or becoming a sophist, but certainly not a philosopher. The sophist has a vested interest in preventing his student from philosophizing, however he hides this from the pupil. The apparently honest relationship between the sophist and the pupil is only a phantom which serves the sophist's agenda. He deceives his pupil no less than his student will deceive his audience when, as an ideal politician, he will meet the crowd.

In case of the sophist's pupil developing and becoming a philosopher he would have to join those who grope after the truth. In such a case, as a philosopher of that period, he would have been involved in a battle involving two fronts: the counter and the neo-conservative dimensions of the cultural arena, which had to be rapidly erased while introduced to an attractive alternative; and at the same time he would be involved in a struggle against nihilistic and hedonistic trends, as well as the sophist's version of questioning respected traditions.

The sophist tries his best, squeezing to the student's cap a magic medicine which will detach him from the responsibility toward a kind of openness to the call, to the quest for this readiness which is inseparable from the call, from the will, from the never-determined transcendence which enables counter-education. Counter-education manifests itself here as an unlearning and as readiness to be called upon. Counter-education as will to overcome the subjectification of the subject, as a commitment to question the self-evident, and as an existential-philosophical-political facing meaninglessness and as a resistance to the violence of the hegemonic education and the comfort it can supply or promise. His rivals are the conservatives, on the one hand, and the philosophers, introducing a free mind and alternative quest, on the other.

Of course, the sophist is unable to share this secret with his pupil and remain his teacher and, as a true sophist, he must mislead his pupil, time and again, becoming ever more enslaved to his endless and meaningless violent educational project. As an "enlightened" educator the sophist represents the disillusion from the traditional realm of self-evidence which he is committed to dissolve. Both his teaching and education are aimed at the destruction of the remaining objective significance of the old myths, values, and truths. At the same time, however, his existence is conditioned in the successful reproduction of the current order of things, especially in its political dimensions.

The prevailing political order secures the realization of *arete* in the public sphere. The candidate for happiness within this arena is carefully selected in the Greek world: he has to be a Greek and not a barbarian, a man and not a woman, an adult and not a boy, a free person and not a slave. It is important to notice that basically the sophist refrains from attacking the accepted order where success in the public sphere was the criterion for revelation and realization of the worthy human characteristics. If he would had attacked it, he would have been prevented from convincing his pupil to pay dearly for his teaching, which promised success in good citizenship and improvement of the existing civic order. Protagoras is one of the finest examples, revealing the double game played by the sophist.

It was no else but Protagoras, the famous relativist who was asked to articulate the constitution of the new coloni Thurii in the year 444 B.C. Needless to say he enthusiastically received this invitation. Even if the story about his expulsion from Athens as a threat to public order is historically true it does not negate our claim that basically he was part and parcel of the prevailing order. As an "enlightened" educator, in fact, the sophist collides with some traditional truths and values and develops a skepticism toward them, but he does not dare to suggest a radical critique nor self-critique. He does not dare to question the longing for fame, glory, and political power as criteria for success of the rhetor. The sophist does not confront the self-evident elements of his pupils,[22] which guarantees their interest in his teaching and their future success in politics. He refrains from revealing his hidden vested interests—especially his dependence on them and on the reproduction of the current order. He hides his conservativism toward the order in which manipulative teacher-pupil are possible and even demanded. This is the sophist's "modernism" at its pick. The sophist avoids questioning his student's realm of self-evidence since at the moment he questions the foundations and aims he will be transformed into his most dangerous rival, the philosopher. Another reason is his own existence as a prisoner within the boundaries set by the violence of the education of the time. And so, structurally and immanently, the sophist is a teacher who cannot but deceive his pupil and, through him, the entire community, and himself.

But is there a possibility for the sophist to be honest with himself as long as he remains a sophist? Can an educator become an emancipator through an anti-moralistic education and by distribution of effective tactics of deception to his pupils? And even more than that, is it possible that inner strains and contradictions would open new possibilities for emancipation of the sophist and his pupil as persons, as philosophers, and as bearers of counter-education? So far we have introduced a partial and indirect answer by reconstructing the teacher-pupil relations as manifested between the sophist and the future politician. There were, however, other options, different educational possibilities, such as anti-political conceptions of *polemos*, which did not promise success by effective deception of the crowd, which were not secretly tied up with the conservatism of the hegemonic group. In what follows we will represent two of these educational possibilities: the first is monological, the second dialogic. The first will be represented by Diogenes, the second by Socrates.

Diogenes of Sinope (400-324 B.C.) was active one generation after Socrates. His entire educational project was founded on his anti-political stand. Facing the dramatic fall of his traditional cultural and political space that had already in the days of Socrates become problematic, Diogenes could not offer the kind of education which would prepare the student for the good life within the traditional order.[23] He also refrained from offering any kind of political alternative and concluded with declared anti-politics, which even explicitly avoided education and its immanent violence toward the Other as an object for manipulation and constitution.

For Diogenes, only within a total avoidance of any political dimension is redemption from the effects of normalizing education possible. This means the very avoidance of human company and collective needs, roles, and aims. Diogenes, however, did not abandon the quest for redemption. In his project redemption is possible only as a personal Odyssey. It is possible by attaining *ataraxia*, peace of mind, which a person might hope to reach only if he dares to free himself of all sophisticated dimensions of politics which are internalized by formal and informal education. The various dimensions of the internalized existence of politics that one has to overcome extend those related to his involvement in the public sphere (such as leading positions on the army, succeeding in the courts, or creating the consensus of a public meeting in the *agora*). Diogenes' alternative education threatened the very quest for fulfillment of the *arete* and the striving for success and happiness in the public sphere.

As a coherent educator who explicitly refuses to educate, Diogenes avoids the polis life and struggles for his ideas as an *idiotes*, as a person who deliberately avoids community life and sets himself outside, in nature, to look there for his fortunes. There, in nature as anti-culture, in the wilderness where law, education, and human protection and repression are absent, he looks for redemption as peace of mind. This sought-for peace of mind is understood to be determined by *autarkia*, self-sufficiency, with its material and spiritual dimensions. Diogenes' way toward this ideal is shaped by avoiding most human needs. The coherence of this thinker, who fulfilled his own aspirations, made him famous, namely, made him an educator, while emphasizing his commitment to refuse all versions of existing political constructions and educational methods. His philosophy, which became known as cynicism, made him famous to a degree that another celebrated figure of the age, Alexander the Great, felt that he had to visit and challenge the strange educator who explicitly refused to teach and to adjust himself to the political order of the day.

Two great figures challenge each other: one is Alexander of Macedonia (known as "The Great"), who represents the quest for the highest realization of *arete*. His longing for peace of mind is conditioned by an unquestioned success in politics and, ideally, in conquering the entire world: as long as there exists any independent political entity, be it even one person who is not enslaved by the Macedonian, then Alexander the Great would be deprived of his peace of mind. His self cannot find itself unless it destroyed all forms and potentials of the autonomy of the Other self and became God. Only as God can he hope to complete the destruction of the otherness of the Other and become himself, in an absolute opposite to the ideal of Diogenes. Fulfilling this project would have deprived Alexander of the possibility of being acknowledged by someone else, that his autonomy and sovereignty are pre-conditions for selfhood, which might acknowledge or negate the subjectivity and the very existence of Alexander as great or even as a persona. This is not a failure of Alexander, but the self-defeating element within the political project. It determines the inherent violence and the self-defeating fate of all versions of politics and its educational alternatives.

The success of Diogenes is determined not by a political height, but rather by the possibility of overcoming politics all together. According to a famous legend, when Alexander was on his way to conquer the east he visited Diogenes. He found Diogenes enjoying the sun outside the barrel which served as his house. "Stand a little less between me and the sun" said Diogenes the Cynic who was given this nickname, as he was known as living a kind of life fit only for dogs.[24] Alexander stopped his men from harming the offender of their king who was to become the sole ruler of the entire known world. He said that if he did not have the fortune to be Alexander, he would chose to be a kind of Diogenes. The story exemplifies the collision between two great alternatives in education. Both, however, avoid counter-education. To our mind counter-education is exemplified by Socrates. The Socratic educational project should not be considered as a middle way. It is the great alternative to all educational versions. As such and according to its central concepts and practices it should be understood as counter-education.

Like the philosophy of Diogenes, the philosophy of Socrates (470-399 B.C.) is fundamentally a way of life. Diogenes tried to overcome politics, but failed to overcome his dialogical essence and the temptation to teach students of his own. His teaching was negative and indirect; from time to time he returned to the *polis*, but only in order to educate in the only possible way left free for him: negation in a symbolic way. And so he would walk along the streets of the city, in broad delight, holding a candle in his hand. When asked for the meaning of his odd behavior he would answer, laconically, that he was searching for something rare, for an honest person in that city. When asked for the reason why he insists on being buried with his feet to the sky he offered the answer that as things were at present it was only logical to expect that sooner or later everything would turn upside down. Diogenes served for the citizens of the polis a permanent symbol which changed conventional meanings and demanded interpretations in a way that required a suspension and even negation of the current realm of self-evidence. The contradictions within his anti-politics were not limited to issues as that he had to live by begging while claiming *autarkia*. Even more important was the fact that he could not really be satisfied by himself for himself: therefore, he had to look for company. This was not in the style as founded by Nietzsche's Zarathustra but in the humanist form of community and dialogue. He was compelled to return to the world of politics in order to negate it. He could not resist caring for the redemption of the Others. This was because without them he could not seriously expect to reach any peace of mind within the depths of his self, as he had promised himself. But if to stay coherent, according to his own philosophy, he could not be redeemed. He was thrown into a helpless position as long as he could not find the way for not caring for the Others' fortune and the critique of the cultural and political arena of his day.

Socrates' education, like that of Diogenes, was too immanently negative and fundamentally indirect while it was a concrete way of life.[25] Like Diogenes, and in opposition to the sophists' teaching, Socrates is the educator of all people and of all generations. He educates for reasons other than gold coins and such rewards. Their ways differed yet their aim was the same: to create a collision between the present "facts" and the truth. The endless devotion of these two utopists stands in total opposition to the sophists, who basically serve and perpetuate the present order of things.

In Diogenes we have found two differing aspects: according to one, the human being searches for the truth within himself, and this adventure is fundamentally machoist and egoistic in nature. According to the second, the person who knows something about truth has to struggle against the world of politics and, at the same time, bring the quest for readiness to the call of *the totally other* to Others, inviting them to unlearn that which was imposed on them by the hegemonic normalizing education.

For Socrates the gap between the ethical "I" and the moral "I" was unclear and from a moral commitment he addresses the infinite responsibility toward the Other's salvation through overcoming meaningless. His concept of responsibility toward the otherness of the Other and his "own" otherness are at the same time anti-autoritarian. This anti-authoritarianism, however, manifest readiness for the *call*. In Heideggers' words "to learn means to make everything we do answer to whatever addresses itself to us as essential."[26] The ideal which influenced his educational praxis was that of a community where people live without doing evil (*Kakos Poein*) to each other. To this ideal Socrates devoted both his life and death. In the dialogue "Crito," Socrates explained why he did not agree to run away and save himself from the death penalty: "We must not do wrong in return, or do evil to anyone in the world, however we may be treated by them."[27] Here is manifested with special visibility the special sense he gives the concept of *arete*. The original meaning of *arete* was talent, but not of the sort every person has, according to his nature, but rather that inherited from glorious ancestors. This is an aristocratic concept par excellence. As we have seen, the sophists gave a "democratic" sense to the concept as it relates to the praxis of teaching, which essentially everyone can buy. Socratic thought was a turning-point in the history of the concept of *arete*. In his thought, the relation between moral and true knowledge is constituted by a Utopian axis. The good as knowledge gets the meaning of a struggle over the salvation of the soul. This battle takes place in light of the good as *absent*, as something never to be formulated in a positive way, never to be positively present: it is always beyond the horizons of every real dialogue. It is beautiful since justice and truth merge there, overcoming time and space, question and answer, pain and happiness.

Socrates is a teacher who re-defined and re-mapped teacher-pupil relations. His educational stand implied that he might teach his pupil something valuable only as someone who knows that he knows nothing. This stand is not an obstacle in his search, but rather on the contrary, a step in his permanent quest for the answer to the great question: "What is the good?" This search can be realized only by fulfilling our dialogical essence as human beings, and because of the fortune of the dialogue, which is synonymous with the fate of the Other. Socrates needs very special pupils which are not yet present.

In a certain sense Socrates' stand is similar to that represented by the sophists, since he too does not know the truth yet refuses to abandon his teaching. Socrates, however, does not pretend to be a teacher who knows; nor does he teach by establishing monological relations between teacher and pupil. In fact, he is not really a traditional "teacher." He manifests the anti-authoritatian stance of the one who resists the quest for avoiding facing meaninglessness and resists the drive to be drawn the Same, the "them," or the consensus. The homelessness of the teacher within an counter-educational alternative is articulated in special clarity by Heidegger who is mistakably considered as taking part in an essentially different tradition: "Teaching," says Heidegger, "is even more difficult than learning. We know that; but we rarely think about it. And why is teaching more difficult than learning? Not because the teacher must have a larger store of information, and have it always ready. Teaching is more difficult than learning because what teaching calls for is this: to let learn. Indeed, the proper teacher lets nothing else be learned than—learning. His conduct, therefore, often produces the impression that we really learn nothing from him, if by 'learning' we now automatically understand merely the procurement of useful information. The teacher is ahead of his apprentices in this alone, that he has still far more to learn than they—he has to learn to let them learn."[28] Socrates devotes his life and death for the realization the negative Utopia of such anti-authoritarian teacher-pupil coexistence. The difference between him and the sophists, however, is even greater. The sophist does not sell his pupil the truth, only practical knowledge about future success in domesticated, castrated, life.

"Enlightened" and enlightened education collide here: both the sophists and Socrates are obliged to educate the pupil and prepare him for worthwhile life, yet they operate within opposing concepts of the good life. The sophist was committed to the current world of facts. He is an ally of the present reality. Socrates, on the other hand, lived in light of the not-yet-here, targeted to the Utopian axis. By negating the present reality in light of negative Utopia, in light of the presence of the absent, Socrates could struggle for redemption already in this world, without positive knowledge, departed from truth, which persists in its existence beyond the current horizons. His irony manifested itself in his daily life and not solely in the dialogues. It was manifested in his political involvement, in his role in duties and rights realized and conceptualized as any free citizen of Athens. We have evidence about his courage as a solder in Potidaea (432 B.C.) Empypholis (422 B.C.), and Dalion (424 B.C.). He was also a member in the Praetania, an institution which administered the democratic institutions of Athens, went to Salamis as a member of the delegation sent there by the oligarchy that ruled Athens for some years and was generally an active citizen. This political involvement led him more than once to a clash with the authorities. At the same time, Socrates lived as an active philosopher, and the political dimension in his life was not minimized by his conviction that the truth was unknown to him. This was because of the relation of the quest for overcoming accepted "truths" and the commitment to love in his life, a commitment that produced the morality of counter-education, which is still valuable for us today. Socrates lived and died for the love of wisdom in a world where knowledge cannot be but false or impossible. But he also knew how to search and for the sake of what he should search for truth. On such an excursion, according to Socrates, one can only transcend himself with and for his fellow humans and for his own sake.[29]

For Socrates, in contrast to the accusations of Nietzsche, the truth was unobtainable but within the struggle over his redemption. This was a part of the dialogical relationship between him, the world, and the Other. Philosophical life meant for him caring about the truth and for the soul.[30] This is why his version of education, an anti-manipulative and non-violent education, is understood by us as a model example of what we call counter-education. As a praxis and as a philosophical stand it can only be realized as responsibility for the Other. It demands education for a special kind of sensitivity. For a kind of hearing that will enable the existential moments within which every person would become simultaneously a pupil and a teacher. Only in such a way would he be able to recover his stolen humanity systematically stolen from him by normalizing education and the power relations of the political arena within which he lives. As a teacher he serves as a midwife.[31] As a representative of counter-education he can refuse and negate the fruits of education, but he cannot introduce a positive alternative, to give birth,[32] by his own. But he can, and should allow, Others to give birth: he helps them to produce not children but thoughts.

As a paradigmatic figure of counter-education Socrates was a teacher to the degree that he was a pupil of his pupil. As a worthy teacher he had to commit himself to the aim of becoming the pupil of his partner to the dialogue. Yet at the same time he himself had to be prepared to present himself as a potential teacher to his teacher-pupil. The realization of this version of counter-education took place at two levels at the same time: dialectical dialogue and ongoing irony.

Enlightened education of this kind, namely counter-education, is determined by the refusal to reproduce the normal relations between teacher and pupil. Within this framework the pupil is no longer an object for the teacher's manipulation (who in his part is himself an object for manipulation by the system he serves as an agent), and the teacher is not the source of authority and knowledge for the pupil. In enlightened education a joint Odyssey, the solidarity and the authentic struggles between the partners and within each of them is the essential element, and they all receive its meaning and goal as aimed at knowledge of what is beyond the self-evident. As a paradigmatic version of counter-education, in contrast to the immanent violence of education as manifested in the sophist example, it is impossible to divide between the love of wisdom and the love of the Other, between moral and epistemology/ontology. However, is this great endless effort for discrepancy from the realm of self-evidence quite justified? In other words, is counter-education better or more justifiable than normalizing education, or in yet another formulation: in what sense is it preferable over the sophist project, that after all is well founded in the present and the given reality and on actual power relations in the world of facts?

This version of enlightened education, which we call counter-education, differs from normalizing education in its dialogical essence. It is realized to the extent that the object of its search is transcendent, absent, and, therefore, determined by Utopia. The absent referent and the representations and the active presence of the absent within the dialogue are a constant source of contradictions. This crisis is the quintessence of Socratic education. It is a call for an aesthetic game in the richest meaning of the term: it is not a "mere" messianic impulse—it is at the same time/terra/impossibility a concrete way of life. Such a dialogue is possible only as a negative Utopia. As a concrete negative Utopia it is possible, yet only when the participants acknowledge and transform their pain into something totally different: *worthy suffering* as a transcendent element within which it is possible to address the presence of the absent as meaninglessness, or, nothingness, as unworthy life, or death. The infinity of nothingness is the impetus of the dialogical movement, solidarity between committed partners in a suffering world, toward the Utopian common good as justice or as educational quest for justice.[33] But this does not mean that this dialogue is an easy way of life or that there are no conflicts between its participants. It is also in danger of diverging from its dialogical essence and being drawn into Fascist aeshtetisized politics.

In certain respects the *elenchus* (logical refutation) in the Socratic dialogue, like the sophist's *eristic* (disputation), is quite similar to the *polemos* in Heraclitus's thought. The counter-educational dialogue is nothing less than a life-and-death struggle—for the sake of the Other. This is a difficult imperative, which has to face refusal or the absence of the partner, as well as the inner striving to give up discrepancy of the self-evident in the inner and outer world of the enlightened educator.[34] It is, however, an imperative which is not determined by its success.[35] Therefore, as a genuine counter-educator, Socrates is ready to sacrifice his body for his and for the Others' souls, his present for the not-yet-here, for *the totally other*[36] than the given reality.

It is important to notice the special context of the sacrifice that Socrates offered to humanity for the possibility of introducing the potentiality of struggling over the Utopia within counter-education. He sacrificed his life in a world in which all sacrifices are justified in order to prevent the sacrifice.[37] In his life and in his death he gave up everything in order to receive back something: worthy life. His Utopia culminates into life in the service of life as a realization of Negative Utopia, an enlightened life. This kind of life is an endless dialogue. This is because he conceives the soul as eternal. He lives within a constant crisis on the edge of infinite abyss, facing its bottom depths, in conflict between the present and "the journey of a thousand years and that that is beyond."[38]

For Socrates the transcendence from the realm of self-evidence by the dialogical route was not easy, yet it was an imperative, "a command of god."[39] However, within this project that suffering is inevitable "the one who struggles to fulfill the actions of justice" is promised "happiness."[40] What looks at first sight as a one-dimensional concept of happiness should be understood within the context of counter-education and the Socratic imperative of questioning, challenging, and negating the self-evident while resisting any positive Utopian alternative. One has to remember that the starting point of the Socratic as well as the Enlightenment's counter-education of late eighteenth century was the Utopian imperative and that it is a dialectical project with dialectical concepts. And so is the concept of happiness. Happiness, *eudemonia* in the traditional

Greek culture, meant happy, blessed with success, enjoying good fortune. And here Socrates transforms the meaning of the concept of happiness from something delightful into a human mission, an aim that will never be fully fulfilled. The concept of happiness is detached by Socrates from its traditional egoistic utilitarian framework into an opposite meaning: the abandoning of self utility in the present order of things. The happiness that Socrates aims for is also different from the peace of mind that Diogenes strove for. For him happiness means "the ability to stand up to troubles as well as against the fortunate events in life."[41] And so, within counter-education, happiness is involved with challenging the perpetuation of suffering amid an evil and meaningless reality. The perpetuation of evil is defined for enlightened education as a negative pedagogical praxis. In such case, however, suffering becomes more humane and worthy. In this respect it is similar to the young Marx's Utopia: "All his *human* relations to the world. . . are in their objective action. . . the appropriation of this object, the appropriation of human reality. The way in which they react to the object is the confirmation of *human reality*. It is human effectiveness and human *suffering*, for suffering humanly considered is an enjoyment of the self for man."[42]

Understanding the role that the dialogue has within the Socratic counter-education is essential for understanding enlightened education. It is possible only if we appreciate the centrality of Utopia. At first glance it looks as though the dialogue is engined by his quest for the idea of the good. However, it is important to realize that the idea of "the good" is both present and absent. There is not even one question which is solved by the knowledge of the good—only from the promise, in light of the hope for the possibility of such knowledge. The promise itself is anchored in the not-yet-here, in what has an undetermined existence beyond our horizons and beyond the dialogue of those who search the good. This is the Utopia. The Utopia is a pre-condition for dialogue, it is both its axis and its presence in present, a presence that is always negative. This is because the good is actualized in the presence by its negation, as evil.[43] In its positive dimension it is never realized in the world life of the partners to the dialogue.

On the good there is very little that is possible to say, as on the Utopian axis which enables the dialogue. And yet in its erotic form[44] the Utopian form is what constitutes the dialogue and determines its possibilities and limitations. The Socratic metaphor of the sun and the discourse of the good in "the republic"[45] is similar to what we see here about the relationship between the Utopian dimension and the issue of the good within the dialogue. What then is the difference between the metaphor of the sun as the truth about the good or the source of the light and the Utopia that we articulate here? The difference is in that the metaphor of the sun refers to something partial, known to us, even if it is impossible to look at it directly and study it in a fully positive way. The potential of the concept of Utopia at the very end is based on its total absence and its presence as an invitation, a clue for the absent totality. And as such it is present in Eros and as Eros, an impetus for the dialogue "for wisdom is a most beautiful thing, and love is of the beautiful; and therefore love is also a philosopher or love of wisdom. . ."[46] The concept of Utopia, not explicitly mentioned here, is central as the metaphor of the sun, yet it is impossible to reduce it to one of the elements of the realm of self-evidence. As an erotic power and as the absence of totality of the good, it establishes moral responsibility, "divine love" as it is called in the Symposium.[47] It sheds light on the links derived from it but in itself it is not determined by any of the chain's rings.

Socrates says that the sun not only aids seeing, it is also a constitutive element of the things' presence and visibility.[48] And so the good also takes part in the existence of being and is not only a condition for the constitution of a new discourse aimed at its perception. The Socratic ontology in this point is diametrically opposed to that of Anaximander, who claimed "that everything comes from the unlimited and he accepts the general principle that things are destroyed into what they came from."[49] For Socrates, seeing and the gazed share a common element with the sun, yet they are not identical with the sun. And so, also the perception and the truth share something central with the good, but differ from the good itself,[50] which is "the reason for science and truth." The Utopia, which always remains beyond the horizons of the dialogue and its manifestation—the idea of the good—will never be truly positively present. This is an anti-positivist-oriented education since within it the good, the justice and the beautiful are conceive to be present only in their absence or in their negation: in worthy suffering, in facing the unbridgeable abyss between ignorance and knowledge, in challenging the incommensurability of the ethical "I" and the moral "I," and in hope. This is the reason for the centrality of the question in the Socratic project. This is what makes such a dramatic difference between this project and that of the sophists. The sophists represents the camp of the answers without being troubled with the questions. The Socratic school is troubled with the wrong questions and lacks the answers.

The sophists' camp dwells in the realm of the present self-evidence and no other option is opened for it. The Socratic dialogue lives in the current reality, which is its starting point (as in the case of all versions of counter-education), but the home it longs for is beyond the current horizons, in the not-yet-here. The sophist strives for success as an efficient egoist; the Socratic educator cares for the Other and her/his suffering. This link between the quest for the truth and the caring for the Other and her/his love is the foundation of the special enlightened education of Socrates and constitutes his teaching. It has been a landmark of counter-education until our days.

The roots of any genuine question are nourished in the fertile earth of uneasiness and despair. A genuine question distinguishes itself from a non-genuine question in its awareness of the absence of foundations and in the limits of its horizons. It distinguishes itself by its willingness to question and crack the self-evident.[51] This is within a struggle for deviation from the self-evident and for the self-constitution of the participants of this counter-educational praxis. In the Socratic dialectic, in the *elenchus*, the question plays a key role. The Socratic question is what makes Socrates into a troubling "gadfly" and a superb "midwife."

The Socratic project is to be considered as counter-education since it does not convince and reproduce the self-evident and its social context. On the contrary, it gives birth to new sets of questions and enables the self-constitution of emancipated participants. Here we find the opposite to what we have found in the sophist's art of rhetoric (both in speech and in debate), where the convincing answer is anchored in the self-evident of the victor and the defeated is drawn into the system or destroyed. What counts here is the development of new questions and new, always temporary, agreements and solitary self-constitution within a dialogue where love is the driving force for responsibility toward the truth and the Others.

The Socratic dialogue emancipates the participants from being imprisoned in "their" realm of self-evidence, from what is described in *The Republic* as "the cave" toward the truth, which is always beyond the present horizons. Because of the special role that the question and the questioning play, and because of its negative Utopianism (as all versions of genuine counter-education), the Socratic project is not aimed at a new, repressive, and totalitarian realm of self-evidence. As genuine counter-education it negates and transcends (those struggling for the realization of their potential for autonomy) from the realm of self-evidence. It is true that abandoning the immanent negativism of counter-education is a real danger. The neglect of the negativism of enlightened education is also real; it is on the edge of becoming "enlightened" education, which constitutes new truths, security, and manipulations. Yet as long as it is true to itself it will avoid being degenerating into education.[52] The truths will be never positive and directly within the current reality for counter-education, and enlightened Socratic educators will refrain from this danger. At the same time it is possible to constitute a new realm of understanding which is inherently unstable, ever-evolving, and offers temporal consensus between the participants who will always see their realm of understanding as a position from which they question both the current realm of self-evidence and their present knowledge and identity. In this version of counter-education, the only stable element is love and a responsibility toward the Other. The quest for overcoming false "truths" and the transcendence into infinity as a totally other truth receives different formations as the dialogue develops.

Departing on this adventure, and it is a philosophical, existential, and political adventure, is erotic. Yet this erotic impulse acknowledges the suffering in an unbearable reality. The suffering is immanent to Eros itself, whose very existence includes eternal dying and recovering.[53]

These experiences of revealing, deciphering, transforming, and merging of horizons and their contents is individualistic per se, namely in the Marxian sense, namely, social. Only a social person is able to realize her/his individuality. The question is an echo of something which calls to the human being, which uses the quest for truth for something higher.[54] Socrates calls it the good; some Christians call it love of God and some mystics call it mystery or "the One."[55] Here we will satisfy our obligation to pinpoint the effects of this calling. The call as a fact higher than the facts of current reality and the question which is awakened by the call and is constituted by "the principle of hope"[56] plants ontological signs which under certain conditions might develop, bloom, and direct people within a dialogue on a quest for partners. Here we are confronted with a magic circle: These partners are the children of the dialogue (*B'nei Siach*, in Hebrew); however, it is only with such partners that the Utopia of the dialogue can realize itself. As a genuine negative Utopist Socrates is willing, and actually has to enter this magic circle and pay with his life for this right.

Socrates has to educate his fellow citizens: he is obliged to ask the frightening and embarrassing questions because he is compelled to look to the partners for constituting the dialogue. And what can he teach them? He cannot really teach them. He can, however, deliver his *love* and share his responsibility for them and with them. He can show them the imperative that might awaken the soul which was drowned into the self-evident, the forgetfulness of love and the seriousness toward one's own life. For such an opportunity he is willing to pay any price. And so, this enlightened educator offered with no hesitation what he was ordered to pay for the opportunity of experiencing philosophy with his partners, deviating meaningless life.

In the dialectics within counter-education, dialogue's special responsibility is realized between the participants: they are obliged to refuse all violence and destructive manipulations. This is because each of them has to ensure the progress of all other participants,[57] and there is no progress unless everyone is emancipated. It is impossible to divide between total devotion to the truth and to each other's actualized autonomy. Redemption is here not salvation: it is either mutual or altogether impossible. It is worthy stating here that the redemption within the dialogue is not solely an advance in the realm of the good or in the revealing of the truth. The concepts of Utopia and redemption support each other here within one project.[58]

Like Diogenes, Socrates also does not disagree on this or that element of the existing political order, but rather on the political principle. However, while Diogenes departed from the power games and lived exiled in the wildness, Socrates decided to struggle from within. Socrates refused to leave the *polis*; within it, however, he is a threatening outsider and its greatest lover. This is the framework for the Odyssey toward the good. This journey cannot take place outside the city and the hope for dialogue. Its starting point is the atomized lonely person and the transcendence from the self-evidence and the prevailing powers. The struggle for love and transcendence takes place within the city and against its present political foes.

In the dialogue, daily activities are suspended together with other dimensions of the logic of politics and are replaced by a discursive game of another kind.[59] This discursive game includes the critique of the lower discursive order and offers it an *Aufhebung*, negation while containing some elements and elevating them to a higher order as higher kind of human intersubjectivity.

The Socratic dialogue reveals the philosophical negation of the sophist's way of life; the sophist playing with his pupil is an essential part of his world. His inner logic is the art of violent manipulation. It is a game founded on cheerful pessimism,[60] which permits one human being to play with another without allowing him even to awaken, revolt, or hope for something which is not-yet-here. Pessimism is here manifested in the denial of truth and in the acceptance of the world of facts as the only arenas where people can realize their *arete*. There is no dimension higher or essentially different than the given facts, and there is no way to struggle against the prevailing order which ensures invisible *subjectification* of the subject, which include immanent impotency to unveil the violences of normalizing education. The hastiness is here manifested in jumping into a closed pessimism, which offers a pleasant life in the world of present repressive order. A "success" of this kind, when it happens, is revealed as a cry of loneliness of persons without a persona,[61] addicted to their self-repression, which is violently externalized by the imperative to enslave or destroy the otherness of their Others. Alexander was a person who tried this way to the limit, within this world to realize his *arete* without really changing the power games for something higher. Fundamentally he could not have been happy. As he became more powerful and as he enslaved more free people, he only became lonelier: thus deprived himself from a possible partner to any dialogue and so from love.

Socratic dialogue and the counter-education which it offers (as opposed to the Macedonian example) manifests a total transformation in power relations, by colliding philosophy with politics: within this negative Utopia the will for truth overcomes the will for power. Moral life and love prevail. Within such a counter-education the pupil unlearns/learns in a non-violent dialogue to the extent that it is possible within an aggressive context; the written texts, the vocal questionings and self-critique, and the general way of life all merge into an alternative to the order already in this world without constituting an alternative totalistic orgy.[62]

The Utopia strives against the foundations of the existing order of things and presents itself as the most radical of all acts. This is because it is a turning-point, which might elevate the dialogic community toward new horizons and a new realm of understanding. It offers new human possibilities. Enlightenment reveals itself in Socratic counter-education by presenting an invitation for dialogue. This dialogue, of course, does not literally elevate the participants. Real struggling persons, by endless efforts, might constitute their identity, knowledge, and roles of the dialogue within the dialogue. All that is, of course, a Utopia, yet it is a concrete Utopia which concrete people can, and within the Socratic project, should, struggle for its realization.

The Eros of the Socratic teaching is manifested already in the invitation for taking part in it; the invitation already contains the interpretive labor for the future teacher-pupil. The emancipation is not reserved solely to the end of the journey and it is partly realized, namely being fought for, in the climbing toward solidarity between the teacher-pupil and the pupil-teacher. The Socratic invitation is extremely outspoken. Socrates seduces to kill him—or join him. No one gets out of the Socratic meeting in the same condition as he came in. Of course, most people avoid the options offered by Socrates and do not side with the first or with the second option. And so, Socrates is the one who is constantly blamed, even by his own pupils, for treating Others as an object for manipulation.[63] This is exactly what we claim that the sophists do in their "enlightened" education.

Out of caring, out of responsibility for the Other and his soul, out of a love of truth, Socrates is not allowed to pass on the invitation in a direct and positive fashion, but in a negative and indirect way. This is because if he avoids this manner he will be transformed into a sophist and his project will become *education* in the accepted sense. He has to set the door half-open for deficiency, for missing the point. And so his metaphysically absent partner will have a chance to find a way to enter and to become enlightened, an Enlightenment which is really his—or totally absent. The Socratic concept of enlightenment as revelation differs from that of Judaism and Christianism, where it is connected to the concept of an omnipotent loving God. As an enlightened counter-educator Socrates is prevented from any positive and direct teaching, such as that of the sophists, because of the nature of truth, which is synonymous with the only open way for striving toward it: a striving which reveals a quest for truth and not for instrumental knowledge. The moral dimension of counter-education is manifested here in refraining from anything which might repress the autonomy of the Other. Socrates is an enlightened educator in the sense that he tries to awaken the Other for enlightening his life on the edge of the abyss, of revealing the possibilities of constituting his own identity, knowledge, and goals. This edge, or "moment," will not pass.

The Socratic invitation is ironic, and it includes his immediate potential colleagues and even those of generations to come.[64] The seed planted by him was nourished by the tumbler of poison he had received from the Athenian court of justice in 399 B.C., and it summarized the teaching and the response of the generation to the Socratic invitation for a dialogue.

If we treat the concept of the idea as a Platonic construct and separate this from the Socratic Utopia we will find that central for him are the responsibility for the Other and for one's own life as an enlightened search and self-constitution. For Plato the eternal, general, non-material idea is reality. For the sophist, reality is the individual in the transient present. Socrates, however, takes the middle ground; on the one hand he is an uncompromising Utopian: the Utopian good which is always beyond the horizons is real for him. It nourishes his commitment to the Other and for the search for what is not-yet-here and the totally other than the present. On the other hand, as a non-foundationalist counter-educator, ultimately, the current dialogue is for Socrates the real. Counter-education must be realized dialogically and as the Socratic example shows, within, it there is place for moral responsibility for the Other, for struggling over the possibility of *transcendence* from a foe to a beloved partner.

For Socrates only the emancipated partner might become a companion for the Odyssey which crosses the prevailing realm of self-evidence toward a new realm of knowledge and existential possibilities. Without the transformation of the Other, the stranger who is an object for manipulation into a beloved one, a partner, the entire aesthetics of the dialectical-critical education is impossible. In such a case Socrates would be blocked from fulfilling his mission.

The arena where the moral Socratic fulfillment is realized in the present is similar to yet different from that of the sophists. The Socratic position connects love of the truth with a love for the Other, between ontology/epistemology and moral, between the present and the future. All this is within the Socratic dialogue as a negative Utopia. From the outside we can see that for Socrates, as for rival "enlightened" educators, the most important thing is the present that has been transformed in the meaning of what Walter Benjamin called "now-time." The penetration of Utopia into the realm of self-evidence enables the dialogue as a concrete way of life. In this sense counter-education is an open *reality*.

Pessimism is revealed as a constitutive element for the Socratic counter-education, since it regards itself as an unending process, which will never reach its telos. Similarly, the struggle against the current limits of the preset reality is also conceived as an unending process. The struggle will never overcome its limits. Even the struggle as a search for a suitable partner is an endless mission with no happy end. This is, however, a (negative) utopian stand: the Socratic counter-education invites not only his immediate listeners, it is a call for all generations and ultimately to all humanity. As such, even if seen as a paternalistic project, in light of his generation's limitations, it is also a humanist position, a counter-education containing some of the central elements which today's counter-education can and should develop. This struggle, however, in contrast to that realized by Socrates, is one in a world deserted by God, where there is no room for an autonomous subject and from which Reason is exiled. In such circumstances today's counter-education is a wordless *prayer* in a Godless world. Under present circumstances we are confronted with the question: "Is the Utopian project still possible and counter-education valuable?" Our answer is a definite "yes".

According to Lessing, if God had offered him the choice between the search for truth and truth itself he would have preferred the search for truth rather than having it. The Socratic counter-education is a revelation which might be realized on meeting another representative of counter-education, with a "Socrates" or a "Nietzsche" of other generations. Socrates, which we deprived of Plato, presents special relationship which are above the current and the self-evident. It is even above truth itself. There are two points worth noting.

1. Every moment of the dialogue, and even a struggle over the possibility of a dialogue, refers to something which transcends the immediate and offers a kind of distancing from the present. The relative detachment from the present opens a range of possibilities. These are differnt from the possibilities offered by the system. They are more than mere reflections of the current system. Already in the evil present, Socrates refers to the good, to which one has to strive from within the actual world and the present discourse. Such a dialogue turns into a concrete way of life for the participants and becomes a composition of an alternative social possibility which includes circular time. On the one hand, such a life is confronted

with the permanent advancement of the dialogue, which does not culminate in a repressive, deceptive, consensus. The dialogical process here is the vital point, which goes along with negative Utopianism and its essential pessimism. On the other hand, such a dialogue in which the impetus is the love of truth and a love for the Other in light of the absent good, becomes an aesthetic game, a way of life. It becomes an ongoing dialogue between generations, their traditions, and that which is beyond. In this sense it is a closed eternal circle, as death is.
2. Socrates manifests pessimism toward the prospects of the dialogue which is so dear to him. This pessimism, however, does not halt the quest for transcendence from the limits of the present horizons. The constant tension between these poles, the absurdity of life within and between two worlds, nourishes the Socratic philosophy of counter-education.

Socrates is positioned within an absurd space. This is the context of his quest for redemption, for the beloved, suitable pupil who will become his teacher. This is the context of his quest for dialogue which will serve as a ladder on which all the participants of the dialogue climb in their search for the truth which enables their self-constitution. It also ensures their leap beyond the lowest depths which separate their realm of self-evidence from *the totally other*. This quest is immanently realized as a struggle, as a negation of the self-evident and the aggressive "more and more" of the politician and his sophist-teacher. These, ultimately, turn out to be naive. This quest, however, is unable to change the totality it transcends: it is a kind of prayer.[65]

Prayer represents the Principle of Hope.[66] It represents the hope that transcendence from the terrible world is possible after all: hope is somewhere, even if it is always a certain distance from the human being. The quest for that which the human subject might become as a real human might constitute the present of those who struggle for deviation from ignorance, loneliness, and temporality. For Socrates, as I have suggested, the central point is the individual journey toward the dialogue and the joint Odyssey within it, and not the consensus as a manifestation of the Platonic idea. Platonic teaching contains a strive toward the end of the "happy science" of search, the end of struggle and self-constitution, as Nietzsche asserts,[67] while Socrates calls for an endless dialogue which does not promise the end of the struggle. The question lies in the absence of an objective yardstick to measure the truth: How can Socrates even dare to call for partners for the dialogue, and what is to be expected from such a dialogue which is deprived of the ideal of consensus and its repression? Within the Socratic project the objective truth is a regulative idea, not a constitutive one. And so, in the absence of a binding consensus of the kind in which one forces on the Others as the successful termination of the discourse the questions arise: "What will be the starting point of the discourse?" "What kind of roles will be accepted for developing the dialogue and other obstacles of which the most problematic is the absence of the participants from the realm where only empty freedom rules and there is no place for *hope*?"

This is where the centrality of the (negative) Utopian element in the Socratic project is so central. In the Socratic version of counter-education the participants depart on what might be seen as a absurd journey in light of the principle of hope. It symbolizes the good which is immanently beyond their horizons and which enables the erotic transcendence for ever new and more human potentialities and possibilities. The dialogue realizes the "I-thou" relations between the self and its potentials, mediated by an object for interpretation, on the one hand, and between different speech communities and what is beyond their horizon, on the other. The Utopia is the framework within which hope, reason, and aim are possible. The God who appears in the Socratic world is a personification of this Utopian element.

The aim of our discussion was to reconstruct critically the philosophical foundations of current humanist and "enlightened" educational alternatives in the Israeli arena. It refers to the essentials of the "enlightened" educator. The reference to the Socratic example avoids the challenges of multiculturalism, gender, post-colonialism, as well as postmodernistic discourses and the questions which challenge today's enlightened educator and creates the current blossoming of the "enlightened" alternative, on the one hand, and the historical downfall of Enlightenment's ideals, on the other. However, the central characteristics and problematic are already manifested by the example of Socratic-sophists.

Today, as a representative of "the progressive forces," the "enlightened" educators actually treat their pupils as objects of manipulation and persuade them in a positive-functionalist manner against certain political trends, but not against educational violence as such. It does not encourage and support them for deviation from the political power games and the current realm of self-evidence.

The current "enlightened" educators in Israel are covered politicians, modern sophists who abandoned the Enlightenment's commitment for critique, transcendence, and revolution. They try to teach in a positive and direct way, "to spread the truth," in order to enslave their students onto a positive action which suits and serves their conceptual limitations, class interests, and ideology. The discourse they offer differs substantially from the ultra-nationalistic and religious-nationalist ethnocentrist militarism. However, it differs substantially from the Socratic dialogue; it does not extract, nor suspend, for the sake of the dialogue, the power games of the world which they are committed to serve and reproduce.

Normally, such "enlightened" educators will criticize the Israeli oppression of the Palestinians, and from time to time will be able to understand the sources of Palestinian violence. But very rarely will they criticize the discourse. Normally they will refrain from criticizing the discourse as a manifestation of violence, and they will probably never challenge violence in all its manifestations, discursive and non-symbolic alike. One takes for granted that such educators will not commit their lives, as did Socrates, for the Utopia of dialogue as a free, rational, open, public, and ongoing human coexistence which commits itself to the transcendence from the present order of things, nor to its total transformation. Such an educator would never cross the dividing line between education and counter-education.

Ultimately, the "enlightened" educator as a standard agent of normalizing education is committed to the denial of counter-education and will remain a sophist. In the Israel of today these sophists will refer to the immediate political context, which is important for counter-education too, but they will remain there and praise functionalism and strategic-oriented theories and instrumental-oriented praxis. The other, philosophically/politically critical reference to the present, which constituted for Socrates a life-and-death dialogical partnership between him and his eternal speech community, is quite irrelevant for "enlightened" educators. They do not want and cannot learn from the Socrates, Buddhas, Jesuses, and Nietzsches of all generations. Not their pessimism but rather their sophism is what constitutes her/his abandonment of counter-education. The naiveté of such educators' stance prohibits them from Utopian pessimism which enables the enlightened educator to struggle for the constitution of the only political solidarity still open: the refusal to submit to current facts and the critique of the present realm of self-evidence and its power apparatuses.

Counter-education and its present Socratic representatives, on the contrary, are committed to the task of transcendence from the realm of self-evidence and defending the autonomy of the subject within a context which systematically negates it and threatens to destroy it. In an age when Reason is exiled and Instrumental Rationality governs, counter-education can find much support in the Socratic example for presenting a new religion, a human seriousness toward Spirit and that which is beyond the governing rationality and the prevailing facts.

The very possibility of the struggle, in light of the hope principle, enables a dialogical coexistence and counter-education. Within such a framework, the enlightened educator can realize the effort to find/create the future partner who will fight for her/his stolen sovereignty, interests, and alternative knowledge and perspectives. As an enlightened educator she/he knows that the Other as a partner is not identical with the Other as someone to care for, to love, to emancipate. She/he knows the dialectics of emancipation which culminates in repression and that between the quest for truth and the quest for freedom. The enlightened educator has no illusions about the dangers and limitations of counter-education, on the one hand, and of the possibilities of the current education, on the other.

In contrast to the "enlightened" educators, the enlightened educator would not evade the crisis nor conceal the limitations and dangers of humanist education today: they would not try to seduce the pupil to the dialogue. On the contrary, they would reveal the questions of humanist-oriented education today. The very existence of the future partner would be challenged in a way which would enable her/him to emancipate herself/himself from the current realm of self-evidence. In destroying the enslavement of the possible partners the enlightened educator will realize the responsibility toward the Others and would invite them to a kind of love of humanity and responsibility toward the Other and toward the alternative realm of understanding, which realizes the impetus of counter-education into an alternative even in the present order of things.

The enlightened educator, however, as a utopian pessimist, is disillusioned regarding the prospects of counter-education. She/he acknowledges that education will have the upper hand, and that the partner will never reach *ataraxia*, the peace of mind within counter-education and the political activism which derives from it. As an enlightened educator, she/he acknowledges that even if a suitable partner is found and the Utopia of the dialogue is realized to a certain degree, transcendence is still an unfulfilled mission[68] and, most important, the world would not be changed unless from the outside, by a catastrophic unperfected event which will suddenly invade the present. Yet the enlightened educator will not abandon her/his mission, not even in the Israeli context. Her/his religious attitude might find much use in Jewish negative theology as opposed to the political theology of the Zionist project. It is precisely the Zionist violence and counter-violence, amid the traditional moral mission of Judaism, which makes counter-education so relevant and imperative in current Israel. However, it must start by deciphering the illusion spread by current "enlightened" education in all its versions.

NOTES

1. Yoram Bar-Gal. *Homeland and Geography in Hundred Years of Zionist Education*, Tel Aviv: Am Oved 1993 (in Hebrew).
2. Ilan Gur-Ze'ev. *Education in the Era of the Postmodern Discourse.* Jerusalem: The Magness Press 1996, 8 (in Hebrew).
3. Nimrod Aloni. "State-National Humanist Educational Network is today's imperative," *Hachinuch Usevivo; Educatin and Context* 19 (1997), 207 (in Hebrew).
4. "Declaration of the Rights of Man and the Citizen," in Dale van Kley (ed.), *The French Idea of Freedom: The Old Regime and the Declaration of Rights of 1789*. Stanford: Stanford University Press, 1994, 1.
5. "The Dunlap Broadside of the Declaration of Independence in Congress, July 4, 1776, a Declaration," in Eduard Dumbauld, *The Declaration of Independence and What it Means Today*, Oklahoma: University of Oklahoma Press 1950, 157.
6. Nimrod Aloni. "A platform for moral education in an era of values crisis," *Hachinuch Usevivo: Education and Context* 18, (1996), 17 (Hebrew).
7. Michel Foucault. *The Order of Things: An Archeology of the Human Sciences.* London: Routledge 1994, 386.
8. Juergen Habermas. *Erkentnis und Interese.* Frankfurt a.M.:Suhrkamp 1968, 386.
9. Nimrod Aloni, *ibid.*, 19.
10. Immanuel Kant, *Education*, Ann Arbor: The University of Michigan Press 1960, 12. See also Immanuel Kant, *What is Enlightenment?*
11. Kant too favored disciplination, which treated the young as an object of manipulation and conceived of them as unsuitable for the truth, equality, and respect for what they are. See: Kant, *ibid.*, 36. Gotthold Ephraim Lessing has the same concept of discipline and asserted that the entire human history was a preparatory lesson for critical education in his generation; Gotthold Ephraim Lessing. *The Education of the Human Race.* London: Anthroposophical Pub. Co. 1927.
12. Jonathan Barnes. *The Presocratic Philosophers.* London and New York: Routledge, 542.
13. Plato. "Protagoras" 328, in *The Works of Plato*, New York: The Modern Library 1928, 206.
14. Plato. "Protagoras," 327, *ibid.*, p. 205.
15. Immanuel Kant, "Beantwortung der Frage: Was ist Aufklerung," in Paul Raabe and William Schmidt Biggerman, *Aufklerung in Deutschland*. Bonn: Hohwacht Verlag 1979, 9-16.
16. Plato. *Protagoras.* Translated by C. W. Taylor, Oxford: Clarendon Press 1976, 328, 20.
17. Plato. *Theaetetus.* Translated by Harold North Fowler, Cambridge: Harvard University Press 1967, 166, 95-96.
18. Diogenes Laertius, ix, 55, De Sophystics elenchnis, 183a.
19. Plato. *Protagoras.* Translated by C. C. W. Taylor, Oxford: Clarendon Press 1976, 318e, 11.
20. "One must know that war is common and right is strife and that all things are happening by strife and necessity." Heraclitus. fragment 80 in: G. S. Kirk (ed.), *Heraclitus: The Cosmic Fragments.* Cambridge: Cambridge University Press 1962,

238. Here Heraclitus on his part refers to Anaximander's ontology and gives it a new turn. The sophists follow the same line of Greek Pessimism.
21 Michel Foucalt. *The Archeology of Knowledge*. Translated by A. M. Sheridan Smith, London: Routledge 1995, 211.
22 Plato. "Euthydemos," in *Early Socratic Dialogues*. Translated by Trevors J. Saunders, Penguin Books, 286, 341.
23 Eduard Zeller. *Outlines of the History of Greek Philosophy*. Translated by L. Palmer, New York: Meridian Books, 1955, 128.
24 Eduard Zeller, *ibid.*, 129.
25 Michael Nill. *Morality and Self Interest in Protagoras, Antiphon, and Democritos*. Leiden: E. Brill 1985, 19.
26 Martin Heidegger. "What calls for thinking?", in *Basic Writings*. London: Routledge 1993, 373.
27 Plato, "Crito" 49, in *Plato*. Translated by Harold North Fowler, Cambridge, Harvard University Press, 173.
28 Heidegger, *ibid.*, 379-380.
29 Plato. "Laches" 200-201, in Trevor J. Saunders (ed.), *Early Socratic Dialogues*. Translated by Iain Lane, Harmodsworth: Penguin Books 1987, 115.
30 Plato. "Apology," in *Plato* 1966, 29, 109.
31 *Ibid.*
32 This is one of the sources of the weakness of counter-education, which cannot hand or realize itself as a durabale comprehensive positive Utopia. Yet as counter-education it has no such arrogance, and it should be tested for what it is: counter-education. As a negation of the self-understood and injustice it does have some "positive" elements, as its very existence as a social entity, as alternative way of life for some who participate in this dialogical praxis. Socrates used this expression to introduce his educational mission because its low social status served his irony and because it was his mother's profession and he used to say that she was a wise woman and continues her profession.
33 Plato. *Early Socratic Dialogues*. "Laches" 200, 114.
34 It is a dialogical concept very different from the one held by some Critical Pedagogy thinkers of our time like Paulo Freire, Henry Giroux, and Peter McLaren.
35 This concept of dialogue difference therefore also from the concept of dialogue developed in current feminist pedagogy by thinkers, as Kathleen Weiler and Elizabeth Ellsworth.
36 On this concept see: Ilan Gur-Ze'ev. *The Frankfurt School and the History of Pessimism*. Jerusalem: Magness press 1996, 229. Max Horkheimer, *Gesammelte Schriften* 7. Frankfurt a.M.: Fischer 1985, 386.
37 Plato. "Apologia," in *Plato* 1966, 29, 107.
38 Plato. "The Republic" 621, in Scott Bauchman (ed.), *The Portable Plato*. New York: The Viking Press, 1955, 696. Socrates manifests a position diametrically opposed to the thesis of Horkheimer and Adorno according to which "the history of culture is the history of the internalization of the sacrifice of the victim," in: Max Horkheimer and Theodor Adorno. *Dialectic of Enlightenment*. Translated by John Cumming, New York: Allen Lane 1972, 62.
39 Plato. "Apology," in *Plato* 1966, 29, 109
40 Plato. "The Republic," 621, in *The Protable Plato*, 696.

41 Plato. "The Republic," 621d, in *The Portable Plato*, 696.
42 Karl Marx. *Early Writings*. Translated by T. B. Bottomore, London: C. A. Watts 1963, 159.
43 Max Horkheimer. *Gesammelte Schriften* 14, Frankfurt a.Main: Fischer 1985, 114.
44 Plato, "Symposium," *The Portable Plato*, translated by Benjamin Jowett, New York: The Viking Press 1955, 166.
45 Plato. "The republic," 507-509, *ibid.*, 539-541.
46 Plato. "Symposium," 204, *ibid.*, 162.
47 Plato. "Symposium," 180, *ibid.*, 133.
48 Plato. "The Republic," 508e, *ibid.*, 540
49 Jonathan Barnes. *The Presocratic Philosophers*, Routledge: London and New York 1989, 33.
50 Plato. "The Republic," 509, *ibid.*, 542.
51 I thank my friend and colleague Adam Tenenbaum for the introduction of the concept "realm of self-evidence." On my understanding of the concept see: Ilan Gur-Ze'ev. *The Frankfurt School and the History of Pessimism*. Jerusalem: Magness Press 1996, 222-224.
52 In Plato's "The Republic" it is seen in the tension between the educational implications of the example of the one emancipated from the cave and his responsibility demands his return to the cave and its prisoners, and the ideal state and its repressive educational system.
53 Plato. "Symposium," 204, *ibid.*, 162.
54 It clings to Heidegger's words: "But if man is to find his way once again into the nearness of Being he must first learn to exist in the nameless. In the same way he must recognize the seductions of the public realm as well as the impotence of the private. Before he speaks man must first let himself be claimed again by Being, taking the risk that under this claim he will seldom have much to say. Only thus will the pricelessness of its essence be once more bestowed upon the word, and upon man a home for dwelling in the truth of being." Martin Heidegger. *Basic Writings*. edited by David Farrell Krell, London: Routledge 1996, 223.
55 Plotinus. *The Enneeads*. Translated by Stephen McKenna, London: Faber and Faber n.d., 623.
56 Ernst Bloch. *The Principle of Hope*. Translated by Neville Plaice, Cambridge: MIT Press, 1986.
57 Hans Georg Gadamer. *Wahrheit und Methode: Grundzuge Einer Philosophische Hermeneutik*. Tuebingen: J. C. B. Mohr 1965, 349.
58 Plato. "Apology," 33 in *Plato* 1966, 119.
59 Adi Ofir. "On philosophy as a serious game," *Yyiun*, 35(1986), 24 (Hebrew).
60 Ilan Gur-Ze'ev. *ibid.*, 13.
61 Jan Masschelein. "Wandel der Oeffentlichkeit und das Problem der Identitaet," *Zeitschrift fuer Pedagogik* 28 (1992), 59-75.
62 The concept of redemption within the aesthetic life Socrates offers is much richer than the romantic alternative Friedrich Schiller offered in his "Aesthetic State," which is also positioned as anti-politics. Yet Schillers' anti-politics is fundamentaly conservative and misses the political implications of the Socratic counter-education. Friedrich Schiller. *On the Aesthetic Education of Man in Series of Letters*. Oxford: Oxford University Press, 1967, 192.

63 Euthydemus has similar feelings toward Socrates, in "The Republic," 486b, 487d, *ibid.*, 509-510, and Alcibiades in the "Symposium," 217 *ibid.*, 177.
64 Plato. "Phaedrus," in *Plato* 1966, 277, 571.
65 Franz Rozenzweig. *The Star of Redemption.* Jerusalem: Magnes Press 1970, 215.
66 Ilan Gur-Ze'ev. *ibid.*, 257-272.
67 Friedrich Nietzsche. *Gesammelte Werke*, 4 "Die Vorplatonische Philosophen," Muenchen o.d. 357.
68 Ilan Gur-Ze'ev, Jan Masschelein, and Nigel Blake. "Reflectivity, reflection and counter-education," in *Studies in Philosophy and Education* 20: 2, 93-106.

CHAPTER 11

The Metaphysics of Traffic Accidents and Education Toward an Alternative Public Sphere

A mighty silence accompanies "traffic accidents," which are conceived in the public sphere[1] as the sacrifice of victims to the Molokh. A regular ritual is breaking this silence to demand a reduction in the number of victims sacrificed, aided by "technical means" like "stronger enforcement of traffic regulations," "more investments in the sub-structure," and "traffic safety education." Issues such as the institutionalization of car accidents and the rationalization of the "mistakes" that allow / produce them are not addressed effectively. In the standard discourse of traffic and road-safety, the enslaving myths of "the car," "driving," and speeding," are also ignored. They function dialectically as regulative ideas ("magnificent," "liberating," "total dynamic," "creative driving") and at the same time as the representation / production of the victim. The sacrifice is not limited to technological progress. It is also an imperative of its ideals and symbols and it is presented in terms of inevitablity: an imperative that, from an impersonal point of view, is rational and desirable. It is not viewed as being non-advantageous, an imperative of *Fortuna* as a manifestation of the allmighty *Moira*, or of other transcendental intervention or heavenly prevention. In contrast to these possibilities, car "accident" victims are viewed as a necessary and even a desirable means for protecting current technological progress and the level / quality of life, which is an aim in itself. This "quality" of life is the essence of "life" at the current historical stage. In this epoch the "quality" of "life" is nothing but an instrument and crystallization of technological progress in a specific form. This form will now be deconstructed and critically reconstructed.

In this context human beings sink into meaninglessness, being is forgotten, and the "life" of the thing is glorified. The car is endowed with a life of its own; its life is valued and its mythological representations are sanctified. This glory marks the conditions that make it possible: a post-modern anti-Christ, a counter-being that is evolving. The car, the motorcycle, the speedboat, and the plane are depicted as "strong," "loyal," "admirable," "beautiful," and "lovable." They are "objects of passion" and they are even perceived as "divine." They do not manifest the reason for decaying spirituality, but rather indicate its camaraderie with the death drive. Eros is enslaved in the service of

Thanatos. The "speeding," "performance," and "charm" of the motor vehicles, which slay the attendants to the uncontrollable, to the quest for the transcendence and authenticity of man, are the adorable, the admired, and the divine—not even, but rather because they are assigned to death. Death is the nothingness of "unsuccessful" life. The traffic "accident" takes the form of the meaningless end of "successful" life. It is conceived as a void bereft of any collective "meaning," value, or transcendental dimension. This is to be attributed to the accomplishments of camouflaging the politics of luck. Under these conditions, death is represented as personal, as an active form of the presence of (private) "bad luck" which, psychologically, is totally unexpected. At the same time, this private "luck" is necessary and carefully calculated and productive from the public or rational point of view. The issue of the unexpected, in the sense of the Roman's *fortuna,* has its role even in a totally administered society or self-regulated system, but this issue normally gets the attention it deserves in an ironic form. Its presence does not get a name; in the present public sphere, the traffic victims do not receive a name, a place, and a "voice." They are voiceless deaths which, by contributing to the public horizon as commodities and statistical data, lead to reproduction and successful advancement of the present order.

Within present horizons, "death and the traffic accident" is just one of the representations of the normal technological functioning of the system. It can be controlled to a large degree, statistically, by rational strategies and known manipulations at a cost that is rationally evaluated in determining the life, and, death balance on the roads. This balance is not a matter of sheer luck, but rather a proof of the effectiveness of the system: its self-control and its systematic operations, self-examination, and reproduction potential. The present reality, and the false consciousness it allocates, symbolizes the continued triumph of the present realm of self-evidence[2] to which human beings are attached and by which they are produced. Within its horizons, present human "normality" and its potentialities are attached to, and reproduced by, Instrumental Rationality's control and its reproduction activities. They produce, present, advance, and reproduce human beings and their normality: they participate in defining it. One of these vital and aggressive manipulations is called "education." Normality, in the play of the production and reproduction of its self-evidence and regulative principles, needs "traffic accidents." It needs the "accident" and the ("bad") "luck" as a productive symbolic energy for the rational organization of truths and meanings, and for the production of objects for interpretation and manipulation.

The organization, control, distribution, and the consummating current normality needs, in the requirement of its being as self-evidence, to be unseen.

It is of vital importance that its essential qualities will not be questioned, identified, and challenged. The importance of being unseen lies in its need to maintain itself without being perceived as limited, totally controlled, and anti-transcendental. For this purpose, the representation of quasi-transcendental predications as "good" and "bad" "luck," which are uncontrolled, unexpected, and unfortunate are very productive. In this manner, traffic "accidents" are part of a special historical normality of the "we"—which is produced by it, reproduced by it, and normally unable to challenge it.

Contrary to common belief, to a certain degree there is truth in the popular expression that "only a total abolition of transportation will prevent traffic accidents." That kind of "accident," as the category of "accident" pinpoints, is not to be totally eliminated, since it is not the intervention of *Moira* here, not a transcendental intervention against the rational constitution of the order of things. It is, on the contrary, the face of this order itself and its inner logic that appears when facing death and suffering in traffic "accidents." This logic is especially crystallized in the logic of motor transportation which has peculiarities and localities in its ontology that are not to be reduced to mere crystallizations of a stronger power. Yet, the current realm of self-evidence and its knowledge networks, dynamics, and power relations is the only framework within which the logic of motor traffic and its "accidents" is possible. It is not just one of its manifestations. Motorized traffic realizes a certain logic that can be criticized. It contains a system of codes of behavior and values that point to passions, interests, fears, and dreams that constitute the reality of motorized road interaction. Traffic also realizes subjects, objects, and truths with which certain institutions are authorized to deal. They reveal a power that is beyond their specific and concrete manifestations when they institutionally / legally / expertly deal with traffic "accidents." Such institutions include the police, hospitals, psychologists, and statisticians. Without death on the roads, without "accidents," practically and logically, there is no life for these institutions and intervention theories, regulations, and practices. Outside or without the existence of those regulations, theories, practices, and institutions there cannot be a network. In the absence of a system and a realm of self-evidence the current way of being is hidden.

At present, the logic of economic efficiency actualizes the purpose principle. It maintains and reassures the present balance of traffic injuries by avoiding "unproductive" or "unreasonable" investments in symbolic, financial, and political changes necessary for saving human lives. It would be a mistake to employ a reductionist explanation, according to which the number of current deaths, injuries, and evils is maintained in the present equilibrium. For the living, on the whole, the victims produce values lower than those who were saved—by not changing the situation that leads to their suffering or death in "accidents."

The balance of evils that people suffer is not determined solely by money. Western societies today are willing to suffer many hardships that have nothing to do with monetary gains: what is at stake here is symbolic capital, much more than financial capital. While being distinct, they are integrated in different networks of power / emotions / knowledge relations. These historically based syntheses determine the balance of evils. In other words, the dynamics of symbolic and financial capital, in their changing context, determine the "good" or "bad" "luck" statistics and the exact range and scope of traffic "accidents" needed to preserve and to develop the present order. By that I do not mean that a change in the rate of traffic deaths and injuries is not possible. I am only showing the procedures and powers determining the chances and the directions of such a possible change. Here one should distinguish between subjective sufferings and evils and the very existence, as individual, temporary, and conscious being of human beings in inter-subjective contexts. That is to say, existence as evil and existence within and as part of an objective will and power which manifests itself in subjective wills and power relations in changing contexts. This objective justification of traffic "accidents" also has a subjective dimension, ranging from the maintenance of present and promised commodities, to those motorized participants who have not yet been hit.

In line with what Heidegger called *Ge-stell*, the technological one-dimensional world hides the possibility of rescuing the uncontrolled potentialities, both in the compromising settlement in the present order of things and in the revolt against it. Within this *existentia*, it is not just that spirit is in the Diaspora—even the reason of protest and revolt has been conquered.[3] Within this order human beings are manipulated, activated, and analyzed in all dimensions and levels of their private and public existence, and the illusion of liberation is one of its most needed symbolic energy focuses. This mirage is not an illusion that activates people; rather it is a material dynamic in the network and appears objectively as a commodity that is manufactured, distributed, marketed, purchased, and consumed. It even has its market price, and what can be more "real" and objective than that? What is at stake here is the transformation of human beings and their relative autonomy, the deconstruction of their dialogic essence and their reflective capabilities, and the industrialized destruction of their bodies. On the roads, specifically, it is realized in two seemingly antagonistic manners: on the one hand, participation in the traffic flow, privately and publicly enjoying its fruits, while on the other hand, suffering its evils and limitations to the degree of threatening public prosperity and destroying the individual.

It is worthwhile to point out the destructive element of the productive dimension of motorized traffic and to emphasize the overall rationality and productivity of man's destruction, which is deciphered, in the case of traffic "accidents," as one aspect of a complex process. Here, a greater integration between the public and the private spheres is provided to the degree of the complete elimination of the private sphere. In other words, it annihilates a potentially spiritual and emotional autonomous realm in which Man's dialogic nature and uniqueness of being enable him to reflect on the conditions of the negation of the conditions for realizing his essence. What is at stake here is not his self-realization, but rather the prevention of his struggle to reflect on the conditions determining his limitations, possibilities, and orientations.

The sterilization of transcendence protects the constitution of a one-dimensional world and one-dimensional man in a realm in which, ideally, everything would be automatized and rationalized with no external threat. Under such circumstances, the energies of reflection, protest, rebellion, and transformation are reconstructed and transformed into productive elements improving the efficiency of the present system. The return of this myth within ever-greater rationalization and an increase in efficiency of the system happens while denoting the individualistic elements of the system and the possibilities for competition, self-decision, and change as open options for every normal human being in the system. An ideal closed Platonic cave is constituted in an anti-idealistic, anti-collectivist, and instrumentalist era: motorized vehicles, especially the fast models, glorify individualistic values in a special context. Within this context, unlimited mobility, total privacy, and individualistic control[4] are praised as part of their destruction.

Within the framework of the current capitalist globalization, technological developments, and the representations of the culture industry, there is less room for counter-education which strives for reflection, struggles for dialogue and transcendence, and offers resistance to the present order of things. The present conditions reduce the social, cultural, conceptual, and existential potential for dialogue and solidarity. Under these conditions there is less room for the individual's struggle to become some one rather than some thing—to become an ethical I, who not only reflects but also commits herself to transcendence in relation to the Other as part of a responsibility toward the Other. The system reproduces itself by reducing the human being into some thing, a mere agent, an efficient producer / consumer. As such, he / she accepts the present realm of self-evidence, identifies with it, and abandons the quest to realize *the totally other as present* in the actual Other. Within the system there is no room for dialogue and solidarian self-positioning, nor self-constitution. We need to ask whether it is possible, within this order, to challenge the present reality through counter-education by offering alternative microscopic and general realities: concepts, experiences, and actions which can ultimately change the system and its cultural, social, gender, and ethnic formations. The reduction of the subject into a "subject" and the development of a contingent, multicultural, fluid, local, and temporal identity, lead to knowledge and value forms that are part of the general reification of the current globalization of capitalism. Within the present culture industry that represents and serves this order, "the individual" is hailed purely in terms of his/her status as a consumer/producer. Free choice and democracy are expressions that find themselves celebrated purely within a rhetoric that serves the reproduction of this anti-humanist order.

The quest for transcendence and the advancement of reflective power represents a movement that is well suited to the metaphor of vertical movement: a movement that is essentially a potentiality and is aimed toward the not-yet-realized, to the absent. Traditionally, this kind of movement was not conditioned by, but rather attached to a different kind of movement. Traditional movement possibilities were dialectical, while the reflective potential manifested "vertical" ("platonic") movement and openness to the eternal and the absolute. It was cyclical and part of the eternal movement of the universe that gave dialogue its transcendental possibilities. At the same time, it was based on the recognition of the human limitations of the horizontal movement possible within the framework of "the realm of necessity."

In Plato's *Phaedrus*, "the being which really is" is in a "region," "above the heavens," and real human existence is to be realized only by transcending the human being from the given "up" into it, "winged" as it were: "The natural property of the wing is to carry what is heavy upwards, lifting it aloft to the region where the race of the gods resides, and in a way, of all the things belonging to the sphere of the body, it has the greatest share in the divine, the divine being noble, good, and everything which is of that kind."[5]

The present possibilities of movement are different. Today's fast traffic is taking place in a context in which "vertical" transcendent movement has become irrelevant and has actually disappeared, while "horizontal" movement within the one-dimensional framework of "the same" is no longer looked upon as limited, hard, and slow. Motorized traffic does not represent a mere technological change. It represents a totally different metaphysics of movement and different human possibilities. "*Speeding* is precisely elimination of expectation and duration.... Shifting the soul this time from the brain to the motor will free man from apprehension about a future that no longer has any raison d'etre, since everything is already there, here and now, present and over at one, in the instantaneous apocalypse of messages and images, in the great old joke at the end of the world!"[6]

Motorized traffic is necessarily a movement of a new kind: movement that is in principle unlimited and borderless. The (inevitable) absence of limits to this movement has two manifestations: speeding ability and the ability to drive anywhere ignoring the question of purpose and meaning. The ability to get anywhere overthrows the traditional concept of movement, a concept that received its meaning in light of its purpose according to physical hardships and limitations as well as practical ambient factors and the slow moving nature of locomotion prior to technological acceleration. The new speedy mobility is unique by being represented and conceived as an expression of privacy and independence, in that drivers are supposed to drive their vehicles as a perfect expression of their free will, unbounded by external limitations or direction. The realization of free will, determination, and the ability to change are conceived, or at least they are supposed to be conceived, as an expression of privacy and autonomy. At any given moment, such privacy may direct itself upon others as an inescapable disaster, or it may generate a form of understanding and cooperation with them, as a way of demonstrating that they are in control of motorized vehicles.

Traditional traffic mobilized men and women and their assets in a linear axis within a recognition of its limits and its passion for an erotic movement which is essentially different from that characterizing the daily round of life where "everything is the same." The essential movement to pre-motorized traffic was driven by an erotic power for transcending man from daily life, from the limited and the defective toward the good, the beautiful, and the right, the real and the eternal.

The essence of today's traffic lies in the void of erotic silence, in the absence that is reproducing "the same all the time." In the present horizon of self-evidence, the phenomenon "same all the time" is recruited into the dialectic between and within horizontal movement in the realm of space (speed) in which speed inherits the realm of time (eternity)—a dialectic that characterized the quest for (vertical) transcendence. Historically, the narcissistic being enclosed within the car with the illusion of overcoming time and of the control of external space, and the motorized vehicle as a locus of "excitement" are replacing religious ecstasy, the traditional quest for eternity, and the Enlightenment's devotion for autonomy and reflexive capacities. The illusion of controlling a man-made machine in a completely self-created and self-controlled environment is today's Tower of Babel. It is different to controlling an animal in the service of human needs. It avoids the question of God, his laws, the problem of not being a God and being outside heaven. However, the realm of self-evidence that the original Tower of Babel builders tried to construct was a religious act of rebellion; it was an alternative to the heavenly enterprise, indeed its foundation, and it was humanistic and earthly.

The illusion suggested by the automobile represents an alternative to previous stages in the history of Western civilization. It also represents an alternative to the cultural stage of commitment to an ideal of a free public sphere, where reason and free men and women are supposed to flourish within a dialogue of concrete social conditions. This transition from one realm of self-evidence to another is technologically very productive. It is also defines the self reproductive possibilities of the system that uses human beings as drivers and travelers—who are transformed into commodities and treated as objects. They become "part of the market" for car dealers, advertisers, and the like. In parallel, they become objects in the sense of work power in which it is useless to make a division between the driver and the machine from a practical or rational point of view. That is not to say that motorized traffic has to manifest itself in the same way in any possible world. It is argued that in a different realm of self-evidence, a different set of passions, myths, procedures, and criteria would be in operation. There would also be another metaphysic at work where traffic behavior would be different.

The productivity of present anti-metaphysics secures the scientific and technological progress within which the myth returns as the sole ruler in science and (instrumental) rationality's name. This reality manifests a false consciousness that reproduces and advances it within the framework of technological progress where it is useless to make any logical distinction between the accident and the mistake. This is because the accident manifests a personal mistake that is logically necessary and productive according to the inner logic of the system. The new myths that determine the causes of traffic "accidents" are scientifically accurate, socially necessary, and technologically productive. In a sense, the highest expressions of individuality have become nothing more than the expressions of the demolition of the subject's autonomy. This reduction represents the destruction of a kind of ideal commitment to a negation of power fields in which the hegemonic discourses produce a consensus that constitutes an ever-evolving realm of understanding in which subjects recognize other subjects and collectives as partners in solidarity in a common movement toward Utopia.

In the current false libertarian consciousness, driving functions as a myth that enables one to see the road networks and the regulation dynamics of present society as the antithesis to the penetrating force of the system in the private sphere. The driver functions as a eunuch, protecting the public and the private spheres from being penetrated by new, vivid, and young myths. The current system is defended against the rough winds of a new realm of common self-evidence that is about to overrun and conquer the aging, dissolved realm of self-evidence that is under pressure. The castration of the erotic essence of movement in the world where motorized traffic was unknown and Instrumental Rationality did not rule might be seen as productive. It is productive from the point of view of the capitalistic commodities market.

Under these conditions, there is such a thing as a normal or an average driver. Every insurance company realizes this possibility. This "normal" driver who identifies with the speedy driving myth is the one who surrenders himself to the systematic castration that the present capitalistic society imposes on its followers. The struggle for freedom and transcendence has no place in a reality where man conceives of himself as one who might be with himself as a driver, as one who "controls the business," and as someone who "acts in a right manner," according to rules which he cannot avoid, even for a moment, with no danger of capital punishment.

In ages when Instrumental Rationality did not reign as sole monarch, driving had a different character. Driving was a manifestation of the gap between the ideal and the present situation. It was conceived as mobilizing and instructing in a reality that is essentially transcendent. For example, in the book of Ecclesiastics 2:3, "My heart conducting itself with wisdom, how yet to lay hold on folly," or in Lamentations 3:2 "He hath led me and caused me to walk in darkness but not into light." Today, when traffic and transportation are viewed with an anti-ontological and nondialectical eye, traffic is conceived as self-regulated movement in an alternative unlimited reality that is self-sufficient—an aim in itself. The comprehension in fashionable conventions and in dominating and repressive administrative procedures of automatic movement that this traffic represents is taking the place of the erotic quest for absolute truth that traditional forms of transportation have represented since the downfall of the Tower of Babel. Even the Enlightenment's vision of the human being in the world, traveling within this framework, still held on to some essential elements of the Judeo-Christian realm of self-evidence. In traffic and in the present context, and especially in the "excitement" of driving at high acceleration (e.g., in a "powerful" B.M.W.), the driver can reassure himself that he has sovereignty over reality and time in the public sphere—overcoming its non-narcissistic regulations—and drive back home, within and into the endless horizons of himself. Giving the driver the private sphere within the public sphere hides the disappearance of both dimensions. It presents neither an accident nor good or bad luck, but rather expresses the efficiency of the system's own realization by reducing human beings into drivers or passengers. The system manifests itself through agents and dynamics as exemplified by drivers and passengers in traffic, and there is no other reality or absolute idea outside of it, as there is no reality to systems outside the realms of self-evidence. By this I do not claim that human beings are mere representations and agencies of the systems that create and imprison them. My thesis reconstructs a dialectic between ontological and historical dimensions. Historically, there are various symbolic and extra-symbolic opportunities and limitations for human beings to transcend the system and its limited horizons. Ontologically, it is important to emphasize the centrality of being and the not-yet-realized, the dimension of potentiality, of *the totally other* as represented in the Principle of Hope. However, the transcendence and the overcoming of limitations and hegemonic strategic attitudes, symbolic and extra-symbolic dynamics, are historically and locally contextualized. That is why the anti-humanistic tendencies in the relatively prosperous West are so effective, as can be seen in the traffic arena. The world of fast traffic is a place where humanistic potentials have no environment in which to be realized and developed. The constant noise of the engine, the density of the traffic, and the impossibility of a determined attitude toward the environment—that is both spiritually and ecologically balanced—contribute to the constitution of the dynamic, speedy intersubjectivity that is an arguable logical and political imperative. Psychologically, speeding and the quest for speed can be characterized as a "quest for danger" and sometimes as a healthy "stress backing." We need to seek out the ontological sign of the success of *Ge-stell* within it, which hides the uncontrollable. In other words, we must search for the unobservable that traditional Western art and *techne*, in the Greek sense of the word, brought into the light of everyday reality out of the realm of mystery as something that is autonomous in this daily reality and not as part of it. Under such circumstances, human possibilities and limitations were different from the ones confronting the new man of today. Today's exciting driving as a mystic experience, as *poisis* in the sense of seeking the limits of the (im)possible, rather than as an expression of the manipulation possibilities of the present system, is a manifestation of stolen freedom and false revolt within a totality where there is no relevance to the concepts of estrangement and repression. On such an earth, there is no place for trying to rebuild the humanist enterprise, as exemplified in the project of the builders of the Tower of Babel or in the enterprise of the Enlightenment.

Within the horizons of the false public sphere, it seems inevitable that, on the public level, rational men and women will contribute their share concerning decisions about issues such as reducing traffic speed, prohibiting driving under the influence of drugs or alcohol, and other regulations of that sort. At the same time, on the private level they are driven both to demand their stolen freedom by the negation of Instrumental Rationality's demands and to preserve the well-being of the system and their own safety as agents of that system and its current dynamics and horizons. In practice, the new man will rebel against the conditions that constitute him, his possibilities, his pleasures, and his miseries at the earliest opportunity. The taboo that *Ge-stell* constituted will be destroyed with extreme joy, real joy, whenever possible, sometimes at all costs. This rebellion is punitive and useless. It reflects the irony of the system that calculated such a reaction and which has called for it under its secret educational agenda.

In conformity with the present order of things, a person realizes himself as a driver. According to the degree of effectiveness in representing himself as one who is "successful," to a large extent the driver is recognized according to the car that he has or does not have. He drives a vehicle that simultaneously enables him to manifest "success" and to rebel against his stolen uniqueness and freedom in the ocean of rules, regulations, and control apparatuses that are maintained by the system. From the "outside" this reaction is identified on a scale ranging from "dangerous driving" to "madness." There are studies emphasizing the incommensurability of the subjective and the objective dimensions in motorized driving.[7] I do not see an incommensurability manifestation, but rather one of the many representations of normality in the present mythic one-dimensional realm of self-evidence. This is a false rebellion because it is planned and controlled by the system, constituted on private and collective repression and guilt consciousness of a supposed primordial sin[8] practiced daily in the earthly hell of normality.

This normality is produced and reproduced by the different elements and dynamics of symbolic energies which enable the destruction of the mere potential of another look at knowledge, man, and the world. The possibility of a utopian glance at the possible non-repressive, non-instrumental attitude that could have represented a comprehensive alternative to a totally different concept of movement and traffic is completely obfuscated.

Within such a utopian alternative, there is room for a different self-motion and intersubjective mobility where there are no rational, calculated, institutionalized traffic "accidents." The self-driven movement is never independent. It is always contextualized and materialistic, but it can struggle for overcoming limitations by deconstructing the realm of self-evidence that is closed within its horizons. It can try to transcend itself by revealing coded social manipulations and truths, validity parameters and consciousness production operations, by deciphering these codes and by denoting their political meaning. In this sense, the alternative universality and the alternative individualism represented in these terms create a potential for liberation that is met by dangerous alternatives to humanist tradition and whatever liberalism is realized in the present political, social, and cultural systems of Western societies. A spiritual alternative to the present order might bring an alternative realm of self-evidence that would be less problematic and more terrible, in light of Enlightenment ideals, humanist values, and liberal social regulations to which present Western societies are committed. The history of motorized transportation reveals the openness, if not the quest, of Western culture to this alternative, where there is no place for autonomous subjects, solitary intersubjectivity, reflective discourse, and dialogical attitudes toward society's challenges.

In modern times, the road networks have become an arena of knowledge that contains its specifications and uniqueness, but basically reflected, tested, and reassured the rationality of each driver and that of the entire system. The logic of the present realm of self-evidence is built within the collective consciousness, in symbolic and commodity distribution and consumption practices. They are present in the education of each person to behave within the given horizons of procedures, rhetoric, and practices that are both universalistic and one-dimensional. The roads and the behavior on them reveal an educational enterprise and examination process of the universality of the symbolic violence of the present education. It has become an arena in which human rationality is tested, realized, and reassured daily by each driver in each second of his or her driving experience. Too much independence, nonconformism, ignorance, or luck of practical experience in this field is sanctioned or rewarded not by a personal teacher, a ruler, a class or interest group, but by the system and Instrumental Rationality in which they themselves function simultaneously as its agents, representations, and victims.

Traffic today represents an important site of Instrumental Rationality and its successes. These successes are manifested everywhere. However, the success of Instrumental Rationality is not totally without problems, as can be seen in ecology, medicine, or transportation. On the roads, its failures are of tremendous magnitude: exactly where it is most vital, traffic becomes ever more intense, costly, and inefficient, as can be seen in traffic jams in the big cities. Yet, as in other fields, Instrumental Rationality's failure is recognized solely according to its own standards, and so are the suggested solutions. This proves to what degree a realm of self-evidence is omnipotent—until its downfall. Traditionally, a realm of self-evidence could be destroyed from the outside or stagnate and disintegrate from within, since it includes or could include antagonistic spiritual elements. The uniqueness of the present Western realm of self-evidence is the absence of spiritually antagonistic elements.

Therefore, dramatic antinomies that represent Instrumental Rationality's total control do not endanger its systems or its perpetual advancement—at all costs, total catastrophe included.

The traffic that in the West is more or less available to all levels of society represents the erosion of reification, repression, and revolt against it. The dynamics of regulations, their realization and their changing conditions, both from the system's point of view and from the users' point of view, are not to be divided. The system is one-dimensional and universalistic. There is no repressive group interest or conception to be revolutionized or challenged. In order to survive as a driver, one must adjust to the system and contribute one's share to its well-being. The driver is a manifestation of the commodity exchange in which even death in a traffic accident is a rational requirement of the market, technological advance, and the continuation of "increasing the standard of living" among the survivors. These ideals and requirements have evolved out of modernity, but they negate its Enlightenment utopia and its concrete social and cultural potentialities.

The world of traffic is only a fragment of a complicated totality, however, it is a major junction between different networks. Here, there is a perfect manifestation of the almost absolute validity of the universality of the system's codes, as understood and performed by the representatives of the different sources. This is not to ignore the fact that in present post-modern conditions, more than ever, people can simultaneously participate in different and sometimes conflicting constellations which may be political, conceptual or psychological, modern, post-modern, and/or pre-modern. The acknowledged pluralism is promoted essentially as a one-dimensional phenomenon, enabled by an irresistible universalistic logic that there is no open public way to resist it or to revolt against it with no immediate punishment. This argument can be seen in the present conditions and rules of traffic and road "accidents." The "accident" is thought to be one of two: either a misunderstanding of those involved in the traffic or "bad luck." The second possibility might take the form of a kind of institutional neglect of road conditions that cause the "accident," which is systematically represented as a personal issue, or "bad luck," as if it were a heavenly punishment. Such is the attitude of many of the cases of the first category, when "bad luck" or "mere coincidence" manifest themselves in the form of a drunken or "bad" driver approaching from the opposite direction.

In contrast to Foucault's thesis concerning the clinic or the jail, I claim that the traffic space is the best normalization and disciplining site: not as a Foucaultian closed site that determines the limits of normality, but rather as a meeting-point between the different networks. This synthesizing process leads to the production, stimulation, and transformation of the various networks and sites as the production of their essence—which is localized by the realm of self-evidence and the dynamics and borders that are possible within it as its concrete and specific realization. The closure as reconstructed in road traffic is not the space and disciplinary form that Foucault examines. The closure/stability of the realm of self-evidence is the form that determines the amounts and the conditions of the openness of systems, their pluralism and permitted difference. It is also that which determines the constructive and deconstructive possibilities of codes, concepts, and practices. As motorized traffic has shown on the roads, there is not an alternative spiritual foundation or social bearer for the renewal of concepts or the rebirth of ideals or for the appearance of a new relevant critique on the current reality and its systems. Within the framework of the current realm of self-evidence, such understanding has become irrelevant, or even a sign for illness or undeniable weakness. Basically, the obfuscation of the possibility of experiencing estrangement toward the current cultural problem is supplied by the erosion of the antagonistic manifestations between the rationality of capitalistic symbolic and commodity production and the humanist ideals of the Enlightenment, which have been completely integrated into the prevailing realm of self-evidence and its systems.

Filippo Tomaso Marinetti understood that speed is a new spirituality, a religion, that "will master time and space," that gives rise to "a new morality"[9] and "a new beauty; the beauty of speed. A racing car whose hood is adorned with great pipes, like serpents of explosive breath—a roaring car that seems to ride on grapeshot—is more beautiful than the *Victory of Samothrace*."[10] A similar, yet very different myth from the one about which Marinetti dreamed was realized to the degree of mastering the current order of things. Some of Marinetti's ideas have a place in this order. Yet the dream has been de-contextualized, transformed, and takes place in a new realm of self-evidence, where the status of concepts and myths are totally changed. The similarity I speak about is not a similarity within the same system, or within the same realm of self-evidence, rather, it is a structural one on a diachronic level. In our post-modern situation, we have many such similarities between local symbolic or political structures and dynamics, while others are totally foreign to one another. More concretely, the Futurist, the Fascist, and the Nazi conception of movement and transportation are very different from that of the modern-Enlightenment, but they do share central aspects and structures with the current transportational metaphysics. Traffic became a subject for "experts" who dealt with separate aspects of it, and it never attracted a philosophical study of its totality.

In the second half of the twentieth century, a new realm of self-evidence started to form, and man was therein reduced to a function as a producer/

consumer. This reduction was provided by the same dynamics that lead to the constitution of emancipatory humanist utopias in the Enlightenment era. Intensified and transformed, these dynamics changed the modern realm of self-evidence into a new realm in which the conceptual possibilities and the ideals, values, dialogue and struggle possibilities that were open in modernity were systematically closed and eroded. If in modernity the human subject was conceived potentially as a site of reflection, dialogue, solidarity and as a focus of emancipatory social action in the second half of the twentieth century, this ideal has now been transformed into a mere sign of a function. Man has become a sign of a function in the context of his producer/consumer abilities: and only as such is he relevant to the self-reproduction of post-industrial society and the development of its symbolic world. This is the context of the flourishing rhetoric about preserving and protecting human life and the awakening of sensitivity regarding the fatality of traffic accidents in an era of their indisputable decrease if we look at the terms of the percentage of casualties.

At the same time, the vitality of traffic "accidents" has become increasingly important for the system. The mass production of commodities has become committed to a vast interchange that has led to the rapid devaluation of goods through the promotion of new fashions and technologies, thereby eliminating ineffective producers and problematic consumers or socially unproductive groups. Their destruction has many modes and, as the system becomes more sophisticated, it is less direct, vulgar, and explicit and ever more efficient. This distraction ensures the continuing production and consumption of new fashions that increase the exchange of commodities and the system's self-reproduction. It protects the workplaces of men and women—though not the people themselves—who become owners of cars, motivated by passions and dreams shaped by the automobile as an agent and as an ideal.

It has become unprofitable to produce cars that will last for a long time. Their rapid replacement is built into the system. The intensified dynamics have been transformed from the means of the system into an end in itself. The movement of commodities increased and revolutionized in many ways by modernity has become, in the new realm of self-evidence, a vital element in stabilizing its systems and protecting its horizons. Therefore, just as human beings have to reflect and advance the system by being agents of increasing dynamism they are also caught up in the same matrix of disposability and become increasingly worn out, rapidly and totally. From the capitalist, that is, rational point of view, traffic accidents are a necessity, a matter of life or death. Yet this is but a manifestation of a deeper development, of progress within the framework of Thanatos, of being hiding from human beings without God, without the possibility of utopia and without anything mysterious or uncontrollable with which they might engage. A real solution to the traffic problem and a dramatic reduction in the number of victims and the attitude toward them is a serious threat to the current order of exchange and the current symbolic understanding space, as well as the mental constitution and the attitude of the drivers.

It is worthwhile, in this context, to denote the connection between a reduction in speed and a reduction in accidents and casualties. "All the empirical data prove that whenever and wherever a speed limit had been introduced, the number of accidents decreased,"[11] argues Hans-Georg Retzco. There are exact details showing the dramatic link between the decrease in the number of accidents, especially in deaths and serious injuries, and the decrease in traffic speed.[12] Spolander argues that the reduction in traffic speed will result in a significant drop in the number of casualties in the accidents that will remain to a ratio of 4:3,[13] even in the case of a minimal reduction of the speed limit.

Accidents are to be understood within the context of interpreting the essence of traffic and the new status of movement in the current realm of self-evidence. This is the starting point for understanding the link between the mistake and the accident, the personal and the public spheres. This is the current status of the realm of understanding and communication possibilities as they are manifested in an era in which the traffic space is a communicative network. It is where the functions of the newest false human subjectivity are produced, represented, destroyed, and reproduced. Men and women become relevant—are alive—as reproducers of motorized movement and as the victims of the symbolic reproduction of the extinction of their human essence. It is a process that is carried out by the very same subjects who are the agents of their systems and manifestations.

On a more political level, why and how is it that there is no agreement on reducing the speed limit, investing more resources in infrastructure, improving the safety dimensions of cars and implementing regulations that will lead to a significant drop in the number of victims? My argument is that philosophically and politically, the present level of suffering among casualties and the continuation of road-deaths represent a rational equilibrium, from the point of view of the existing order. Traffic safety education is of special importance because it has the quickest and the largest rhetorical impact while being politically the least expensive and, philosophically, the least problematic. In the Israeli arena, this might be exemplified by Eliahu Richter, a traffic researcher who says that "the myth that there is a need to increase safety education and drivers preparation education in order to decrease the slaugther on the roads by higher awareness has been proven wrong again and again."[14] Another Israeli researcher, Irit Uchmann, presents a similar argument. She maintains that while the National Israeli Institution for Driving Preparation gives courses for about 90,000 drivers annually, the usefulness of these courses is never actually checked. The manager of the Israeli National Institution for Safe Driving declared frankly that "Most of the course is directed toward re-studying traffic regulations. . . . It is nothing but a waste of time, and even a terrible waste of money and energy."[15]

The American economists, Lester and Charles Law, calculated that the cost of saving one person's life from a traffic "accident" is worth 850,000 hours of extra driving time. And since the average life of an American is equal to 600,000 hours, they have "proved" that it is irrational to save a person's life at the cost required under present conditions. Saving one victim under such conditions is described (somewhat un-scientifically?) scientifically as a lousy deal.[16] They also state, explicitly, that society is clearly not prepared to increase traffic safety by decreasing the mobility and comfort of people. Society is unwilling to deprive poor people from the right to drive unsafe cars if the alternative is that they would not be car owners at all.[17] According to these researchers, this is the reason for the lack of investment in a sub-structure that would drastically lower the number of victims. I do agree with their conclusion that a substantial decrease in the number of traffic victims is possible. To a certain degree, I even share their conclusion that "society" is not interested in reducing the number of casualties. As things stand today, the demand for lowering the injuries ratio is completely irrational. However, in contrast to these researchers, I do not think that we should see this issue as a manifestation of society's free will, or as a manifestation of genuine social and cultural progress.

By claiming that a substantial reduction in the number of traffic victims is irrational from the point of view of the system, I do not mean that such a reduction is in itself irrational, since the current system does not value life and does not view the victim's life since it does not consider the life of the victim as anything that is valuable in itself. My claim refers to the economic and symbolic energy that the system has to invest in order to change the present balance. The symbolic energy and economic cost of creating social, cultural, and physical conditions that will substantially reduce the number of traffic victims is irrational, under the current system. The level of rational control is such that in facing the data of the experts, the conditions of society would have already changed unless such a change was merely irrational, as it seems to be according to the present order of things. Normally, hegemonic rhetoric masks this imperative of the current system, but sometimes the functionalist symbolic exchange reveals its truth. Treating the internal rhetoric of researchers working for insurance companies, transport, and road works might be of some use, but even their public publications are sometimes good enough for this purpose.

A. D. Reynolds and R. F. Dawson's rhetoric might demonstrate Instrumental Rationality in action, in their devotion to an "objectivist," "neutral," and functionalist attitude. Already in the 1970s, they were occupied in calculating the rationally justified investment in preventing car accidents and their victims. In their report, they treated the problem in such terms as "the cost of a death is not less than the loss of the output which the deceased person would have produced" if he or she had not been killed in the accident.[18] The experts discuss questions about the economic worth of the life and death of a car accident's victim and in these reports "it is sometimes argued that if society loses an accident victim's output, it also gains the consumption that he will no longer need." An accurate calculation of the economic value of one person's life is very precise in such reports; in addition, they even differentiate between the value of women's and men's lives. Dawson, for example, found that the British economy loses L 4360. in each fatal accident in which a man is the victim, but gains L 1120. in the case of the victim being a woman: "Since the work done by housewives was given a low value in the calculations, society could be said to gain on average. . . when women are killed in road accidents."[19]

Norbert Elias is one of the few thinkers that has placed the traffic issue in a nonmarginal place in his social and cultural critique. In the spirit of Aristotle and Kant, Norbert Elias presents an essentialist concept, according to which human essence is manifested in self-control and self-regulation. For Elias, this is realized within the framework of present reality, with the traditions and regulations shaping its formations and dynamics. Unlike Aristotle and Kant, however, he identifies self-control and regulation with technical control. More specifically, self-control is realized and tested functionally on the motorized road traffic: "Controlling the car (which includes its maintenance) is nothing but an extension of the driver's self-control or self-regulation."[20] For Elias, cultural development is a universal educational process of humanity. One of the major forces of education, according to Elias, is the progress of technization of a given society. Here, he places technization—the historical process of transportation—in a special position. The supreme trial of every culture is its ability to develop an ever-higher degree of self-control, and this is manifested in the issue of traffic in general and accidents in particular. In consonance with the thesis presented here, Elias also argues that it is wrong to make a division between traffic accidents and the status of knowledge and the dynamics constructing the present shape of society.[21]

Elias maintains that it is not only that the victims of traffic accidents in the developed culture of Western societies are inevitable, the truth is that they are an indication of the extent to which Western culture has gone in making technological development one of its most important parameters. He sees a connection between further advancing technization of traffic and improving self-control as indications for cultural progress. His findings show that it is possible to identify a considerable gap between the rate of traffic accidents in Western societies and that in non-Western societies.[22]

Elias uses his data in order to defend the special stand of Western culture and the advantages that Western societies have over non-Western ones. The differences are substantial and noticeable in the effectiveness of social standards that concern self-control and regulation. The major cause of traffic accidents, according to Elias's thesis, is the driver, and the degree of self-control of the driver is an outcome of the level of his cultural development. The degree of cultural development is evident in the self-control of the individual, a component responsible for causing the accidents and responsible for their victims.[23] I do agree with Elias that road accidents are not a matter of luck or chance and that, in fact, they are not "accidents."

Elias refers to the cultural progress of the West as a manifestation of the progress of rationality and the advancement toward a higher degree of integration. From that respect, too, traffic accidents are a manifestation of rationality (or the degree to which society has been rationalized), on the one hand, and a justified punishment or a pedagogically necessary treatment that non-Western societies have to suffer, on the other. Although his thesis has to be rejected on a few grounds, his thesis is still an important one. It is important since it implicitly presents the road as an arena in which rationality is tested objectively, by manipulating the vehicles, drivers, and their communication abilities with other drivers in the context of their intersubjectivity. They are examined in parallel on their ability to know and understand agreed conventional codes and regulations, and on their ability to do this by realizing the needed amount of self-control in the equalization of man with the car, airplane, or speedboat.

I do not agree with Elias's conclusion, when he claims that the degree of traffic efficiency reveals the degree of a culture. However, his studies are useful, for the deconstruction of the cultural context and philosophical essence in the transformational (re-constructive) transformation of its potentials and cultural essence. More than that, I can make use of some of his findings as an example for my argument concerning the success of the purpose principle within the framework of advancing Instrumental Rationality that develops vital elements of hegemonic forces in post-industrial society. This rationality has a special presence in interchange networks: transportation, the representation of knowledge, its agents, and other commodities. The efficiency of the system is manifested by motorized traffic and not in the cultural and social stage, as Elias tries to convince us. Thus, the level of traffic accidents does not represent any punishment, or luck or "accident," in which its essential characteristics lie in its being an incident, an inevitable catastrophe. In contrast to Elias and other conservatives defending the present anti-humanistic Western order of things, I see in traffic "accidents" the logic of the system, the forces constructing its rationality and its self-presentation and manipulations. Since this rationality is instrumental in its essence, it is not determined by values and is attracted to the mission of the anti-transcendental being, an aim of self-reproduction and advancement of nothingness, of Thanatos. This concrete representation of Instrumental Rationality has social, economic, and technological results in the public sphere and in the remains of what could have been the public sphere of the individual.

Therefore, the implementation of a policy that would lead to a real reduction in traffic "accidents" might clash with the purpose principle, which is indifferent to any value-oriented obligation. It would also be at odds with transcendental ideals, as the supremacy of preserving and developing human life and its well-being and preferring it over further technological advancement possibilities, as well as other elements of protecting the life of the control and repression potentialities of the system. Four possibilities are to be raised in referring to the limits of the rationality of a praxis that will substantially reduce the number of traffic "accidents" and their victims.

A. *A further reduction is needed in the speed of traffic.* In such a case, the symbolic function of driving might bring the driving and other related networks into total chaos. This should be understood in terms of a space where killing time and extrinsic controlled self-constitution have become central and productive educational and political dimensions of prolonging the life of the system.

B. *Substantial changes will be needed in traffic organization, in car structuring, and especially in the representation of the producer/consumer as man-machine.* In such a case, the erotic passion between the driver and the car might be confused, and a demand might come to constitute different social borders, relations, and dynamics in which an erotic state between human beings might be constituted. There is even the danger of lightening the educational contribution of a false erotica between man and motorized vehicles under the new cultural conditions. Such a critical light might reveal the part that modern speed driving plays in the self-forgetfulness of man in his refusal to transcendence and in his forgetfulness of forgetfulness.

C. *The dangers of the traffic routes as sites of knowledge exchange and realization.* A consideration of the dangers involved in fast driving and an essential change in the ways in which the dangers on the roads are represented might damage its economic, social, and cultural production. The productivity of the relation to the danger involved in speedy traffic is based on the dual structure of this kind of danger: as an enemy and as an object of strong passion. This danger is represented as something that has to be overcome. By the same token, as a dimension of "otherness" in the heart of a one-dimensional world it demands the release of surplus energy and frustration in such a way that in the final analysis it will secure present normalization strategies, power hierarchies, and dynamics. These elements protect, serve, and hide themselves as self-evidence. Life on the edge, as philosophy on the edge, might be an erotic reflection of health, as Nietzsche proclaimed. However, in certain systems like ours, looking for the danger and running away from unplanned and uncontrolled life are two dimensions of one and the same trend: Thanatos's track of self-forgetfulness, which is also the forgetfulness of being, the nothingness. "And so everything rushes at man, man-target is assailed on all sides, and our only salvation now is to be found in illusion, in flight from the reality of the movement, from the loss of free will. . . "[24]

D. *The changes about which I speak threaten the very possibility of struggling for the realization of human freedom, solidarity, and dialog in history.* This is the case because there is not a way to totally ignore the essential difference between self and intersubjective understanding / realization and freedom, between Eros and Thanatos. Traffic is an arena where the possibility of dialogical solidarity and alternative communication is tested daily. Today's roads provide an exemplary manifestation of rationality, of "healthy" competition and cooperation between people as if there were a vivid dimension of a free and democratic public sphere. The aforementioned possible changes in symbolic and traffic operation might crack the self-understandability of some apparatuses and strategies of the system, endangering other entities—that of traffic—and thus endangering the entire system. Cracking vital self-evident dimensions will question the ways of production and reproduction of the conceptual apparatus, the hegemonic collective consciousness, normalization strategies, and educational manipulations responsible for reproduction of the necessary public attitude and criteria and so forth. Essentially, different forms of approach to evaluation, communication, and intervention might penetrate along radical alternative driving and traffic philosophy. As such, they might bring about an alternative human condition. Such an order must represent a different intersubjective grammar and a different human attachment to human beings, technology, and ecology as well as toward the unspeakable or uncontrollable. The object of such a transformation is not identifiable within the borders of the current realm of self-evidence. Such a transcendence must be of a utopian order that philosophically denotes the primacy of the potential over the actual: it must be politically aggressive or be smashed by the hegemonic educational dynamics of the system and its despair.

A radical examination of motorized traffic and the reconstruction of the function of accidents, as well as a study of the possibility of alternative education for safe transportation, all demand a critique of Instrumental Rationality, its context, and its operation. What I am suggesting here engages only one dimension of the issue: the political dimension; and it is at odds with the philosophical one.

Motorized traffic and accidents are but one mode of being's games of revealing and hiding: its way of motivating man into realizing himself as "being toward death."[25] Within this questioning, I think that we should try to understand the philosophical dimension of technological and transportational progress. Heidegger's ontological questioning, as well as the understanding of the procedures of the human body, soul, and truths according to Foucault, still leave room for the Habermasian critical reconstruction and that of Adorno's critique on Instrumental Rationality. These elements are vital elements of the theoretical attitude that I suggest. The theory suggested here is "pessimistic" but, by the same token, it is Utopian. It understands the current advancement of transportation and education for safe transportation as manifestations of nothingness. At the same time, it treats the contingent historical stand of concrete systems as a real world. It is where happiness, falsity, possibilities of hope, and concrete opportunities are present and deserve protection in the struggle for their development, especially through the de-construction of the current realm of self-evidence to the greatest possible degree.

Education on the issue of safer transportation and the call for more careful behavior on the roads might become an important part of a struggle against the powers manifested in the slaughter on the roads, namely countering the logic of the current Western realm of self-evidence. Such an education, even under the present circumstances, might be aided by presently existing antagonistic sites in the system or newly developed focuses that contain the potential of becoming vital elements of the coming realm of self-evidence. Specifically, I am referring to the destructive / educational potential of the tradition of the free public sphere in modern Western culture.

Essentially, this tradition is conservative in its self-understanding, but for our purposes the more central issue revolves around the very separation between the public and the private sphere. This rich tradition contains (and might reproduce) the explicit and implicit codes and parameters that guide behavior in the public sphere and the alternative possibilities of the human subject. Normally, this is the basis of producing and controlling the subject in accordance with the hegemony concepts and interests, or power balance in the system. At the same time, however, this power might be directed against the system, might serve as part of a transformation that would enable a more autonomous and less controllable subject and intersubjectivity. Human life might thus become richer and contain new possibilities, as part of an enterprise that opens new horizons and drives toward new dangerous normalization systems and opportunities for liberation.

Countering the present reproduction of traffic accidents, resisting the current ways of distribution and consumption of "the problem" and its suggested solutions, might become parts of such a utopian struggle. Such a struggle must become a radical political and philosophical praxis. It is important here to denote some conservative elements and pinpoint the possibility of their transformation within this Utopian struggle. After all, the alternative education for safety transportation is but one of its bearers and builders. Such an alternative education is impossible without maturity manifestations such as a new type of communicative action that is not under the control of the purpose principle, overcoming anti-narcissistic self-forgetfulness and the reestablishment of refinement in the public sphere of behavior. However, all these elements and their attributes are impossible in the face of the absence of dramatic change in concrete social and cultural conditions. I do not share Habermas's optimism and positive utopianism concerning the possibility of communicative action and scientifically based advancement toward the "ideal speech situation" that would constitute a solidarian partner in dialogue. In this instance, I see more relevance in Jean Baudrillard's conception of a communication which cannot see a way out of our present situation. However, that is the end of Baudrillard's truth and the opening opportunities for an alternative communication / traffic education. It is a project that targets the realization of new ways of driving—as a representation of transcending traditional kinds of solidarity within a new aesthetic motorized movement—as part of the entrance of challenging the exile of Spirit and its alternative power / knowledge relations.

The term *derech eretz* (the way of respect) contains in Hebrew a vital importance for any education for safe driving and for any alternative communicational praxis. It exceeds the traffic issue and completes it. In Judaism, there is a unique synthesis between *Torah* (the Jewish written law) and *Torah Shebeal-pe* (the Jewish oral law) as a reflection of the dialectic of the earthly life and the heavenly world, nature and man. In Judaism, the heavenly world does not reduce earthly life and material things such as the body to something of a lower degree. The written *Torah* proclaims the sanctity of the ways of this world and the sanctity of the human soul, the body and its passions and needs. That is why Judaism praises human worldly ways of conduct as an autonomous dimension that is not of a lower degree and is never totally separated from heaven in principle, the written *Torah* and oral tradition—*Torah Shebeal-pe*—cannot be separated. These worldly ways and man's conduct in earthly matters are not to be separated from God's imperative, from the truth of the *Torah* and from heavenly eternity. In this sense, while having its history, different interpretations, and educational and political manifestations,[26] *derech eretz* delineates a religious dimension. While representing the earthly dimension in human life, *derech eretz* manifests the redemptive aspects in our daily life. As such, it also represents the general human utopian axis of humanity's enlightenment as developed by figures such as Schiller, Kant, Hegel, and Marx. They represented a mature conception of *derech eretz* in which acknowledging the absence of the traditional God does not negate utopia or the moral value of daily matters and the acknowledgment of different ways of life. As it was written in *Masechet Derech Eretz Zuta*, 71, 2: "*Kol drachecha yieyu leshem shamaim*" (Let all your ways be for the sake of heaven).[27] I would like to develop this concept into a general humanistic educational attitude, as exemplified in the traffic issue. That is to say, alternative traffic education is connected to an alternative conception of movement and to an alternative, utopian conception of the public sphere.

The concept of *derech eretz* on the roads has two aspects: one of knowledge and the other of action. Each of them is contained in two different contexts: private and public. In the public sphere, *derech eretz* is conditioned by the recognition of an epistemological system that is conceived as legitimate and is enabling knowledge concerning relevant codes and norms in the current public sphere.

Unlike mere politeness, behavior manifesting *derech eretz* is conditioned not only on the act being conceived as polite, but that other men and women might be trained to behave in accordance with it. This follows because it is conditioned by knowledge; therefore, it is not a matter of making people behave "properly" (which would leave open the issue of repression), but rather it is a question of a real educational enterprise. Under this interpretation, *derech eretz* is not merely an epistemological issue, and it cannot be realized only as a concrete moral, obligatory, conscious action. In this sense, *derech eretz* is not a mere epistemic function or a framework. It is conditioned by a special sort of knowledge, one that is morally oriented, namely, courteous behavior that is shaped by the acknowledgment of the other's identity, needs, rights, hopes, and limits, and ultimately directed toward a common transcendence. According to this perspective, education for *derech eretz* on the roads might be realized only as the politics of overcoming the purpose principle, which constitutes the heart of Instrumental Rationality and capitalist practice.[28] Marx suggests the utopian movement in sexual relations between free men and women as a concrete criterion for true communism,[29] namely, for the overcoming of the purpose principle that is the essence of both capitalism and vulgar communism. This kind of intersubjectivity, which is determined by recognition of the other as Other, as different, and as a partner for critical dialogue and creative solidarity, is manifested in the Jewish category of *derech eretz*.

The *derech eretz* education that I am suggesting is but a revolt against the totality of the present reality and is directed toward its questioning and deconstruction. In contrast to postmodern educational rhetorics, however, such an education is committed to overcoming the driver as an ego with no essence that realizes itself by negating the Other's otherness. This kind of education has a utopian axis: a commitment to the revelation of the idea of a human being as an autonomous site, as an agent of solidarity, and as a guardian of being even when defending a rational, open, and free public sphere. This humanistic renaissance avoids being just one more manifestation of the narcissistic power that is produced by the current culture industry. This humanistic Utopia connects, again, the private man to a public sphere which is being constantly criticized and re-formulated daily by the individuals creating it. Human beings become social again, namely, real human beings, individuals.

Today, the very possibility of educating people against the current trend toward de-personalization and indifference in regard to the other is conditioned by the effectiveness and strength of Instrumental Rationality's manifestations. Education for *derech eretz* on the roads brings man home to himself and can liberate him from the system's hegemony, as a piece of statistical data and as an almost totally controlled function. This "almost" is important for any possible counter-education. Education for *derech eretz* on the roads transcends the level of treating the issue as a mere private, or economic "safety" matter to a political, moral, philosophical, and existential one. Even as a utopian enterprise, this is impossible when one is deprived of any tradition. Therefore, the educational project that I suggest must be established via a hermeneutic approach to the tradition or traditions denoting the moral and spiritual dimensions of manners and making it possible to demand that *derech eretz* be realized.

The project suggested here is a Jewish one, while emphasizing its multicultural, yet universal-humanist implications. Judaism might be interpreted in an anti-ethnocentric way, as part of a universal enterprise of edifying, transcending, and liberating. It can avoid ethnocentrism and cultural neocolonialism by avoiding the mistakes of both current conservative universalist and multiculturalist discourses. As a humanist alternative, it should cross the existing borders between classic critical theory and Foucault's project in suggesting the possibility of a new critical dialog and political praxis. Reinterpreting concepts such as *derech eretz* and educating for alternative transportational reality and traffic education, against its conservative understanding, on the one hand, and as part of a dialogue with other cultural concepts, on the other, might evolve into a meaningful defense for reason and a more human order of things.

An alternative education of the kind I suggest is very different from the prevailing one. Such an education must deconstruct the inner logic of the current realm of self-evidence and subject it to interrogation. It must be questioned if there is to be the possibility of redeeming a sense of estrangement toward it to the degree that it may become enlightened. Instrumental Rationality and ethnocentrism must be challenged in order to reestablish human attachment to one another and to Utopia through the opening up of a dialogue.

Deciphering the essence of "traffic accidents" must face the contingency of the formation of the realm of self-evidence and the systems reflecting it.[30] A realm of self-evidence creates or is being realized in local social-cultural systems which struggle and communicate with one another and which are violent by their nature. The system is not to be identified with a national sovereignty. It crosses political borders and is much closer to cultural spaces, but it is not identified with it since it includes local social hierarchies, their financial and symbolic power struggles and political praxes. Systems can change characters and borders, as well as the direct dynamics and limits within their subjects, consciousness, and working political strategy.

The utopia overcoming the present realm of self-evidence and deconstructing local systems and their power relations is based on the principle of hope that is about to storm it every minute and every day. However, this concrete utopia cannot but rely on and refer to the concrete capitalistic and nationalistic reality in order to challenge it by counter-education, as by *derech eretz* on the roads. Here I do not refer to an abstract individual as a contingent supreme standard. I speak about the constitution of new values, new myths, and a new heroism of sacrifice for the totally different, the transcendent. In its nature, such an education is opposed to the "education for safe driving on the roads." Such an approach is determined to de-construct present reality and transcend itself. It aims to generate this project without being non-humanistic, but with the determination to transcend humanism and to save it from the presence it wants to deconstruct. Such a determination requires considering institutionalized "accidents," their production, selection, and designing apparatuses even on the roads. Counter-education must support itself on this acknowledgment and on making use of interests and dynamics that are currently shaping the local systems. On one level, it has to use insurance companies and other interest focuses that are for the moment opposed to those of the car industry, importers, and the government. On another level, it can make use of the remains of the nation-building myth and Kantian moral conceptions in anti-conservative contexts, which can be directed toward concrete action against this aspect of the death industry known as "normal traffic conditions." The remnants of national fanaticism may be of some use, too, in a counter-educational action against the world of "traffic accidents."

Such an action is conditioned by the refusal to accept the forgetfulness of forgetfulness, against the refusal to rebel against the self-understood and specifically against hegemony trends in the Israeli system. One might assume that such an education is really going to decrease the number of traffic victims. Such an instrumentalist might succeed, but only by acting in such a way that will ultimately advance and fortify the system in which a revolt functions in the form of actual or potential "traffic accidents," that is, as any commodity. The counter-education is fed by the hope principle, from the transcendental impotence that has no power to reduce the number of casualties. In principle, it cannot be "successful." It can only appear as a refusal for "success," normality and self-understanding, as a negation of nothingness that the present reality manifests.

Even so, we have to demand education for a negation of the current ways of the Western system and a total refusal of its self-evidence. Such a refusal must include the acceptance of the liberation of the oppressed (intellectually, psychologically, and economically) potentialities. The realization of the demand for such an education is possible only if the entire social horizon can be changed and a real public sphere can flourish. In such a utopia, a new place for technology and transportation will be provided by the new human being. There is the place for an essentially different kind of traffic, which has a different telos to the current one. There and only there will an equal status be attained for all traffic victims. Even then, will they be victims of a way that is not theirs? And what will be the form of an alternative that we cannot positively describe? All that we can do is act against the negation of its possibility and rebel against the Evil Industry that constitutes the one-dimensionality of the present reality.

NOTES

1 Juergen Habermas. *The Structural Transformation of the Public Sphere.* Cambridge: MIT Press 1992.
2 Ilan Gur-Ze'ev. *The Frankfurt School and The History of Pessimism.* Jerusalem: Magnes 1996 (in Hebrew).
3 Herbert Marcuse. *One-Dimensional Man.* Boston: Beacon Press 1964, 123-143.
4 Mary Tiles and Hans Oberdiek. *Living in a Technological Culture.* London and New York 1995: Routledge 130.
5 Plato. *Phaedrus.* Translated by C. J. Rowe, Warminister 1986, 61.
6 Paul Virilio. *The Art of the Motor.* Translated by Julie Rose, Minneapolis: University of Minnesota Press 1996, 92.
7 Lester and Charles Lave. "Barriers to increasing highway safety," in Peter Rothe (ed.), *Challenging the Old Order; Toward New Directions in Traffic Safety.* New Brunswick and London: Theory Transaction Publishers 1990, 78.
8 Sigmund Freud. "Totem and Taboo," in: *The Standard Edition of the Complete Psychological Works of Sigmund Freud,* 18. Translated by James Strachey, London 1971.
9 Filipo Tomaso Marinetti. "The new religion-morality of speed," in: R. W. Flint (ed.), *Marinetti; Selected Writings.* London 1972, 94.
10 Filipo Tomaso Marinetti. "The founding and manifesto of Futurism," *ibid.,* 41.
11 Hans-Georg Retzko. "Speed and accidents in German motorways," in: *International Proceedings Conference on New Ways and Means for Improved Safety,* Tel-Aviv February 20-23 1989, 6.
12 Krister Spolander. "How to reduce speeding," *ibid.,* 73.
13 *Ibid.*
14 Eliahu Richter. "A national or a scientific failure?" in: *Universita,* Jerusalem 1993, 9 (in Hebrew).
15 Irit Uchman. "A rational approach toward traffic accidents," *Tnua Vetachbura,* 27, 1990, 21 (in Hebrew).
16 Laster B. and Charles A. Lave. "Barriers to increasing highway safety," in: Peter Rothe, *Challenging the Old Order* Cambridge: Polity Press 89.
17 *Ibid.,* 23.
18 C. H. Sharp. *Transport Economics.* Tiptree 1973, 67.
19 *Ibid.*
20 Norbert Elias. "Technization and civilization," *Theory, Culture & Society,* 12 (1995), 25.
21 Norbert Elias. "Technization and civilization," *Theory, Culture & Society,* 12: 3 (August 1995), 8-9.
22 *Ibid.,* 23-34.
23 *Ibid.,* 24-25.
24 Paul Virilio. *The Art of the Motor.* Translated by Julie Rose, Minneapolis: University of Minnesota Press 1995, 132.
25 Martin Heidegger. *Sein und Zeit.* Tuebingen: M. Niermeyer 1963, 265-266.
26 Mordechai Broier (ed.) *Persons and Roads.* Tel-Aviv 1987 (in Hebrew).
27 Rabbi Asher Frizker. *Masechtot Derech Eretz.* Tel-Aviv 1950, 19 (in Hebrew).
28 Karl Marx. "On the Jewish question," in: *Early Texts.* Translated by David Mclellan, Oxford: Blackwell 1971, 114.
29 Karl Marx. "Economic and philosophical manuscripts," in: *Early Texts.* Translated by David McLellan, Oxford: Blackwell 1971, 147.
30 Ilan Gur-Ze'ev. *The Frankfurt School and the History of Pessimism.* Jerusalem: Magnes Press 1996, 222-224 (in Hebrew).

Index

Subject

Action, 11, 21, 96, 101, 139, 188, 192, 217, 219, 301-302, 311, 341
research, 217
Actuality, 15, 276, 278
authentic, 3, 6, 13, 70, 92, 108, 177, 186, 204-206, 215, 222, 319
Autonomy/Autonomous, 2, 11, 109, 112, 116, 123-124, 133, 145, 164-166, 170, 172-173, 198, 200, 207, 217, 223, 261, 268, 270, 282, 287, 309, 312

Banality of Forgetfulness, The (Auron), 83
Being, 3-4, 12, 21, 48, 70, 92, 100, 102, 206-208, 117, 151, 177, 206, 208, 211, 217, 245, 284, 303
Bildung, 123, 144, 161-162, 165, 168, 172, 221
Beitar, 31
Bund, 177

Capitalism, 10, 12, 14-15, 17, 44, 69, 90, 101, 108, 110-112, 115-116, 125, 133-139, 141, 145, 180-181, 183, 192-193, 168, 221, 247, 257, 259, 262, 322-323, 326, 331-332, 342-343
advanced capitalism, 5, 133, 230-231, 263
Collective, 8, 17-18, 21, 25, 27-29, 31, 33, 36, 38, 40-3, 69, 70, 73-8, 81-2, 85, 90, 96-99, 103, 119-120, 243-7, 244, 290, 319, 325, 328-9, 338-339
and nationalism 225-226, 234, 251-252, 254-257, 259-260, 262-3, 266
'I', 108
memory, 8, 13, 16-17, 19, 33, 69, 73, 91-92, 96, 99, 206, 213
identity, 25, 29, 37, 40, 69, 71-72, 74, 76, 87, 89, 93, 97, 121, 215-216, 221, 227, 236, 243, 246, 277
Colonization/decolonization, 5, 18, 27, 42-43, 64, 73, 80, 100, 120, 177, 182, 189, 200, 206-207
Consensus, 114, 139, 184, 195, 198, 219, 221, 251, 278, 280, 288-290, 295, 298 304, 210, 325
Counter-education, 2-3, 5, 7-8, 10-21, 27, 48, 62, 64, 98, 101, 103, 141, 153, 177, 181, 185-186, 191, 194, 197-200, 211, 213, 216, 219, 237, 280, 293-4, 296, 299-313, 322-323, 342-344
Critical humanism, 88, 149-150, 278

Critical literacy, 210, 215, 217-218, 235, 237-238
Critical Pedagogy, 7, 10-1, 14-15, 88, 98, 191, 208, 218, 235, 237
Critical Philosophy, 4-5, 7, 9-11, 15, 19, 199
Critical Theory, 9, 15, 63, 88, 102-103, 139-140, 147, 149, 164, 166, 181, 202, 234-236, 339, 343
Cynicism, 7, 81, 114, 144, 234, 276, 284, 295-296

Dialogue, 4, 11, 13-14, 19-20, 28, 38, 42, 45, 51, 60-61, 63-64, 71, 78, 81, 85-6, 96, 100-101, 110, 131, 145, 147-152, 165, 172, 186-187, 190-191, 193-195, 198, 204-205, 207, 210-212, 215-218, 222-224, 226, 233-235, 238, 279, 285-6, 294, 296-297, 299-306, 308-313, 321-323, 246, 271, 325, 329, 332, 338, 340, 342-343
Diaspora, 16, 29, 31, 33-36, 41, 43-44, 52, 62, 64, 73-77, 80, 88-89, 102, 104, 119, 121, 129, 134, 176, 178-179, 194, 243, 249, 252, 274, 321
Difference, 4, 6, 10, 15, 101, 103, 113, 118, 156, 164, 172, 174, 177-8, 184, 186, 188-191, 194, 198, 236, 240, 253, 262, 331
Discourse, 11, 14, 16, 18, 53, 56, 60-1, 71, 82, 99, 101-3, 125, 131, 135, 140, 147-151, 157-158, 168-169, 179, 183-184, 189-193, 195, 200, 204-210, 212-213, 215-238, 254, 261, 268, 276-277, 286, 288, 291, 302, 309, 311, 325, 329, 343

Emancipation, 2, 7, 12-3, 15, 19-65, 70, 77, 80, 99-100, 143, 143, 160, 172-178, 192, 194, 197, 206, 218, 143, 153, 332
Enlightenment, 18, 63, 77, 81, 97, 99, 101, 111, 122-123, 125, 128, 133, 150-151, 159-160, 163, 165-166, 168, 170, 173, 191, 195, 199, 220-221, 223-224, 230, 259-260, 278, 282-285, 302, 307-308, 311, 324, 326-327, 329, 330-331, 341
Eros, 11, 17, 81, 112, 114-115, 123, 133, 137, 150, 158, 160, 165, 169, 171, 173, 221, 223-224, 233, 238, 265-268, 281, 302, 305, 307, 311, 319, 324, 326, 328-329, 337-338
Essential/ism, 5, 7, 10, 27, 29-30, 33-34, 111, 149, 151-152, 178-179, 186, 190, 197, 284, 311, 335

Ethical "I", 6, 11-12, 19-85, 95, 99, 101, 125, 185, 224, 297, 303, 323
Exile, 1, 3, 17, 25-7, 29, 33, 35, 37-41, 43-6, 58, 63, 76-7, 92, 97, 100, 108, 116, 163, 173, 190, 201, 254, 283, 286, 306, 309, 312, 340
Factuality, 4, 7, 12, 20, 108, 135
Feminism, 11, 15, 127, 131-135, 140, 143-150, 152-153, 189, 200, 218, 235, 237, 240
Forgetfulness, 4, 21, 83, 90, 96, 337-338, 340, 344-345
Frankfurt School, 15, 63, 102, 204

Globalization, 18, 25, 29-30, 33-37, 40-41, 43, 45-46, 48, 51-65, 70-76, 80-103, 177-178, 194, 210- 211, 219, 229, 263

Hebrew University, 162, 231
Hegel's dialectics, 72
Heimat, *See* homeland
Hermeneutics, 219
Home/land, 16, 25-30, 32-48, 63, 76, 80, 90, 93, 115, 144, 182, 231, 284, 254, 267, 273, 303, 326, 342
Homelessness, 26-27, 33, 35, 38, 46-48, 298
Hope, 7, 10, 12, 19, 30, 21, 60, 65, 71, 80, 103, 111-112, 147, 152-153, 185, 205, 207-208, 215, 218, 224, 227-8, 234, 236, 249, 285, 291, 295, 302, 305-6, 311-312, 357, 339, 342
Hope Principle, 10, 102-103, 205, 207, 219, 310, 327, 343-344
Human, 1-10, 12-14, 17-19, 21, 26, 28, 33, 36, 40, 45, 52, 59, 63, 65, 69, 71, 73-76, 78, 81-87, 85, 87, 94-96, 99-101, 159-160, 172, 112-117, 120, 122-124, 126, 128, 130, 137, 145-152, 180-182, 185-186, 188, 190, 194-195, 197, 200, 200, 205-207, 209, 214, 217-219, 221-225, 232, 243-247, 249, 255-256, 262, 264-265, 262, 284-287, 289-291, 293, 295, 297-299, 302, 305-307, 310-312, 318-327, 329, 332-333, 335, 337-338, 340-343
essence, 96, 148-149, 177, 208, 218, 333, 335
Humanism, 55, 58, 64, 69, 75-76, 81-85, 87, 90-91, 93-56, 99, 101-102, 108-109, 111-112, 124-126, 128, 138, 142, 145, 149-151, 159, 162, 166, 168-170, 173, 180, 182-184, 192, 194, 196-197, 199, 212, 214, 229, 237, 243, 260-261, 276, 278, 280-286, 296, 309, 311, 313, 327, 329, 331, 337, 341-344
Humanity, 2, 40, 85, 102, 124, 128, 133, 150, 152, 159, 162, 168, 172, 192, 219-220, 222, 255, 268-269, 290-291, 299, 309, 313, 335, 341

Ideal, 3, 7, 11, 13-14, 18, 31, 35, 37-38, 42-44, 69, 73, 75-77, 80-82, 85, 87, 89, 95-97, 100-101, 112, 114-117, 121, 123-124, 126, 129, 132, 137-138, 140, 143-144, 146, 148-149, 151, 153, 158, 160-161, 164, 170, 172-173, 177, 179, 183, 185-156, 192, 195-196, 198, 205, 221, 223-225, 227-228, 231, 234, 244, 248, 250, 252-257, 260-261, 263, 268, 270, 279, 282-284, 289-292, 295, 297, 311, 318, 322, 325-326, 329-332, 337, 340

Idealism, 17, 81, 186, 225, 260, 279, 322
Identity, 2, 11, 16, 18, 25-26, 28-30, 32-41, 44-5, 47, 51-52, 54, 64, 69-70, 72-74, 76, 78-83, 85, 87, 89-93, 96, 99-100, 103, 115-116, 119, 121, 125, 128, 136, 142, 145-146, 148-149, 165, 172, 177-178, 181-182, 186, 189-190, 193-194, 205-207, 213-218, 227, 234,236, 243-247, 253, 277, 288, 305, 307-308, 323, 341
Image, 8, 14, 19, 26, 31, 41, 47, 57, 68, 70, 100, 128, 133, 141, 147, 247, 256, 266, 324
Infinity, 4, 14, 21, 117, 177, 185, 201, 245, 301, 305
Intersubjectivity, 2-3, 19, 28, 68-9, 77, 110, 115, 189, 213-6, 218, 225, 243, 246-247, 289, 306, 327-329, 336, 338, 340, 342
Invisibility, 5-6, 20, 25, 30-6, 39-48, 53-60, 62-3, 69, 72-3, 75-81, 83-6, 89-94, 96-98, 102, 108, 113, 120-2, 124, 129, 131, 133-137, 143, 146, 148, 166-167, 172, 176-179, 182-185, 194-196, 198-200, 212, 217, 220, 225-227, 229, 231, 269, 277, 279, 284, 313

Jewish, 16-20, 243-4, 248-255, 258-260, 262, 265, 268, 340, 342
messianism, 17, 33, 97, 243
telos, 35, 46, 48, 97-98, 182, 194
victimhood, 34, 43, 47, 75

Knowledge, 2, 6, 8-9, 12, 52, 68-71, 73, 75, 80-81, 83-84, 94, 96, 108, 110, 116, 121-9, 131-132, 133-134, 136-138, 140-141, 144-145, 152-153, 157-158, 160-161, 164-167, 169-172, 176-177, 179, 187, 193, 196, 198, 205-208, 212-218, 221-222, 225, 227, 230-231, 236, 246, 251, 257, 264, 267, 269, 279, 287-288, 298-300, 302-303, 305, 313
about, 68, 158-9, 161, 288
bodies of, 19, 68, 121, 126-127, 132-133, 136, 140-141, 146, 161-163, 170, 216, 224, 256
constitution of, 7, 64, 121, 126-127, 140, 152, 157, 169, 181, 269, 298, 307-308
controlling, 180, 225
image of, 8, 14, 18-19, 68-69, 115, 133, 158, 162, 164-6, 170-171, 198, 204, 206, 216, 224, 232, 234, 247, 256, 266
instrumentalization of, 93-94, 98, 100, 126, 151, 167, 171, 173, 180, 210, 308
reproduction of, 83, 141, 164, 167, 172, 236

Literacy, 70, 204-242, 253
Love, 7, 11-2, 14, 21, 26-8, 42, 44, 53, 102, 114, 116-7, 147, 151, 164, 172-173, 186-187, 190, 216, 218, 227, 233, 265, 285, 291, 299-300, 303-308, 310, 313

Marxism, 33, 56, 80, 261, 268
Media, 34, 79, 87, 89, 99, 180-2, 184, 210, 225, 229, 232, 281
Meaninglessness, 13, 22, 38, 113, 224, 256, 293, 298, 301, 318

Index

Messianism, 4, 12-3, 15, 17, 181, 243
  moment, 4, 12, 190
Modernity, 12, 15, 69, 84, 123-124, 180, 182-183, 189, 225, 229, 247, 257, 261, 264-268, 270, 282, 330, 332, 333
  post-modernity, 15, 17, 142, 180-181, 261, 268
  crisis of, 70-8, 80-7, 90-103, 113, 128, 137, 150, 153, 164, 183, 210, 219, 225, 279, 286, 289, 291-2, 297-300, 303, 307-8, 313
Moral, 2, 7-8, 10-1, 20, 43, 456, 48, 52-5, 58, 62, 159-160, 162, 178, 186, 188, 246, 248, 252, 260, 331, 341-342, 344
  education, 71-3, 88, 97, 99, 102, 102, 123, 294
  "I", 20, 99, 185, 224, 297, 303
Multicultural/ism, 11, 15,-6, 18, 63, 65, 82, 99, 101, 103, 157, 172, 178-9, 183-184, 186-188, 189-191, 193, 196, 199-200, 237, 246, 248, 252, 260, 311, 323, 342-343
  education for, 191-3, 195-9
Multicultural Education, 11, 176, 186-187, 188-191, 193-194, 198-199, 488
Myth, 4, 7, 12, 17, 31, 37, 42, 57, 69-70, 72-75, 80-82, 86, 88, 93, 96, 111, 121, 124-125, 127, 130, 135-136, 141-144, 179-181, 206, 210, 212, 225, 228, 230-232, 248-250, 255-258, 260-261, 263-265, 267-271, 279-281, 289, 293, 318, 322, 325-326, 328, 331, 333-334

Nakbah, 17, 25, 27, 29, 36-37, 39-41, 45, 52, 61-63, 85
  as homeland, 25, 39
  Holocaust/Nakbah dialectics, 41, 46-47, 52, 55, 61
  Holocaust/Nakbah memories, 51-67
  Holocaust/Nakbah representation, 47, 52
Nationalism, 28, 52, 56, 63, 125, 182, 187, 194, 167, 249, 277, 281
Nazism, 34, 46-47, 52-5, 57-60, 62, 75, 79, 89, 91-94, 98, 169, 250, 331
Nihilism, 7, 173, 265, 276, 281, 283-4, 293
Normality, 3, 6, 13, 36, 129, 190, 224, 234, 243, 264, 319-320, 328, 330, 334
Normalizing education, 1-5, 7-10, 12, 14-21, 25-30, 33-5, 38, 43, 47-8, 68-69, 72, 82, 98-99, 122, 146, 176-177, 179-180, 182, 187, 190-192, 195, 197-198, 214, 217, 224, 234, 243-244, 248, 252-254, 267-268, 271, 289, 291-292, 295, 297, 299-300, 306, 312, 330, 328, 340

Ontology, 9-10, 35, 62, 70, 86, 101, 123-124, 148-152, 167, 205, 211, 280, 289-300, 303, 305, 308, 320, 326-127, 339
Other, 2, 3, 5-6, 8, 11-12, 15, 17, 19-20, 25, 27-29, 35, 37-39, 46, 48, 51-2, 54-56, 61-62, 65, 68, 70, 74-75, 78, 84, 87-88, 94, 96, 98-103, 112, 125, 129-130, 151, 176-178, 184-186, 192, 194-195, 197-198, 164-165, 173, 204-206, 214, 218, 227, 233-234, 243, 246-247, 249-250, 253, 259-260, 267, 286, 290-291, 294-297, 299, 301, 305-308, 310-311, 313, 322, 341-343
Otherness, 2-6, 10-12, 19, 27-8, 33, 37, 51-2, 55, 65, 137, 148-149, 178, 184-186, 193-194, 171, 243, 246, 249-250, 286, 290, 295, 297, 253, 260, 264, 306, 338, 342

Palestine, 8, 16, 18, 21, 25, 30-5, 37-48, 51, 59-61, 73, 77, 80, 108, 120, 128, 136, 183, 249, 254, 259, 263
Paternalism, 79, 128, 151, 237, 309
Performative Principle, 225, 263, 269
Pessimism, 100-1, 149, 153, 166, 216, 222, 285, 306, 309-310, 312, 339
  heroic, 250
  philosophical, 108, 167
  utopian, 103, 149, 312-3
Phalogocentrism, 108, 115, 117, 165
Postmodern/ism, 9, 115, 151, 220, 224
  and memory, 56
  and Palestinians, 37-38, 56, 237, 267
  and pessimism, 100, 166, 222
  and truth, 110, 112, 115, 117, 164-166, 171-3, 222, 224, 236
  and the university, 110-112, 114-117, 163-165, 168-172
  and violence, 9, 112, 114-115, 260, 270, 282, 311
  constitution of the human subject, 64, 114-115, 149-150, 170, 172, 223, 236, 282
  discourse, 18, 56, 101-102, 110, 150, 158, 165, 169, 172, 222-223, 237, 311
  education, 85-86, 101, 116, 158, 171-173, 235-237, 282, 311, 342
  feminism, 15, 149, 172, 234, 237
Power, 4, 6-7, 17, 20-21, 25, 28, 30, 40-41, 43, 48, 69, 71, 73-74, 76, 80, 85-96, 98, 100, 103, 119, 121-123, 125, 127, 129, 131-132, 134, 136, 139, 142-144, 146, 148, 152-153, 157, 159, 161, 163, 166, 168-169, 171, 173, 176-177, 179, 181-182, 190, 192, 199, 108, 112-114, 205, 207-208, 215-219, 222-223, 225, 228-230, 233, 235-238, 243-246, 251-252, 254, 261-263, 267-268, 270, 281, 284, 286-288, 290-291, 294, 300, 303, 306-307, 311-312, 320-326, 338-340, 342, 344
  and empowerment, 2, 9, 43-44, 47-48, 77, 91, 101, 188, 198, 206, 208, 214, 227, 235, 238, 264, 266-7, 289
  relations, 1, 3, 6, 13, 15, 85, 110, 123, 136, 143, 150-151, 153, 190, 195, 198, 207, 218, 237, 271, 278, 299, 307, 321, 343
  struggles, 80, 144, 151-152, 158, 164
  symbolic, 80, 113, 130, 204, 207
Principle of Hope, 10, 102-103, 305, 310-312, 205, 207, 219, 236, 327, 344
Principle of Individuation, 243
Purpose Principle, 320, 337, 340, 342-343

Reality Principle, 128, 130, 152

Redemption, 33-34, 42-43, 52, 59, 75-78, 85, 96-97, 114, 120-122, 125-126, 171, 173, 183, 199, 219, 223, 227, 263, 295, 297, 299, 306, 310, 341
Reflection, 2, 4, 7, 11-12, 14-15, 20, 25, 52, 54, 63, 91, 111, 114, 116, 126, 140, 204, 211, 215, 217, 219, 222, 234, 163, 180, 245-246, 248, 251, 267, 270, 321-323, 328-9, 332, 338, 340, 343
Relativism, 10-11, 61, 65, 96, 149, 223, 279, 293
Rhetoric, 9, 28, 69, 83, 86, 101-102, 112, 115-116, 128, 207, 212, 225, 227-228, 232, 235, 237, 157-159, 161, 167-172, 184, 188, 199, 260, 281, 286, 288-292, 304, 323, 329, 322, 333-335, 342

Same, 4-5, 10, 13-14, 25-27, 117, 298, 245, 323-324
Science, 68, 115, 133, 157, 159-161, 163, 168, 171, 286, 288, 303, 310, 325
   as ideology, 133, 166
   as poesis, 171
   metaphysical pretensions and, 163
   as profession, 165
   as vocation, 160-161, 165
Self, 1-3, 25-28, 38, 40, 68, 70, 102, 124, 130, 145, 165, 169, 204, 206, 224, 233-234, 246, 249-250, 283, 288, 295-296, 302, 311, 319, 338
   constitution, 7, 9, 12, 19-20, 28, 34, 51, 62, 87-8, 93, 121, 148, 153, 165, 181, 193, 216-217, 219, 221, 225, 233-234, 245-246, 265, 289, 295, 304, 308, 310, 323-324, 337
   control, 18, 319, 324, 335-336
   forgetfulness, 5, 111, 286, 291, 295, 337-338, 340
   identity, 76, 205, 207, 245, 247
   positioning, 52, 231, 323
   realization, 3, 28, 244, 250, 322
   regulated system, 65, 170, 181, 209, 319, 325-326, 332, 335, 337
   sacrifice, 38, 141, 225, 248, 250, 255, 265
Sex, 20, 141, 143, 150, 164, 172, 188-189, 233, 342
Sophist, 121, 124, 169, 285-294, 297-301, 303, 307-308, 310-313
Soul, 2, 4, 84-5, 89, 98-99, 109, 121, 127, 129, 142, 151, 176-7, 219, 223, 230, 233-4, 256, 266, 284, 298-9, 301, 305, 307, 323, 329, 341
Spirit/ual, 2, 18, 28, 31, 71, 78, 83, 85, 97, 109, 111, 114, 122, 128, 139, 144-5, 159-160, 165, 167-168, 177-180, 182-183, 191, 220, 230, 233, 245, 247-250, 252, 264, 266-267, 277, 281, 284-5, 312, 318, 329-331, 335, 342
   and violence, 78, 255, 270-271, 256
   critical, 20, 112
   education, 71
   exile of, 1, 17, 85, 268, 270, 284, 322, 340
   instrumental, 71, 97, 99, 123, 133, 138, 168, 180, 182, 191
   Jewish, 17, 31, 85, 102, 179, 182
   Zionist, 42, 71, 82-3, 85, 93, 98, 109, 142, 179, 182-3, 227-8, 265, 270, 278
   western, 182, 260

Subjectivity, 6, 122, 197, 286, 290-291, 296, 333
Symbol, 12, 16-17, 19, 27, 29, 31, 38-39, 43, 51, 69, 75, 81, 89, 99, 111, 124, 137, 139, 145, 150, 157, 159, 170, 180, 204-5, 207, 222-3, 228, 246, 248, 250, 254, 256, 259-260, 265, 267, 271, 277-8, 284, 288-289, 312, 318-319, 327, 329, 331-333, 335, 337-338,
   as commodity, 111, 331
   capital, 276, 321
   energy, 248, 256,267, 221, 319, 321, 328, 334
   exchange, of, 208, 224, 254, 260, 335
   power, 16, 53, 83, 122, 158, 130, 204, 245, 248, 158, 204, 221, 226, 343
   violence, 6, 8-9, 16, 27, 29, 35, 39, 47, 53, 64-65, 89, 122, 157, 176, 181, 190, 243, 204, 226, 246-248, 290, 329

Teacher, 9, 75, 79, 83, 119-121, 127-8, 162, 165, 214, 216, 220, 279, 285, 298, 300, 329
   And student, 120, 286-7, 290, 292-4, 296, 298, 307, 310
   mission of, 119, 121-153, 279, 286, 287, 288, 300, 305, 307, 312
   status of, 17, 119-153
Teaching, 8, 19, 70, 72, 84-87, 95, 97, 178, 212-214, 216, 221, 230, 238, 278, 285-286, 288, 293-294, 296-298, 304, 307, 310
   as agency of the system, 68, 121, 127, 181, 213, 215, 229, 250, 278, 284, 300
   as emancipators, 88, 279, 285, 295-297, 215, 218
   mission of, 83, 206, 227, 286, 293, 303, 307
   zionist, 119-153
Technology/Technological, 16, 44, 68, 80, 121, 132, 182-183, 158-159, 188, 205-207, 247, 258-259, 266, 276, 280, 318-319, 322-325, 332, 337-338
   and knowledge, 115, 132, 137, 158, 163, 165-167, 172
   and Instrumental Rationality, 17, 97, 131-132, 182, 197
   and utopia, 109, 334
   post-industrial, 69, 115, 132, 165, 279
   progress, 14, 69, 89, 116, 134-137, 151, 158, 179, 184, 160, 163, 166-167, 172, 207, 254, 282, 325, 330, 336-337, 339
Totally Other, 1-5, 7, 10-12, 19, 21, 25, 74, 122, 147, 150, 207, 215, 224, 233, 249, 257, 322, 327
Transcendence, 3-5, 7, 11-14, 21,25, 68, 71, 74, 81, 99-100, 113-114, 116, 145, 164, 180, 185-186, 190-2, 206, 211, 216, 219-220, 222, 224, 233, 245, 249, 283, 293, 301, 305-306, 310-313, 319, 322-324, 326-327, 337, 339, 342
Truth, 26, 99, 123-124, 128-129, 131, 140-141, 153, 281, 283-299, 303-13, 319-320, 326, 328, 334, 336, 339-341

Universalism, 64, 115, 185, 223, 329
   and Enlightenment, 123, 150, 163, 166, 195

Index

Universal/ity, 32, 47, 123-124, 144, 146, 149, 152, 166, 171, 186
   and emancipation, 19, 77, 80-81, 85, 99, 123, 125-126, 128, 165, 171, 173, 198, 263
   and nationalism, 33, 47
   and humanity, 85, 93, 166, 172, 222, 330
   and Judaism, 16, 76, 96, 102, 194, 263
   and meaning, 72, 93-4, 103, 188, 222
   and morality, 47, 77, 81, 93-4
   and multiculturalism, 342-3
   and symbolic violence, 329-330
   and values, 9, 281
   implications of the Holocaust, 52, 55, 58-9, 61, 64, 90-4, 101
Utopia, 3, 6, 10-13, 80, 99-100, 102, 112, 114, 123, 125, 128, 132-133, 139, 143, 147-9, 152-3, 160, 195-6, 159-160, 164, 171, 173, 206, 216, 219, 254, 297, 300-303, 305-309, 311-313, 325, 333, 341-344
   and Enlightenment, 119, 164, 167, 173, 313, 330
   and humanism, 102, 112-113, 115, 332, 341-342
   axis, 4, 33, 71, 133, 150, 152, 205, 222, 298, 299, 302
   concrete, 13, 21, 150, 185, 206, 307, 343
   Jewish, 32,-3, 119, 249
   negative, 2, 7, 12, 19-20, 113-117, 217-218, 298-301, 304, 307-308, 310
   pessimism, 103, 149, 309-310, 312-313, 339
   positive, 2-4, 12, 20, 73, 109, 111, 114, 116, 196, 139, 152, 222, 235, 340
   postmodern, 101, 164
   project, 15, 80, 98, 285, 309, 344
   struggle, 340

Zionist, 32, 76, 109, 128, 226, 249, 252

Victim, 5, 21, 27, 41, 93, 95, 98, 100, 135, 234, 318, 320, 329, 334, 344
   as/and victimizer, 2, 20-1, 36, 41, 45, 47, 160, 179, 181, 245
   eternal, 74, 101
   Holocaust, 45, 74, 83, 89, 91, 93, 98
   Jews as eternal, 33-34, 36, 40-41, 74, 79-80, 96, 98
   Palestinians as victims of the, 35, 40, 43, 45-48, 90-92, 216
   of symbolic reproduction, 2, 20, 160, 234, 247, 253, 333, 336
   of traffic accidents, 318-319, 333-335, 337, 344
Victimhood, 27, 34, 36, 39, 46-47
Victimization, 5, 15, 20, 25, 35-6, 40-1, 43, 46-8, 93
Violence, 1, 4-6, 8-9, 11, 15, 20, 27, 35, 40, 47, 76-77, 79, 93, 101, 111, 113-5, 157, 163, 168, 171, 173, 176-201, 243, 247, 251-5, 258, 260-261, 264-265, 267, 271, 277, 282, 290-291, 299, 305-307, 312
   conflicting, 15, 20, 28-29, 45, 48, 122, 179-180, 190, 198, 243, 245, 253, 260, 271
   constituting the human subject, 1, 5, 20, 43, 76, 127, 130, 197, 244, 246, 266
   constituting reality, 5-6, 129, 181, 244-246, 250-251, 264, 343
   Judaism and, 77-8, 85, 90, 177, 181, 243-4, 258, 263
   metaphysical 245, 271
   productivity of, 5-6, 9, 15-17, 27, 120, 122, 129-130, 177, 181, 245, 250, 264, 266, 268
   structural, 16
   symbolic, 8-9, 16, 29, 35, 45, 47, 176, 181, 190, 243, 246, 290, 329

Name

Achimeir, A., 126
Adorno, T., 14, 17, 46, 102, 147, 163, 165, 221, 224, 235, 261
   and Instrumental Rationality, 339
Ahimeir, A., 32, 187, 249, 252, 253, 264
Alboim-Dror, R., 120, 128
Al-Ghuri, E., 53
Al-Haj, M., 135
al-Husayni, H. A., 52, 60
Almatukal, T., 54, 91
Altermann, N., 252
Alush, N., 53
Anaximander, 303
Applegate, C., 26
Arafat, Y., 59, 76
Aristotle, 335

Arlozorov, H., 32, 36
Aron, R., 161
Auron, Y., 82, 83, 85, 91, 93, 95
Avitbul, M., 85
Ayalon, A., 262, 269

Bacon, F., 170
Baje, A., 167
Bakri, M., 91
Bar-Adon, A., 128
Barak, E., 212
Barth, R., 12, 222
Bashir, S., 56
Baudrillard, J., 65, 167, 222, 223, 340
Bauman, Z., 223, 234
Beck, L., 102

Beck, U., 181
Begin, M., 32, 36
Beilin, Y., 88
Ben-Amos, A., 58
Ben-Eliezer, U, 244
Ben-Gurion, D., 32, 36, 58, 178, 251, 252, 263
   and the Israeli Defense Forces, 254
Benjamin, W., 102, 309
Ben-Naftali, M., 58
Berdichevskyi, M., 32
Bhabah, H., 125, 186, 237
Bishara, A., 45, 52, 54, 55, 56, 60, 61, 63, 90, 267
Bloom, E., 151
Borochov, D., 32, 36
Bourdieu, P., 170, 206
Brecht, B., 92
Brosh, H., 212
Buber, M., 76, 125, 126, 162, 173
Bulata, K., 47, 54, 92
Burbules, N., 165, 216

Cohen, H., 89, 173

Dagan, M., 229
Darwish, M., 38, 40, 47, 92
Daskal, M., 168
Davis, N., 221
Dawson, R. F., 335
Deleuse, G., 125
Demjanjuk, J., 89
Derrida, J., 10, 17, 101, 113, 116, 163, 166, 181
Dilthey, F., 223
Diner, D., 58
Dinur, B. Z., 34, 74, 84, 125, 178, 194, 226
Diogenes, 294-95, 302

Einstein, A., 92, 173
Eisenberg, S., 180
Eisner, K., 160
Elbaz, F., 215
Eldad, Y., 127, 253
Elias, N., 335, 336
Elkana, Y., 90, 98
Ellsworth, E., 237
Ezrahi, E., 168

Finkerfeld-Amir, A., 43
Foucault, M., 20, 101, 122, 166, 217, 221, 224, 236, 282, 330, 331, 339
Firer, R., 82
Fisher, S., 189
Freire, P., 208, 218, 224, 235, 237
Freud, S., 130, 167, 221, 232
Fulman, S., 212

Garudy, R., 58
Giroux, H., 14, 140, 208, 218, 235, 236, 237
Goldhagen, D., 59
Gor, J., 237

Gordon, A.D., 30, 36, 42, 256
Gorias, 287
Grinberg, U.-Z., 32, 126, 187, 255, 258, 264
Gur-Ze'ev, I, 52, 56, 58, 61, 62, 64
Ha'am, A., 31
Habermas, J., 151, 153, 162, 165, 195, 224, 235, 261, 340
Habibi, E., 55, 92
Hammer, Z., 84
Har-Zion, M., 256
Hegel, G. W. F., 234, 341
Heidegger, M., 158, 181, 256, 264, 297, 298, 321, 339
Heraclitus, 289
Hertz-Lazarowitz, R., 212, 213
Herzl, T., 31, 231
Hess, M., 32, 36
Hirsh, D., 151
Hitler, A., 75, 76, 93
Hobsbaum, E., 125
Horkheimer, M., 11, 17, 102, 124, 147, 173, 234, 235, 261
Horowitz, M., 52
Hussein, S., 76, 98

Irving, D., 58
Issawi, C., 58

Jabotinsky, Z., 32, 36, 127, 179, 248, 251, 252, 253, 254
Jamson, F., 224
Juenger, E., 250, 254, 264

Kahane, M., 97, 258
Kant, E., 123, 159, 165, 167, 221, 282, 335, 341
Katzenelson, B., 73
Klachkin, Y., 187
Kook, Z. Y. H., 258
Kuziminsky, E., 216

Laclau, E., 17
Landauer, G., 160
Law, C., 334
Law, L., 334
Lehmann, Z., 127
Leibowitz, Y., 77
Lessing, G., 123, 219, 220, 309
Levinas, E., 1, 11, 20
Luther, M., 219
Lyotard, J.-F., 5, 100, 101, 161, 164, 270

MacIntyre, A., 162
Many, M., 167
Marbach, A., 212
Marcuse, H., 130, 150, 152, 166
Marinetti, F. T., 331
Marx, K., 150, 341, 342
Masschlein, J., 14
Masschelein, J., 207

Index

Mattar, P., 53
McLaren, P., 14
Moritz, K. P., 26
Muhafaza, A., 53
Nazur, G. A., 76
Ne'emann, A., 119
Netanyahu, B., 58, 212, 225
Nevo, J., 52, 54
Newman, J. H., 161, 168
Nietzsche, F. W., 233, 256, 296, 299

Offir, A., 169
Orlev, Z., 228
Ovadia, S. B., 92
Oz, A., 46

Papon, M., 59
Pappe, I., 56, 61, 62, 63, 64
Parech, B., 193
Peres, S., 82
Petri, R., 26
Plato, 121, 158, 160, 233
Protagoras, 285, 286, 293

Rabin, Y., 52, 82, 99, 183, 258
Retzco, H.-G., 333
Reynolds, A. D., 335
Richter, E., 333
Ringer, F., 162
Rorty, R., 169, 192, 193, 195
Rozenzweig, F., 86, 102
Rot, H., 76, 126
Rubinstein, A., 95

Sadeh, Y., 252
Said, E., 38, 40, 45, 46, 55, 59, 60, 61, 125, 177, 205, 236, 256
   and the Holocaust, 47
   and homelessness, 48
   Palestinian response to Holocaust, 57

Sarayah, H., 56
Saria, N., 93
Schiller, F., 165, 341
Schleiermacher, F., 223
Sextus, 285
Shapiro, J., 129
Sharabi, H., 44
Shoshani, S., 212, 229
Simon, E., 76, 121, 125
Simon, L., 119, 120
Socrates, 121, 285, 294, 297-99
   and counter-education, 296
   as an enlightened education, 308
Spolander, K., 333
Sterenhel, Z., 168, 169
Stirner, M., 265

Tabenkin, Y., 252
Taylor, C., 216
Tierney, W. G., 164, 172
Trumpeldor, J., 31, 254, 256

Uchmann, I., 334

von Humboldt, W., 163, 165, 167, 168, 221

Walden, Z., 212
Walters, B., 59
Wasserman, H., 168, 169
Weber, M., 124, 125, 159, 160, 221
Wertheimer, S., 212
   and Utopianism, 230

Yahari, M., 252
Yang, R., 237
Yosef, S. B., 248

Zelermeier, M., 215
Zweig, S., 92

Studies in the Postmodern Theory of Education

General Editors
Joe L. Kincheloe & Shirley R. Steinberg

Counterpoints publishes the most compelling and imaginative books being written in education today. Grounded on the theoretical advances in criticalism, feminism, and postmodernism in the last two decades of the twentieth century, Counterpoints engages the meaning of these innovations in various forms of educational expression. Committed to the proposition that theoretical literature should be accessible to a variety of audiences, the series insists that its authors avoid esoteric and jargonistic languages that transform educational scholarship into an elite discourse for the initiated. Scholarly work matters only to the degree it affects consciousness and practice at multiple sites. Counterpoints' editorial policy is based on these principles and the ability of scholars to break new ground, to open new conversations, to go where educators have never gone before.

For additional information about this series or for the submission of manuscripts, please contact:

    Joe L. Kincheloe & Shirley R. Steinberg
    c/o Peter Lang Publishing, Inc.
    275 Seventh Avenue, 28th floor
    New York, New York 10001

To order other books in this series, please contact our Customer Service Department:

    (800) 770-LANG (within the U.S.)
    (212) 647-7706 (outside the U.S.)
    (212) 647-7707 FAX

Or browse online by series:
    www.peterlangusa.com